Beginning Shell Scripting

Eric Foster-Johnson, John C. Welch, and Micah Anderson

Wiley Publishing, Inc.

Beginning Shell Scripting

Published by
Wiley Publishing, Inc.
10475 Crosspoint Boulevard
Indianapolis, IN 46256
www.wiley.com

ISBN-13: 978-0-7645-8320-9
ISBN-10: 0-7645-8320-4

Manufactured in the United States of America

10 9 8 7 6 5 4 3 2 1

1MA/QW/QU/QV/IN

For general information on our other products and services or to obtain technical support, please contact our Customer Care Department within the U.S. at (800) 762-2974, outside the U.S. at (317) 572-3993 or fax (317) 572-4002.

Wiley also publishes its books in a variety of electronic formats. Some content that appears in print may not be available in electronic books.

Library of Congress Cataloging-in-Publication Data

Foster-Johnson, Eric.
  Beginning shell scripting / Eric Foster-Johnson, John C. Welch, and Micah Anderson.
    p. cm.
  Includes index.
  ISBN-13: 978-0-7645-8320-9
  ISBN-10: 0-7645-8320-4 (paper/website)
  1. Operating systems (Computers) I. Welch, John C., 1967– II. Anderson, Micah, 1974– III. Title.
  QA76.76.O63F59717 2005
  005.4' 3—dc22
                              2005002075

About the Authors

Eric Foster-Johnson (Arden Hills, MN) is a veteran programmer who works daily with Linux, Unix, Windows, Mac OS X, and other operating systems. By day, he writes enterprise Java software for ObjectPartners, a Minnesota consulting firm. He has authored a number of Linux and Unix titles including *Red Hat RPM Guide*, *Teach Yourself Linux*, *Teach Yourself Unix*, and *Perl Modules*.

To Katya and Nalana.

John C. Welch (Boston, MA) has more than ten years of Mac experience in the trenches of the IT world. He packs the hall at Macworld Expo where he's a regular speaker, sharing his experiences and knowledge on using Macs effectively in business and enterprise IT environments. John's articles are frequently featured in *MacTech Magazine* and *WorkingMac.com*, and he is semi-regularly featured on *The Mac Show* conducting interviews with the geekier side of the Mac community. He's recently been touring the country presenting seminars on Mac OS X administration to IT professionals from coast to coast.

First and foremost, this is dedicated to my son, Alex, who is always the angel on my shoulder.

As an only child, I've "adopted" my own family over the years to make up for the one I didn't grow up with, so in no particular order: Adrian, Jenny, Melissa, Sly, Web, Karen, Skip, Gypsye, Schoun, Harv, Jessica, the MacTech Crew, Sam, Steve, Shawn, Hilary, the YML list, the list that is never named, and too many others who help me out in myriad ways.

Oh, and to Randy Milholland, whose work has kept me sane in this very odd world.

Micah Anderson has been a Unix system administrator for more than a decade. He is a Debian GNU/Linux developer and works as an independent consultant building alternative communication infrastructure and supporting the technology needs of positive grassroots alternatives.

This is dedicated to my parents, who got me started hacking on the Timex Sinclair and have always supported me, no matter what I do. This is also dedicated to those around the world who have struggled for horizontal self-determination in the face of oppression: those who inspire people to dream of a better world by doing something about it. Slow and steady wins the race.

Credits

Acquisitions Editor
Debra Williams Cauley

Development Editor
Sara Shlaer

Technical Editor
Dilip Thomas

Copy Editors
Nancy Rapoport
Luann Rouff

Editorial Manager
Mary Beth Wakefield

Vice President & Executive Group Publisher
Richard Swadley

Vice President and Publisher
Joseph B. Wikert

Project Coordinator
Erin Smith

Graphics and Production Specialists
Carrie Foster
Lauren Goddard
Denny Hager
Joyce Haughey
Jennifer Heleine
Barry Offringa

Quality Control Technician
Laura Albert

Proofreading and Indexing
TECHBOOKS Production Services

Contents

Contents

Contents

Contents

Contents

Contents

Contents

Introduction

A shell is a program that takes commands typed by the user and calls the operating system to run those commands. For example, you may use the shell to enter a command to list the files in a directory, such as ls, or a command to copy a file, such as cp. A shell acts as a form of wrapper around the operating system, hence the term *shell*.

Unix and Linux systems support many different kinds of shells, each with its own command syntax. You can run a shell window to enter shell commands from a graphical desktop environment.

Shell scripts combine commands together and act similarly to batch files. With a shell and shell scripts, you can customize your system, automate tedious daily tasks, better perform your work, and get more out of your computers.

No matter how nice a graphical user interface your system sports, adding the power of a shell can dramatically increase the speed and efficiency of what you can do on your computer. Shells provide greater control over your system and allow you to do some things that simply cannot be done from the graphical environment. Shells often allow you to perform tasks remotely, which proves useful if you need to do something to a large number of computers, or computers located at another site.

Furthermore, Apple Computer chose Unix, an inherently scriptable operating system, as the basis for Mac OS X. In the Macintosh environment, you get the ability to create scripts along with a really neat desktop user interface.

As many small devices grow in functionality, you'll find shells even on low-end PDAs and handheld computers.

Many users fear the command line, which does seem kind of retro in this era of graphical user interfaces. But the immense power of shell scripts makes it worthwhile to learn about the shell and scripting.

This book covers shells, shell scripts, and a vast array of techniques for getting the most out of your systems with scripts.

Whom This Book Is For

This book is aimed at anyone who wants to get more out of their computer systems. This especially includes Mac OS X users who want to take advantage of the powerful underpinnings of Mac OS X, and Linux users who want to learn more about their systems.

Windows users can take advantage of shells and shell scripts to work around some of the brain-dead features of that operating system.

You do not need to have any prior experience writing programs or scripts. Wrox "Beginning" books start with the basics and lead you through the entire process. If you do happen to have programming experience, many of the topics will prove easier to pick up.

What Does This Book Cover?

This book covers shells and shell scripting with a special emphasis on the Bourne shell, the most commonly available shell. Special features of the C shell, bash, and Korn shells are also covered, but the emphasis is on scripts that are compatible with the Bourne shell. This will allow your scripts to work on the largest number of systems.

This book starts with the basics of shells and then covers how to make shell scripts. Special chapters cover interacting with the operating system and more complicated programming techniques. After reading this book, you should have a thorough grounding in how to create shell scripts, as well as the ability to find out more, an important task in today's ever-changing world of technology.

Throughout this book, you'll find a plethora of practical examples. We promise not to show how clever we are and instead focus on what works.

How This Book Is Structured

The first five chapters of the book cover the basics of shell scripting. Chapters 6 to 11 address more advanced scripting topics, including awk and sed, two commands that are used in a great many scripts. The final chapters of the book show how to apply scripting to status monitoring, systems administration, and the desktop.

The following is a summary of the topics covered in each chapter:

❑ **Chapter 1, Introducing Shells:** In this first chapter, you see what a shell is and how shells work. You discover the great variety of shells as well as how to find the shell on your system. You learn how to call up shell windows so that you can type in commands. You also learn about the default shells on Mac OS X, Windows (under Cygwin), Linux, QNX, and other systems.

❑ **Chapter 2, Introducing Shell Scripts:** This chapter extends the discussion of shells to introduce shell scripts. You find out what a script is, how to create scripts, as well as how to run scripts. Because scripting requires a text editor, you'll find a review and recommendation of editors for Linux, Unix, Windows, and Mac OS X.

❑ **Chapter 3, Controlling How Scripts Run:** This chapter introduces how scripts run, as well as how you can control which commands in your scripts get executed. You find out how to have your scripts make decisions and take alternate paths as needed.

❑ **Chapter 4, Interacting with the Environment:** No shell is an island. This chapter covers how your shells can find out about the surrounding environment. This chapter delves into how to pass data to a shell script and how to modify the environment. Furthermore, you'll see how the magic #! line works and you'll learn how to create executable commands from your scripts.

❑ **Chapter 5, Scripting with Files:** Virtually all modern operating systems allow you to store data in files. This is important so that most scripts interact with files of some sort. To help with this, Chapter 5 covers how to create, read, modify, and remove files.

❑ **Chapter 6, Processing Text with sed:** Sed provides a stream, or batch-mode text editor. Using sed for text editing would be excruciatingly painful. But, using sed from scripts allows you to transform files with simple shell commands. This chapter covers how to call on sed's power from your scripts.

❑ **Chapter 7, Processing Text with awk:** Awk is a special tool for working with text. Zillions of shell scripts use awk for sophisticated parsing and control over text. This chapter introduces awk and how you can call on awk from your scripts.

❑ **Chapter 8, Creating Command Pipelines:** Shells and shell scripts come out of the ancient Unix traditions. These traditions include the quaint notion that each command should perform one task and one task only. The Unix philosophy includes the ability to combine these building-block commands into more complex commands. Chapter 8 covers how to create command pipelines, where the shell sends the output of one command to the input of another.

❑ **Chapter 9, Controlling Processes:** Chapter 9 discusses the terms "program," "process," and "process IDs." It shows how you can query about processes, kill processes, and gather information about what is running on your system. This chapter also covers how to call on other processes from your scripts and then query how the processes ran, such as whether the processes succeeded or failed.

❑ **Chapter 10, Shell Scripting Functions:** As your shell scripts grow in size and complexity, you can use functions to help simplify your scripts. Functions also make it easier to reuse parts of a script in other scripts you write. Chapter 10 covers functions as they pertain to shell scripts, how to create functions, and how to use them.

❑ **Chapter 11, Debugging Shell Scripts:** Much as you'd like, no script is perfect. Software, all software, sports little problems called *bugs*. Debugging is the art of locating and destroying these problems. This chapter covers techniques for finding bugs as well as tips to reduce the occurrence of bugs before they happen.

❑ **Chapter 12, Graphing Data with MRTG:** MRTG is a really clever package for showing complex data sets as graphs. MRTG works especially well for graphing aspects of your computing environment such as network throughput, memory resources, and disk usage. Chapter 12 shows how you can call MRTG from your scripts and use MRTG to help monitor your systems.

❑ **Chapter 13, Scripting for Administrators:** Chapter 13 extends the discussion in Chapter 12 to cover more general techniques for administering systems using shell scripts.

❑ **Chapter 14, Scripting for the Desktop:** Scripts are often associated with server systems only, but you'd be surprised at how well scripts can work on the desktop. This chapter covers how to call on your desktop applications from scripts, such as office suites, multimedia applications, and especially the Mac OS X desktop.

❑ **Appendixes:** Appendix A contains the answers to chapter exercises. Appendix B covers the most useful commands available on Unix, Linux, Mac OS X, and Windows (under Cygwin).

What Do You Need to Use This Book?

This book covers shell scripting. To try out the examples, you will need the following.

❑   A shell, such as the Bourne shell

❑   Text-editing software

Chapter 1 covers the shell requirements in depth and describes how to find the shell on your system. For Windows users, you should download and install the Cygwin package, also described in Chapter 1.

Chapter 2 covers text-editing software as these packages relate to shells. You'll find a list of editors, as well as recommendations.

Conventions

To help you get the most from the text and keep track of what's happening, a number of conventions are used throughout the book:

> **Boxes like this one hold important, not-to-be forgotten information that is directly relevant to the surrounding text.**

Tips, hints, tricks, and asides to the current discussion are offset and placed in italics like this.

As for styles in the text:

❑   Important words are *italicized* when first introduced.

❑   Keyboard strokes appear like this: Ctrl-A.

❑   Code within the text appears in a monospaced typeface, like this: `persistence.properties`.

❑   Code examples are presented in the following way:

```
Code examples appear in monofont with a gray background.
```

❑   Within code blocks containing both input and output text, input appears in **bold** font.

Keyboards differ between systems. For example, Windows and Linux systems usually sport a keyboard with an Enter key. Mac OS X keyboards from Apple Computer label the key Return instead. This book uses Enter as this is the most common form.

Source Code

As you work through the examples in this book, you may choose either to type all the code manually or use the source code files that accompany the book. All the source code used in this book is available for download at `www.wrox.com`. Once at the site, simply locate the book's title (either by using the Search box or by using one of the title lists) and click the Download Code link on the book's detail page to obtain all the source code for the book.

Because many books have similar titles, you may find it easiest to search by ISBN; this book's ISBN is 0-7645-8320-4.

After you download the code, just decompress it with your favorite compression tool. Alternatively, you can go to the main Wrox code download page at www.wrox.com/dynamic/books/download.aspx to see the code available for this book and all other Wrox books.

Errata

We make every effort to ensure that there are no errors in the text or in the code. However, no one is perfect, and mistakes do occur. If you find an error in one of our books, like a spelling mistake or faulty piece of code, we would be very grateful for your feedback. By sending in errata you may save another reader hours of frustration; at the same time, you will be helping us provide even higher quality information.

To find the errata page for this book, go to www.wrox.com and locate the title using the Search box or one of the title lists. Then, on the book's details page, click the Book Errata link. On this page, you can view all errata that has been submitted for this book and posted by Wrox editors. A complete book list including links to each book's errata is also available at www.wrox.com/misc-pages/booklist.shtml.

If you don't spot "your" error on the Book Errata page, go to www.wrox.com/contact/techsupport.shtml and complete the form there to send us the error you have found. We'll check the information and, if appropriate, post a message to the book's errata page and fix the problem in subsequent editions of the book.

p2p.wrox.com

For author and peer discussion, join the P2P forums at p2p.wrox.com. The forums are a Web-based system for you to post messages relating to Wrox books and related technologies and interact with other readers and technology users. The forums offer a subscription feature to email you topics of interest of your choosing when new posts are made to the forums. Wrox authors, editors, other industry experts, and your fellow readers are present on these forums.

At http://p2p.wrox.com you will find a number of different forums that will help you not only as you read this book, but also as you develop your own applications. To join the forums, just follow these steps:

1. Go to p2p.wrox.com and click the Register link.
2. Read the terms of use and click Agree.
3. Complete the required information to join as well as any optional information you wish to provide and click Submit.
4. You will receive an email with information describing how to verify your account and complete the joining process.

You can read messages in the forums without joining P2P, but in order to post your own messages, you must join.

Once you join, you can post new messages and respond to messages other users post. You can read messages at any time on the Web. If you would like to have new messages from a particular forum emailed to you, click the Subscribe to this Forum icon by the forum name in the forum listing.

For more information about how to use the Wrox P2P, be sure to read the P2P FAQs for answers to questions about how the forum software works as well as many common questions specific to P2P and Wrox books. To read the FAQs, click the FAQ link on any P2P page.

Introducing Shells

This chapter introduces the shell, obviously the most important component for shell scripting. It describes the choices among shells, as well as how to find out which shells are available. In modern graphical desktop environments, it is not always easy to find the shell, but you'd be surprised at how many systems actually support shells, from Zaurus PDAs to Audrey network appliances to the beautifully designed Mac OS X systems.

No matter how nice a graphical user interface your system sports, adding the power of a shell can dramatically increase the speed and efficiency of what you can do on your computer. Shells provide greater control over your system and allow you to do some things that simply cannot be done from the graphical environment. Shells often allow you to perform tasks remotely, which is especially useful if you need to do something to a large number of computers or computers located at another site.

Even in an environment such as Apple's Mac OS X, shell scripting is a useful, powerful tool in anyone's kit. Apple had the forethought to make it possible to connect shell scripts to the GUI environment via a number of custom utilities that ship with the OS, so you can link UI-level scripts done in AppleScript to the shell environment for more power than either environment alone would have.

Because shells exist to accept your commands, each shell provides help for entering complicated commands, a set of sometimes-complicated shortcuts that can speed up your work immensely. These shortcuts include special editing modes, based on the two traditional text editors, `emacs` and `vi`.

In this chapter, I discuss the following:

❑ Understanding shells, including a number of different shells with interesting names such as bash, ksh, and csh.

❑ Finding your shell, which is not always easy in a graphical desktop environment.

❑ Entering commands into shells, editing those commands, and storing a history of your commands.

❑ Using wildcards in your commands.

If you're already familiar with the shell, parts of this chapter will likely cover material you already know. If so, you may want to skim through for anything new and then jump to the next chapter.

What Is a Shell?

A *shell* is a program that takes commands typed by the user and calls the operating system to run those commands. The shell interprets your commands. For example, you may use the shell to enter a command to list the files in a directory, such as ls, or a command to copy a file, such as cp.

There are a number of different shells, which are introduced later in this chapter.

Here's a short example to give you a taste of using a shell. Launch a shell window, or access a shell. Type the following command to list all the files in the current directory:

If you don't know how to launch a shell window on the desktop or log into a shell, that's okay. See the section Determining Which Shell You Are Running for more on how to track down the elusive shell on your system.

```
$ ls
configuration   eclipse    icon.xpm     plugins   startup.jar
cpl-v10.html    features   notice.html  readme    workspace
```

In this example, you simply type ls and press Enter (or Return, depending on your keyboard). The $ is the shell prompt, which tells you the shell awaits your commands. The remaining lines are the names of the files in the current directory.

Just going over the basics of running a simple command introduces a lot of complex topics, as shells are not all that simple. If the following sections don't make sense, don't worry. Each topic will be covered in detail later in this book.

The shell displays its prompt, shown here as $, and then passively awaits your commands. When you type a command and press Enter (or Return on Mac OS X systems), you are telling the shell to execute your command.

The shell looks for a program—that is, a file with execute permissions—with the name ls. The shell looks at all the directories in your command path. The shell runs the first program found that matches the name (and the execute permissions) and then displays the results of the program to your screen, as in the second and third lines in the code example.

The command path is stored in the environment variable named PATH. Read more on environment variables in Chapter 4.

The way the shell interprets commands and executes programs is fairly complicated. Back when shells were first created, their developers thought shells were pretty nifty. The fact that you're reading this book now, more than 30 years later, means those developers were right.

Back in the ancient days of computing, computers ran no shell, or the shell, if it existed, was so connected to the operating system that it was indistinguishable. You can still see the legacy of these single-shell systems in the MS-DOS shell on Windows.

Don't worry, I'll show you how to break free of the single-shell monopoly on Windows.

A shell acts as a form of wrapper around the OS, hence the term *shell*. (Nowadays, with object-oriented parlance, a shell would be called something like a CommandReadingOperatingSystemDecorator.)

Shells were designed long before graphical interfaces existed. As graphical environments mature, most users explicitly run shells less and less for their daily work. But a shell can automate some very complex sequences of commands. In addition, most Linux systems are designed to be updated from typed-in commands — that is, from a shell. Furthermore, whether you know it or not, a shell often powers many of the graphical commands users run. Learning the shell can help you better understand your computer.

Why Use Shells?

Unix was the first popular operating system to break free of the single-shell monopoly. In Unix (and Linux), a shell is simply a program. What makes the shell special is that a shell is the program run when most users log in. (You can configure which program [shell] gets run.)

As such, the shell fits in well with the Unix philosophy that each command should do one thing and do it well. Complex commands are then built by combining small commands. In this context, a shell is simply another command — a command that facilitates combining other commands.

You can use shell scripts to automate administrative tasks, encapsulate complex configuration details, and get at the full power of the operating system. The ability to combine commands allows you to create new commands, thereby adding value to your operating system. Furthermore, combining a shell with a graphical desktop environment allows you to get the best of both worlds. You get all the friendliness of the graphical user interface and all the power of the command line.

On Unix and Unix-like systems such as Linux, a shell interprets your commands, running one or more programs for each command you enter. In addition, most shells allow you to group a number of commands in a file, called a *shell script*. When you run the shell script file, the shell executes the commands in the script file in order.

For example, you can create a shell script to look for all files that have the text string `"abc"` in the file name and then sort those files by the date they were last modified and back up those files that contain the most recent changes. The same script could send you an email when it finishes its work and also deliver an affirmation that you are a good person.

Each shell provides a different syntax as to what you can enter. The syntax supported by most shells includes a lot of support for working with files. For example, you can list all the files that start with an uppercase *A* or a lowercase *a*, using a simple command like the following:

```
$ ls [Aa]*
```

3

The ls part tells the shell to launch the command named ls (which lists file names). The [Aa]* part is interpreted by the shell and is part of the syntax supported by most shells.

The bracket syntax, [Aa], is considered a regular expression. Many commands, such as grep, support regular expressions, sometimes with a slightly different syntax. See the Working with Wildcards section for more on regular expressions and wildcards.

What Kind of Shells Are There?

Since there is no monopoly on shells, you are free to run any shell you desire. That's all well and good, but choosing a shell without knowing the alternatives isn't very helpful. The following sections introduce the main shells.

The Bourne Shell

The original Unix shell is known as sh, short for *shell* or the Bourne shell, named for Steven Bourne, the creator of sh. As shells go, sh remains fairly primitive, but it was quite advanced for the 1970s, when it first appeared (as part of the Seventh Edition Bell Labs Research version of Unix). The Bourne shell has been considered a standard part of Unix for decades. Thus, sh should be available on almost all systems that support Unix or Unix-like commands, including Linux, Unix, and Mac OS X systems.

The Bourne shell feature set, therefore, forms the least common denominator when it comes to shells. If you truly need to write portable shell scripts, stick to only the features supported by sh. (I'll highlight where I go beyond these features in the examples.)

The basic Bourne shell supports only the most limited command-line editing. You can type characters, remove characters one at a time with the Backspace key, and press Enter to execute the command. If the command line gets messed up, you can press Ctrl-C to cancel the whole command. That's about it. Even so, the Bourne shell supports variables and scripting, and remains in wide use today, especially for system administration scripts.

For many years, the Bourne shell was all that was available for interactive Unix usage. Then along came the C shell, or csh, the first major alternative to the Bourne shell.

The C Shell

Designed by Bill Joy at the University of California at Berkeley, the C shell was so named because much of its syntax parallels that of the C programming language, at least according to the official documentation. Finding similarities is not always that easy, so don't expect C programming skills to help with the C shell, unfortunately. What is true, however, is that a great many C programmers use the C shell.

The C shell caught on quickly and became the default shell on Unix systems derived from the Berkeley Software Distribution, or BSD, flavors of Unix. Among the surviving players today, Solaris, based originally on BSD Unix and later on System V Unix, has many die-hard C shell users.

Csh added some neat features to the Bourne shell, especially the ability to recall previous commands (and parts of previous commands) to help create future commands. Because it is very likely you will need to execute more than one command to perform a particular task, this C shell capability is very useful.

The most commonly used special C shell commands include !! to execute the previous command again and !$ to insert the last argument of the previous command. See the section Entering Commands for more on these handy shorthand commands.

> *Note how virtually all shells have sh in their names, such as csh, ksh, bash, and so on. The major exception is the rc shell, covered later in this chapter.*

For many years, the C shell and the Bourne shell were the only games in town. Anyone who used Unix heavily in the 1980s or early 1990s likely learned the C shell for its superior feature set and command-line editing capabilities. Most Bourne shell scripts, however, will not run in the C shell because of differences in syntax.

The C shell was an essential part of the Berkeley, BSD, version of Unix. And the C shell formed one of the reasons why users wanted to run BSD Unix instead of the official Unix, which came from AT&T at the time. During this period of rivalry between West Coast Unix (BSD) followers and East Coast Unix (AT&T) followers, the AT&T folks created an alternative to the C shell called the Korn shell.

The Korn Shell

The Korn shell became one of the main salvos in AT&T's response to the growing popularity of BSD Unix. When AT&T developed System V (five) Unix, the developers realized they needed a shell to match the capabilities of the C shell. (As per software developers everywhere, they chose not to use the freely licensed C shell that already existed but instead created something new.)

Created by David Korn at AT&T Bell Laboratories, the Korn shell, or ksh, offers the same kind of enhancements offered by the C shell, with one important difference: The Korn shell is backward compatible with the older Bourne shell syntax. While the C shell created a brand-new syntax, the Korn shell follows the earlier Bourne shell syntax, extending the syntax as needed. This means that the Korn shell can run most Bourne shell scripts. The C shell cannot.

> *You can find out more about the Korn shell at www.kornshell.com.*

The Korn shell has been standardized as part of POSIX, the Unix suite of standards, covered later in the chapter.

The Korn shell ships as a standard part of System V Unix. This means that everyone with a commercial version of Unix, such as AIX, HP-UX, or Solaris, has the Korn shell (and this is likely the default shell, too). Users of Berkeley Unix and Linux, however, had no access to the proprietary Korn shell. And that was a shame because users liked the features of the Korn shell. The proprietary nature of the Korn shell created a rift. Just about everything in Unix could be made to run on any other version of Unix. But users of commercial versions of Unix had the Korn shell. Users of free versions of Unix did not because there was no free alternative for the Korn shell. That meant that Korn shell scripts would not run on the free versions of Unix. Furthermore, many organizations ran both commercial and free versions of Unix, adding to the problem of having scripts that run on one system and not on another. The whole idea of Open Systems, especially promoted by Unix, was that programs could run on any Unix or Unix-like system. The Korn shell was one of the first major programs that broke this covenant. The rise of Linux just made the problem worse because Linux did not run the Korn shell as well, as covered following.

This situation left Unix administrators pulling their hair out because the shells available on different flavors of Unix acted differently.

To help with this problem, Eric Gisin wrote a public domain Korn shell, called pdksh, that remains popular today. Years later, the source code to the official Korn shell was released under an open-source license. But this all occurred too late to stop the rise of bash.

The Korn shell was king of the shells on proprietary Unix, but that now pales in comparison to the installed base of Linux. Linux, a Unix work-alike operating system, grew faster than anyone predicted, and Linux users wanted an advanced shell with features like that of the Korn shell. But Linux users needed a shell that was freely available under an open-source license. This led to the development of bash.

Where the Korn shell was a form of answer to the success of the C shell, the bash shell can be considered an answer to the Korn shell.

Bash, the Bourne Again Shell

The bash shell answered a clear need, a need shown by the initial success of the Korn shell. Users wanted a shell that was compatible with Bourne shell scripts but with advanced features such as command-line editing. Users also needed a freely available shell, free of proprietary licenses. All of this led to bash, or the Bourne Again shell, a play on words to link it to the earlier Bourne shell.

Bash offers command-line editing like the Korn shell, file-name completion like the C shell, and a host of other advanced features. Many users view bash as having the best of the Korn and C shells in one shell. That's good because the Korn shell was available only on System V Unix systems. It was not available on BSD Unix, Linux, or other systems. On these systems, bash filled in the gap left by the lack of a Korn shell. All this occurred as Linux grew at a spectacular rate, often at the expense of Unix systems. This led to the situation today, where there are far more bash users than Korn shell users.

Years later, the Korn shell sources were released under an open-source license, but it was too late. Bash rules the roost now. Bash is by far the most popular shell and forms the default shell on Linux and Mac OS X systems. The examples in this book focus on the Bourne shell with the extensions provided by bash.

> Be aware: Linux and Mac OS X systems actually use the bash (Bourne Again) shell as the default shell. Bash then masquerades as sh, the Bourne shell. But on standards-compliant Unix systems such as Solaris, from Sun Microsystems, the sh command is supposed to be the Korn shell, ksh (covered following). This can lead to a conflict, unless — and this is very important — you stick to just the older Bourne shell features supported by both bash and ksh. Another "gotcha" for Mac OS X is that versions of that environment prior to 10.3.X used tcsh, or T shell, as the default, which is a csh, or C shell derivative. Because most shell scripts are assuming sh or an sh derivative, not checking which shell your script is running in can cause problems. Luckily, there's an easy way to deal with this, and you learn about it in the book.

tcsh, the T C Shell

Linux systems popularized the T C shell, or tcsh. Tcsh extends the traditional csh to add command editing, file-name completion, and more. For example, tcsh will complete file and directory names when you press the Tab key (the same key as used in bash). The older C shell did not support this feature.

For the most part, tcsh acts as a C shell on steroids. It is mostly backward compatible with the C shell. In fact, on Linux, tcsh is the program that acts both as csh and tcsh, so many Linux C shell users are really running the enhanced tcsh instead.

Other Shells

Over the years, a number of other shells have appeared, each with a small but devoted following. These shells include ash, zsh, and rc.

Created by Kenneth Almquist, ash is a Bourne shell–compatible shell that is smaller than bash and runs certain scripts more accurately than bash. Almquist created ash on NetBSD Unix to better run INN, a program for exchanging newsgroup postings with other computers. INN had troubles running under bash.

Ash is the default shell and appears as sh on the Cygwin environment for Windows.

The Z shell, or zsh, focuses on interactive usage. Zsh offers a zillion extended options for working with wildcards, file listings, directories and paths. These are all very useful on Unix or Linux systems, which all have a very deep directory hierarchy.

See www.zsh.org for more on the Z shell.

The rc shell comes from the Plan 9 operating system, developed by Bell Laboratories, where Unix originated. Plan 9 sports some interesting features and takes the Unix philosophy to the next level. With Plan 9, users can log in to any system on the network and see their home directory, regardless of where the directory is actually stored. A small number of users adopted rc outside of Plan 9.

Graphical Shells

At a time when Unix vendors felt they could compete against Windows in the desktop software arena, these vendors created a number of graphical extensions to shells, particularly the Korn shell. The Common Desktop Environment, or CDE, was meant to provide a standard desktop experience for Unix users. CDE combined elements developed by Hewlett-Packard, Sun, and other Unix workstation vendors. In the end, however, CDE was too little, too late. It wasn't until years later, with the development of the Mac OS X operating system's Aqua UI, and the Linux GNOME and KDE desktop software, that Unix systems could really compete with Windows on the desktop.

Out of the CDE effort, however, came dtksh, short for the desktop Korn shell (many CDE programs sport names that start with *dt*). Dtksh is the Korn shell and supports all the standard ksh features. In addition, you can create windows, menus, dialog boxes, and text-input fields using shell commands built into dtksh.

Another shell with graphical commands is tksh, which combines the Tk (pronounced *tee kay*) graphical toolkit that comes with the Tcl (pronounced *tickle*) scripting language with the Korn shell. Tksh extends the Korn shell with graphical commands but otherwise uses the Korn shell syntax in place of the Tcl syntax.

For more on tksh, see www.cs.princeton.edu/~jlk/tksh/.

The Official POSIX Shell

POSIX, the Portable Operating System Interface for Computer Environments standard, defines a standard for writing portable applications. This is really a standard for writing portable applications at the source code level on systems that look similar to Unix. Because many applications depend on a shell (especially for installation), POSIX also standardizes on a shell — the Korn shell.

The POSIX shell, however, is called sh. This means that a host of slightly different applications all masquerade as sh, the venerable Bourne shell:

❑ Some Unix systems still include the AT&T-created Bourne shell.

❑ Most modern commercial Unix systems, however, include the POSIX shell, which is really ksh under the covers in a POSIX compatibility mode.

❑ On Mac OS X and Linux systems, bash acts as sh.

❑ On the Cygwin environment for Windows, as well as NetBSD Unix, ash acts as sh. Each of these shells can act mostly like the Bourne shell, but all sport some differences. As you can imagine, this situation can lead to problems when trying to write portable shell scripts.

Note that bash should conform to most of the POSIX 1003.2 standard. The problem occurs, however, when script writers make assumptions based on whichever shells act as sh for their systems.

To help resolve these problems, you can run bash with the --posix command-line option. This option tells bash to operate with the POSIX standard default operations instead of the bash-specific operations where they differ. In other words, this makes bash act more like a POSIX shell. See the Command-Line Options section for more on how to use command-line options.

Default Shells

The default shell on Linux and Mac OS X is bash, the Bourne Again shell. Bash provides a modern shell with many features, and it runs on many, many systems where it is not the default. Hence, I use bash as the primary shell for the examples throughout this book.

Barring extra configuration, the default shells for many systems appear in the following table.

Operating System	Default Shell
Mac OS X	bash (Mac OS X 10.3, earlier versions use tcsh)
Solaris, HP-UX, System V Unix	ksh
QNX 6	ksh
Zaurus PDA	bash
Yopy PDA	bash
Windows with Cygwin	bash
Windows with Services for Unix	ksh (not a full version, however)

If your system does not have bash, you can download the sources from www.gnu.org/software/bash/.

Choosing a Shell

Unless you are the administrator or have administrator permissions, you are stuck with the default shell as defined by your administrator. That's usually okay because modern shells are all pretty good, and you may need to deal with assumptions regarding shells as you work. For example, when administrators assume everyone runs the Korn shell, they may set up parts of the environment that break in strange ways for users of other shells, particularly users of the C shells. This often happens with commands that are not specifically shell scripts. And these types of problems can be really hard to track down.

So your best bet is to stick with the default shell as defined by your administrator. If you are the administrator or you have administrator permissions, you can change your startup shell to run the shell you prefer.

If you are free to choose but you don't have any particular requirements or a history with a particular shell, choose bash if it is available. Bash is under active development and forms the default shell on a great many systems.

If you don't have bash available, go with the Korn shell if it is available. (This is sad to say, coming from a die-hard C shell user.) The C shell was the best thing around in its day, but bash is clearly the most-used shell today. Bash has most of the good features of the C shell, too.

If you do have a history with a particular shell, go ahead and use that shell, as you will be the most productive with a familiar shell.

Changing Your Default Shell

The chsh command, if available, allows you to change your default, or login, shell. This is handy if you just hate your current shell and your administrator is not open to changing your shell for you. The chsh command, short for *change shell*, allows you to modify the system environment for your login. The basic syntax follows:

```
chsh username new_default_shell
```

For example, to change user ericfj to use bash, run the chsh command as follows:

```
$ chsh ericfj /bin/bash
```

Note that you need to enter the full path to the shell. The chsh command will likely require you to type in your password, so that only you and the administrator can change your default shell. The new login shell will be available for use the next time you log in. (You can log out and log back in to run the new shell.)

On Linux, you need a slightly different syntax:

```
chsh -s new_default_shell username
```

On BSD Unix, use the chpass command, which requires the following syntax:

```
chpass -s new_default_shell username
```

On Mac OS X, there are a number of ways to change your shell, depending on your setup. First, you can run either chpass or chsh (they are both the same program), using the chpass syntax listed previously. The second and more common way is to change the settings in the Terminal application. (You talk to the shell in Mac OS X via Terminal, which is just a, well, terminal to the shell environment in Mac OS X.) From the /Applications/Utilities directory open the Terminal application. From the Application menu, select Preferences, or press ⌘-, (the Command key plus the comma key). The Terminal Preferences window opens. Select the "Execute this command (specify complete path):" button, and enter the full path to that shell, such as /bin/tcsh (as shown in Figure 1-1). Note that this method changes the default shell that Terminal uses for every physical user on that system, so if there's more than one person and you change the shell, you may have some irate people on your hands.

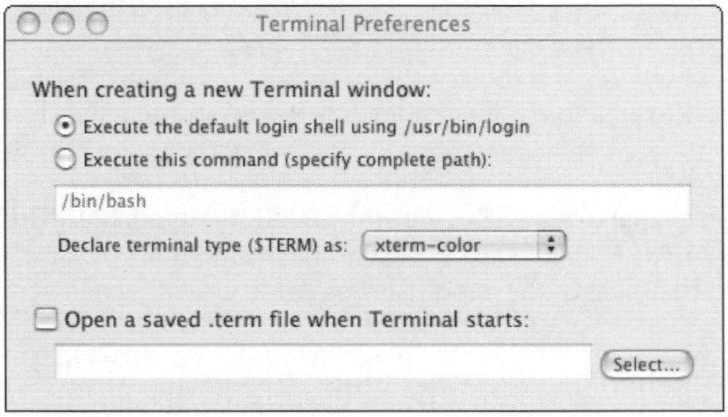

Figure 1-1

Another way to change the shell for a specific user is to use NetInfo Manager, which is the GUI interface to the directory system Mac OS X uses to store user account settings. From the /Applications/Utilities/ directory, open up NetInfo Manager. NetInfo Manager displays a hierarchy of settings in a columnar fashion; the root is on the left, and the current branch opens to the right. In the middle column, click the "users" entry, and find your short username (in our example, "admin") Notice that when you click admin, the bottom window displays various settings for that user, as shown in Figure 1-2.

To make changes, click the "Click the lock to make changes" button. You must be an admin user to authenticate; otherwise, you won't be allowed to change your shell here. After you've authenticated, scroll down in the settings area of the window until you see the "shell" entry. Double-click the path for the current default shell in the Value(s) column, and enter the full path to the new default shell, as in Figure 1-3.

Figure 1-2

After you've entered the new shell path, hit ⌘-S to save. You'll be asked if you really want to do this. Click "Update this copy" to save your changes, and quit NetInfo Manager. You should see your change reflected in Terminal immediately, but if not, log out and log back into your account, and you'll see the changes.

Figure 1-3

Running a Shell from Within Another Shell

Shells are simply programs. Because a shell can run programs, nothing is stopping you from running a shell from within a shell, or a shell within a shell within a shell, and so on. To do this, simply type in the shell command you want to run. For example, if your default shell is bash, but you want to try the features of tcsh, simply type in **tcsh** and try it out:

```
$ tcsh
$
```

The tcsh program responds with a prompt, ready for your commands. Remember now, however, that you are running a different shell, so the syntax of some commands may differ.

Finding Out More About the Shell

Use the man command to display more information, a lot more information, on your shell. For example, to learn about the bash shell, use the following command:

```
$ man bash
```

You should see copious output.

How Do Shells Fit into a Graphical Environment?

The shell, combined with the cryptic commands it supports, such as cp and rm, helped form the impression that Unix and Linux systems are hard to use. Today, just about every system offers a graphical desktop environment that makes using the computer a lot easier.

As the various desktop environments mature, users tend to run shells less and less. Some users may even end up believing that there is no such thing as a shell. For example, you can work with a Macintosh system for a long time and never need a shell. That's good. The shell just gives you extra power and flexibility.

The problem of how to embed a shell into a graphical environment was solved years ago with the Unix xterm application and the Macintosh Programmer's Workshop (MPW). In both these cases, the shell runs inside a window on the normal desktop display. The problem was, prior to Mac OS X, the OS didn't have the concept of a shell, so it was always a bit of a kludge. Now that Mac OS X is based on BSD Unix, you now have the full abilities of a true Unix shell environment available, a great improvement over earlier attempts. This provides a very powerful tool. Shell windows typically add scroll bars, control over fonts and font sizes, and, most important, the ability to copy and paste text. Place two or more shell windows on your display, and you have a powerful environment because you can run commands in one window and then select text for placement into commands entered in another.

The image in Figure 1-4 shows a typical power-user Linux desktop with multiple shell windows.

Because a great many shell commands work on files, you can often use a graphical file manager to eliminate the need for a shell. Graphical file manager programs, however, don't work well for those tasks that shells work best at. For example, if you want to change the case of all the file names in a directory from uppercase to lowercase, shells work far better than file managers. Also, if you want to copy those files that have been modified after a certain date, for a backup perhaps, shells again work better than file managers.

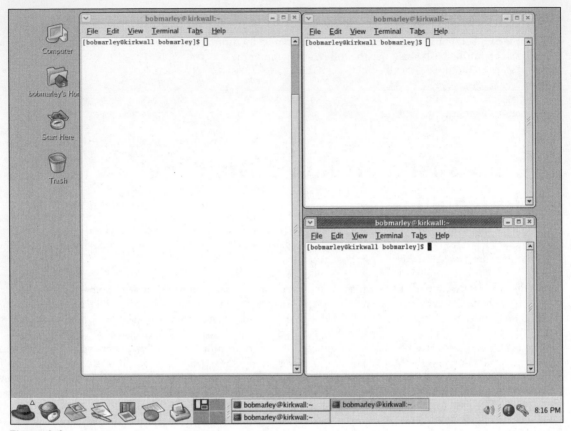

Figure 1-4

Once you determine you need a shell, the next step is to find it.

In modern desktop environments, shells run inside special shell windows that hold a shell-based command line. Most shell windows also support scroll bars that allow you to review the output of past commands.

If the shell is the first program run when you log in to a system, it seems odd to have to find the shell. But on today's modern operating systems, the desktop environments often hide the shell on purpose. The intent is not to stop you from using the shell; instead, the goal is to reduce the level of fear of users taught that Unix-like systems are difficult to use.

If you are logging in using the telnet or ssh programs, then the first program you see will likely be a shell. Problem solved. You've found your shell. If instead you run a graphical desktop environment, you may need to look around. The following sections describe how to start a shell window for a number of Unix and Unix-like systems, starting with Linux.

Running Shells on Linux

Linux systems typically run one of two major desktop environments, GNOME or KDE. Both the GNOME and KDE environments, however, try to appear somewhat like Windows, with the Linux equivalent of the Windows Start menu usually appearing in the lower-left corner.

On a Fedora or Red Hat Linux system with a GNOME or KDE desktop, choose Terminal from the System Tools menu. With the default KDE environment, choose Terminal from the System menu.

Your Linux system may sport slightly different menus, but the concept is the same. Nowadays, the shell is considered a tool or utility and will be available on a sub-menu under the main system menu.

These applications are called terminals or terminal windows because they create a pseudo, or virtual, terminal, which mimics the behavior of an old-fashioned ASCII terminal. To the underlying operating system, these actually are terminals, albeit software-only terminals.

Running the GNOME Shell Window

Figure 1-5 shows the gnome-terminal window, which provides the default shell under the GNOME desktop. Choose Terminal from the System Tools menu to launch this program. (The KDE terminal window looks similar to the gnome-terminal window, as covered in the following section.)

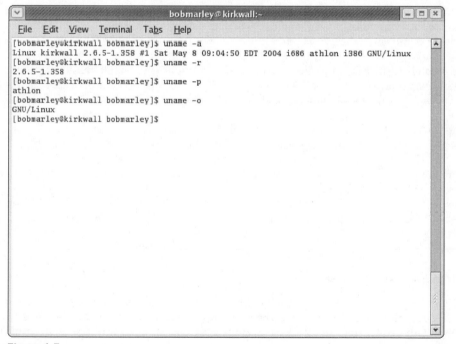

Figure 1-5

The first thing you should notice about the gnome-terminal window is the menu bar, which spans the top of the window. The menus on this menu bar allow you to customize the terminal window. For example, you can control the size of the text from the View menu.

The second thing to notice is the very handy scroll bar along the side, which allows you to scroll through the output. For example, if you list all the files in a large directory, the listing will scroll because there are likely more file names to display than will fit within the window.

The third thing to notice is the shell prompt, usually ending with a $ character, which shows the shell running inside the window awaits your commands. The gnome-terminal window will launch your default shell, usually bash. (As with most things, you can configure this in the profile settings within the gnome-terminal window.)

To configure the gnome-terminal window, select Edit ➪ Current Profile. You can define the command launched in the shell window, the text size, text fonts, colors, and other details such as how many lines to save in the scroll buffer.

The other shell windows on Linux all appear very similar to the gnome-terminal window. There's not much you can do with a shell window, anyway.

Running the KDE Shell Window

The KDE shell window, called konsole, looks and feels very similar to the gnome-terminal window. The konsole application offers a comparable set of features to the GNOME offering. The konsole program extends what the gnome-terminal offers, however, with greater support for multiple sessions.

Each session is really a separate instance of the shell running. By default, sessions appear in separate tabs within the konsole window. (The gnome-terminal also supports multiple sessions, each in its own tab.) You can click the tabs to switch to additional shells.

Another excellent feature of the konsole application is support for bookmarks. Unlike web pages, konsole allows you to bookmark directories. Choose the Add Bookmark choice from the Bookmarks menu to store the current directory as a bookmark. You can then select the bookmark directory from the Bookmarks menu to jump immediately to that directory. The konsole application does this by issuing a cd command to change to the bookmarked directory.

> *The KDE konsole window uses Shift-Ins (or Insert) to paste, while the gnome-terminal window uses Shift-Ctrl-V. These shortcut differences can make it difficult to go back and forth between terminal windows. It is usually better to stick with one type of terminal window.*

Active Select and Paste

One thing that may confuse people used to Macintosh or Windows systems is the active select and paste model used by the X Window System. The X Window System, or X, provides the low-level graphics on Linux and Unix systems. (You can also run X on Mac OS X or Windows systems, in emulation.)

With X, selected text is instantly available for other programs to use. You can use the left mouse button to select text and then paste that text into a different window. Typically, the middle mouse button of a three-button mouse pastes the currently selected text. (Press the two buttons simultaneously on a two-button mouse to emulate the missing middle button.)

This may seem like the traditional copy and paste model, but you get to skip the copy step. With the X Window System's active select and paste model, you can simply select and paste.

In addition, X supports the normal copy and paste model with a clipboard. You can place some text in the clipboard while selecting other text for active pasting.

A long time ago in a galaxy far, far away, you could be really productive using active select and paste with the vi text editor in multiple shell windows. Nowadays, most users run graphical text editors, covered in Chapter 2, instead of vi.

Running Shells on Mac OS X

On Mac OS X, you'll find a shell window available by using the Terminal application, located in the /Applications/Utilities/ folder. It defaults to a base terminal window for your default shell. Because Mac OS X ships with a single-button mouse, there are some oddities that you don't find in other systems. With a single-button mouse, or the trackpad on a portable, to emulate the second button, you Control-click (press the Control key and click the mouse). This brings up a contextual menu that allows you to make use of features like pasting the selected text without going to the keyboard, as shown in Figure 1-6.

If you find Ctrl-clicking annoying, just replace the standard Mac mouse with a mouse or trackball that you prefer. Without any added software, Mac OS X supports two buttons and a scroll wheel. Most of the better mice from Microsoft or Kensington come with improved drivers so you can program the extra buttons for specific tasks.

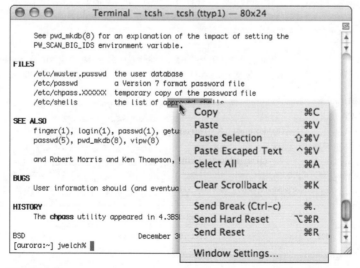

Figure 1-6

If you want to use the Xterm application to get to your shell environment under OS X, you can do that with Apple's X11 application (in Mac OS X 10.3 or later, it's a custom install), or by using XFree86. (X11 is Apple's implementation of XFree86, so they're essentially the same thing.) X11 lives in the /Applications/Utilities/ folder, and when you start it, it opens an xterm window for you by default. To emulate the second and third buttons, use Option-click and Command-click.

Running Shells on Unix Systems

On Unix systems under the CDE, or Common Desktop Environment, click the terminal icon that appears on the taskbar at the bottom of the screen. You'll see a dtterm window.

The dtterm program appears similar to that of the gnome-terminal or konsole window, although dtterm supports fewer options from the menu bar.

With the GNOME desktop environment making inroads into commercial Unix systems, especially Sun's Solaris, CDE is being used less and less.

Running Shells on Windows — Isn't command.com Enough?

MS-DOS provides a primitive shell called command.com, or cmd.exe, depending on the version of Windows. Command.com is the old name for the program that provided the MS-DOS command line on PCs. On modern Windows systems, you can still see the legacy of command.com with the MS-DOS Prompt window, the Windows equivalent of a shell window.

This shell, however, doesn't offer the features of modern Unix and Linux shells, especially when it comes to shell scripting. Because of this, if you want to write shell scripts on Windows, you need to install another shell.

Installing Cygwin on Windows

Cygwin is the name for a set of packages that provide a surprisingly large number of Unix-like utilities for Windows systems. With Cygwin installed, you can make your Windows system act very much like a Unix system, at least from a user perspective.

For shells, Cygwin includes ash, bash, tcsh, zsh, and pdksh. The default shell is bash, which you should use for the examples in this book. Download the Cygwin package from www.cygwin.com.

> **By default, Cygwin installs in** `C:\cygwin`, **which becomes the virtual root directory of the Cygwin environment. When you run the Cygwin bash shell, for example, the shell starts in your user home directory, from the perspective of Cygwin. This directory is /home/*username*, such as /home/ericfj for a user named ericfj. In reality, however, this directory is located in C:\cygwin\home\ericfj. From the bash shell, however, this appears as /home/ericfj. You need to pay attention to this if you work with files.**

To launch a Cygwin shell, use the Windows Start menu.

Because the Cygwin package includes a number of shells, as well as a plethora of commands, this is probably the best shell package for Windows users. But you may decide to instead install Microsoft's Windows Services for UNIX.

Installing the Korn Shell on Windows

Microsoft's Windows Services for UNIX provide a number of Unix commands on Windows. For shells, this package offers both the Korn shell and the C shell but not bash. Furthermore, the Korn shell as part of this package is not a complete Korn shell. Because of this, you are better off, from a shell-scripting perspective, to load Cygwin instead.

For more on the Microsoft's Windows Services for UNIX, see http://www.microsoft.com/windows /sfu/default.asp.

Running Shells on PDAs and Other Systems

In addition to running shells on desktop and server systems, you can also run shells on quite a few small systems such as PDAs, especially Linux-based PDAs.

On the Yopy PDA, click the Linupy menu (similar to the Windows Start menu), and choose Terminal from the Utilities menu. The Yopy will start a shell window running bash. On low-resolution PDA displays such as that on the Yopy, however, you will likely see only part of the width of each line, which makes entering commands and editing files more difficult.

The latest Zaurus PDAs solve the screen resolution problem by providing a 480×640 pixel screen in portrait mode and 640×480 in landscape mode. In both modes, you can see the entire width of a line.

On the Zaurus, choose Terminal from the Applications menu to launch a shell window. Or click the Home button to see the application launcher. Click the Applications tab, and select the Terminal icon. Figure 1-7 shows a bash shell window running on the Zaurus.

With QNX 6.0 on an Audrey Internet appliance, choose Terminal from the main Infinity menu (for those using the Infinity operating system images).

In most cases, it is not that hard to launch a shell window, regardless of the system you use. As you can see from these examples, even PDAs and Internet applications sport shell windows, ready for you to play with.

Once you have a shell available, the next step is to start entering shell commands. Shell commands form the basis of shell scripting.

Figure 1-7

Entering Commands

Shells display a command prompt and then await your commands. The prompt indicates the shell is ready.

The prompt usually ends with a dollar sign ($), a percent sign (%) for C shell users, or a hash mark (#, also called a sharp sign) if you are logged in as the root, or super user. Modern shells often come configured to show your username, machine name, and current directory in the prompt.

For example, the following line shows the default tcsh prompt for user ericfj on a machine named kirkwall, in the user's bin directory:

```
[ericfj@kirkwall ~/bin]$
```

Note that the tilde character, ~, is shorthand for the user's home directory.

Bash, by default, shows a prompt like the following on Linux systems:

```
[ericfj@kirkwall bin]$
```

Note how bash just displays the current directory name relative to its parent directory. You can really see the difference when you change to a user's home directory. The following shows a bash prompt for the user's home directory:

```
[ericfj@kirkwall ericfj]$
```

But if you use tcsh, you will see a prompt like the following:

```
[ericfj@kirkwall ~]$
```

Prompts are configurable, so your system may differ. In many cases, however, the default prompt is useful enough so that you don't need to change it. These examples come from a Fedora Core 2 Linux system.

In this book, a dollar sign ($) will act as a shorthand for your shell prompt. While the prompts may differ, shells all act the same: they patiently await your commands. The examples in this book show $ for the shell prompt and # for the shell prompt of the root user.

This patience has limits. On some Unix systems, for example, the C shell defaults to a 60-minute automatic logout setting. If you enter no commands for an hour, the shell quits and logs you out. This time period is also configurable.

Determining Which Shell You Are Running

Once you launch a shell window, the next step is to determine which shell you are running.

Try It Out   Which Shell Am I Running?

If you don't already know what kind of shell it is, try the following command:

```
$ echo $SHELL
/bin/bash
```

How It Works

The basic format of a shell command follows:

```
command argument1 argument2 ...
```

The *command* part is the name of a command, a program or shell script, or other file that is somehow marked as an executable command. In this example, echo is the command. Shells on Windows systems, for example, would look for commands named echo.exe, echo.com, or echo.bat to execute because Windows uses file-name extensions (.exe, .com, .bat, and so on) to mark files as executable. Linux and Unix systems, on the other hand, use file permissions to mark files as executable. Shells on Linux and Unix systems would look for an executable file named echo in this example.

Shells look for the commands in directories the shell recognizes as the command path. See Chapter 4 for more on how to modify your shell's command path.

Shells expect commands to appear first. After the command, you can pass a number of arguments to the command. These are values passed directly to the command, which then interprets the arguments as it sees fit. (There are also command-line options, covered following.)

This example uses the `echo` command, which displays a line of text, the text you provide. `Echo` is so named because it echoes back whatever you provide. This may seem like a very dumb idea for a command, but `echo` is surprisingly useful. The `echo` command allows you to present text to the user or lets you know details of how a command will run. To use `echo`, pass the data you want to display as arguments to the `echo` command.

The example passes `$SHELL` as an argument to echo. You might expect echo to print out `$SHELL`, but the leading dollar sign informs the shell that this is a special value. In this case, the dollar sign indicates that `SHELL` is a shell variable. The shell then expands the command by replacing `$SHELL` with the value of the shell variable named, appropriately enough, `SHELL`. Shells usually include quite a few shell variables populated with values about the computing environment, which is why shell variables are often called *environment variables*. While you can quibble over the differences, in most respects, shell variables are the same as environment variables.

On Linux and Unix systems, the SHELL environment variable holds the name — that is, the program file — of the user's default shell. In this case, /bin/bash indicates that the shell is bash, running as the bash command in the directory /bin. Other results include /bin/tcsh for the T C shell and /bin/ksh for the Korn shell.

> **Be careful not to depend too much on the paths, such as /bin/bash. On Unix systems, except for Mac OS X, bash will likely not be installed in /usr/bin. Instead, bash, as an add-on package, would be installed in /usr/local/bin or some other directory for commands added at a particular site. This is because bash is not standard equipment on a Unix system (other than Mac OS X and other versions of BSD Unix). On the flip side, Unix systems based on System V Unix will likely have the Korn shell installed as standard equipment. Linux systems, however, will likely not. So you may find ksh, the Korn shell, in alternate locations on BSD Unix and Linux systems.**
>
> **Non-Unix or Linux systems may install shells in entirely different locations. For example, the default shell on the QNX-based Audrey is ksh, but the command is located in /nto/bin.**

It is the shell that expands $SHELL to the value of the user's default shell. Thus, in this example, the `echo` command is passed the argument /bin/bash, which echo dutifully prints back.

Each command interprets its arguments differently, although usually arguments are file or directory names. Each command may also accept command-line options that control how the command behaves.

Command-Line Options

In most cases, a command-line *argument* provides data for a command to work on, while a command-line *option* selects among the command's many options for how to work on the data. This distinction is not always clear. In the end, you are at the mercy of whoever wrote the command in the first place. The options and arguments differ by command and are often strangely named.

Unix, which popularized these concepts and commands, has a long, long history that doesn't always make sense. For example, the command that alerts users to newly received email is called `biff`, after the name of a dog that barked when the postal carrier brought the mail.

So you should always check the documentation for each command you intend to use to see what options are supported by the command. The basic format for a command can be expanded to include the following:

```
command option1 option2 ... argument1 argument2 ...
```

Command-line options almost always come first. And command-line options almost always start with a dash character, -. Newer commands (meaning anytime after the late 1980s) often support options that start with two dashes, --.

Nowadays, the two-dash and the one-dash folks have mostly come to a *détente,* where the two-dash options are used with longer, more understandable, names for the options, and the one-dash options are used with single-letter options. The two-dash options are also often designed for infrequent use, with the single-dash short options used for the most common options.

For example, the -v option is often (although not always) used to request verbose output. The long form of this option is often --verbose. You can choose -v or --verbose as you see fit for those commands that support both options. In most cases, there will be a long option that corresponds to each single-letter option.

> *What you consider verbose and what the creator of the command considers verbose may differ greatly. Verbose may merely mean outputting a few cryptic hex numbers.*

On MS-DOS, a forward slash, /, is used in place of a dash for many command options. This is especially disconcerting to Unix and Linux users, as these systems use a forward dash to separate directories. Many MS-DOS commands accept either the slash or dash to precede options.

Try It Out   Using Command-Line Options

To see more about how command-line options work, first try the following command without any options:

```
$ uname
Linux
```

The `uname` command, originally short for *Unix name,* displays information about the operating system. By default — that is, with no options — `uname` prints out the kernel name, in this case, Linux.

Now try adding options. For example, the -o option shows the following on Linux:

```
$ uname -o
GNU/Linux
```

You can also try the longer options. For example, try the following command:

```
$ uname --hardware-platform
i386
```

With Linux on an Intel-architecture system, the hardware platform is listed as i386. The -p option provides the processor architecture. On Linux, you may see the following:

```
$ uname -p
athlon
```

Note that this Linux system uses an AMD processor.

You can combine all the uname options by using -a, or --all. For example:

```
$ uname --all
Linux kirkwall 2.6.5-1.358 #1 Sat May 8 09:04:50 EDT 2004 i686 athlon
i386 GNU/Linux
$ uname -a
Linux kirkwall 2.6.5-1.358 #1 Sat May 8 09:04:50 EDT 2004 i686 athlon i386
GNU/Linux
```

How It Works

The uname command prints out information about a system. This is important if you need to write shell scripts that can handle different computing environments and operating systems.

The uname command is one of those handy commands that can help your shell scripts determine the platform the script is running on. But the uname command also shows how not all commands run the same on all systems.

You can determine what options a command supports and, more important, what these options mean by using the online manuals. The man command displays the online manual entry for a given command. The basic format follows:

```
man command_name
```

For example:

```
$ man uname
UNAME(1)                        User Commands                        UNAME(1)

NAME
       uname - print system information

SYNOPSIS
       uname [OPTION]...
```

```
DESCRIPTION
       Print certain system information.  With no OPTION, same as -s.

       -a, --all
              print all information, in the following order:

       -s, --kernel-name
              print the kernel name

       -n, --nodename
              print the network node hostname

       -r, --kernel-release
              print the kernel release
    :
```

The man command displays the manual entries one screenful at a time, using the more command. (See Chapter 8 for details on how to create command pipelines using the more and less commands.) You can use the man command to determine the available command-line options.

> *The man command is your friend. This is one of the best commands on Unix and Linux systems and can tell you a lot about your system.*

To show how Unix and Linux commands differ, you can try the uname command on another system, such as Mac OS X.

Try It Out   Using Command-Line Options on Mac OS X

On a Mac OS X system, you'll see the following response for the uname command:

```
$ uname
Darwin
```

Darwin is the name of the Mac OS X version of BSD Unix. The -p option tells the uname command to output the processor type. On a Mac OS X PowerPC system, you will see the following:

```
$ uname -p
powerpc
```

How It Works

The uname command performs the same function on Mac OS X as on Linux or Unix systems. But the uname command differs in the support of command-line options. The Mac OS X uname command, for example, does not support the --all option, as it just prints out an illegal-option message. Mac OS X does support the -a option, however:

```
$ uname --all

uname: illegal option - l
usage: uname [-amnprsv]

$ uname -a
```

```
Darwin Eric-Foster-Johnsons-Computer.local 7.5.0 Darwin Kernel Version 7.5.0: Thu
Aug 5 19:26:16 PDT 2004; root:xnu/xnu-517.7.21.obj~3/RELEASE_PPC Power Macintosh
powerpc
```

The Mac OS X `uname` command also doesn't support the `-o` or `--hardware-platform` options. This is very important. Not all Unix and Unix work-alike systems support the same command-line options.

Combining Options

The normal format for command-line options is to precede the option letter with a dash, as in the following command:

```
$ uname -r
2.6.5-1.358
```

You can typically provide more than one option. For example:

```
$ uname -r -p
2.6.5-1.358 athlon
```

Most Unix and Linux commands also support combining a number of options with just a single dash. For example:

```
$ uname -rp
2.6.5-1.358 athlon
```

This example combines the `-r` and the `-p` option but places both on the command line with a single dash, as `-rp`. This command has the same effect as if the options were presented separately.

Strange Options

As mentioned earlier, most Unix and Linux commands support options starting with a single dash. Some newer commands, especially those that come from the GNU project (www.gnu.org), support longer-named options starting with two dashes.

A few options don't use either the single or double dash. The `dd` command, for example, supports a very different command-line option format. With `dd` (short for data dumper), the options take the following format:

```
dd option1=value1 option2=value2 ...
```

For example:

```
$ dd if=backup.iso of=/dev/tape bs=20b
```

The `dd`, `cpio`, and `tar` commands, all related to backups (at least originally), take radically different command-line options and syntax. This is just one of the quirks with Unix and its long history.

See the online manual entry for dd for more details. Just remember that Unix and Linux commands are not all consistent. You should look up the commands you need to use in the online manuals.

With the ability to create long, complex command lines, it becomes essential that you be able to edit the command line to create these commands. That is where a number of shell features come in handy.

Command Editing

The original command-line editing feature was essentially just the Backspace key. You could delete from the end and retype commands. Pressing Ctrl-C cancels the entire command. This is useful if your command is so messed up, it is no longer worth it to fix. Since those early days, shells have advanced quite far, and now most offer a plethora of features to help edit complex commands.

The original Bourne shell supports only Backspace and Ctrl-C editing of commands. But since the C shell, all new shells have supported ways to help edit commands. The facilities shells offer include the ability to repeat previous commands, or parts of previous commands, to recall commands from a history of commands and the ability to use real text editors to edit commands.

> **Unfortunately, command editing also brings out the differences between shells. The format and syntax differ greatly between shells.**

Command Substitution

Most Unix and Linux commands deal with files and directories. Furthermore, the file system supports a deep hierarchy of directories, something that comes from the rich command sets on Unix and Linux, which leads to long, complicated commands. Type in a directory name incorrectly and you may wipe out crucial data, miss an important backup, or inadvertently damage your system.

One thing shell designers noticed right away was that commands usually occur in a sequence. That is, you will typically enter a number of commands, all of which repeat parts of the previous commands. For example, you may enter a number of commands that work within a given directory. This can be as simple as copying a number of files to the same directory or changing the permissions of a number of files or directories.

To help with this, shells offer a number of ways to repeat parts or all of previous commands.

Repeating Previous Commands

The C shell introduced the double-exclamation mark syntax, ! !. This command repeats the previous command in its entirety. Now, why in the world would anyone want to repeat a command that just ran? Didn't the command already do its work? Actually, not always. Trying a command again after an error is one of the most common reasons for repetition. Other reasons you may want to repeat a previous command include the following:

❏ **To check the status of a system or application:** For example, if users report problems with an Oracle database, you may want to issue a command to check its status. If Oracle appears to be down, you may want to restart Oracle in another shell window and then repeat the command to check the status of Oracle until you verify that the database is running again.

❏ **To rebuild a software application, especially after modifying files:** Software developers do this all the time. You may edit a file with a graphical editor and then want to rebuild the software to see if you have fixed a problem or that everything is working properly. (See the Tools to Edit Shell Scripts section in Chapter 2 for more on graphical text editors.)

Attempting the same thing over and over again but expecting different results is considered a sign of insanity.

Try It Out   Repeating Commands with !!

With the C shell, T C shell, and the Bourne Again shell, use the !! syntax to repeat the previous command. For example:

```
$ df -k
Filesystem            1K-blocks       Used Available Use% Mounted on
/dev/hda2             24193540    3679032  19285536  17% /
/dev/hda1               101086       5943     89924   7% /boot
none                    502380          0    502380   0% /dev/shm
/dev/hda5             48592392   21111488  25012520  46% /home2
/dev/sda1               499968     286432    213536  58% /mnt/sd
$ !!
df -k
Filesystem            1K-blocks       Used Available Use% Mounted on
/dev/hda2             24193540    3678992  19285576  17% /
/dev/hda1               101086       5943     89924   7% /boot
none                    502380          0    502380   0% /dev/shm
/dev/hda5             48592392   21111488  25012520  46% /home2
/dev/sda1               499968     286432    213536  58% /mnt/sd
```

How It Works

Shells such as bash, csh, tcsh, or ksh keep track of the previous command, which the !! syntax recalls.

The exclamation mark character, !, is often called a bang. So !! is bang, bang.

The !! command is interpreted entirely by the shell. You won't find a command program on disk named !!. With bash, tcsh, or csh, !! will display the previous command, df -k in this example, and then execute that command.

The df command prints information on how much disk space remains free (df is short for *disk free*). The -k option tells df to output in kilobytes rather than 512-byte blocks.

Why check the amount of disk space remaining twice in a row? Because another process may have changed it (or because you are obsessive). Note how the amount of free space changed for /, or the root file system, between calls. In this case, you have a small amount of additional space. In real life, however, you'll most often use the df command as a disk fills. This can be especially important when a disk is filling rapidly.

See the section Viewing the Command History for more on repeating previous commands.

For another example, the ping command checks network connectivity to a given machine, represented by the machine's hostname or network (IP) address. The name ping comes from the pinging sound of submarine radar systems. Ping sends a certain type of network packet to another system, which should then send the packet back.

For example, the following command runs the ping command to a system identified by an IP address:

```
$ ping 192.168.0.4
PING 192.168.0.4 (192.168.0.4) 56(84) bytes of data.

--- 192.168.0.4 ping statistics ---
11 packets transmitted, 0 received, 100% packet loss, time 9998ms
```

The ping command runs forever unless it encounters a very serious error. In most cases, you need to terminate ping by pressing Ctrl-C. When you press Ctrl-C, ping displays some statistics, as shown at the end of the output in the example.

This example shows that you cannot reach the system identified by its IP address 192.168.0.4 (a system on the local network). This may lead you to check network cables and routers and whether the remote system is even running.

The ping command is not a full network testing application. If ping works, you know your system can reach the remote system on the network. If ping doesn't work, however, you cannot always assume the network is down. Many network firewalls disable ping messages. Or, the remote system may not run the process that responds to pings.

A better means to test network connectivity is usually trying to connect to the remote application you are interested in, such as a remote Web server, file server, database, or other application.

Once you think the network link is repaired, you can try the command again. For example:

```
$ !!
ping 192.168.0.4
PING 192.168.0.4 (192.168.0.4) 56(84) bytes of data.
64 bytes from 192.168.0.4: icmp_seq=0 ttl=64 time=0.069 ms
64 bytes from 192.168.0.4: icmp_seq=1 ttl=64 time=0.062 ms
64 bytes from 192.168.0.4: icmp_seq=2 ttl=64 time=0.060 ms
64 bytes from 192.168.0.4: icmp_seq=3 ttl=64 time=0.059 ms
64 bytes from 192.168.0.4: icmp_seq=4 ttl=64 time=0.061 ms
64 bytes from 192.168.0.4: icmp_seq=5 ttl=64 time=0.063 ms
64 bytes from 192.168.0.4: icmp_seq=6 ttl=64 time=0.060 ms
64 bytes from 192.168.0.4: icmp_seq=7 ttl=64 time=0.060 ms

--- 192.168.0.4 ping statistics ---
8 packets transmitted, 8 received, 0% packet loss, time 6998ms
rtt min/avg/max/mdev = 0.059/0.061/0.069/0.010 ms, pipe 2
```

In this case, the `ping` command succeeded in reaching the other system.

The Korn shell uses the r command instead of !! to repeat the previous command. You must first set up the command history feature, however. See the section Viewing the Command History for more on command histories.

Repeating Parts of Previous Commands

In addition to repeating the entire previous command, you can also ask the shell to insert parts of the previous command in any new command. The most useful feature is the ability to type !$ in place of the last item on the previous command.

The !$ syntax does not work on the Korn shell.

Try It Out   **Replacing the Last Item on the Previous Command**

When you put !$ in a command in the bash, csh, or tcsh shell, the shell replaces the !$ with the last item, usually the last argument, of the previous command. For example:

```
$ mkdir web_files
$ cp *.html !$
cp *.html web_files
$
```

How It Works

The shell doesn't do much with the !$ because the shell merely replaces the last item from the previous command, the directory web_files in this example. You can continue using !$ again and again, but remember, it repeats only the last item of the most recent command. For example:

```
$ mkdir web_files
$ cp *.html !$
cp *.html web_files
$ cd !$
cd web_files
$ cp ~/web/external/index.html !$
cp ~/web/external/index.html web_files
cp: cannot create regular file `web_files/index.html': No such file or directory
```

Notice how once you've changed directories, the subdirectory name web_files no longer applies, because you are in that directory. Also, note that the !$ syntax repeats the last item on the command line from the previous command. This is not always what you want. For example:

```
$ file index.html
index.html: HTML document text
$ cat !$ | more
cat index.html | more
<html>
<head>
<title>Near to the Barking Seals</title>
<link rel="stylesheet" type="text/css" href="pconline.css" />
<LINK REL="SHORTCUT ICON" HREF="favicon.ico">
```

```
</head>
<body bgcolor="#FFFFFF">
$ tail !$
tail more
tail: cannot open `more' for reading: No such file or directory
```

In this example, the `file` command examines the file index.html to try to determine its file type, which it assumes is HTML text. The `cat` command prints out the file to the screen, using `!$` to refer to the file name. The pipe character, `|`, sends the output of the `cat` command to the input of the next command, `more`. (This is a command pipeline, covered in Chapter 8.) The `more` command displays one screen at a time. Use the spacebar to advance to the next screen and the Esc key to quit the `more` command.

The next command line, `tail !$`, passes the last item from the previous command to the `tail` command. But there's a problem. The last item of the previous command was not the file name, but instead the `more` command. So this command fails (unless you have a file in the current directory named `more`.

Even with the limitation that you have to pay attention to what the previous command held, the `!$` syntax is one of the most useful features provided by the shell. This feature originated with the C shell and was also picked up for the bash shell. The Korn shell doesn't support this feature, unfortunately.

Using the Up and Down Arrows

In addition to using `!!` to repeat the last command and `!$` to repeat the last item from the last command, you can use the up and down arrows to cycle through the previous command.

You can edit each command that appears, modifying the command. Or you can simply run the command again.

This is one of the few features that appeared to come from the MS-DOS world and the old doskey program. Normally, features in Unix and Linux find their way into Windows and MS-DOS, not the other way around.

Viewing the Command History

The shell can keep track of more than just the previous command. In fact, you can ask the shell to keep an entire history of the commands you typed in, as the up and down arrows show.

The command-history feature originated with the C shell. The Korn shell uses a different syntax, and bash supports both the C shell and the Korn shell syntaxes.

In the C shell, you can enable the command history with a command like the following:

```
$ set history=60
```

This command tells the C shell to store the 60 previous commands in its history. When the history list fills, the shell will dump the oldest entry to make room for a new entry. See the section Customizing Your Account in Chapter 4 for more on setting up the command history when you log in.

Once set up, you can use the `history` command to view the command history, as shown following:

```
$ history
    1  12:30    echo $history
    2  12:30    history
    3  12:30    pwd
    4  12:30    cd web_files/
    5  12:31    history
```

In this example, only a few commands are in the history, all executed at about the same time, 12:30. If the history is long, you may want to pipe the output to the `more` or `less` command.

The history holds a number for each command. You can use the number with the exclamation mark, `!`, to repeat that command from the history. For example:

```
$ !3
pwd
/home2/ericfj/writing/beginning_shell_scripting/web_files
```

In this case, command number 3 in the history is the `pwd` command, which prints the current working directory.

You can also use the exclamation mark with the start of a command in the history to repeat that command. For example, the previous command, `pwd`, starts with *p*. Use the following example as a guide:

```
$ !p
pwd
/home2/ericfj/writing/beginning_shell_scripting/web_files
```

You don't have to use the first letter. You can provide one or more characters. Usually providing a number of characters ensures that you get the right command. In Unix and Linux, for example, the `rlogin` command, which logs in to a remote system, and the `rm` command, which deletes files, both start with *r*. Unless you want to accidentally delete files, you should include a number of characters when running a command from the history.

The Korn shell supports a command history as well but uses the `r` command instead of an exclamation mark. Like the C shell, you may need to set up the history feature first, but set the `HISTSIZE` value instead of the C shell's history:

```
$ HISTSIZE=60
```

Once set up, run the `fc` command (short for *fix command*) to view the history, with the `-l` (ell) option:

```
$ fc -l
1       set -o vi
2       fc
3       pwd
4       pwd
5       fc -l
```

The `fc` command can also call up an editor.

When you've selected a command, you can execute that command by number or partial text, similar to the feature in the C shell. Remember to use the r command in the Korn shell, as ksh does not support the exclamation-mark syntax.

The bash shell supports most of the C shell and Korn shell history features. Like the C shell, bash supports the history command for listing the command history. Bash supports the !!, !number, and !partial_txt means to execute previous commands. Like the Korn shell, you can execute the fc -l command to list the command history. Bash uses the Korn shell HISTSIZE setting to control the size of the command history. Bash does not support the Korn shell r commands.

The following table shows the main shell history commands.

Shell	List Command History	Run Last	Run by Text	Run from Number
bash	history, fc -l	!!	!partial_text	!number
csh	history	!!	!partial_text	!number
ksh	fc -l	r	r partial_text	r number
tcsh	history	!!	!partial_text	!number

Calling Up an Editor

In addition to executing commands from the history list, you can call up a text editor to edit any particularly complex command. Of course, you have to imagine you live in a parallel universe where only two text editors exist: vi and emacs. Even so, this can be handy in rare occasions where you face a particularly troublesome command.

Each shell, excluding csh, supports a set of editing commands. You can turn on the vi or emacs editing mode with a command, set -o for bash and ksh or bindkey with tcsh.

This style of command editing is not supported by csh. The tcsh shell adds this ability (one of the additional features tcsh adds to the csh feature set).

The following table shows the commands to control the editing mode.

Shell	Set vi Editing	Set emacs Editing
bash	set -o vi	set -o emacs
csh	not supported	not supported
ksh	set -o vi	set -o emacs
tcsh	bindkey -v	bindkey -e

Once you have set up a particular editing style, you can use the various key sequences supported by these text editors to work on the command line. For example, in emacs mode, Ctrl-A moves the cursor to the beginning of the line. If you use vi or emacs for text editing, these key combinations should come naturally to you. If you don't, you're likely better off using the text editor of your choice to create command lines or full scripts.

The bash and ksh shells also support the ability to call up a full-screen editor. The `fc` command, used previously to list the command history, can call up a text editor. Type **fc** alone to call up an editor, vi or emacs, on the previous command. Pass a number to `fc` to edit the given command in the history, such as `fc 3` to edit command 3 in the history. Pass some text of a previous command, such as `fc cp`, to edit the previous command that starts with the given text.

See Chapter 2 for more on vi, emacs, and other text editors.

Using File-Name Completion

File-name completion occurs when the shell offers to help you enter file and directory names. This is one of the most useful shell features because Unix and Linux systems have many, many directories. To ask the shell to complete a file name, simply start typing the name and then press Tab to expand the name. For example, type the following:

```
$ ls /usr/lo
```

Now press the Tab key. The shell will expand /usr/lo to /usr/local/:

```
$ ls /usr/local/
```

Now type **b**, the start of *bin*, and press the Tab key:

```
$ ls /usr/local/b <Tab>
```

The shell will expand the *b* to *bin:*

```
$ ls /usr/local/bin
```

> *Press Esc-\ in ksh in vi editing mode. Ksh doesn't support the Tab character for file-name completion. Bash supports Tab or Esc-/. Note the difference between Esc-/ (bash) and Esc-\ (ksh).*

The bash shell also supports a few more features for completing commands. If there is more than one name the shell can use, press Esc-? to see a list of all the possible files. Type **ls /usr/local/** and then press Tab. Nothing will happen because there is more than one name the shell can expand. Then press Esc-? to see all the possible files, as shown in the following example.

```
$ ls /usr/local/ Esc-?
bin        games    lib       man      share
etc        include  libexec   sbin     src
```

> *Use Ctrl-D in the C shell (and tcsh), or Esc-= in the Korn shell to list all the possible names.*

The bash shell goes further. Use Esc-~ to expand a username. Use Esc-$ to expand shell variables (a topic covered in Chapter 2). The Esc-~ comes from the use of a tilde character, ~, to refer to your home directory.

Working with Wildcards

Shells support a rich set of wildcards to help work with files. A *wildcard* is an expression that the shell uses to expand to a number of file names — that is, to all files that match the expression.

Wildcards are often called globs. The use of globs is called globbing.

The * Wildcard

The main wildcard is a star, or asterisk (*), character. (Java programmers sometimes call this a *splat*.) A star alone matches anything and nothing, sort of Zen-like. Typically, you need to pair a star with some other characters to form a more specific expression. For example, *.txt matches all file names ending with .txt, including all of the following:

```
.txt
a.txt
a_very_long_name.txt
A_FILE_NAME_WITH_UPPERCASE_LETTERS.txt
```

The * means that you don't care what letters there are before the *.txt*.

Typically, an expression such as *.txt will match all text files. You can refine the wildcard expression further. For example, a*.txt matches all file names that start with a lowercase letter a and end with .txt. Again, the * means you don't care about any letters in between. Using the files from the previous list, a*.txt would match just the following:

```
a.txt
a_very_long_name.txt
```

If you want files that start with an uppercase *A* or a lowercase *a* and end with *.txt*, use the expression [Aa]*.txt. This expression would match the following files:

```
a.txt
a_very_long_name.txt
A_FILE_NAME_WITH_UPPERCASE_LETTERS.txt
```

You can use the star more than once — for example, with the expression a*v*.txt. This expression would match only one file in the example list of files:

```
a_very_long_name.txt
```

On MS-DOS, each program has to support wildcards on its own. A few DOS commands, such as DIR, support a limited number of wildcard expressions. This is very different with Unix and Linux, as the shell supports the wildcard expressions so each program doesn't have to.

Try It Out   **Using Wildcards**

You can use the `ls` command to get a handle on how wildcard expressions work. For example:

```
$ ls /usr/lib/l*z*.a
/usr/lib/libbz2.a      /usr/lib/libkudzu_loader.a   /usr/lib/libz.a
/usr/lib/libkudzu.a    /usr/lib/libmusicbrainz.a    /usr/lib/libzvt.a
```

How It Works

In this example, the `ls` command lists files in the /usr/lib directory, a directory with a lot of files, most of which start with the lowercase letter *l* (short for *library*). In this example, the shell will expand the wildcard expression to all files with names starting with the lowercase letter *l* that also have a lowercase *z* somewhere in the file name and end with .a (a common file-name extension for libraries).

You can combine expressions, such as the following:

```
$ ls /usr/lib/l*[Az]*
/usr/lib/libbz2.a                           /usr/lib/libkudzu_loader.a
/usr/lib/libbz2.so                          /usr/lib/libmusicbrainz.a
/usr/lib/libbz2.so.1                        /usr/lib/libmusicbrainz.so
/usr/lib/libbz2.so.1.0.2                    /usr/lib/libmusicbrainz.so.2
/usr/lib/libFLAC++.so.2                     /usr/lib/libmusicbrainz.so.2.0.1
/usr/lib/libFLAC++.so.2.1.2                 /usr/lib/libOggFLAC++.so.0
/usr/lib/libFLAC.so.4                       /usr/lib/libOggFLAC++.so.0.0.4
/usr/lib/libFLAC.so.4.1.2                   /usr/lib/libOggFLAC.so.1
/usr/lib/libkdeinit_kaddprinterwizard.la    /usr/lib/libOggFLAC.so.1.0.2
/usr/lib/libkdeinit_kaddprinterwizard.so    /usr/lib/libz.a
/usr/lib/libkorganizer_eventviewer.la       /usr/lib/libz.so
/usr/lib/libkorganizer_eventviewer.so.1     /usr/lib/libz.so.1
/usr/lib/libkorganizer_eventviewer.so.1.0.0 /usr/lib/libz.so.1.2.1.1
/usr/lib/libkorganizer.la                   /usr/lib/libzvt.a
/usr/lib/libkorganizer.so.1                 /usr/lib/libzvt.so
/usr/lib/libkorganizer.so.1.0.0             /usr/lib/libzvt.so.2
/usr/lib/libkudzu.a                         /usr/lib/libzvt.so.2.2.10
```

This command lists files in the /usr/lib directory that start with a lowercase *l* and have an uppercase *A* or a lowercase *z* in their names. Unlike the previous example, this expression does not require that the file end in .*a*, or any extension for that matter.

You can use more than two letters inside the square brackets. For example:

```
$ ls /usr/lib/l*[AFLz]*.a
/usr/lib/libBrokenLocale.a   /usr/lib/libkudzu_loader.a   /usr/lib/libSDL_mixer.a
/usr/lib/libbz2.a            /usr/lib/libmusicbrainz.a    /usr/lib/libSDL_net.a
/usr/lib/libIDL-2.a          /usr/lib/libSDL.a            /usr/lib/libz.a
/usr/lib/libIDL.a            /usr/lib/libSDL_image.a      /usr/lib/libzvt.a
/usr/lib/libkudzu.a          /usr/lib/libSDLmain.a
```

This example lists all files in /usr/lib that start with *l*; have an uppercase *A*, *F*, *L*, or lowercase *z* in their names; and end with .a.

The ? Wildcard

While the star expression matches all or nothing, the question-mark expression, ?, matches precisely one character. You might need the question mark to winnow a long list of files names down to a few.

In addition, the question mark proves very useful when working with dot files. *Dot files* are files and directories that start with a period, or dot. In Unix and Linux systems, dot files are normally hidden. The ls command, for example, will skip dot files unless you explicitly ask for them.

A big problem with dot files and wildcard expressions is that the current directory has a name of a single period (.), and the parent of the current directory has a name of two periods (..), which creates a big problem if you use a wildcard expression such as .* to list all files that start with a dot. The shell can simply treat all files in the current directory as having a name that begins with ./, which refers to files in the current directory, such as ./a.txt. Also, files in the parent directory can be accessed as ../file_name, such as ../a.txt.

If you just want to view dot files and directories, use the question-mark syntax. In this case, you can start with all files with names beginning with a period and having at least two more characters, which eliminates the . and .. directories. For example:

```
$ ls .??*
```

On a typical Linux system, you will likely have hundreds of files matching this expression. (Mac OS X systems, by default, sport far fewer dot files and directories.) When you have a better idea what files are available, you can further refine expressions. For example:

```
$ ls .j*
.jedit:
abbrevs       jars        modes                   recent.xml
activity.log  jars-cache  perspective.xml         session
dtds          jtidy       PluginManager.download  settings-backup
history       macros      properties              startup

.jpi_cache:
file  jar
```

This command lists all files starting with a *.j* or all files in a directory with a directory name starting with *.j*.

Running Commands in the Background

When you run a shell command, the shell waits until the command finishes. You cannot execute any more commands, at least in that shell, until the command finishes or you kill it (typically by pressing Ctrl-C). All the operating systems discussed in this book, however, support multitasking. So why doesn't the shell? It does. Place an ampersand after a command to run it in the background. For example:

```
$ xmms &
[1] 2280
$
```

The shell responds with the process ID of the command. (See Chapter 9 for more on processes and how you can use this process ID.) Next, the shell displays a prompt. It is ready for further commands. When the background task completes, you'll see an extra message from the shell, such as the following:

```
[1]+  Done                    xmms
```

Summary

This chapter introduced the shell, the program that accepts your commands on Unix and Unix-like systems such as Linux. Shells provide the main interface to the underlying operating system. In this chapter you learned:

❑ Even if you run a graphical environment, you'll find one or more shells under the hood, running commands. Using these shells gives you access to the full power of your system.

❑ Unix and Linux systems offer a plethora of shells. Of these, the most popular shell is bash, the Bourne Again shell. Bash is the default shell on Linux and the current version of Mac OS X.

❑ Each shell offers a number of features to help enter commands, such as command-line editing and a history of commands.

❑ Shells differ in syntax, especially between the C shell and the Korn shell. That's unfortunate because it makes using a shell harder if you need to switch systems. Luckily, the bash shell supports many features of the Korn shell and the C shell. For example, bash supports both the `history` and the `fc -l` commands to list the command history.

The next chapter takes you from shells to shell scripting.

Introducing Shell Scripts

Chapter 1 introduced the shell, a program that patiently awaits your input in the form of commands. These commands range from a simple ls command to complex command lines made up of multiple commands. Each shell, such as bash, ksh, or csh, requires a slightly different syntax for entering commands, although the basics are very similar. Commands often require command-line options as arguments. All of this can make for complex commands.

Furthermore, you often need to issue a number of commands to accomplish your task. Add this all together and you can see why Unix has the reputation for being hard to use.

Shell scripts help slice through this mess. Shell scripts can hide the complex command syntax, specialized command-line options, and the long directory paths needed for many commands. Shell scripts can gather multiple commands together into one script and thereby act as a single command.

But shells aren't the only way to write scripts. Specialized scripting languages provide another means to write scripts for your system. These specialized languages include Perl, Python, and Tcl.

This chapter introduces shell scripts, as well as writing scripts to interact with the user. It addresses other scripting languages and the tools needed to create your own scripts.

This chapter covers the basics for shell scripts, including:

- ❑ Writing your first scripts
- ❑ Choosing a text editor for creating your scripts
- ❑ Writing scripts to remember strange commands, commands you won't likely remember
- ❑ Outputting text in your scripts, to provide data to the user
- ❑ Storing values in variables
- ❑ Gathering input from the user

The chapters to follow examine major topics in shell scripting in depth. For now, the best way to learn is to get started writing scripts.

What Are Shell Scripts?

A *shell script* is a text file that contains one or more commands. This seems pretty simple after all this buildup, but that's all a script really is. The power of shell scripts, however, lies not in the simplicity of the concept, but in what you can do with these files.

In a shell script, the shell assumes each line of the text file holds a separate command. These commands appear for the most part as if you had typed them in at a shell window. (There are a few differences, covered in the chapters to follow.) For example, this code shows two commands:

```
df -k
ls
```

The following Try It Out shows you how to make these two commands into a script and run it. You'll see a number of very short examples that should provide a quick overview to scripting.

Try It Out   Creating a First Script

Type these two commands into a text file. (See the section Tools to Edit Shell Scripts later in this chapter for more on choices for text editors on various platforms.) Save the file and name it `script1`.

You can then run `script1` with the `sh` command:

```
$ sh script1
Filesystem            1K-blocks      Used Available Use% Mounted on
/dev/hda2              24193540   3712320  19252248  17% /
/dev/hda1                101086      5943     89924   7% /boot
none                     502380         0    502380   0% /dev/shm
/dev/hda5              48592392  25468844  20655164  56% /home2
/dev/sda1                499968    286640    213328  58% /mnt/sd
readpipe.tcl   script1  tktext.pl  vercompare.py
```

Chapter 4 shows how to turn a shell script into a command and how to specify the shell to run for the script.

Running the `script1` script generates the same output as if you had typed the two commands, `df` and `ls`, at the shell prompt.

How It Works

This example passes the name of a file, `script1`, as an argument to the `sh` command, which is, of course, the name of the Bourne shell command.

Remember that sh may really be bash or ksh on some systems. This, and the other examples in this chapter, stick to just the syntax supported by the Bourne shell and so should run on all versions of sh.

The `sh` command reads in the `script1` file one line at a time and executes the commands it encounters. This is very important to remember: A shell runs every shell script. There is no magic involved. The shell command, `sh`, accepts a file name as an argument and executes the named file. Executing the file involves executing each command in the file one line at a time.

The `script1` script file lists two commands, `df -k` and `ls`, both commands introduced in Chapter 1. The `df` command lists the amount of disk space free on the available file systems. The `ls` command lists out the files in the current directory. Because of this, the output on your system will differ, based on the amount of free disk space on your file systems and the files in your directory. The shell outputs the results of the commands.

Notice that the output of the `df` command blends right into the output of the `ls` command. There is no separation or any explanation as to what is going on. See the section Outputting Text for more on how to change this.

You can use wildcards in your shell scripts, too, just as if you were entering commands at the command line. The following Try It Out shows you how to use wildcards.

Try It Out   Using Wildcards in a Script

Enter the following command into a text file, and save the file under the name `script2`:

```
ls /usr/lib/l*z*a
```

You can then run the command with `sh`:

```
$ sh script2
/usr/lib/libbz2.a                          /usr/lib/libkudzu_loader.a
/usr/lib/libkdeinit_kaddprinterwizard.la   /usr/lib/libmusicbrainz.a
/usr/lib/libkorganizer_eventviewer.la      /usr/lib/libz.a
/usr/lib/libkorganizer.la                  /usr/lib/libzvt.a
/usr/lib/libkudzu.a
```

How It Works

Just as if you had entered the `ls` command at the command line, the asterisks (*) in the argument are expanded by the shell to a list of those files in the /usr/lib directory that start with *l* (ell), have a *z*, and end with an *a*. The shell outputs the results of the command.

This is very similar to the wildcard examples in Chapter 1, but this time, you're using the wildcard expressions inside a script.

You have to be careful, however, with the commands you place in your shell scripts. Interactive commands, especially full-screen commands, don't tend to work very well. The following Try It Out lets you experiment with how shell scripts work when you invoke an interactive command.

Try It Out   Running an Interactive Command

Enter the following command into a text file and save the file under the name `script3`:

```
vi
ls
```

Then run the script using the following command:

```
$ sh script3
readpipe.tcl   script1   script2   script3   tktext.pl   vercompare.py
```

How It Works

Before you see the final output in the preceding example, you will see the entire shell window area get taken over by the vi command. The shell will pause script3 until the vi command ends.

The vi text editor, discussed in the section Learning vi Modes, will wait until you enter the proper cryptic vi command to exit. If you are not familiar with vi, try :q! — that is, colon, *q*, bang (exclamation point). This will exit the vi command. The shell will then execute the next command in the script3 file, ls in this example.

Chapter 9 covers some mechanisms to execute programs and capture the output instead of just waiting for the program to terminate.

If for some reason you make a mistake in a shell script file, the shell will quit executing the command and display an error message. In many cases, but not always, an error will stop execution of the whole script. For example, if you accidentally typed the vi command as *vex* (because that is what it does to many), you would have a script like the following:

```
vex
ls
```

Enter this text and save the file under the name error. Now you can run the script:

```
$ sh error
error: line 1: vex: command not found
error   readpipe.tcl   script1   script2   script3   tktext.pl   vercompare.py
```

In this example, the shell continued executing the script even after the error on Linux and Mac OS X.

Chapter 11 covers more on handling errors and debugging scripts.

Alternatives to Shells:
Other Scripting Languages

Shells each provide their own scripting language. For example, C shell scripts are not the same as Bourne shell scripts. You can choose from any shell you have available for scripting (although the Bourne shell and bash are good shells to stick with, for reasons explained in the last chapter). In addition, you can create scripts in a number of specialized languages, languages created just for scripting.

Note that there are a number of reasons why you should write your scripts for the Bourne shell instead of the C shell. See www.faqs.org/faqs/unix-faq/shell/csh-whynot/ for an interesting list of reasons why you should avoid the C shell for scripts. The C shell provides a great interactive shell, but you probably want to use sh or bash to run your scripts. This book covers the C shell, but the main focus remains on bash and sh.

While this book focuses on shell scripting, you should be aware that there are alternatives. Only you can determine which language fits your needs.

Some of the reasons to choose one language over another include the following:

❑ **Your experience and comfort level:** This is similar to the old saying, "If all you have is a hammer, then all your problems look like nails." If you know just one scripting language, that language is the right choice for you. And this is not really a bad idea. There is quite an overlap across scripting languages.

❑ **The experience and comfort level of others in your organization:** If your organization needs to maintain a number of scripts for a long time, then you'll want to choose the language that works best for the rest of the team.

❑ **Availability:** Some languages may be available, and others may not. For example, if you want to script a web site, then the two most available languages are PHP and Perl. These are the languages supported by the majority of web-hosting firms.

❑ **What feels right:** Some scripting languages support syntaxes that seem, well, downright odd. This is really a matter of personal preference. But if you really hate the syntax of a language, you should probably pick another.

❑ **What you need to learn:** One of the advantages of using the shell for scripting is that you need to learn the shell as well, just to enter commands. Scripting doesn't add much more to learn than what you already need to know about the shell. This is not true for other scripting languages, where you need to learn an entirely new language.

This book, obviously, focuses on shell scripting. But the following sections should provide a flavor of other major scripting languages to help you decide. There are literally hundreds of scripting languages, but three of the most popular are Perl, Python, and Tcl.

Perl

Short for *Practical Extraction and Reporting Language, Perl* originated as a tool to help system administrators generate reports on system activities. Perl excels at generating reports.

Perl includes many of the powerful text-processing abilities of another language called Awk, covered in Chapter 7. In addition, thousands of add-on modules provide extra features for Perl, such as networking and database access.

Perl runs on Windows, Linux, Unix, Mac OS X, and a host of other systems. Furthermore, most web-site hosting firms support Perl, allowing you to write Perl scripts to process web requests. (These are called *CGI*, or *common gateway interface*, scripts.)

The following shows a Perl script:

```perl
#!/usr/bin/perl -w

#
# Reads DBM file, printing entries.
#
# Usage:
#   Perl sdbm2.pl database

use SDBM_File;
use Fcntl;

# Print format for STDOUT.
format STDOUT=
@<<<<<<<<<<<<<<<<<<<<<   @<<<<<<<<<<<<<<<<<<<<<<<<<<<<<<<<<
$key, $value
.


format STDOUT_TOP=
Program         File Name           page @<<<
$%
.


$database  = $ARGV[0];


# Open DBM database.

$mode = 0666;

$flags =  O_RDONLY | binary();

tie(%execs, 'SDBM_File', $database, $flags, $mode)
    or die
  "Can't open \"$database\" due to $!";

  # Process entries.
while ( ($key,$value) = each(%execs) ) {

    write;
}

# Close database.
untie(%execs);



# Subroutine to return
# O_BINARY value on Windows,
# and nothing if not on Windows.
#
sub binary() {
  return O_BINARY if is_windows();
}
```

```
#
# Subroutine to detect if running under
# Windows.
#
sub is_windows() {
    return $^O =~ /^(MS)?Win/;
}
```

This script reads through a DBM database, printing out all the values using a Perl report format. Many of the concepts in this script, including using a hash or sharp sign, #, for comments, come originally from shell scripting.

Note how the first line uses the #! format to specify the program to run the script, /usr/bin/perl in this case. In addition, note how Perl uses double quotes similar to the Bourne shell. When you want to place double quotes within a double-quoted text string, you need to use a backslash character, \, to escape the quotes.

Detractors of Perl don't like the large amount of punctuation you see in even the simplest Perl scripts. Perl uses a $, @, and % to reference variable values, depending on the type of variable. Perl supports many more special variables, such as $!, than the shell does. This can also make Perl scripts harder to understand.

For more on Perl, see Cross-Platform Perl, Second Edition by Eric Foster-Johnson (Wiley, 2000).

Python

Python, named for the Monty Python comedy troupe, provides a relatively modern scripting language, at least compared to Perl, Tcl, bash, ksh, and csh. Python supports object-oriented development and in its most controversial feature, uses program indenting to define blocks of commands.

The following is a sample Python script:

```
#!/usr/bin/python

# Reads in package header, compares to installed package.
# Usage:
# python vercompare.py rpm_file.rpm
#

import rpm, os, sys

def readRpmHeader(ts, filename):
    """ Read an rpm header. """
    fd = os.open(filename, os.O_RDONLY)

    h = ts.hdrFromFdno(fd)

    os.close(fd)
    return h


ts = rpm.TransactionSet()
h  = readRpmHeader( ts, sys.argv[1] )
```

```
pkg_ds = h.dsOfHeader()
for inst_h in ts.dbMatch('name', h['name']):
    inst_ds = inst_h.dsOfHeader()

    if pkg_ds.EVR() >= inst_ds.EVR():
        print "Package file is same or newer, OK to upgrade."
    else:
        print "Package file is older than installed version."
```

This Python script compares a software package in RPM format with an RPM file to see which package should be considered more recent: the installed package or the package file. Most Linux systems use RPM (short for *RPM Package Manager*) to manage installed applications.

Python is well known for using whitespace, such as the tab character, to define blocks. While a Bourne shell script will start an if statement with `if` and go until the `fi` statement, Python starts with `if` and then all indented lines underneath form the block. While indenting your scripts can improve readability, mandating the indenting has been the most controversial feature of Python.

Python is more object-oriented than Perl or shell scripts. Although you can create object-oriented scripts in any language, if you have experience in Java or C++, then Python is more likely to appeal to you.

Tcl

Tcl, pronounced *tickle*, stands for *Tool Command Language*. Tcl was created as a lightweight means to add scripting to applications such as word processors, integrated-circuit testers, and spreadsheets.

Tcl sports a simpler syntax than most shells but even so has proved itself highly useful. The following script shows how to open a pipe to a program, a topic covered for shell scripting in Chapter 8.

```
# Opening a pipe for reading.

#
# Opens command as a pipe for reading.
# Pass command without the leading | character.
#
proc read_pipe { command } {

    # Initialize
    set data ""

    # Start piped command.
    set fileid [open |$command r]

    if { $fileid != "" } {

        # Read data.
        set data [read $fileid]

        close $fileid
    }

    return $data
```

```
    }

# readpipe.tcl
```

Tcl has been compared by many to appearing as LISP without all the parentheses. If you know LISP, Tcl will be easy to learn. Tcl works best if you have a C or C++ program for which you want to add scripting. The Tcl interpreter can easily be embedded within a C or C++ application, allowing you to run scripts from within the application.

You will find that Tcl shares many features with shell scripts, including using a dollar sign, $, to reference variables.

These sample scripts should give you at least a flavor of these different languages, enabling you to better decide if one of these will meet your needs.

MS-DOS Batch Files

You could consider MS-DOS batch files as another form of scripting language. While you can write scripts using the MS-DOS batch syntax, even sophisticated scripts, the batch syntax misses a number of features provided by modern shells such as bash or ksh. For example, DOS does not support file globbing using wildcards. A true shell scripter, therefore, will look disdainfully on MS-DOS batch files as being inadequate.

Even so, MS-DOS batch files are proof that scripting has shown itself useful in just about every environment.

Once you have selected a scripting environment (*hint*: pick sh or bash), the next step is to choose a tool for editing shell scripts. Because shell scripts are merely text files, the tool you need to select is a text editor.

Tools to Edit Shell Scripts

To write shell scripts, you really need two tools:

❑   A shell

❑   A text editor

The main tool you need to edit shell scripts is a text editor. This makes sense because shell scripts are simply text files, albeit special text files. If you've programmed in any computer language, chances are you have selected a text editor that meets your needs. By all means, stay with any editor that has proved productive for your work. There is no reason to change.

If you haven't selected an editor, or you are running on an operating system you have not used much before, then the following sections will prove useful.

Using Legacy Editors

Unix, Linux, Mac OS X, and many other operating systems support two legacy editors: emacs and vi. These are editors that have been around for years and run on nearly every platform you can think of.

As of 10.3.5, Mac OS X actually uses vim, or vi Improved. If you're new to vi, this won't really make a difference, although differences between vi and VIM are noted in this book as needed.

The mere mention of these editors makes some people shudder in fear. They aren't that bad. Really. Older than many software developers, these editors sport a certain retro feel. They are useful for three main reasons:

❑ Many people have been trained on these editors. You would be amazed at how muscle memory works; just watch diehard emacs or vi users as their fingers fly over the keyboard. True diehards don't even use the arrow keys or other such modern innovations. These people are most entertaining when they use Macintosh systems.

❑ These editors are available anywhere. Well, mostly anywhere. There once was an awful Unix system from Prime Computer that didn't even have vi, but that is thankfully long gone. You can run vi on PDAs and supercomputers and most everything in between. Vi used to even be an example program for the Borland C compiler on DOS.

❑ These editors don't require a graphical environment. If you connect to a remote system via telnet or ssh, for example, graphical editors will likely not work. Vi or emacs will, however. For this reason alone, you may want to learn one of these text editors.

The following sections introduce these two retro text editors. Imagine you are back in the 1970s. Disco is big. Computers are rare and expensive. Computers actually work. And you have an ASCII terminal as your only means to access computers.

Delving into emacs

If there is a wonder editor that can meet all needs for all people, it is emacs. A product of the GNU project, emacs can do anything. Literally anything. That's because emacs has a built-in LISP program interpreter. Originally written by Richard Stallman, leader of the Free Software Foundation and a champion of free software, emacs provides an extensible text editor with a plethora of features. You can read your email, browse the news, and even play games, all from within emacs.

Emacs does not ship with all versions of Unix. For example, System V Unix does not include emacs. You can download emacs from www.gnu.org/software/emacs/emacs.html.

Unlike vi (covered following), emacs is a modeless text editor. So with emacs, you can just type. This makes editing documents easy. The hard part, however, comes when you want to perform a command in the editor, such as saving a file. Because emacs is modeless, you need some way to let the emacs program know you want to save the file. In modern applications, you'd simply choose Save from the File menu. Emacs, however, predates the common usage of the mouse and graphical desktops, although modern versions of emacs work with both.

Like modern desktop applications, emacs uses the equivalent of keyboard shortcuts, but emacs uses these key combinations for *every* editor command, and there are hundreds of commands. Thus, for emacs commands, two keys are important: Control and Meta. Most keyboards show Control as Ctrl, with Macintosh keyboards showing "control." The Meta key, however, is nowhere to be found. There used to be systems that actually showed a Meta key, but for modern keyboards emacs usually maps Meta to the Alt or Esc key. In most cases, this will be Esc, but you should check the emacs documentation or online help for your system. (Directions for consulting the emacs documentation and online help appear later in this section.) On Mac OS X systems, the Meta key maps to the option key, which, on most Mac keyboards, reads as "option" but may read "alt" instead.

Emacs includes extensive online help available within the application from the Help menu or from help commands. In the emacs documentation, the key combinations appear as C-x or M-x, short for Ctrl-X and Alt-X or Esc-X (based on your Meta key mapping). So, for example, the command to save the current text is C-x C-s. This translates to Ctrl-X, Ctrl-S. The key combination C-x b for jumping to the next buffer translates to pressing Ctrl-X and then B. The tables following use the same conventions to get you used to the emacs way of documenting key combinations.

To get started with emacs, simply type the emacs command:

```
$ emacs
```

This launches either an emacs window or the text-only version of emacs. Both versions work the same, but the graphical version provides extra help in the form of menus and scroll bars. You may find emacs available from the system menus, usually in a programming or tools section, as emacs is most used by software developers.

Emacs starts up with a handy help screen unless you provide a command-line argument of a file name or have otherwise told emacs not to display this help.

Figure 2-1 shows the default emacs help screen.

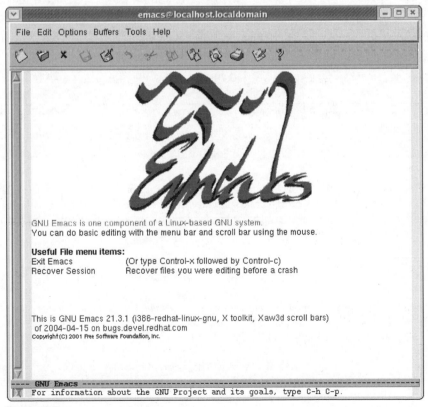

Figure 2-1

As you can see in the figure, modern versions of emacs include a menu bar. The commands available from the menu bar are invaluable for learning emacs. You don't have to remember all the strange key combinations. Many of the menu choices show the corresponding key combination, which helps you learn emacs gradually instead of all at once.

Emacs can be highly customized. Your version of emacs may differ. Don't worry. Use the online help to get started.

You can also tell the emacs command to load a particular file or files on startup, speeding up your work. For example, to start an emacs session with the script1 file from the first example in this chapter, use the following command:

```
$ emacs script1
```

This command tells emacs to load the file named script1 in the current directory.

The most important commands for using emacs appear in the following table.

Emacs Key Combination	Editing Command	Long Name
C-x C-s	Save text in the current buffer with the current filename.	save-buffer
C-x C-c	Save and quit. Saves text in the current buffer and exits emacs.	save-buffers-kill-emacs
C-x C-w	Save text in current buffer under a different file name.	write-file
C-x C-f	Open file.	find-file
C-g	Magic operation to cancel a running operation that appears hung.	keyboard-quit

In the previous table, the long name is the official emacs name for the given operation. The long name is useful should you decide to customize emacs, an advanced topic. The long names also give you an idea of how emacs names its commands and what kinds of commands are available. You can run a long command by pressing M-x and then typing the command name.

Press Enter after typing in the command name. For example, to open a new file, you can choose Open File from the File menu; type C-x C-f; or, to prove you know emacs, type M-x find-file.

The great claim that emacs is modeless isn't entirely true, as you can find out if you try the M-x key combination to run an emacs command. M-x won't always work because of hidden emacs modes. Try M-x in a buffer that you can edit, which is not a help buffer.

Emacs supports an extensive online help system. This is great because unless you've been trained with emacs, most newcomers get confused by the huge number of editor commands available. The following table lists the main help commands.

Emacs Key Combination	Help Command	Long Name
C-h C-h	Get help on using emacs help	help-for-help
C-h i	View the emacs manuals	info
C-h c *key*	Show the long command for the given key	describe-key-briefly
C-h k *key*	Show more description for the given key	describe-key
C-h t	Enter the emacs tutorial	help-with-tutorial
Ch-x *command*	List the keys for a given long command name	where-is
C-h b	List all key bindings (long)	describe-bindings
C-h a *text*	List all commands containing text	command-apropos

The Help menu also provides a lot of options. You'd be amazed to see all the online material on emacs available from the Help menu. The emacs manuals support a primitive type of hypertext, called *info*. The info system was created long before the Internet and HTML became popular.

Because there are so many key combinations, emacs provides a lot of help to figure out which key does what. You can use the C h c or C h k combination to figure out which command emacs will execute for a given key. With either the C-h c or C-h k combination, you need to press the actual key combination to see the description. For example, to determine what the C-h t combination does, press C-h c C-h t.

The area at the bottom of the emacs window, called the *minibuffer,* should then display the following:

```
C-h t runs the command help-with-tutorial
```

This feature is great if you try one of the commands listed in this chapter and it doesn't do what you think it should.

Emacs provides a huge number of commands to navigate through a file. Remember that emacs was designed before users could rely on having arrow keys, let alone a mouse or a standardized keyboard. The following table shows the main emacs navigation commands.

Emacs Key Combination	Navigation Command	Long Name
C-f	Jump forward one character	forward-char
C-b	Jump backward one character	backward-char
C-n	Jump down one line	next-line
C-p	Jump up one line.	previous-line
M -f	Move forward one word	forward-word

Table continued on following page

Emacs Key Combination	Navigation Command	Long Name
M-b	Move back one word	backward-word
C-a	Move to beginning of the line	beginning-of-line
C-e	Move to the end of the line	end-of-line
M-<	Move to beginning of file	beginning-of-buffer
M->	Move to end of file	end-of-buffer
C-v	Jump forward one screen	scroll-up
M-v	Jump backward one screen	scroll-down
C-l	Clear screen, move cursor to center of file, and redraw	recenter
C-s	Search forward	isearch-forward
C-r	Search backward	isearch-backward

Yow. Don't worry, though. If you run the graphical version of emacs, you can use the scroll bar, the mouse, Page Up and Down keys, arrow keys, and other modern features you'd expect. In addition, most versions of emacs come preconfigured for standard PC keyboards. So, for example, the Home key should move the cursor to the beginning of the line, and the End key should move the cursor to the end of the line.

> In older versions of emacs, pressing the Home key moved you to the start of the whole file, while End moved you to the end of the file. You may still see this behavior, depending on how emacs has been customized for your platform.

To type at a particular location, just click the mouse where you want to type.

Emacs supports a powerful search engine. Type C-s to start searching. As you type the text to search for, emacs already starts searching. This is called an *incremental search,* and it proves very powerful and fast. To search for the next occurrence of the text, type C-s again, and so on. Use C-r to search backward.

Emacs uses a block cursor that may confuse you. The Macintosh pioneered the idea that the cursor appears between two characters, which simplified a lot of issues for how selections and keys should work. Emacs, however, always places the cursor on a character position rather than between characters. This can be a bit disconcerting at first.

Emacs also causes confusion with its support for copy and paste. The keys chosen by emacs, at least by default, conflict with the standardized shortcuts for cut, copy, and paste on most platforms. The following table shows the emacs copy and paste commands.

Emacs Key Combination	Copy and Paste Command	Long Name
C-w	Cut selected text	kill-region
M-w	Copy selected text	kill-ring-save
C-y	Paste text	yank

Emacs provides a powerful concept called a *kill buffer*. A *buffer* in emacs is an area that holds text. The kill buffer is where emacs places text that has been cut. You can bring text back from the kill buffer (what most people call a paste operation). To copy or paste text, select the text you want with the mouse. You can also mark text by moving the cursor to the beginning of the text block, marking the start, moving the cursor to the end of the text block and marking the end, and then cutting or copying the text. Using the mouse proves a lot easier.

See the online help within emacs for more on how to mark text.

The classic emacs keys for cut, C-w, and paste, C-y, were chosen long, long ago, before the Macintosh appeared, before IBM's CUA (Common User Access) interface guidelines (the guidelines for the Windows interface), even before DECwindows. These keys become a problem, however, when you try to work with other applications. Now you can do everything, really everything, in emacs But, most users also run other programs such as word processors, web browsers, and so on.

Microsoft Word in particular conflicts with emacs. C-y, which is the default shortcut for paste in emacs, is redo in Word (and also in the OpenOffice.org Writer application). C-w, which is the default shortcut for cut in emacs, closes the current window in both Word and Writer (and in many other applications).

You can remap keys in emacs to help mitigate this problem with interoperability. But C-x, which should be the cut command in Word, is problematic because C-x is the prefix used for a huge number of emacs commands.

To be fair, emacs predates Word, Writer, and most other desktop applications. That's no consolation, however, when you try to work with multiple applications together.

In addition to cutting selected text, emacs provides a number of commands to delete text, from characters to words to lines. The following table lists these commands.

Emacs Key Combination	Text Deletion Command	Long Name
Delete, C-d	Deletes the character under the cursor	delete-char
Backspace	Deletes the character to the left	backward-delete-char-untabify
C-Delete, M-d	Deletes word, to the right of the cursor	kill-word
C-k	Deletes to the end of the line	kill-line
C-t	Transposes (swaps) two characters	transpose-chars
Insert	Toggles overwrite mode	overwrite-mode

As usual, these key combinations can be customized, so your version of emacs may differ slightly.

As mentioned previously, emacs is an old application, appearing prior to graphical windowing systems. Over the years, however, emacs developed its own text-based windowing system. These textual windows are called buffers.

A *buffer* is both an area of memory that holds text and a subwindow in the emacs window. Sometimes this second meaning is called a window, but the documentation is not always consistent. Separate top-level windows in emacs are called *frames*.

With emacs, the C-x 2 key combination splits the current window into two buffers. That is, press Ctrl-X, followed by 2. You can edit two separate files, one in each buffer. Or both windows can refer to the same buffer, allowing you to view and edit at two places in the file at once. This feature can prove very convenient.

The following table lists the emacs buffer-related commands.

Emacs Key Combination	Buffer-Related Command	Long Name
C-x 2	Split window	split-window-vertically
C-x 1	Return to one window	delete-other-windows
C-x b	Jump to next buffer	switch-to-buffer
C-x b *buffer*	Switch to the named buffer	switch-to-buffer
C-x 4 b	Jump to next buffer and create a subwindow for it	switch-to-buffer-other-window
C-x C-b	List current buffers	list-buffers
C-x C-f	Load file into buffer	find-file
C-x 4 f	Load file into new subwindow	find-file-other-window
C-x C-s	Save current buffer to current file name	save-buffer

In addition to splitting the current window into two subwindows, emacs keeps a list of buffers. You can have a number of buffers hidden off-screen, such as the kill buffer. The C-x b key combination jumps to the next buffer in the buffer list. The C-x C-b combination lists all the available buffers.

Once you can find your way around a file and edit text, you can make use of the interactive shell inside emacs. Using the M-x `eshell` command starts an eshell, or emacs shell, inside an emacs buffer. This shell appears in Figure 2-2.

Because this shell appears inside an emacs buffer, you can select text, copy and paste from other buffers, and grab previous shell commands. Thus, you can edit a shell script in one emacs window while trying out the commands in another window.

As you can imagine, back in the day emacs was a very, very productive tool. Nowadays, emacs shows its age, but it still has many users. The embedded shell helps when writing shell scripts.

> *There is another version of emacs called xemacs, available at www.xemacs.org. Xemacs provides more support for graphical environments. The two versions differ, and there seems to have been a bit of conflict in the past between the emacs and xemacs partisans. Choose whichever version of emacs you prefer.*

Figure 2-2

Learning vi Modes

Emacs may show its age, but before there was an emacs, vi was the best thing around. The fact that vi is still here, and still being used, shows that it, like shells and shell scripts, still serves a purpose for many users. Vi, short for *visual editor*, is a modal editor. In vi, there are two modes: insert and command. In insert mode, the text you type gets entered into the file you are editing. In command mode, the keys you type are interpreted as vi commands, short cryptic commands that can have a major effect on your files.

To start vi, simply enter the vi command:

```
$ vi
```

You can also start vi with a session editing a particular file. For example:

```
$ vi script1
```

This command tells vi to edit a file named script1 in the current directory. Vi can create the file if it does not exist.

You can pass more than one file name on the command line. For example:

```
$ vi script1 script2 script3
```

Vi shows each file one at a time. The :n command (see the second table following) jumps to the next file.

When you start vi, the editor places you in command mode. Thus, any keys you start typing are assumed to be commands. Unlike emacs, you cannot just start typing text. Instead, you have to enter a command to switch to insert mode. The most common command to enter insert mode is a lowercase i, short for insert.

The following table lists the commands to switch over to insert mode.

Vi Insert Command	Purpose
i	Inserts before the current character
I	Inserts at the beginning of the line
a	Appends after (to the right of) the current character
A	Appends at the end of the current line
o	Inserts a new line after the current line
O	Inserts a new line before the current line

Once in insert mode, the text you type gets entered into the file you are editing. Press Esc to exit insert mode.

Some versions of vi display text at the bottom of the editor telling you that you are in insert mode, such as the following:

```
-- INSERT --
```

But many versions of vi provide no feedback as to which mode you are in. If you're ever unsure, just press Esc twice. If you are already in command mode, vi merely beeps at you. When you get into command mode, vi beeps at you.

> *One of the best descriptions of vi is that it is a program that beeps at you a lot.*

In command mode, you can use the arrow keys to navigate through the file. You can also use special keys to navigate, as listed in the following table.

Vi Navigation Key	Purpose
h	Move one character left.
j	Move one line down.
k	Move one line up.

Vi Navigation Key	Purpose
l	Move one character right.
Ctrl-D	Move down one-half page.
Ctrl-U	Move up one-half page.
Ctrl-F	Move forward one page.
Ctrl-B	Move back one page.
G	Jump to the end of the file.
1G	Jump to the first line.
number G	Jump to the given line number.

The G command takes you to a given line number. This is very useful when you get an error from the shell about a shell script. Usually the error message tells you which line had the error. While this may not always be accurate, you can use the G command to quickly jump to the line in question. Simply enter the line number and then an uppercase G, and vi takes you there.

Chapter 11 covers how to deal with errors and fix them in your scripts.

You can use this method of placing a number before a command to perform the command that many times. For example, 4j moves the cursor down four lines.

Remember, you must be in command mode for these commands to work.

Vi supports a number of file-related operations, as you'd expect from any text editor. The following table lists the main file-related operations.

Vi File-Related Command	Usage
ZZ	Save current file and quit vi.
:w	Save current file.
:wq	Save current file and quit vi.
:q	Quit vi. Does not save.
:q!	Really quit vi. (Like shouting.)
:n	Jump to the next file.
:rew	Go back to the first file.
:w *filename*	Save the current text under a different *filename*.
:f	Report the name of the current file and the current position.

Vi supports a number of special commands that start with a colon character (:). These include :w to write the current contents to disk (under the current file name) and :q to quit vi. If you try to quit vi without saving, vi beeps at you. You can force vi to quit with the :q! command. The exclamation mark, !, acts as a way to force vi to do your bidding. You can use it with other commands, such as :n! to jump to the next file without saving the current file. Note that any changes you made will be lost, the same as if you quit without saving.

You can also use :w! to overwrite a read-only file if you are logged in as root.

Like emacs, vi supports yanking (copying and pasting) text, although with a different set of commands, as shown in the following table.

Vi Copy and Paste Command	Usage
yy	Yanks current line into buffer, similar to copying to the clipboard.
p	Puts the yanked text on the next line after the current position of the cursor.
number yy	Yanks more than one line, as specified by number.
u	Undoes the last command.
r	Redo, when called after an undo, performs the undone command again. Not supported by default in vim.
.	Repeats the last command.

You can yank, or copy, four lines of text with the 4yy command. You can then move the cursor about and paste the lines into the text with the p command.

You can search in vi with the / command. Just type / and then the text to search for. The following table summarizes the vi search commands.

Vi Search Command	Usage
/text	Search for text going forward.
/	Search again for the same text, going forward.
?text	Search for text going backward.
?	Search again for the same text, going backward.
n	Repeat last search.
N	Repeat last search, but reverse the direction.

Over the years, versions of vi have advanced far beyond the original simple program that beeps a lot. A version of vi called vim, short for *vi improved*, adds a host of new features to vi. Vim provides for syntax highlighting for programming files, including shell scripts, and an amazing amount of extended functionality. Vim includes extensive online help and multiple split windows.

Linux ships with vim as the default implementation of vi. Thus, if you type vi or vim, you get the `vim` command. Mac OS X does the same, using vim for vi.

> *See www.vim.org for more on vim. Vim is free but considered charityware. The vim web site asks that if you find vim useful, you consider helping needy children in Uganda.*

You may also want to load Cream for Vim, a graphical front-end to vim. This add-on makes vim appear almost as a fully graphical editor, including scroll bars and menus.

> *Download Cream for Vim from cream.sourceforge.net.*

If vi or emacs isn't your cup of tea, you can choose from a large variety of graphical modern text editors.

Moving to Graphical Text Editors

In addition to the legacy text editors, you can choose from a wide variety of more modern graphical text editors. These editors usually include menus, the ability to change the text font, and scroll bars — all useful features for text editors.

Editors are personal tools. Just as different people like different types of cars, people have different tastes in text editors. What works for one person may bug the heck out of another. There's no one right editor for everyone, so choose one that works for you.

If you are starting with Linux, Mac OS X, or Unix, then you should begin with a more modern editor. And there are modern editors for just about every taste. You can choose from editors that just run on a particular platform, such as Mac OS X, or choose from a number of excellent cross-platform editors.

Cross-Platform Editors

Moving between systems can be hard. If you work on any combination of Mac OS X, Linux, Windows, or Unix systems, you'll be faced with learning how each system operates over and over. Even something as simple as quitting an application or closing a window differs by platform. This problem only gets worse when dealing with text editors, something most script developers use for hours a day.

If you need to work on different systems, especially Linux and Windows systems, you probably want to get a cross-platform text editor. Instead of having to relearn all the special options for text editors on each platform, you can learn an editor once and then reuse your skills on multiple boxes. These are all programs that can run on multiple operating systems and should act the same, or nearly the same, on all supported systems.

> *Note that emacs and vi are cross-platform editors as well. You can download versions of either editor for a plethora of systems. See the section Using Legacy Editors for more on emacs and vi.*

jEdit provides one of the favorite cross-platform text editors. Available at www.jedit.org, jEdit runs on any system that supports Java on the desktop, including all the desktop systems listed so far. jEdit requires a Java Runtime Environment available from www.java.com, to execute. jEdit is too large a program for most PDAs, however.

jEdit supports syntax highlighting, showing comments, for example, in a different color. jEdit supports most source file formats and includes a lot of features. You can download plugins that extend jEdit, adding new functionality. jEdit can manage the task of downloading and installing plugins, which makes this whole process painless. In addition, you can customize the jEdit display to place, or dock, windows where you want them.

jEdit appears in Figure 2-3.

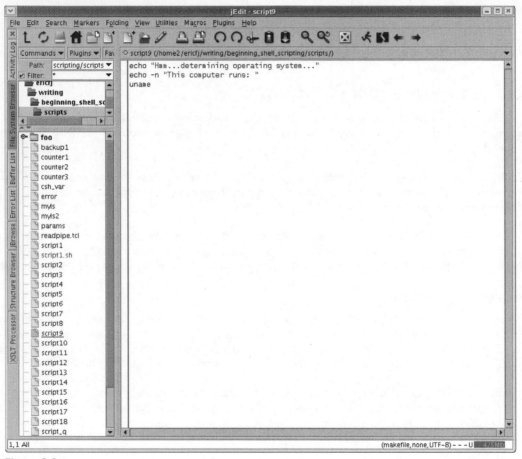

Figure 2-3

Another cross-platform editor, known simply as J, includes a huge amount of functionality right out of the box. J supports special modes for editing Java, JavaScript, XML, and a number of other file syntaxes. J works the same for all formats, providing a consistent editing environment. J supports reading and sending email and the CVS source code control system. There are other neat aspects to J that you just have to discover.

In addition, J doesn't barrage you with a huge number of options. This is also the downside of J. You have to be able to edit J's property files to customize the editor. If you work in a text editor for a large part of every day, J can prove quite productive.

Like jEdit, J runs on any system that supports Java on the desktop. Download J from http://armedbear-j .sourceforge.net.

Jext provides yet another Java-based text editor. Jext, available from www.jext.org, provides a simply beautiful text editor with a host of features. Like jEdit, Jext supports plugins to extend the functionality of the editor.

Of these three Java-based text editors, jEdit provides the largest number of features.

Eclipse is a full-blown IDE (Integrated Development Environment) for developing Java applications. A handy editing plugin called color editor performs syntax highlighting on approximately a hundred file formats, including shell scripts. The color editor plugin actually uses the jEdit syntax definition files to highlight the source code.

Download Eclipse from www.eclipse.org and the color editor plugin from http://gstaff.org/colorEditor/. You will also need a Java Runtime Environment.

Another popular editor for those who work with software is SlickEdit, an editor that runs on Windows, Linux, Mac OS X, and most popular Unix systems. You need to get a different version of SlickEdit for each platform. You can purchase SlickEdit from www.slickedit.com.

Mac OS X Editors

For text editors on Mac OS X, you have an embarrassment of riches. Along with the editors mentioned previously, you have a number of free, shareware, and commercial editors that exist only for Mac OS X and take advantage of some of the unique features of the Mac operating system.

Luckily, you get one for free, namely TextEdit. This lives in the /Applications folder and is a basic text editor, with some additional features. One feature that you have to watch out for is that by default, TextEdit uses RTF, not plain text, for its normal format. Because RTF is not usable for shell scripts, you want to make sure that you select Make Plain Text from the Format menu, as shown in Figure 2-4. This ensures that the file you save is a plain text file, as required for shell scripts.

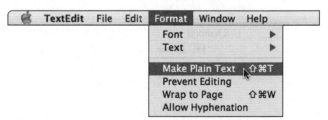

Figure 2-4

While TextEdit is a good basic editor, it's really not designed for shell scripting. It's a bit of a station wagon in that it does everything *okay*, whereas you want something that's built with your needs in mind.

There are a lot of editors out there, but the best one that won't cost you a lot of money is SubEthaEdit, by the appropriately named Coding Monkeys, at www.codingmonkeys.de/subethaedit/. SubEthaEdit is a programmer's editor and has a lot of the things you want out of such a beast. First, everything is plain text. Second, it supports features like syntax highlighting. It's reasonably extensible. It also allows other people using SubEthaEdit on your local network to collaborate with you on a document at the same time. Aside from the shared editing, it also supports features such as regular expression searching (introduced in Chapter 1), the ability to jump to different parts of your script, and split-screen views, which are great for things such as long scripts where you have one part of the script relying on another part, and there are 8 billion lines of code between them. Split-screen views let you see both at once, so you spend more time scripting and less time coding.

If you're using SubEthaEdit for personal use (*read*: not in a commercial environment), then it's free. If you're using it in a commercial environment, then the cost for three licenses is $35 U.S., which is pretty reasonable for such an amazing product.

But the true leader in the Mac OS X text-editor race is BBEdit from Bare Bones Software, at www.bare bones.com/products/bbedit/. BBEdit is one of those products that have so many tricks and shortcuts you don't even realize how badly you need it until you use it. To start with, if you're an emacs user, you can tell BBEdit to use emacs keybindings, or keyboard commands, so that your muscle memory still works. BBEdit has command-line components, so if you're in a shell window, you can open a file in BBEdit directly from the shell, edit it, close it, and never have to deal with the Mac OS X open/save dialog boxes. BBEdit is shown in Figure 2-5.

> *BBEdit doesn't support every emacs shortcut. (For all its coolness, it's only a text editor. You can't send email from it. Although if you need to send email from something with a Bare Bones logo, they'll happily sell you an email program.)*

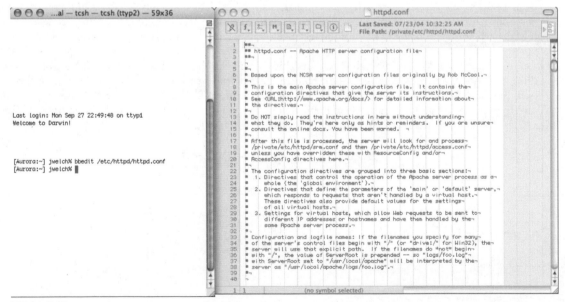

Figure 2-5

But wait, there's more! BBEdit has built-in support for regular expressions and can apply them to multiple files in multiple folders at once. It's tightly integrated into the shell environment, so you can run the scripts you're working on from within BBEdit and never have to switch between BBEdit and a Terminal window.

Do you want to use Perl or Python within BBEdit? It's in there. Want to be able to connect to a remote machine securely via SFTP to edit scripts there? Built in. Want to open those remote files from the shell in BBEdit via SFTP? Can do. Want to use BBEdit from the shell to check differences between two or more files? In two or more folders? Got it. BBEdit's not shareware, nor is it Open Source, but if you want the ultimate text tool on Mac OS X, then BBEdit is what you want.

Linux Editors

Each of the Linux desktop environments includes one or more text editors, and you can choose from a plethora of other graphical text editors for Linux.

For the GNOME desktop, one of the main editors is gedit, which appears in Figure 2-6.

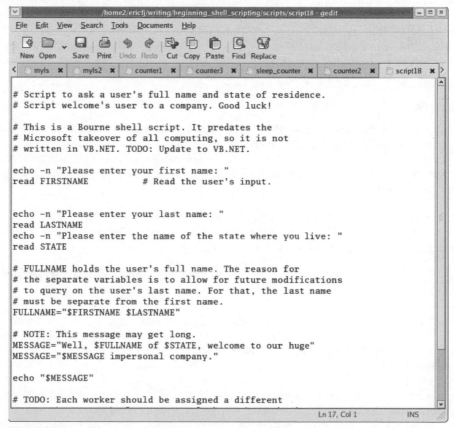

Figure 2-6

Gedit provides a basic text editor in a friendly-looking window. In addition to basic text editing, gedit supports the syntax of a number of programming and markup languages, such as Java, C++, XML, and HTML. Gedit does not highlight shell scripts, unfortunately.

A special gedit plugin allows you to run commands, such as shell scripts, and capture the output of these commands. Gedit shows the output in a separate window. As with the emacs editor, the ability to run shell scripts from within the text editor is a great help.

For the KDE desktop, kate defines the main KDE text editor. Kate provides a full-featured text editor, supporting many more features than gedit, including the capability to manage projects. Each project includes a number of files, and this feature is very useful for Web site development or programming.

You can rearrange the kate interface, moving and customizing toolbars and keyboard shortcuts. Kate supports plugins to extend its functionality. For example, the default kate installation includes plugins for working with C++ programs, HTML web pages, and XML documents.

Cute, available at http://cute.sourceforge.net, provides a text editor aimed at beginners. This editor is built on the Qt (pronounced *cute*) libraries. Qt forms the base of the KDE desktop software.

Other graphical editors for Linux include SciTE and Glimmer. SciTE, from www.scintilla.org/SciTE.html, started as a demonstration application that evolved into a comprehensive programmer's text editor. Glimmer, from http://glimmer.sourceforge.net, provides another graphical editor with syntax highlighting for shell scripts and other programmer-related file formats.

Unix Editors

Just about all the Linux editors can work on Unix, although the GNOME or KDE editors may require too many Linux libraries to make the porting effort worthwhile. For example, unless you have the full GNOME desktop for your Unix system, it is unlikely you can get an editor such as gedit to work. That's because GNOME (and KDE) applications have a large number of dependencies on libraries that come with the full desktop environments.

The standard Unix desktop is called CDE (Common Desktop Environment). CDE should be available on most commercial versions of Unix such as Solaris or HP-UX, except for Mac OS X, where there is no reason to run the CDE in place of the Macintosh desktop interface.

The CDE desktop includes a text editor, available from an icon on the task bar. This is a fairly bare-bones editor but friendlier than vi or emacs.

A favorite Unix text editor is NEdit. NEdit, available at www.nedit.org, requires the Motif libraries (now freely available for most platforms as OpenMotif from www.openmotif.org). Motif forms the basis of the CDE as well. You can download prebuilt versions of NEdit for Linux and most versions of Unix from the NEdit web site.

NEdit looks a bit dated with the standard Motif look, but don't let that put you off. For Unix text editors, NEdit provides an amazing amount of power and simplicity. NEdit has been optimized for speed and keyboard efficiency. It supports shell scripts and lots of other programming-related file formats, such as C, Java, and so on. You can see NEdit in Figure 2-7.

```
  ┌──────────────────────────────────────────────────────────────────────┐
  │ ▼ ▓▓▓ script18 - /home2/ericfj/writing/beginning_shell_scripting/scripts/ ▓▓▓  □ ▫ ▫ ✕ │
  ├──────────────────────────────────────────────────────────────────────┤
  │  File   Edit   Search   Preferences   Shell   Macro   Windows         Help │
  ├──────────────────────────────────────────────────────────────────────┤
  │ # Script to ask a user's full name and state of residence.            ▲ │
  │ # Script welcome's user to a company. Good luck!                      │ │
  │                                                                       │ │
  │ # This is a Bourne shell script. It predates the                     │ │
  │ # Microsoft takeover of all computing, so it is not                  │ │
  │ # written in VB.NET. TODO: Update to VB.NET.                         │ │
  │                                                                       │ │
  │ echo -n "Please enter your first name: "                             │ │
  │ read FIRSTNAME              # Read the user's input.                 │ │
  │                                                                       │ │
  │ echo -n "Please enter your last name: "                              │ │
  │ read LASTNAME                                                         │ │
  │ echo -n "Please enter the name of the state where you live: "        │ │
  │ read STATE                                                            │ │
  │                                                                       │ │
  │ # FULLNAME holds the user's full name. The reason for                │ │
  │ # the separate variables is to allow for future modifications        │ │
  │ # to query on the user's last name. For that, the last name          │ │
  │ # must be separate from the first name.                              │ │
  │ FULLNAME="$FIRSTNAME $LASTNAME"                                      │ │
  │                                                                       │ │
  │ # NOTE: This message may get long.                                   ▼ │
  └──────────────────────────────────────────────────────────────────────┘
```

Figure 2-7

In addition, NEdit can run in a server mode. You can type in the nc command to launch an NEdit window with a given file or, if NEdit is already running, call up the given file in the running NEdit. This proves very handy when you browse directories and want to edit or view files.

A networking package also has a command named nc, so you may find conflicts, especially on Linux, where nedit and its nc command are located in /usr/X11R6/bin while the networking nc command is located in /usr/bin.

Microsoft Windows Editors

Microsoft Windows includes an ancient editor called Notepad. Generally, because of the way Notepad handles the end-of-line characters, you should not use this editor for scripting or programming.

Instead, Textpad provides a very good Windows editor. Like many of the other editors listed here, Textpad highlights the syntax of shell scripts. You can download specific syntax definitions for the Bourne, C, and Korn shells. Textpad is one of the fastest and most responsive editors for Windows. There are lots of additional editors to choose from on Windows.

You can download Textpad from www.textpad.com. It is a shareware application.

When you have selected a text editor, you can begin to create shell scripts in earnest. The next sections cover some of the basics for scripting. The next few chapters continue with the basics.

Writing Scripts

Writing scripts is as simple as editing text files with the commands you want in your scripts. The hard part comes when you need to enter the commands correctly and tie the commands together into useful scripts. The following sections introduce the basics of scripting, starting with a very useful task: letting scripts remember for you.

Remembering Commands So You Don't Have To

A lot of commands sport complex, hard-to-remember arguments. You may find yourself looking up the online manual pages for a command each time you want to run it. If you run this command a lot, you'll start to remember. But if you run this command infrequently, you'll likely forget.

Even if the commands are simple with a few options, you may want to store the commands in scripts so that you can simply execute the scripts instead of remembering and typing the whole commands. The following Try It Out examples illustrate this procedure.

Try It Out   Launching a Music Player

Xmms plays music on Linux systems (so do a number of other programs). You can collect a number of songs into a playlist and store this playlist in a file. Passing the name of this file as a command-line argument will tell xmms to play the songs on that list.

All of this involves a lot of typing. Instead, create a script like the following:

```
xmms $HOME/multi/mp3/reggae_playlist.m3u
```

Save this script under a name such as `reggae` (the style of music) or `favorites` or `irieriddims` or any other name that makes sense.

How It Works

This script runs the `xmms` command and passes the name of a playlist file to the command. This script foreshadows the deep, dark subject of variables. `$HOME` refers to your home directory on Unix, Linux, and Mac OS X. You can then run your script in place of typing in the full command.

You need to create the playlist itself inside xmms and then save the playlist to a file. You can replace the playlist file in the previous script with the name of your playlist file.

You can use this script as a guide for other commands or your own playlists. Of course you like reggae music, but you may have chosen to store your files in a non-optimal location (as this example shows the one true location to store music files).

Just kidding. Anyone who tells you that there is one true location for something is just wrong, plain wrong. Any such person deserves to be trapped in a corner while you patiently explain, again and again, about how the variable factors such as file system types, inode allocations, and disk-partitioning schemes impact the true correct location for any particular type of file. Just kidding again. The best bet is to distract these annoying people by asking which is best: FreeBSD, OpenBSD, or NetBSD Unix. Get the discussion started and then quietly walk away.

Try It Out   Running an Application from Its Installation Directory

As another example, the BuddySpace instant messaging (IM) client communicates with Jabber servers and also the common protocols for MSN, AIM, Yahoo!, and ICQ instant messaging. BuddySpace is written in Java, making it another cross-platform tool.

Cross-platform tools are, by definition, good.

BuddySpace, however, requires that it be started from its installation directory. Otherwise, it may not find all the needed files.

Enter the following script and save it under the name `jabber`:

```
cd $HOME/java/im/BS252pro-complete ; sh buddySpace.sh
```

How It Works

This command appears in two parts. The first part changes the working directory to the java/im/BS252pro-complete subdirectory of your home directory (using $HOME again). The second part uses the sh command to launch a shell script. (Yep, a script can launch another script.)

This example shows another new technique. You can place two commands on one command line. Use a semicolon to separate the commands.

Download BuddySpace from buddyspace.sourceforge.net.

Outputting Text

Most scripts need to output text of some sort. The output may be the results of a command, covered in Chapter 8. Or you may just want to prompt the user to enter data for the script. In any case, the primary way to output text from a script is the echo command, introduced in Chapter 1. Recall that the basic syntax is:

```
echo text_to_output
```

Pass echo the text you want to output. The following example shows how to use echo in a script.

Try It Out   **Creating a Hello World Script**

Enter the following into a file and name the file `script4`:

```
echo "Hello World"
```

When you run this script, you'll see the following output:

```
$ sh script4
Hello World
$
```

How It Works

The echo command simply outputs the text you pass to it. The text "Hello World" is required for any programming book.

I'm violating convention here by using a name other than helloworld for the script, however. I'm an iconoclast.

After your script completes, you should see the prompt for the next command. The shell isn't impatient; it's just telling you it is ready for the next command. This prompt can prove important with the −n option to the echo command, as in the following example.

Using echo without Newlines

You can pass a −n command-line parameter to echo to tell echo not to print a new line after the text. By default, echo outputs a new line when complete. To see this at work, enter the following into a file. Name the file script5:

```
echo -n "No newline"
```

Run this script with the sh command:

```
$ sh script5
No newline[ericfj@kirkwall scripts]$
```

How It Works

With the −n command-line option, echo prints out its text with no new line.

> *The term new line handles a yucky abstraction. For years, Unix and Linux systems used a line-feed character (ASCII 10) to mark the end of a line of text. MS-DOS and Windows use a carriage-return character (ASCII 13) and a line-feed character to mark the end of a line. Macintosh systems, up through Mac OS 9, used a carriage-return character to mark the end of a line. Thus, there were three main ways to signify the end of a line of text, depending on the platform. Programming and scripting languages have had to deal with this issue for years. For shell scripts, the term new line means whatever character or characters are needed for a given platform to mark the end of a line of text.*

Note how the bash prompt for the next command, [ericfj@kirkwall scripts]$, appears right after the text from script5, No newline. In this example, the text appears as a confusing mush, but this technique is very useful when asking for user input (see below).

In addition, you can use the −n option to echo to build up an output message on a number of lines. This can make your output messages easier to understand inside your script. That is, your script becomes easier to read should you ever need to look at it again.

> *Comments, covered below, also make scripts easier to read.*

Writing Palindromic Scripts

This example shows a palindrome output a bit at a time. Enter this text and save to a file named script6:

```
echo -n "A man,"
echo -n " a plan,"
echo -n " a canal,"
echo " Panama."
```

When you run this script, you'll see this output:

```
$ sh script6
A man, a plan, a canal, Panama.
```

How It Works

This script merely uses the echo command, with and without the -n command-line option. But it introduces a key point to remember when creating output text.

The output text here is essentially the user interface for your script. Your scripts should be easy to use and easy to understand.

The key point is that you need to insert spaces to separate items. Note how the second, third, and fourth lines output a space first. This separates the output from the previous line. You can put the spaces on the initial line, or the line below, as needed. The spaces make the output clear.

In addition, the punctuation, commas, and a period in this example also help make the output more understandable. Try making the script without spaces or punctuation. Enter the following text and name the file script7:

```
echo -n "A man"
echo -n "a plan"
echo -n "a canal"
echo "Panama"
```

When you run this script, you'll see a less understandable output:

```
$ sh script7
A mana plana canalPanama
```

The -n option to the echo command works very well if you want to explain the output of a command or just show that the computer is magical, as in the following Try It Out.

Try It Out   Mixing Commands with Text Output from echo

This script shows how the computer can do magic. Enter the script that follows and save under the file name script8:

```
echo "I will guess your user name."
echo -n "It is: "
whoami
```

When you run this script with sh, you should see output similar to the following:

```
$ sh script8
I will guess your user name.
It is: ericfj
```

Your username should appear in place of ericfj.

How It Works

The first `echo` command outputs a sentence that explains what the script will do, using the word `guess` to imply that the script has intelligence. The second `echo` command outputs text that will appear just prior to the output of the third command, `whoami`.

The `whoami` command, short for *who am I*, outputs the name of the current user, your username. When put together, through the clever use of `echo -n`, it looks like the script has guessed your username.

The `whoami` command does not exist on all platforms. If that is the case for your system, try the following script, named `script9`, instead:

```
echo "Hmm...determining operating system..."
echo -n "This computer runs: "
uname
```

This script sports less magic but shows the same concepts. When you run this script, you should see:

```
$ sh script9
Hmm...determining operating system...
This computer runs: Linux
```

The output should differ based on your operating system. In Mac OS X, for example, you should see:

```
$ sh script9
Hmm...determining operating system...
This computer runs: Darwin
```

On an Audrey (which does not provide the `whoami` command), you will see:

```
# sh script9
Hmm...determining operating system...
This computer runs: QNX
```

Note that you are logged in, by default, as the root user on an Audrey.

These examples show how to build up messages with the `echo` command to make your scripts look better and provide more information about what they do.

Following on the topic of letting the computer, in the form of shell scripts, remember data for you, you can use the `echo` command to remind yourself of hard-to-remember data as well, as in the following Try It Out.

Try It Out   Remembering Data for You with Scripts

The Yopy PDA connects to a Linux system using networking over a USB port. When you plug in the PDA, you can type in the proper command to start up the USB networking. (Or you could configure the Linux system to automatically start USB networking, but that's not the topic here. There is usually more than one way to perform a given task.)

To save on brain cells, you can fill in the proper command to start USB networking into a script. Plug in the PDA, and run the script. The following is an example of such a script:

```
/sbin/ifconfig usb0 192.168.1.1
echo "Yopy is on 192.168.1.1"
```

Name this script yopy. When you run this script, you'll see the following output:

```
$ sh yopy
Yopy is on 192.168.1.1
```

Make sure your PDA is on and plugged into the USB port prior to running this script.

How It Works

This script really isn't that hard to remember. The ifconfig command configures networking interfaces. It is a system administrator command, so you will likely find it in /sbin or /usr/sbin. The device refers to a USB port, so usb0 sounds right. And Internet addresses in the 192.168.*x.x* range refer to a private network. Remembering that it is 192.168.1.1, however, can be a pain, especially if your local network runs on a different address range.

The first command sets up networking on the USB port. The second command displays a message to the user that the networking is set up. And it helpfully outputs the Internet address for the USB device.

In addition to these uses, the echo command proves very useful to prompt the user to enter data. You want the user to enter the right data, so you need a prompt to tell the user what to enter. See the section Gathering Input later in this chapter for more on this.

Variables

As shown in Chapter 1, the echo command can output more than just plain text. You can also store values in variables and have echo output those values. As with programming, a *variable* is a named item that can hold a value. You can store a value in a variable and later use the variable as a placeholder for that value. This proves very useful for shell scripts.

With scripts, each variable has a name and a value. You assign the named variable to a value. You can then access the variable's value using a special syntax. This syntax is:

```
VARIABLE_NAME=VALUE
```

The VARIABLE_NAME is the name of the variable. Variable names must start with a letter or an underscore (_). Subsequent characters in variable names can be letters, numbers, or underscores. You cannot use spaces in variable names. Most older scripts tend to use all uppercase letters for variables, as this was considered the most portable across systems. This is not necessary, however. Even from the beginning of the Bourne shell, you could create variables with lowercase letters.

This syntax applies to the Bourne shell, bash, and ksh. The C shell uses a different syntax, discussed later.

Do not place a space or anything else between the variable name, the equal sign, and the value.

To access the value of a variable, use a dollar sign, $, as a prefix to the variable name:

```
$VARIABLE1
```

This syntax tells the shell to replace the text $VARIABLE1 with the value held in the variable VARIABLE1.

The shell expands the text with the variable name, not the individual commands.

Try It Out   Using Variables

Here is one of the simplest uses for shell script variables. Enter this text and save it under the file name script10:

```
VARIABLE1=Value
echo "My variable holds: $VARIABLE1"
```

Run this script with sh:

```
$ sh script10
My variable holds: Value
```

How It Works

This simple example sets the variable named VARIABLE1 to a value, conveniently enough, Value. Setting the variable does nothing other than place the value into a named area of the computer's memory. The echo command line then accesses the value of the variable. The shell, sh in this case, replaces the text $VARIABLE1 with the value of the variable, Value.

If you need to place a space in a variable value, use double quotes around the entire value, as in the following Try It Out.

Try It Out   Using Double Quotes with Variables

In this example, you can see the use of double quotes to keep a string containing spaces as a single value:

```
VARIABLE1="A value"
echo "My variable holds: $VARIABLE1"
```

Save this text under the file name script11. When you run this script with sh, you will see the following output:

```
$ sh script11
My variable holds: A value
```

How It Works

This script works the same as `script10`. In this case, however, the variable `VARIABLE1` holds the text `A value`. Because the text has a space in it, to get the space into the variable you need to enclose the value in double quotes.

Variables and the C Shell

The syntax shown so far for setting variables does not work with the C shell (or the T C shell). For example, if you run `script11` with the C shell, you will see the following error messages:

```
$ csh script11
VARIABLE1=A value: Command not found.
VARIABLE1: Undefined variable.
```

With the C shell, you need to use the `set` command:

```
set variable_name = value
```

Typically, you should use lowercase variable names with the C shell. You must use the `set` command. You can place spaces around the equal sign. Spaces are not required but can often add clarity to your scripts.

The following example shows how to set a variable from the C shell:

```
set variable1="A value"
echo "My variable holds: $variable1"
```

This script is essentially the same as the `script11` script for the Bourne shell. If you run this script, however, you need to run it with the `csh` command, not `sh`:

```
$ csh csh_var
My variable holds: A value
```

If you skipped past it in Chapter 1, see www.faqs.org/faqs/unix-faq/shell/csh-whynot/ for a list of reasons why you should avoid the C shell for scripts. This document is very technical, but suffice it to say that industry practice is to use sh, not csh, for scripts.

Combining Variables

You can combine more than one variable in a script, as well as in an individual command line. Practice with the following Try It Out and then let your imagination run wild.

Try It Out   Mixing Variables and Commands

This example shows two variables. Name this file `script12`:

```
VARIABLE1=Cool
VARIABLE2="this system runs "
echo -n "$VARIABLE1 $VARIABLE2"
uname
```

Run this script with sh:

```
$ sh script12
Cool this system runs Linux
```

How It Works

This example sets two variables, VARIABLE1 and VARIABLE2. Note how there is no leading space in VARIABLE2 nor a trailing space in VARIABLE1. A space does separate the values, but this space comes from the arguments passed to the echo command.

The echo command gets a -n option to tell it to skip the new line at the end of the output. This makes the output of the next command, uname, appear on the same line.

Building Up Commands with Variables

The script12 example shows the start of building up a command line with variables. The following examples show how to continue this task and create commands entirely from variables.

Try It Out   Listing Directories

First, you can build up the command-line argument or arguments from a variable. For example:

```
DIRECTORY=/usr/local
ls $DIRECTORY
```

Save the script as script13. Run this script with sh:

```
$ sh script13
bin  etc  games  include  lib  libexec  man  sbin  share  src
```

How It Works

The shell expands the value of the variable DIRECTORY, /usr/local, and passes this value as an argument to the ls command, which lists the files in that directory.

Try It Out   Running Commands from Variables

Second, you can place a command within a variable as well. For example:

```
DIRECTORY=/usr/local
LS=ls
$LS $DIRECTORY
```

Save the script as script14.

The output should remain the same. This script performs the same action, in the end, as the previous script. For example:

```
$ sh script14
bin  etc  games  include  lib  libexec  man  sbin  share  src
```

How It Works

This example extends the previous example to set the `ls` command into a variable, `LS`. Note how the command line now is entirely made up of variables. The shell will gladly expand both variables to create the command to execute.

This may not seem that useful, but if you are writing cross-platform scripts, you may need different command names for the same purpose on different platforms. For example, some Unix systems do not have a command named `install`. On those systems you need to use the `cp` (copy) command instead. You can use a variable to hide this difference:

```
INSTALL=install
```

Or, on other systems, use a different value:

```
INSTALL=cp
```

The difference in the script is then isolated to one section. The rest of this hypothetical installation script would remain the same regardless of the platform.

As a similar example, the C compiler (for programs written in the C language, not for the C shell) usually has a name of `cc`. The GNU C compiler may be named `gcc`. A compiler from a company named LPI may be named `lcc`. You can hide these differences by setting a variable named `CC` to the C compiler command for a particular platform.

You may or may not have a command named cc that executes gcc. On Mac OS X systems, you have to do a separate install of the developer tools to get gcc. If you are going to be doing a lot of shell scripting in Mac OS X, it is highly recommended that you do this install, because it is free and installs quite a few nifty tools for you.

Try It Out   **Storing a Full Command in a Variable**

In this Try It Out, you extend the previous examples to create the entire command as a variable. For example:

```
DIRECTORY=/usr/local
LS=ls
CMD="$LS $DIRECTORY"
$CMD
```

Save the script as `script15`.

The output should remain the same. This script performs the same task, in the end, as the previous two scripts. For example:

```
$ sh script15
bin  etc  games  include  lib  libexec  man  sbin  share  src
```

How It Works

By now, you've seen that it doesn't matter how you create a command to execute, so long as it results in a valid command. You can use variables and combine variables to your heart's content.

De-assigning Variables

To de-assign a variable, use the `unset` command:

```
unset VARIABLE1
```

This command essentially removes the variable named `VARIABLE1`. Do not try to access this variable again without setting it to a new value.

Up to now, I've concentrated on the display of output and storing values. The next step is to gather input, especially input from the user.

Gathering Input

The `read` command reads in data from the terminal (really, the keyboard). The `read` command takes in whatever the user types and places the text into the variable you name. The syntax is:

```
read VARIABLE_NAME
```

Because you are setting a variable value, do not use a dollar sign, $, with the variable name.

You can try out the `read` command with the following example, which shows prompting the user for input and then, lo and behold, reading in the input from the user.

Try It Out   Reading User Input

Enter the following script and name the file `script16`:

```
echo -n "Please enter the new position: "
read POSITION
echo
echo "Congratulations, $POSITION!"
```

Now run the script with `sh`:

```
$ sh script16
Please enter the new position: Grand High Pooh-Bah

Congratulations, Grand High Pooh-Bah!
```

You need to enter the name of a position, *Grand High Pooh-Bah* in this example. Type the text and press Enter.

How It Works

This script uses echo with the -n option to display a prompt, asking the user to enter the name of a new position. I assume here that you have been promoted at work. Note how the prompt message has a colon to help signify the computer awaits the user's input. The prompt also ends with a space to separate the user's input from the prompt. This is a common technique.

After displaying the prompt, the script waits patiently for you to type in the name of the new position. If you make a mistake while entering the text, you can use the Backspace key to edit the input. Once you press Enter, however, the text has gone into the variable.

The next command shows a lonely echo. It has no arguments, so this echo command just prints out a new line. This just shows how you can have greater control over the output. The last echo command prints out the value you typed in, preceded by a message of congratulations.

You are not limited to just one read command in your scripts. You can prompt the user and read in as many values as you need, as shown in the following Try It Out.

Try It Out   Reading Multiple Values

You can use the read command more than once to capture a number of values from the user. For example:

```
echo -n "Please enter your first name: "
read FIRSTNAME
echo -n "Please enter your last name: "
read LASTNAME
echo -n "Please enter the name of the state where you live: "
read STATE

FULLNAME="$FIRSTNAME $LASTNAME"
MESSAGE="Well, $FULLNAME of $STATE, welcome to our huge"
MESSAGE="$MESSAGE impersonal company."

echo "$MESSAGE"
echo "You will now be known as Worker Unit 10236."
```

Save this script as script17 and run it with sh:

```
$ sh script17
Please enter your first name: Eric
Please enter your last name: FJ
Please enter the name of the state where you live: Minnesota
Well, Eric FJ of Minnesota, welcome to our huge impersonal company.
You will now be known as Worker Unit 10236.
```

How It Works

This example illustrates the same concepts as the previous example, except that now you add more than one `read` command to read in three values from the user.

The script sets the FULLNAME variable to the user's first and last name, separated by a space.

Note how the output is built up over a number of lines. First, the MESSAGE variable gets filled with the start of the message. Then the script sets the value of the MESSAGE variable again, this time using the old value of the MESSAGE variable itself as part of the new value. This is a method you can use to augment the value of a variable.

Commenting Your Scripts

Up to now, all of the example scripts have been short and very easy to understand. You don't need to engage in detective work to decipher these scripts. But when you start writing real scripts, your scripts will likely be a lot more complex. To help with this, you can enter comments in your scripts.

Comments are messages to yourself and to future archaeologists (other users) that describe what a script is supposed to do and how it works. Comments help others understand your script. Comments also help you understand your own script, should you need to examine the script months after writing it.

Your memory is never as good as you think it is. No matter what your IQ is, Murphy's law dictates that when the script you wrote in a panic at 2 a.m. to keep your company afloat and your job intact finally breaks six months after you wrote it, you're going to look at it and wonder just how much caffeine is required for you to keep track of 300 variables all named x1, x2, and so on. Comments are, all too often, the only documentation you will ever have for your code or anyone else's code. Comments: Use them, love them.

Comments are especially useful if you found some very clever technique to create a command. Others of lesser intelligence may not understand the full might of your cleverness. (This will not be a problem when you take over the world. But until then, comments can help.)

Another way to pass on knowledge is to sit around a campfire, or at a bar, at night and tell others the crucial details that ought to have been placed in comments. This technique works best on your last day at an organization. Refuse to write anything down. Some companies actually use this technique. And they can see nothing wrong with this method. Until something breaks.

To enter comments in your script, start each comment line with a sharp sign (#). For example:

```
# This is a comment.
```

The # sign is often called a pound sign, a hash, or a sharp. British users cringe at the use of # as a pound sign, because # looks nothing like the symbol for pounds sterling.

With a comment, the shell ignores all the text from the sharp sign to the end of the line. You can place commands inside a comment, but the shell will not execute them. For example:

```
# This is a comment with a command, ls /
```

You can place a comment after a command so long as you use the sharp sign to start the comment. For example:

```
ls /usr/local   # List the files in the directory /usr/local
```

The following Try It Out provides some practice in commenting a script.

Try It Out   Commenting Your Scripts

The following script shows an example of some comments:

```
# Script to ask a user's full name and state of residence.
# Script welcomes the user to a company. Good luck!

# This is a Bourne shell script. It predates the
# Microsoft takeover of all computing, so it is not
# written in VB.NET. TODO: Update to VB.NET.

echo -n "Please enter your first name: "
read FIRSTNAME          # Read the user's input.


echo -n "Please enter your last name: "
read LASTNAME
echo -n "Please enter the name of the state where you live: "
read STATE

# FULLNAME holds the user's full name. The reason for
# the separate variables is to allow for future modifications
# to query on the user's last name. For that, the last name
# must be separate from the first name.
FULLNAME="$FIRSTNAME $LASTNAME"

# NOTE: This message may get long.
MESSAGE="Well, $FULLNAME of $STATE, welcome to our huge"
MESSAGE="$MESSAGE impersonal company."

echo "$MESSAGE"

# TODO: Each worker should be assigned a different
# WU number. Use the last name to look up the worker's
# WUN.
echo "You will now be known as Worker Unit 10236."

# end of script18
```

Save this script under the file name script18. The script should work the same as script17 because none of the commands changed, only the comments. Run the script with sh:

```
$ sh script18
Please enter your first name: Eric
Please enter your last name: FJ
```

```
Please enter the name of the state where you live: Minnesota
Well, Eric FJ of Minnesota, welcome to our huge impersonal company.
You will now be known as Worker Unit 10236.
```

How It Works

Note that this script is essentially the same as `script17`. Just the comments are new. The comments serve a number of purposes:

- ❑ Comments explain what the script does.

- ❑ Comments explain what kind of script this is — a Bourne shell script in this case. You may want to also comment how to run a script.

- ❑ Comments explain why certain techniques were used. This will keep people from second-guessing the scriptwriter's intentions later on.

- ❑ Comments provide warnings for potential problem areas. The note that the output message may grow too long is one example of this type of comment.

- ❑ Comments show areas that are left for future extension. This not only tells you the script writer was thinking ahead but also shows areas you will need to work on should you need to extend the script.

- ❑ Comments show areas that are not yet finished. Often, a message will start with TODO, a combination of *To Do*.

For a script this short, it has a lot of comments — too many, really.

To create good comments, don't describe the obvious in boring detail. Instead, with each script, you should describe, briefly, what the script does. Particularly tricky parts of the script deserve extra comments to help explain what is going on.

You can lie in your comments, but that is not a good idea. You end up merely confusing yourself. You should also skip profanity, if only to avoid future embarrassment. When the source code for parts of Microsoft Windows appeared on the Internet, people were amazed at the amount of profanity in the code. This is one thing that nontechnical people can see and understand in otherwise incomprehensible source code.

Another thing to avoid are names that have, shall we say, insulting connotations. When Mac OS X was released, people who had never dealt with Unix before, or the rather unique sense of humor of the Unix community, went browsing through the various shell scripts that are a part of the system startup and ran across the term "luser" (rhymes with "loser"). A long time ago, it was short for "local user" or someone sitting at the physical computer versus someone on a remote terminal. Well, people read comments by an Apple employee talking about "keeping the lusers from doing something stupid" and were rather snarky about the whole thing. In general, even if you're in a bad mood, save the pejoratives for the bar after work.

Continuing Lines

Most shells, including bash, sh, ksh, and csh, support the capability to type in long commands. You can keep typing away until you enter the entire command. But very long lines are hard to read and harder to understand. Because of this, you can break up your command using the line-continuation marker. Type a backslash, \, at the end of a line to continue a command on the next line, as in the following Try It Out.

Try It Out   Continuing Commands On and On and On

This example illustrates the use of the backslash character to continue a command on the next line:

```
$ ls \
> -CF \
> -1 \
> /usr/local
bin/
etc/
games/
include/
lib/
libexec/
man/
sbin/
share/
src/
```

This forms an extreme example, but you can use this technique when you have to type in long lines.

If you're using Mac OS X and coming to shell from an AppleScript background, the backslash is similar to the AppleScript continuation character you get when you hit Option-Return.

How It Works

When you end a line with a backslash, the shell should display a level-two prompt to show you that the command is not yet complete. Bash presents a > in this example. A question mark, ?, is also common. (You can configure this prompt.)

In this example, the command starts with 1s, the name of the command. A line-continuation marker appears immediately, continuing the command to the next line. The next line holds two options, -CF, equivalent to -C and -F, and continues the command again. The next line holds a simple option, -1 (one), and continues on to the next line, thankfully the last. This line presents a directory, /usr/local, as an argument to the 1s command.

This technique, or course, proves of greater use when the command line would really stretch out. For example, the following command launches a Java application with some complex options and arguments:

```
exec $JAVACMD $JAVA_OPTS \
      -classpath "$CLASSWORLDS_CLASSPATH" \
      -Dprogram.name="$PROGNAME" \
      -Dclassworlds.conf="$CLASSWORLDS_CONF" \
      -Dgroovy.home="$GROOVY_HOME" \
      -Dtools.jar="$TOOLS_JAR" \
      org.codehaus.classworlds.Launcher "$@"
```

The "$@" is a special construct. It refers to command-line arguments passed to the script.

This command uses a lot of continuations to make the script, called groovy, easier to understand. Note how each major command-line option or argument appears on a line by itself. The earlier parts of the script, not shown here, fill in all the variables. Otherwise, the command would be far longer. For example, on Mac OS X, the TOOLS_JAR variable is set as follows (but appearing on one line, with no wrap):

```
TOOLS_JAR="/System/Library/Frameworks/JavaVM.framework/Versions/CurrentJDK/Classes/
classes.jar"
```

As this example shows, a good way to help learn shell scripting is to examine existing scripts, especially networking scripts or scripts that launch complex commands.

The example also uses the exec command to launch the rest of the command. See Chapter 9 for more on exec.

Summary

This chapter presents the basics for creating shell scripts. Starting with your choice in text editors, you can create your own scripts.

❑ For editors, you can choose from a plethora of choices including emacs and vi, two legacy editors, as well as a number of graphical editors that sport more modern interfaces.

❑ Shell scripting is not the only scripting language. There are quite a few others, including Perl, Python, and Tcl, discussed in this chapter.

❑ When beginning with scripts, some of the first tasks include displaying output, or text, to the user. For scripts, the echo command provides the main way to output text to the user. You can use echo with a command-line option, -n, to skip outputting a new line after the text. This is most useful when creating prompts for user input.

❑ Most scripts need to store data in some way. For scripts, you can store values in named variables. These variables can be combined, set to new values, or accessed (read) using the dollar-sign character, $.

❑ To gather input from the user, use the read command. The read command reads in one line of user input, terminated by the Enter key. Read places the user input into a variable, the variable you pass to the read command.

❑ You can (and should) place comments in your script with the # character. You can use the \ character to continue a command on the next line.

The next chapter covers how you can use scripts to make decisions and perform different commands in the case of different conditions, an important technique for writing your own real-world shell scripts.

Exercises

1. Try at least two text editors and choose one that you find productive.

2. Regardless of which editor you picked in Exercise 1, try entering at least three of the example scripts in this chapter with vi. Try three more scripts with emacs. Discuss what you like and dislike about each editor.

3. Write a script to output the text message "A man, a plan, a canal, Panama" with as many commands as possible. Each command must perform something useful for the script. Furthermore, comments don't count for the total. See how many commands you can use in your most inefficient script. Use only the shell scripting concepts introduced so far.

4. Write a command to list the contents of the /usr/bin directory (or a directory that has many commands). You can only set and evaluate variables in your script. You cannot call any commands directly. Extend this script to add some command-line options for the file listing. Try -1 (one) to list the files in one column.

5. Modify the example `script17` file for users in Canada. Instead of asking for the state the user lives in, Canadian users should be asked which province they live in. Extra credit goes to those who can output all text in both English and French.

6. To prove you are truly an emacs guru, use `M-x backward-char` and `M-x forward-char`, the long commands, instead of the left and right arrow keys when modifying the `script17` file for the previous question. Aren't you glad emacs provides this option?

7. Do the same thing with vi when modifying the file `script17`. Show disdain for the arrow keys and use h, j, k, and l exclusively. If you start to like these keys *and* become productive, be afraid. Be very afraid.

3

Controlling How Scripts Run

Once you get beyond some trivial scripts, you'll soon find that a script that just runs command after command after command doesn't work for most real-world scripts. Instead, you need the capability to perform some sort of logic within the program, test conditions, and take alternative measures if certain tests fail. You may need to perform some operation on each file in a directory or back up only selected files. Shell scripting languages offer a variety of ways to test values and then execute different commands based on the results of the tests. All of these things fall under the concept of *controlling how your scripts run*.

This chapter covers:

❑   Advanced variable referencing, useful for conditionals and iteration

❑   Iterating with the `for` and `foreach` statements

❑   Using `if-then-else` statements to test values and execute different commands based on the results

❑   Testing for a variety of values using the `switch-case` statements

❑   Looping while a condition is true

Referencing Variables

Chapter 2 introduced the concepts of variables, named *data holders*. Each variable can hold a value, which you can later reference by placing a dollar sign in front of the variable name. When it comes to looping and conditional tests, however, you often need more options for referencing variables. This section shows you some of those options.

The Bourne shell, along with bash and ksh, provides another means to reference the value of a variable. The normal means is with a dollar sign:

```
$variable_name
```

This example references the value of the variable *variable_name*. If you have not set a value into *variable_name*, you will get no value. This is not an error.

You can also use curly braces to reference a variable's value:

```
${variable_name}
```

This method uses the curly braces to clearly delineate the start and end of the variable name. With just the dollar sign, you have a clear separation for the start of the variable name but not the end.

This alternate method proves very useful if you want to place a variable with other text immediately adjacent or, better still, when you need to append something to the value of the variable. For example, if you have a variable with the value abc and want to output abcdef, the natural way to do this would be to place the variable name next to the text def. Unfortunately, the following would output nothing except for a new line:

```
myvar=abc
echo $myvardef        # nothing
```

Note how the shell sees nothing to separate the name of the variable, myvar, from the text def. Thus, the shell interprets $myvardef as referencing a variable named myvardef. If you have not set this variable, which is likely, then myvardef will hold nothing.

But if you use the ${variable_name} alternate format, you can then make a clean separation between the variable name and the remaining text:

```
${myvar}def
```

Try It Out   Referencing Variables

To better understand how to reference variables, try the following script:

```
# Set the initial value.
myvar=abc

echo "Test 1 ======"
echo $myvar           # abc
echo ${myvar}         # same as above, abc
echo {$myvar}         # {abc}

echo "Test 2 ======"
echo myvar            # Just the text myvar
echo "myvar"          # Just the text myvar
echo "$myvar"         # abc
echo "\$myvar"        # $myvar

echo "Test 3 ======"
echo $myvardef        # Empty line
echo ${myvar}def      # abcdef
```

```
echo "Test 4 ======"
echo $myvar$myvar       # abcabc
echo ${myvar}${myvar}   # abcabc

echo "Test 5 ======"
# Reset variable value, with spaces
myvar="a    b    c"
echo "$myvar"           # a    b    c
echo $myvar             # a b c
```

Save this file under the name `var_refs`. This script goes over the various choices for referencing variables. When you run the script, you'll see output like the following:

```
$ sh var_refs
Test 1 ======
abc
abc
{abc}
Test 2 ======
myvar
myvar
abc
$myvar
Test 3 ======

abcdef
Test 4 ======
abcabc
abcabc
Test 5 ======
a    b    c
a b c
```

Should any of the variable references appear confusing, check over the script, its comments, and the output shown here. These are tricky concepts.

How It Works

For such a short script, this example is complex. You should go over the output one line at a time to better understand how the shell treats these variables. For such a simple subject, this can get surprisingly tricky.

Test 1 shows the normal ways to reference the value of a variable. The script sets the variable `myvar` to the value `abc`. The construct `$myvar`, familiar from Chapter 2, references the value of the variable. The shell will replace `$myvar` with the value `abc`.

The construct `${myvar}` does the same thing. The shell will replace `${myvar}` with the value `abc`.

The construct `{$myvar}` combines normal curly braces, `{` and `}`, with the first construct, `$myvar`. As before, the shell will replace `$myvar` with the value `abc`. The `echo` command will output the curly braces, creating `{abc}`.

In most cases, the construct {$myvar} is a typo. The user likely intended this to be ${myvar} but got the leading curly brace positioned incorrectly.

Test 2 shows what happens if you skip the dollar sign with the variable name. Without the dollar sign, the text `myvar` is just a plain string of text. There is nothing special about `myvar`, even though you named a variable with the same string of text.

The construct `myvar` is just the text `myvar`. So is the construct `"myvar"`, which will appear as `myvar`. The quotes delimit the text. In both these cases, you can guess that the user forgot to include the dollar sign to reference the value of the `myvar` variable rather than the plain text `myvar`.

The construct `"$myvar"` outputs `abc` because `$myvar` references the value of the variable `myvar`. The quotes merely delimit the text. So how can you get the dollar sign to appear? That's what the next construct, `"\$myvar"`, does.

The construct `"\$myvar"` outputs what looks like a variable reference: $myvar. The backslash, \, acts as a special character, telling the shell to use the following special character, $, as a character instead of a means to reference a variable. That is, \$ refers to a plain character $, removing the special meaning $ normally holds. Thus, the ending text is `"$"` and `"myvar"`, or $myvar when output.

The \$ format is called escaping the dollar sign. You can also use a backslash to escape other characters, such as quotes needed inside a quoted text string. Additional examples of escaping appear throughout this book.

Test 3 shows how to combine the values of more than one variable into the same output.

The construct `$myvardef` references the value of the variable `myvardef`, which this script has not set. The `echo` command outputs a new line with no text because there is no value for the variable. In most cases, however, this construct was meant to output the value of the variable `myvar`, with the string of text `def`, making `abcdef`.

The construct `${myvar}def` shows how to do just that. This construct combines the value of the `myvar` variable, `abc`, with the string of text `def`, making `abcdef`.

If you want a space between the variable values, none of this will be an issue. Just place one variable reference, a space, and then another variable reference.

Test 4 continues the use of placing data immediately after a variable by using two variables. Both lines output the same text: the value of the `myvar` variable appearing twice.

The first construct, `$myvar$myvar`, handily provides two dollar signs, each of which can delimit the construct. This way, the shell knows that the second dollar sign starts another variable reference, in this case to the same variable.

The second construct, `${myvar}${myvar}`, makes a clearer separation between the two variable references. Use this format to be most clear should you need to combine variable values.

It may not be clear right now why you'd want to combine variable values with text or other variables, but this is used quite a lot in scripting. Imagine writing a backup script, for example. If you have the name of a file in the variable *filename*, you can construct a backup file name using, for example, $*filename*.bak, with the .bak extension, short for *backup*. See the examples in the Looping over Files section for this construct.

This is one of the differences between script-oriented languages such as shell scripting languages and traditional programming languages such as C, C++, and Java. Scripting languages tend to allow you to place the text you want in your script. Bare text, such as def, is assumed to be text. Variables are denoted with a special syntax, $ in shell scripts. With traditional programming languages, on the other hand, bare text is assumed to be the names of variables. Any text you want to output must be delimited by quotes. This isn't a hard-and-fast rule, but it shows some of the assumptions behind each type of language.

Test 5 shows the difference between using quotes and plain references. This test sets the myvar variable to a new value. It still holds a, b, and c, but this time the test sets the values with spaces in between each element. The quotes on the line that sets myvar to the new value preserve the spaces.

When referencing these variables, you can see the difference between using the quotes, which preserves spaces, and not using them, which treats all the values as individual elements. Because shell scripting was designed around the command line, each element is placed with a single space to separate it from the next element.

The first construct, "$myvar", preserves the spaces in the value of myvar. The second construct, $myvar, which leaves the bare values on the command line, does not preserve the spaces.

If some of this is confusing, don't worry. The best way to learn the intricacies of shell scripting is by experimenting. You can vary the var_refs script to see how different constructs work together. In addition, you can experiment with later scripts to see what works and what doesn't.

These variable constructs are useful when you start to test variable values and use variables to control the flow of how your scripts run. One of the most common means to control the flow in a script is through looping.

Looping and Iteration

Looping is the process of repeating the same script elements a given number of times. Looping works best when applied to one of the following tasks:

❑   Performing the same operation on a number of files

❑   Performing an operation for a fixed number of times, such as trying to reconnect to the network three times (and then giving up if the connection cannot be re-established)

❑   Performing an operation on a given number of items

For all of these iterative tasks, you can use the shell `for` loop. The basic syntax of the `for` loop is:

```
for variable in list_of_items
do
    command1
    command2
    ...
    last_command
done
```

You need to provide the name of a variable. The shell will set the variable to the current value on each iteration through the loop. The commands between the `do` and the `done` statements get executed on each iteration.

The `list_of_items` differs depending on what you want to use for iteration, such as a list of files.

Looping over Files

Quite a few shell scripts need to loop over a list of files. Backup scripts, for example, might check each file in a directory to see if the file is newer than the last backup. If the file has been modified since the last backup, then you may want a script to back up the file.

The basic syntax for looping over a number of files is to use the `for` loop with a list of items that resolves to the files. For example:

```
for filename in *
do
    command1
    command2
    ...
    last_command
done
```

In this example, the `*` resolves to the list of files in the current directory. The `for` loop then iterates over each file, setting the variable `filename` to the name of the current file.

Try It Out   Making a Primitive ls

You can use this example technique to write a primitive `ls` script for listing file names. Enter the following script and name the file `myls`:

```
# Example to look at files in a directory and
# print out the file names.

for filename in *
do
    echo $filename
done
```

When you run this script, you should see the names of the files in the current directory. For example:

```
$ sh myls
Makefile
backup1
case_os
check_csh
counter1
counter2
csh_var
error
find_shells
find_shells2
myls
myls2
nested_for1
readpipe.tcl
return0
return1
```

Your output will differ based on the files in your directory.

How It Works

The for loop in the myls script loops, or iterates, over each item in the list. This list is identified by an asterisk, *, which does nothing magic. As covered in Chapter 1, the asterisk is called a wildcard or a glob. The shell expands the asterisk to the names of all the files in the current directory.

*Note that hidden files—that is, files with names that start with a period—are not included in the * glob.*

The for loop iterates over all the file names in the current directory. The block of commands between the do and the done uses the echo command to output the file name. Thus, the myls script outputs one file name per line.

You can place as many commands as you need between the do and the done, or as few, including no commands.

Try It Out   **A More Extensive ls**

The previous example uses the echo command to print out each file name. You can modify this script to print out the file's size along with its name by switching to a different command. Enter the following script and save it under the name myls2:

```
# Another example to look at files in a directory and
# print out the file names.

for filename in *
do
    # Show the amount of bytes in each file
    # with the file name. The wc command
```

```
      # outputs both.
      wc -c $filename
done
```

When you run this script, you should see output like the following:

```
$ sh myls2
    24 Makefile
   187 backup1
   412 case_os
   232 check_csh
   150 counter1
   179 counter2
    61 csh_var
     8 error
   764 find_shells
   262 find_shells2
   121 myls
   235 myls2
   214 nested_for1
   395 readpipe.tcl
     7 return0
     7 return1
```

Your output will differ based on the files in your current directory.

How It Works

This script iterates over the same type of list, the names of all the files in the current directory. Between the do and the done, the myls2 script still has just one command (plus the comments). The command, however, differs. The myls script used the echo command. The myls2 script uses the wc command, short for *word count*. The wc command can count the number of bytes, characters, and lines in a file, as well as approximate the number of words. (The approximation comes from the fact that wc uses a simple set of rules to determine where words start and end. The wc command does not understand natural text in English or any other language; it just uses rules to determine word boundaries.)

Typically, the wc command outputs all the counts it generates. With the -c option, however, wc outputs only the count of the bytes in the file, not the characters or lines. With the -c option, wc outputs the byte-count, or size, of each file and the file name. Thus, the myls2 script does not need to call the echo command.

Iterating over all the files in a directory is a very common operation in shell scripts.

As another example, you can use the for loop to help create a backup script. Backup scripts save a copy of files to some form of external storage. In most larger environments, administrators run incremental backups. With incremental backups, administrators first perform a full backup of all files and then selectively back up only those files that have changed since the last full backup. Typically, administrators start the process again every so often, such as performing a full backup every month or every week. Every day in between, however, administrators perform incremental backups.

Chapter 13 covers more on administrative tasks such as backups.

Try It Out   **Creating a Simple Backup Script**

You can create a simple backup script using a `for` loop:

```
# Example backup script, for files with names
# ending in .doc
#

for filename in *.doc
do
    echo "Copying $filename to $filename.bak"
    cp $filename $filename.bak
done
```

Save this script under the name `backup1`. When you run this script, you should see output like the following:

```
$ sh ../backup1
Copying 2005_Q1.doc to 2005_Q1.doc.bak
Copying 2005_Q2.doc to 2005_Q2.doc.bak
Copying business_plan.doc to business_plan.doc.bak
Copying ent_whitepaper.doc to ent_whitepaper.doc.bak
Copying lin_proposal.doc to lin_proposal.doc.bak
Copying lin_stmt_of_work.doc to lin_stmt_of_work.doc.bak
Copying proposal1.doc to proposal1.doc.bak
Copying world_takeover.doc to world_takeover.doc.bak
```

Note that the output on your system will differ based on what files are located in your current directory.

How It Works

The `backup1` script loops through all the files in the current directory with names ending in `.doc`, presumably word processor files. The commands in the `for` loop copy each file to a file with the same name but with an extra `.bak` extension. Note that this will result in files with names in the format of `filename.doc.bak`, a sort of double extension. For the most part, shells don't treat the file name extension as a special part of the file name. So in the `backup1` script, the `filename` variable holds the name of the file, such as `2005_Q2.doc`, rather than `2005_Q2`.

Note that a real backup script would likely need to verify whether the item was a file or a directory and perhaps check when the file was last modified. In shell scripting terms, this means you need to combine the loop with conditionals to verify whether a file is one the script should back up or not. See the section Checking Conditions with if for more on conditionals.

Looping for a Fixed Number of Iterations

In addition to looping over a set of files, you can write scripts that loop for a fixed number of iterations.

The previous example scripts have allowed the shell to fill in the *list_of_items* from a listing of files. You can also indicate specific items to iterate over. For example, to teach an expensive computer to count, you can set up a `for` loop like the following:

```
for i in 1 2 3 4 5 6 7 8 9 10
do

done
```

In this example, the `for` loop will set the variable *i* to each of the values 1, 2, 3, 4, 5, 6, 7, 8, 9, and 10, performing whatever commands are in the do-done block.

Try It Out   Counting to Ten

For example, create the following script and save under the name `counter1`:

```
# Counts by looping for a fixed number of times

for i in 1 2 3 4 5 6 7 8 9 10
do
    echo -n "...$i"
done

echo    # Clean up for next shell prompt
```

When you run this script, you will see the following output:

```
$ sh counter1
...1...2...3...4...5...6...7...8...9...10
```

How It Works

This script uses the same `for` loop syntax but places specific values for the list of items to iterate over, where the previous scripts used the shell and the wildcard, or globbing, mechanism of the shell.

In each iteration through the loop, the `echo -n` command outputs the current item, such as 1, 2, or 3. The `-n` command-line option tells the `echo` command to place the output on one line. The final `echo` command prints out a new line so that the next shell prompt won't appear immediately after the 10.

You can place the `for` loop and the `do` statement on the same line, but you must separate the two elements with a semicolon as if they were separate commands (which in a sense, they are). For example:

```
# Counts by looping for a fixed number of times

# Note do on same line requires semicolon.

for i in 1 2 3 4 5 6 7 8 9 10; do
    echo -n "...$i"
done

echo    # Output newline
```

The resulting output will be identical to the previous example.

As you can guess from the way the example scripts specify the values to iterate over, there is nothing stopping you from making a `for` loop count backward. For example:

```
# Counts backwards

for i in 10 9 8 7 6 5 4 3 2 1
do
    echo -n "...$i"
done

echo    # Output new line
echo "Blast off!"
```

Enter this script and save it under the name `counter2`. When you run this script, you should see the following output:

```
$ sh counter2
...10...9...8...7...6...5...4...3...2...1
Blast off!
```

This is the same loop as before, only the values are listed in reverse order. There is also a final `echo` statement making a space-flight reference. You can place values in any order.

The previous example shows a very efficient countdown to launching a spacecraft because there is no pause between iterations. By the time you see the 10, you should also see the 1. The craft is ready to launch. Aside from the remarkable efficiency, you may want to put some kind of wait into a script of this type. You can do that with the `sleep` command.

The `sleep` command takes one command-line argument, the length of time to sleep in seconds. (See the online manuals on the `sleep` command for using other units of sleep time.) For example:

```
sleep 5
```

This command causes the shell to wait for five seconds before going on to the next command.

Note that the sleep amount will not be exact, as your computer will be performing other work (running other programs) at the same time. It should be at least five seconds, however, with an amount very close to five seconds.

Try It Out   **Sleeping between Iterations**

You can try out the `sleep` command with a `for` loop script:

```
# Counts backwards and waits each loop iteration.

for i in 10 9 8 7 6 5 4 3 2 1
do
    echo -n "$i... "
    sleep 1
done

echo    # Output new line
echo "Blast off!"
```

Enter this script and save it under the name sleep_counter. If you run this script, you should see the following when the output is complete:

```
$ sh sleep_counter
10... 9... 8... 7... 6... 5... 4... 3... 2... 1...
Blast off!
```

Note that all the numbers appear with a second delay between each number.

How It Works

This script is the same as the counter2 script except for the use of the sleep command to impose a delay between iterations. (In addition, the three periods are placed after the numbers rather than before.)

The numbers should appear slowly, with a second delay between 10... and 9..., for example. So you will first see the following:

```
10...
```

After a second delay, you see:

```
10... 9...
```

This continues until you see the following:

```
10... 9... 8... 7... 6... 5... 4... 3... 2... 1...
```

After a final one-second delay, you see the blast-off message:

```
10... 9... 8... 7... 6... 5... 4... 3... 2... 1...
Blast off!
```

Looping Like a C Program — the bash Shell

The bash shell supports a for loop syntax that appears a lot like that of the C programming language. The basic syntax is:

```
max=upper_limit
for ((i=1; i <= max ; i++))
do
    commands...
done
```

This is like the C programming language, not the C shell.

In this example, the variable *max* holds the upper limit, such as 10. The for loop will iterate using the variable *i*, where *i* starts at 1 and continues until it reaches a value greater than 10. The *i++* syntax refers to incrementing the variable *i*.

Some things to note in the syntax include:

❑ You need two sets of parentheses on each side, ((and)).

❑ You reference the loop iteration variable, *i* in this case, without the $.

❑ This syntax is supported by the bash shell, although you may find it works with the Bourne shell on systems where bash also provides the Bourne shell, such as Linux and Mac OS X.

If you are familiar with C programming, then this syntax will appear like a C for loop, with some modifications for use in a shell. Otherwise, you probably want to avoid this syntax.

Try It Out   **Looping Like C Programs**

Enter the following script and name the file c_for:

```
# C-language-like for loop.
# Must be run with bash.

max=10

for ((i=1; i <= max ; i++))
do
    echo -n "$i..."
done

echo
```

When you run this script in a bash shell, you will see the following output, like that of the previous scripts:

```
$ bash c_for
1...2...3...4...5...6...7...8...9...10...
```

If you run this script with the Bourne shell, sh, you may see an error like the following:

```
$ sh c_for
c_for: 6: Syntax error: Bad for loop variable
```

How It Works

The double-parenthesis syntax allows for a finer grain of control over a for loop, with much more compact code than trying to create the same loop using the Bourne shell syntax. Another advantage is that you do not need a list of all the items to iterate. Instead, you just need a start value and an end value (1 and 10, respectively, in the example). You'll often find it is far easier to come up with start and end values than it is to create a full list of items.

On the downside, however, you must run your script with bash. The bash shell isn't available on all systems, so you may have a problem. In addition, while this syntax requires bash, some bash-ized versions of sh will also support this syntax. Because of the uncertainty, you probably want to avoid using this syntax.

Looping in the C Shell

The C shell doesn't support the for loop but does support something similar, a foreach loop. The syntax for foreach is:

```
foreach variable (list_of_items)
    command1
    command2
    ...
    last_command
end
```

The loop executes once for each value in the list of items. On each iteration, the shell sets the variable to the current value from the list of items.

Some differences from the Bourne shell for syntax include:

❑   Use foreach instead of for.

❑   There is no in.

❑   There is no do to start the block of commands.

❑   Instead of done, the C shell uses end.

❑   The list of items must be enclosed within parentheses.

Try It Out   Creating a C Shell foreach Loop

The following example shows the C shell foreach loop. Enter this script and save it under the name myls_csh:

```
# C shell foreach

foreach filename (*)
    echo $filename
end
```

When you run this script, you will see a listing of the files in the current directory:

```
$ csh myls_csh
eden.txt
mail
Mail
motif2.txt
myls_csh
oracle.detect
PL2BAT.BAT
rpmlast
signature.asc
tclbook1.txt
tmp
vpkg-provides.sh
```

This list will differ based on which files are located in your current directory.

How It Works

The `myls_csh` script provides the C shell equivalent to the Bourne shell syntax in the `myls` example script. The `foreach` statement is nearly the same as the Bourne shell `for` statement. In the `myls_csh` script, the shell sets the variable *filename* to the name of a file in the directory on each iteration.

> **This syntax is supported only by the C shell, not the Bourne shell.**

If you try to run this script from the Bourne shell, you will see the following output:

```
$ sh myls_csh
myls_csh: line 3: syntax error near unexpected token `(`
myls_csh: line 3: `foreach filename (*)`
```

Nested Loops

You can nest `for` loops. Nope, this isn't about purchasing a really cool High Definition plasma television and staying at home eating popcorn. In shell script terms, *nesting* means putting inside. So nested `for` loops are loops within loops.

Try It Out   Nested for Loops

For example, enter the following script and save the file under the name `nested_for`:

```
# Nested for loop

for i in 1 2 3 4 5 6 7 8 9 10
do
    echo -n "Row $i: "

    for j in 1 2 3 4 5 6 7 8 9 10
    do
        sleep 1
        echo -n "$j "
    done

    echo    # Output newline
done
```

When you run this script, you will see the following:

```
$ sh nested_for
Row 1: 1 2 3 4 5 6 7 8 9 10
Row 2: 1 2 3 4 5 6 7 8 9 10
Row 3: 1 2 3 4 5 6 7 8 9 10
Row 4: 1 2 3 4 5 6 7 8 9 10
Row 5: 1 2 3 4 5 6 7 8 9 10
Row 6: 1 2 3 4 5 6 7 8 9 10
```

```
Row 7: 1 2 3 4 5 6 7 8 9 10
Row 8: 1 2 3 4 5 6 7 8 9 10
Row 9: 1 2 3 4 5 6 7 8 9 10
Row 10: 1 2 3 4 5 6 7 8 9 10
```

Note that this output will appear one item at a time, as this script runs slowly. Put on some spacey music and enjoy the numbers appearing on your screen.

How It Works

This example breaks no new ground. It just shows that you can place for loops within for loops. Just remember a few important points:

❑   Use different variables in each loop, or the loops will likely conflict with one another.

❑   You need to keep the do-done code blocks correct. Each do needs a done. The outer loop do-done block must enclose the inner block entirely.

❑   Note how indenting the script can really help separate the loops.

You can nest loops as deeply as you need; just follow these rules for each for loop.

Checking Conditions with if

The Bourne shell if statement checks whether a condition is true. If so, the shell executes the block of code associated with the if statement. If the condition is not true, the shell jumps beyond the end of the if statement block and continues on. Only if the condition is true will the shell execute the block.

The basic syntax of the sh if statement follows:

```
if (condition_command) then
    command1
    command2
    ...
    last_command
fi
```

If the condition_command resolves to a true value (see the section What Is Truth? for more on truth and falsehood), then the shell executes the commands in the block: command1, command2, and so on to the last_command in the block. Note how if statements end with a fi (if spelled backward). The fi ends the block of commands.

The condition_command includes numerical and textual comparisons, but it can also be any command that returns a status of zero when it succeeds and some other value when it fails.

The if statement is a part of just about every programming language. If you are not familiar with an if statement, however, think of the following general-purpose tasks:

❑ If a file has been modified since the last backup, then back up the file.

❑ If the Oracle database is not running, then send an email message to an administrator.

❑ If a new version of a software package, such as the Mozilla Firefox Web browser, has been released, then update the software package.

If you were assigned any of these tasks — that is, writing a shell script to perform these functions — you would use an if statement. If you are tasked with assignments like these, however, you may need to reword the assignments. For example, the following tasks mirror those from the preceding list but don't use that handy word *if*:

❑ Only modify those files that have been modified since the last backup.

❑ Whenever the Oracle database is not running, send an email message to an administrator.

❑ Update all applications for which a new package is available.

These task statements don't include if, but if you think about it for a while, the if statement fits right in. All of these statements involve a condition. If the condition is true, then the script is supposed to take some action. This type of task fits well with the if statement.

Another good use for an if statement (or a case statement, covered below) is a script that tries to figure out the proper commands to use on different operating systems. For example, if a script is running on Windows, the file copy command will be copy. If the script is running on Unix, then the copy command will be cp. Handling operating system issues is another good use for an if statement.

Whenever you have a task like these, think of the if statement. The What Is Truth? section later in this chapter includes examples to show how to create if statements in your scripts.

Or Else, What?

In addition to the normal if statement, you can extend the if statement with an else block. The basic idea is that if the condition is true, then execute the if block. If the condition is false, then execute the else block. The basic syntax is:

```
if (condition_command) then
    command1
    command2
    ...
    last_command
else
    command1
    command2
    ...
    last_command
fi
```

Again, the entire statement ends with a `fi`, *if* spelled backward. If the `condition_command` is true, then the shell executes the first block of commands. If the `condition_command` is not true, then the shell executes the second block of commands.

There is also an elif that combines the else with a nested if statement. See the related section later in the chapter for more on elif.

What Is Truth?

By convention, Unix commands return a command result of 0 (zero) on success. On errors, most commands return a negative number, although some return a positive number such as 1 (one). Because the Bourne shell `if` statement is tied to running a program and testing for success, it only makes sense that 0 be considered true and 1, or any nonzero number, false. Commands return these numbers when they exit.

Try the following scripts to get an idea of how the `if` statement works, and especially the focus on running commands.

Try It Out   Determining Truth in Scripts

You can simulate a command returning a value by calling the `exit` command. The `exit` command terminates your script. You can also pass a number as a command-line argument to the `exit` command. This number will be the number the shell sees as coming back from your script. Therefore, this is the number the `if` statement will examine.

So you can make a script that returns a success code, 0, with just the `exit` command:

```
exit 0
```

Type in this very long script and save it under the file name `return0`.

You can also make a script that returns a failure code, 1, or any nonzero number you want to use:

```
exit 1
```

Type in this very long script and save it under the file name `return1`.

You now have two scripts, one to create a true condition and one to create a false condition.

Enter the following script and save it under the file name `truth0`:

```
if (sh return0) then
    echo "Command returned true."
else
    echo "Command returned false."
fi
```

When you run this script, you should see a report of a true value:

```
$ sh truth0
Command returned true.
```

How It Works

The truth0 script uses the if statement with the command sh return0. If this command returns true, then the script outputs the line Command returned true. If the command returns false, then the script outputs the line Command returned false. In this case, that command is sh return0. The sh command runs the Bourne shell with the name of a script, return0, and the return0 script calls the exit command with an exit code of 0, or success. Thus, sh return0 is a command that returns 0, or success.

So wrapping this call up, the if statement resolves to true.

You can test the opposite result. Enter the following script and save it under the name truth1:

```
if (sh return1) then
    echo "Command returned true."
else
    echo "Command returned false."
fi
```

Notice how only one line changed: the if statement at the beginning of the script. Instead of calling sh return0, this test calls sh return1, running the return1 script.

When you run this script, you will see a failure message:

```
$ sh truth1
Command returned false.
```

This is because the return1 script calls exit with a command-line argument of 1, a nonsuccess exit code.

Try out these two scripts until you are comfortable with the way shells handle if statements. Just about every programming language has an if statement. Shells, however, by calling on a program to handle the condition, can appear odd to anyone who has a programming background. That's because the if statement usually compares variables in other programming languages instead of running commands.

Note that you can run the test command to compare variable values. See the section Testing with the test Command for more on this topic.

In addition to the return0 and return1 scripts shown here, Unix and Linux systems include two special programs, true and false, that return a true status and a false status, respectively. These are actual programs on disk (usually in /bin). Some shells include true and false as built-in commands. Bash, for example, does this.

Try It Out   True and False

You can try out the true and false commands with the if statement:

```
if (true) then
    echo "true is true"
else
    echo "true is false"
fi
```

```
if (false) then
   echo "false is true"
else
    echo "false is false"
fi
```

Save this script under the name `truth_tf`. Run the script, and you will see:

```
$ sh truth_tf
true is true
false is false
```

With output like this, you get some reassurance that the universe is indeed operating correctly, at least the Unix and Linux parts.

How It Works

The `truth_tf` script includes two `if` statements. One `if` statement checks the value of the `true` command. The other checks the `false` command. As you'd hope, the `true` command is indeed considered true. And the `false` command is indeed considered false.

Remember that the `if` statement wants to run a command. The `if` statement then examines the results of the command to decide whether the results were true. You can then use `if` with different commands to see the results.

For example, you can call the `make` command, which is used to control the compiling of software applications, especially C and C++ programs. The `make` command will return a success exit code (0) if everything went fine and `make` successfully built whatever it was supposed to build. The `make` command will return a failure exit code on any errors.

Note that you may need to install the make command if the command is not available on your system. See your system documentation for more on installing software packages. The following section assumes you have installed make.

Try It Out   Testing Commands

Try testing the `make` command with the following script:

```
if (make) then
   echo "make returned true."
else
    echo "make returned false."
fi
```

When you first run this command, you will likely see the following output:

```
$ sh truth_make
make: *** No targets specified and no makefile found.  Stop.
make returned false.
```

This is because the current directory has not yet been set up for the make command. To do so, you need to create a file named Makefile. Enter the following and save it to a file named Makefile:

```
all:
    echo "make all"
```

Note that it is very important to place a tab character at the start of the line with the echo command. If you don't, make will fail.

Now, you can run the truth_make script and see the following output:

```
$ sh truth_make
echo "make all"
make all
make returned true.
```

How It Works

The Makefile holds a set of rules that tells the make command how to compile and link your application. The example here merely creates a dummy Makefile that performs no compiling.

Think of this example as an idea generator should you use the make command at your organization.

But because the example Makefile has a rule named all (something the make command looks for), then make reports that it performed all commands as instructed. This, then, is a success status.

Notice how make, by default, outputs the commands it will run—echo "make all" in this case—and then make actually runs the command, resulting in the second line of output, make all. The truth_make script then outputs the fact that make returned true. This is a lot for such a short script!

If your system does not have a make command, you will see output like the following:

```
$ sh truth_make
truth_make: line 1: make: command not found
make returned false.
```

The first line of the output comes from the shell, telling you that the command make was not found. The second line of the output comes from the script, truth_make. The call to the make command resulted in an error. In other words, the command resolved to a false value. Note that this error and the failure code come from the shell, not from make (which does not exist on this system).

As mentioned previously, you can call any command as the condition for an if statement. If the command returns 0, then the result is considered true. Otherwise, the shell considers the result false. Most commands return 0 if the command succeeded, even if the command does not really perform a test or comparison.

For example, you can call the ls command as an if condition, as the following shows:

```
if (ls) then
    echo "ls is true"
else
    echo "ls is false"
fi
```

The ls command will succeed so long as it can list the files specified. (With no command-line argument, ls lists the files in the current directory.) Thus, ls, as used in this example, should succeed.

If you try an example like this, however, you'll soon see a problem. The ls command wasn't designed for testing. Instead, ls was designed for output. Thus, you'll get a listing of the files in the current directory as part of this if condition. In most cases, however, you'd like the if conditions to remain silent, outputting no data. To help with this, you can redirect the output, as explained in the next section.

Redirecting Output

Most Unix and Linux commands output their results. The ls command, for example, outputs the listing of the files as requested by you, the user. Use a greater-than sign, >, to redirect the standard output of a command to a given file. The basic syntax is:

```
command > output_file
```

You can try this with the ls command. For example:

```
$ ls > listing.txt
```

This command sends the output of the ls command into the file listing.txt. If the file doesn't exist, the shell creates the file. If the file already exists, the shell truncates the file. When the command completes, you should be able to view the contents of the file listing.txt, which should hold the same data as if the ls command sent its output to the screen.

To get rid of a command's output, redirect the output to /dev/null. You can try this at the command line:

```
$  ls > /dev/null
$
```

The system should respond with another prompt with no output from ls. The greater-than sign, >, redirects the output of the command (ls in this case). Here, the > redirects the output of the ls command to the file /dev/null, often called the *null device* or the *bit bucket*. That's because /dev/null is a special file that the operating system considers a device. In this case, /dev/null consumes all input sent to it, kind of like a black-hole star.

> *The /dev directory is a special directory that holds what are called device files or device drivers, special code that interfaces with devices such as hard disks, DVD drives, USB keychain flash drives, and so on.*

Chapter 8 covers more on redirecting the standard input, output, and error files. For now, just treat this command as sending the output of the ls command to the null device, which consumes all the bytes sent to it.

> *Note that you can also capture the output of a command into a variable. See the section Capturing the Output of Processes in Chapter 9 for more on this topic.*

To get a taste of redirecting, try the following example, which combines redirection with the ls command inside an if-then conditional statement.

Try It Out   Redirecting Output

Enter the following script and save it as the file `truth_ls`:

```
if (ls > /dev/null) then
    echo "ls is true"
else
    echo "ls is false"
fi
```

When you run this script, you will see:

```
$ sh truth_ls
ls is true
```

How It Works

The `ls` command is true. So are most commands, unless they detect an error. In the `truth_ls` script, however, the `if` condition has more than just the `ls` command. The command runs `ls` but sends all the normal output of `ls` to the file `/dev/null`:

```
ls > /dev/null
```

This command should return `true` because in virtually all cases, you can list the contents of the current directory. Unlike the previous example with the `ls` command, in an `if-then` conditional, you should not see any output of the `ls` command unless an error occurs.

You can force `ls` to generate an error by asking `ls` to list the contents of a directory that does not exist. For example:

```
$ ls /fred > /dev/null
ls: /fred: No such file or directory
```

Unless your system has a directory named `/fred`, `ls` will generate an error.

If you are new to redirection in commands, this command also raises some questions. Didn't you just redirect the output of the `ls` command to `/dev/null`? If so, why do you see `ls` outputting an error message? This is the result of a very old tradition in Unix (and brought into Linux and Mac OS X). Programs in Unix, all the way from ancient versions of Unix to modern versions today, have three standard files associated with each program. In most cases, these are not really files but instead devices, represented in the operating system as special device files unless redirected.

These files are:

❑   `stdin`, or standard input, is the keyboard.

❑   `stdout`, or standard output, is the shell window, or screen.

❑   `stderr`, or standard error, is the shell window, or screen. Only error messages should be written to `stderr`.

All of these standard files can be redirected to real files or to other programs.

107

Note how programs have two channels for output: stdout for the normal output and stderr for errors. The previous example used > to redirect standard output for the ls command, not standard error. You can redirect standard error with 2> (in sh, ksh, and bash). For example:

```
$ ls /fred > /dev/null 2> /dev/null
$
```

This example redirects the normal output from ls, as well as the error messages.

> **You typically don't want to redirect error messages to** /dev/null. **You may be hiding something very important.**

See Chapter 8 for more on the topic of redirecting program output and input, as well as how to redirect standard error for csh and tcsh.

You can use these redirection techniques to create a script that tests for the existence of various shells.

Try It Out   Checking for Shells

The following script tests to see which of the most common shells you have installed. Enter this script and save it under the name find_shells:

```
e
echo "Checking your command path for shells..."

if (sh -c exit > /dev/null 2> /dev/null) then
    echo "sh found."
else
     echo "sh NOT found."
fi

if (bash -c exit  > /dev/null 2> /dev/null) then
    echo "bash found."
else
     echo "bash NOT found."
fi

if (ksh -c exit > /dev/null 2> /dev/null ) then
    echo "ksh found."
else
     echo "ksh NOT found."
fi

if (csh -c exit > /dev/null 2> /dev/null ) then
    echo "csh found."
else
     echo "csh NOT found."
fi
```

```
if (tcsh -c exit > /dev/null 2> /dev/null ) then
    echo "tcsh found."
else
     echo "tcsh NOT found."
fi

if (zsh -c exit > /dev/null 2> /dev/null ) then
    echo "zsh found."
else
     echo "zsh NOT found."
fi

if (ash  -c exit > /dev/null 2> /dev/null ) then
    echo "ash found."
else
     echo "ash NOT found."
```

When you run this script, it should display output similar to the following:

```
$ sh find_shells
Checking your command path for shells...
sh found.
bash found.
ksh NOT found.
csh found.
tcsh found.
zsh NOT found.
ash found.
```

Note that your results will differ based on which shells you have installed.

How It Works

The find_shells script repeats a very similar if statement for each of the shells it checks. Each check tries to run the shell with the -c option. The -c option, supported in all the shells tested here, runs commands from command-line arguments. So a -c exit command line tells each shell to run the exit command. The exit command tells the shell to exit. That is, you start up a shell program, asking it to exit right away.

Put together, this runs commands like the following:

```
sh -c exit
csh -c exit
ksh -c exit
```

Now, if your system does not have one of these shells, you will see an error. For example, if you do not have the Korn shell installed, you will see the following (typing in the command at the shell prompt):

```
$ ksh -c exit
bash: ksh: command not found
```

If your system does have a shell installed, you will see output like the following:

```
$ bash -c exit
$
```

So if the command works, the command quits right away. If the command fails, you get an error. Put the command into an `if` statement and you have a test for success (truth) or failure (falsehood).

> *Note that there are a few issues with this approach to finding shells, including the fact that you may have a shell installed but not in your shell's command path. Don't worry about these other issues. The purpose of these examples is to show if statements, not handle all possible conditions.*

If a shell is not installed on your system, however, you shouldn't have to slog through a number of error messages. You can get rid of all program output, if you'd like.

The command passed to the `if` statements redirects the standard output of each command to `/dev/null`. If the command cannot be found, the shell generates an error, which would normally be sent to standard error. The command passed to the `if` statements, however, also redirects standard error to `/dev/null`.

For example, to test for the existence of the `sh` command, you can use:

```
$ sh -c exit > /dev/null 2> /dev/null
```

Note that this command is fairly worthless on the command line because all output gets redirected. Inside an `if` statement condition, however, this works fine, relying on the error or success return code from the command.

You can also try using the `which` command to test for a program's existence. The `which` command displays the full path to a command, if the command exists. If the command does not exist, the `which` command generates an error. For example:

```
$ which ash
/bin/ash
$ which zsh
/usr/bin/which: no zsh in
(/usr/kerberos/bin:/usr/local/bin:/usr/bin:/bin:/usr/X11R6/bin:
/home2/ericfj/bin:/usr/java/j2sdk1.4.1_03/bin:/opt/jext/bin)
```

The `which` command in Mac OS X and the Cygwin utilities for Windows does not support returning a true or untrue value. The `which` command always returns a true value. Thus, the tests in the `find_shells` script generate falsely positive results.

Look at the repetition in the `find_shells` script. Such repetition cries out for using functions, the topic of Chapter 10. You can also use other techniques to reduce the duplication.

Try It Out   Finding Shells with a Shorter Script

If you combine the `if` tests in the `find_shells` script with the `for` loop, you can write a version of the `find_shells` script that is much shorter. Enter the following script and name it `find_shells2`:

```
echo "Checking your command path for shells..."

for check_for in sh bash ksh csh tcsh zsh ash
do
    cmd="$check_for -c exit"

    if ($cmd > /dev/null 2> /dev/null) then
        echo "$check_for found."
    else
        echo "$check_for NOT found."
    fi
done
```

When you run this script, you should see output like that of the find_shells script. The main change has been to shorten the script; the basic functionality remains the same.

How It Works

Note that the find_shells2 script is much shorter and easier to understand than the find_shells script. The for loop in the script iterates over the list of shells. This eliminates the duplicated code in the find_shells script.

The do-done block in the find_shells2 script builds up a command to check for the shell. As before, the command is basically an attempt to run each shell, where the shell is one of sh, csh, and so on. The cmd variable holds the full command to execute. If this command returns true, then the shell was found. Otherwise, the shell was not found.

Using elif (Short for else If)

The Bourne shell syntax for the if statement allows an else block that gets executed if the test is not true. You can nest if statements, allowing for multiple conditions. As an alternative, you can use the elif construct, short for *else if*. The basic syntax is:

```
if (condition_command) then
    command1
    command2
    ...
    last_command
elif (condition_command2) then
    command1
    command2
    ...
    last_command
else
    command1
    command2
    ...
    last_command
fi
```

With the normal `if` statement, and in this case, if the `condition_command` returns zero (true), then the shell executes the commands underneath. In this case, if the `condition_command` returns a nonzero status, or `false`, then the shell will jump to the next condition to check, the `condition_command2`. If the `condition_command2` returns zero, then the commands shell executes the commands underneath the `elif` statement. Otherwise, the shell executes the commands underneath the `else` statement.

Theoretically, the `elif` keyword is not needed, as you can nest `if` statements. But in most cases, `if` makes your scripts easier to understand.

Try It Out   Using elif

Enter the following script and name the file `check_csh`:

```
echo -n "Checking for a C shell: "

if (which csh > /dev/null 2> /dev/null ) then
    echo "csh found."
elif (which tcsh > /dev/null 2> /dev/null ) then
    echo "tcsh found, which works like csh."
else
    echo "csh NOT found."
fi
```

When you run this script, you should see output that differs depending on which shells you have installed. For example:

```
$ sh check_csh
Checking for a C shell: csh found.
```

If your system does not have csh but does have tcsh, you will see:

```
$ sh check_csh
Checking for a C shell: tcsh found, which works like csh.
```

And if your system has neither csh nor tcsh, you will see:

```
$ sh check_csh
Checking for a C shell: csh NOT found.
```

How It Works

The `check_csh` script tries to determine whether you have a C shell installed. Borrowing the tests from the `find_shells` script, the `check_csh` script first checks for csh. If found, the script is done. If not found, the script tests for tcsh, in case you have tcsh installed but not csh. In this script, tcsh is considered good enough to act as csh because tcsh is an extended version of the C shell. Finally, if all else fails, the script outputs a message that csh was not found.

The script logic follows:

```
echo -n "Checking for a C shell: "

if (csh_is_present) then
    echo "csh found."
elif (tcsh_is_present) then
    echo "tcsh found, which works like csh."
else
    echo "csh NOT found."
fi
```

Note that this is not valid shell syntax, as *csh_is_present* and *tcsh_is_present* are placeholders for the real testing code shown in the check_csh script.

You can include more than one elif construct within an if statement, as many as you need.

Nesting if Statements

As with for loops, you can nest if statements, although using the elif construct eliminates many of the nested if statements that would be required without it.

If you nest too many if statements, your scripts will become very hard to read. After two or three nested if statements, you should stop.

The following example shows how you can nest if statements.

Try It Out   **Nesting if Statements**

Enter the following script and save it under the name truth_nested:

```
if (true) then

    # Only if the first condition is true will
    # we get here.

    if (false) then
        echo "The universe is wrong."
    else
        echo "All is well in the universe."
    fi
fi
```

When you run this script, you should see the reassuring message that everything is okay:

```
$ sh truth_nested
All is well in the universe.
```

Rest assured, all is well.

How It Works

This example contains two if statements. If the first if statement resolves to true, then the shell will execute the block inside the if statement. This block contains another if statement. If that statement is true (as well as the first statement, or the shell would not be executing this code), then the script executes the then part. If the second if statement is not true, then the shell executes the else part.

In this example, the first test runs the true command (or shell built-in command). This command returns true (always). So the shell executes the block of commands inside the if statement. The second test runs the false command (or shell built-in command). This command should return false. If not, the shell outputs a message questioning the foundation of existence.

Testing with the test Command

Because the Bourne shell if statement was designed to work with commands, and because many scripts need to compare values, the Bourne shell includes the test command. The test command forms a sort of all-encompassing means to test files, values, and most everything else. Depending on the command-line options you pass, test can compare values, check for file permissions, and even look for whether files exist. The test command is normally implemented by the shell as a built-in command. But test also exists as a program on disk, typically in /usr/bin.

To control what kind of test is performed, you must figure out the needed command-line options for the test command to build up an expression to test. The test command uses the command-line options to determine what comparisons to make. Then the test command exits and returns a 0 if the expression tested was true and a nonzero value (1) if the expression was false. If test encounters an error, it returns a number greater than 1.

To build up a test, you use the command-line options to specify how to compare values. For example:

```
test $x -eq $y
```

This example tests whether the value of x is equal to that of y, using the -eq command-line option. This is assumed to be a numeric equality test. The shell will try to make numbers out of strings if needed.

Comparing Numbers

The following table shows the numeric test options. The variables x and y should have a numeric value, obviously.

Test	Usage
$x -eq $y	Returns true if x equals y
$x -ne $y	Returns true if x does not equal y
$x -gt $y	Returns true if x is greater than y
$x -ge $y	Returns true if x is greater than or equal to y

Test	Usage
$x -lt $y	Returns true if x is less than y
$x -le $y	Returns true if x is less than or equal to y

Passing no test to test results in a false value.

Try It Out   **Testing Numbers**

This Try It Out shows the syntax for various numeric comparisons. Enter the following script and save it under the file name `test_num`:

```
# Number test.


echo "**** Numeric comparisons."
x=5
y=10

echo -n "test -eq: "
if (test $x -eq $y)  then
    echo "X = Y."
else
    echo "X != Y. Expected."
fi

echo -n "test -eq: "
if (test $x -eq $x)  then
    echo "X  = X. Expected."
else
    echo "X != X. "
fi

echo -n "test -eq: "
if (test $x -eq 5)  then
    echo "X  = 5. Expected."
else
    echo "X != 5. "
fi

echo -n "test -eq: "
if (test $x -eq "5")  then
   echo "X = \"5\". Expected."
else
    echo "X != \"5\". "
fi


echo -n "test -ne: "
if (test $x -ne 5)  then
    echo "X != 5. "
```

```
else
    echo "X  = 5. Expected."
fi


echo -n "test -ne: "
if (test $x -ne $y)  then
    echo "X != Y. Expected."
else
    echo "X = Y."
fi

# Note extra ! for "not".
echo -n "test -ne: "
if (test ! $x -eq $y)  then
    echo "X != Y. Expected."
else
    echo "X = Y."
fi


echo -n "test -lt: "
if (test $x -lt 5)  then
    echo "X < 5. "
else
    echo "X  = 5. Expected."
fi

echo -n "test -le: "
if (test $x -le 5)  then
    echo "X <= 5. Expected."
else
    echo "X  = 5."
fi
```

When you run this script, you should see the following output:

```
$ sh test_num
**** Numeric comparisons.
test -eq: X != Y. Expected.
test -eq: X  = X. Expected.
test -eq: X  = 5. Expected.
test -eq: X = "5". Expected.
test -ne: X  = 5. Expected.
test -ne: X != Y. Expected.
test -ne: X != Y. Expected.
test -lt: X  = 5. Expected.
test -le: X <= 5. Expected.
```

In each case, you get the expected results.

How It Works

The `test_num` script has a lot of `if` statements showing different types of numeric comparisons. The tests compare x, set to 5, and y, set to 10.

The script outputs a message with the `echo` command prior to each `if` statement. This should help identify the test by printing out the test on the same line as the result. The script also shows the expected result, true or false, of the test. For example:

```
echo -n "test -le: "
if (test $x -le 5)  then
    echo "X <= 5. Expected."
else
    echo "X  = 5."
fi
```

In this case, the variable x is indeed less than or equal to 5 because x was assigned to the value 5. The `echo` statement that outputs the expected result includes the word `Expected` to make it very obvious when you run this script which result you should see. Furthermore, the `echo` statements include a shorthand to indicate the comparison, such as X = 5 for X is equal to 5, X != Y for X does not equal Y, and X <= 5 for X is less than or equal to 5. This shorthand text does not use the shell syntax for brevity in the output.

The tests in the test_num script show how to use the test command in general, as well as numeric comparisons. Look over all the if statements in the test_num script until you are confident of the results. This is very important. The test command is used everywhere. You need to master this material.

In addition to comparing numbers, you can compare text strings.

Comparing Text Strings

The `test` command can also compare text strings. The `test` command compares text strings by comparing each character in each string. The characters must match for the comparison to be true.

For some reason, text has been called strings or text strings in just about every programming language. The usage comes from the idea of a text string as a string of characters (often of bytes), one after another. The analogy doesn't really hold up, but the terminology has.

You can compare based on the text string values or check whether a string is empty or not. The following table shows the text string test options.

Test	Usage
"$s1" = "$s2"	Returns true if s1 equals s2
"$s1" != "$s2"	Returns true if s1 does not equal s2
$s1	Returns true if s1 is not null

Table continued on following page

Test	Usage
$s1 -z	Returns true if the length of s1 (the number of characters in s1) is zero
$s1 -n	Returns true if the length of s1 (the number of characters in s1) is not zero

The following Try It Out shows the tests from this table in use in a shell script.

Try It Out   Comparing Strings

Enter the following script and save it under the name `test_strings`:

```
# String test.


echo "**** String comparisons."
string="In Xanadu did Kublai Khan..."

echo -n "test of a string: "
if (test "$string") then
    echo "We have a non-null \$string. Expected."
else
    echo "\$string is null."
fi

echo -n "test of a string: "
if (test $notset) then
    echo "How did \$notset get a value?"
else
    echo "\$notset has not been set. Expected."
fi

echo -n "test -z: "
if (test -z $notset) then
    echo "Length of \$notset is zero. Expected."
else
    echo "Length of \$notset is NOT zero."
fi

# Note quotes around multi-word string.
echo -n "test -z: "
if (test -z "$string") then
    echo "Length of \$string is zero."
else
    echo "Length of \$string is NOT zero. Expected."
fi

echo -n "test -n: "
if (test -n "$string") then
    echo "Length of \$string is NOT zero. Expected."
else
```

```
        echo "Length of \$string is zero."
fi


echo -n "test =: "
if (test "$string" = "$string") then
    echo "Strings are equal. Expected."
else
    echo "Strings are not equal."
fi

# Tricky one. Notice the difference.
echo -n "test =: "
if (test "$string" = "$string ") then
    echo "Strings are equal. "
else
    echo "Strings are not equal. Expected"
fi


echo -n "test =: "
if (test "$string" = "In Xanadu did Kublai Khan...") then
    echo "Strings are equal. Expected."
else
    echo "Strings are not equal."
fi


echo -n "test !=: "
if (test "$string" != "In Xanadu did Kublai Khan...") then
    echo "Strings are equal."
else
    echo "Strings are not equal. Expected."
fi

echo -n "test !=: "
if (test "$string" != "$notset" ) then
    echo "Strings are not equal. Expected."
else
    echo "Strings are equal."
fi

echo
```

When you run this script, you should see the following output:

```
$ sh test_strings
**** String comparisons.
test of a string: We have a non-null $string. Expected.
test of a string: $notset has not been set. Expected.
test -z: Length of $notset is zero. Expected.
test -z: Length of $string is NOT zero. Expected.
test -n: Length of $string is NOT zero. Expected.
test =: Strings are equal. Expected.
```

```
test =: Strings are not equal. Expected
test =: Strings are equal. Expected.
test !=: Strings are not equal. Expected.
test !=: Strings are not equal. Expected.
```

As before, all tests work as expected.

How It Works

As with the previous example, the `test_strings` script contains a number of `if` statements, each trying out a different form of `test`. This test uses two variables: *string*, which is initialized to the start of a poem, and *notset*, which is not set and hence has a null value.

As with the previous example, look over the tests to ensure you understand the material. Some of the tests are tricky. For example, the following differs only by a space:

```
if (test "$string" = "$string ") then
    echo "Strings are equal. "
else
    echo "Strings are not equal. Expected"
fi
```

Each space can be very important when comparing text strings. Note also how empty strings have zero lengths:

```
if (test -z $notset) then
    echo "Length of \$notset is zero. Expected."
else
    echo "Length of \$notset is NOT zero."
fi
```

This may seem obvious, but many computer languages would generate an error instead, reserving a zero length for strings that exist but have no value. With shell scripts, you can compare variables that have never been set and so don't exist.

Testing Files

In addition to the numeric and string tests, you can use the `test` command to test files. In fact, testing files is the primary use of the `test` command in most scripts.

The following table lists the file options for the `test` commands.

Test	Usage
-d *filename*	Returns true if the file name exists and is a directory
-e *filename*	Returns true if the file name exists
-f *filename*	Returns true if the file name exists and is a regular file

Test	Usage
-r *filename*	Returns true if the file name exists and you have read permissions
-s *filename*	Returns true if the file name exists and is not empty (has a size greater than zero)
-w *filename*	Returns true if the file name exists and you have write permissions
-x filename	Returns true if the file name exists and you have execute permissions

These tests are described in Chapter 5.

Using the Binary and Not Operators

Each of the test options introduced so far works alone. You can combine tests using the binary and negation tests. The following table shows these add-in tests.

Test	Usage
!	Negates the test.
-a	Returns true if two tests are both true and false otherwise. This is an AND operation.

With the negation test, !, you can negate any of the other tests. So, for example, if you use the -eq option to compare two numeric values for equality, you can use the ! to negate the test, in other words to check for inequality:

```
if (test ! $x -eq $y )  then
    echo "x != y. Expected."
else
    echo "false: x = y."
fi
```

In this example, the $x -eq $y tests if the value of *x* equals the value of *y*. The test will return true if the values are equal and false if they are not equal. Placing an exclamation mark into the test converts the test to return true if the values are not equal and false if they are equal. (Try this test in the test_binary script following in this section.)

The options -a and -o form the binary test options. But even though these are listed as binary comparisons — that is, checks at the bit level — in most cases you can treat -a as a logical AND. Treat -o as a logical OR. For example:

```
x=3
y=10

if (test $x -eq $x -a  $y -eq $y)  then
    echo "x = x and y = y. Expected."
else
    echo "false: x = x and y = y."
fi
```

In this case, *x* equals *x* and *y* equals *y*. In addition:

```
if (test $x -eq $x -a  $y -ne $y)  then
    echo "x = x and y = y."
else
    echo "false: x = x and y != y. Expected."
fi
```

This example tests whether *x* equals *x* and *y* does not equal *y*. This is obviously false.

The -a option takes precedence over the -o option if both appear in the same call to the test command.

You can try out the AND, OR, and negation tests with the following example. These tests tend to get complex because each of these new tests requires an additional test (!) or tests (-a and -o) to run.

Try It Out   Combining Tests

Enter the following script and save it under the name test_binary:

```
# Binary test.

echo "**** Binary comparisons."
x=3
y=10

echo -n "test !: "
if (test ! $x -eq $y) then
    echo "x != y. Expected."
else
    echo "false: x = y."
fi

echo -n "test -a: "
if (test $x -eq $x -a  $y -eq $y)  then
    echo "x = x and y = y. Expected."
else
    echo "false: x = x and y = y."
fi


echo -n "test -a: "
if (test $x -eq $x -a  $y -ne $y)  then
    echo "x = x and y = y."
```

```
    else
        echo "false: x = x and y != y. Expected."
    fi

    echo -n "test -o: "
    if (test $x -eq $x -o  $y -ne $y)   then
        echo "x = x or y != y. Expected"
    else
        echo "false: x = x or y != y is not true."
    fi
```

When you run this script, you should see the following output:

```
$ sh test_binary
**** Binary comparisons.
test !: x != y. Expected.
test -a: x = x and y = y. Expected.
test -a: false: x = x and y != y. Expected.
test -o: x = x or y != y. Expected
```

How It Works

The binary tests often prove confusing, especially since these tests do not compare at the bit level.

The first test uses the negation operator, !, to negate an equals test:

```
if (test ! $x -eq $y) then
    echo "x != y. Expected."
else
    echo "false: x = y."
fi
```

In this case, x holds a value of 3 and y holds a value of 10. These two values are clearly not equal. Thus, the -eq test will return false. The ! test, however, reverses this test, and so the final test will return true.

The second test insists that two equals tests must both be true, as does the third test. The fourth test uses the OR operator, -o, to allow one or the other (or both) of two tests to be true.

———————————

Creating Shorthand Tests with [

In addition to the test command, you can write your tests using [, a shorthand for test. It may seem weird, but [is actually a command. You can check this with the which command:

```
$ which [
/usr/bin/[
```

Note that] is not a command. The] is interpreted as a command-line argument to the [command.

Even though it is a command, [, like test, is often built into the shell. Shells such as bash, for example, come with a built-in test and [commands. You can see this by using the type command in bash:

```
$ type [
[ is a shell builtin
$ type test
test is a shell builtin
```

Note that `type` is also a built-in shell command:

```
$ type type
type is a shell builtin
```

If you use `type` with the name of a command, you will see output like the following:

```
$ type rm
rm is /bin/rm
```

This indicates that `rm`, for *removing*, or deleting, files, is a command. Shells such as bash, csh, and tcsh support *aliases*, where you can enter in an alias name and use the alias in place of a command. The `type` command on bash can also tell you about whether a command is aliased or not. For example:

```
$ type ls
ls is aliased to `ls --color=tty'
```

The `alias` command lists all the aliases. When you run this command with bash, you will see output like the following:

```
$ alias
alias l.='ls -d .* --color=tty'
alias ll='ls -l --color=tty'
alias ls='ls --color=tty'
alias vi='vim'
```

The output on your system may differ, depending on what aliases are set up in your shell.

With tcsh or csh, the output will appear slightly different. For example:

```
$ alias
h        history
l.       ls -d .* --color=tty
ll       ls -l --color=tty
ls       (ls -CF)
qtopia   /opt/Qtopia/bin/qtopiadesktop
rm       (rm -i)
vi       vim
xcd      cd !*; echo  n "^[]2;$cwd^G"
```

As before, the output on your system may differ, depending on what aliases are set up in your shell.

Tying this together, you can write your tests using `test` or `[`, as you prefer. The syntax is:

```
if [ test_options ]
then
    commands
else
    commands
fi
```

Use square brackets, [and], around the `test` options. Note that this example places the `then` construct on the next line. This is needed because this example skips the parenthesis. You can keep the `then` on the same line if you include parentheses, but this syntax looks odd:

```
if ( [ test_options ] ) then
    commands
else
    commands
fi
```

The `test_options` should be the command-line options and arguments normally passed to the test command. For example:

```
x=5
y=10

if [ $x -eq $y ]
then
    echo "X = Y."
else
    echo "X != Y. Expected."
fi
```

The `[` syntax is supposed to make the tests easier to understand, but using `[` can be confusing because of the way `[` was implemented as a command. Even so, this syntax is used in most scripts in place of the `test` command.

Making Complex Decisions with case

Nested `if` statements work well, but as soon as you are confronted with a number of possible actions to take, nested `if` statements start to confuse. You can simplify complex tests with the `case` statement. Whenever you have a question or test with a number of choices and a script that requires specific actions for each choice, you can use the `case` statement. The `case` statement is similar to a set of `if-elif` constructs.

The syntax of the `case` statement follows:

```
case word in
value1)
    command1
    command2
```

```
     ...
     last_command
;;
value2)
     command1
     command2
     ...
     last_command
;;
esac
```

With this syntax, you compare a word, usually the value of a variable, against a number of values. If there is a match, the shell executes the commands from the given value up to the two semicolons (;;) that end an individual case.

The entire statement ends with esac, *case* spelled backward.

Try It Out   Choosing Favorites

The following script shows an example of the case statement. Enter this script and save it under the name choice1:

```
echo "Which would you rather have,"
echo "ksh, a platypus, or"
echo -n "MS Word for Windows for Windows for Macintosh? "
read choice

case $choice in
ksh)
  echo "There are a lot of neat things you"
    echo "can do with the Korn shell."
;;
platypus)
   echo "The Platypus Society thanks you."
;;
"MS Word for Windows for Windows for Macintosh")
    echo "This is not a real product, you know."
;;
esac
```

When you run this script, you will be prompted to provide an answer:

```
$ sh choose1
Which would you rather have,
ksh, a platypus, or
MS Word for Windows for Windows for Macintosh? ksh
There are a lot of neat things you
can do with the Korn shell.
```

Each time you run the choose1 script, you can enter a different answer. For example:

```
$ sh choose1
Which would you rather have,
ksh, a platypus, or
MS Word for Windows for Windows for Macintosh? platypus
The Platypus Society thanks you.
```

Entering in the last value is left as an exercise.

How It Works

This script offers the choice among three very similar items: a shell, an animal, and an imaginary software product. (You can decide which is which.)

Depending on how you answer, the script outputs a different message. In real-world scripts, you are likely to set a number of variables to different values depending on the match in the case statement. For example, you may have a script that determines the operating system using the uname command and then uses a case statement to specify the paths to the CD-ROM drive based on the operating system. This type of script is very common.

For another example usage, a networking script may need to take different options if the networking is a wired Ethernet link, a wireless 802.1x link, or an IP over USB connection. These choices would result in different commands needed to start up networking, or at least different command-line options. The case statement is a good choice for these types of problems.

Handling Problematic Input

There is a big problem with the choose1 script, however. You can see this problem if you enter something unexpected. For example:

```
$ sh choose1
Which would you rather have,
ksh, a platypus, or
MS Word for Windows for Windows for Macintosh? fred
$
```

If you enter an unexpected value, such as fred, the script does nothing. It cannot handle unexpected input. Of course, this means the choose1 script is not very robust and will likely fail if you release this software to the wide world.

To deal with this situation, the case statement also includes a catch-all value of *, which you can use to capture values that would normally fall through a case statement, matching nothing. The syntax follows:

```
case word in
value1)
    command1
    command2
    ...
```

```
        last_command
;;
value2)
        command1
        command2
        ...
        last_command
;;
*)
        command1
        command2
        ...
        last_command
;;
esac
```

Try It Out   Handling Unexpected Input

The following script handles unexpected input as part of a quiz on operating system favorites:

```
echo "Please enter your favorite operating system, "
echo -n "linux, macosx, windows, amigados, or beos: "
read os

case $os in

linux)
    echo "Way cool, you like Linux."
;;
macosx)
    echo "You like Roman numerals."
;;
windows)
    echo "Time to check for a virus."
;;
amigados)
    echo "AmigaDOS will never die."
;;
beos)
    echo "Count yourself lucky."
;;
*)
    echo "Why did you choose $os?"
;;
esac
```

When you run this script, you will be asked to enter your favorite operating system. For example:

```
$ sh case_os
Please enter your favorite operating system,
linux, macosx, windows, amigados, or beos: beos
Count yourself lucky.
```

Each value displays a different message. For example:

```
$ sh case_os
Please enter your favorite operating system,
linux, macosx, windows, amigados, or beos: macosx
You like Roman numerals.
```

If you enter an unexpected value, you will see output like the following:

```
$ sh case_os
Please enter your favorite operating system,
linux, macosx, windows, amigados, or beos: Macintosh System 7
Why did you choose Macintosh System 7?
```

How It Works

This script uses the techniques of the last example script but adds a *) construct to handle input that does not match any of the other values. Thus, if you enter *Macintosh System 7*, as shown shown previously, then the shell executes the *) construct to handle unexpected input. (This is doubly unexpected, as Mac OS X is so much better.)

Note that this example is case-sensitive, so BeOS, for example, would not match beos.

This quiz, while being completely objective, does allow the user to enter in unexpected values, sort of like a write-in candidate in an election. As a general rule, all case statements should include the *) construct to handle unexpected values.

Using case with the C Shell

The C shell doesn't support the case statement like the Bourne shell. The C shell, however, does provide a switch statement, very similar to the Bourne shell case statement.

The C shell syntax is:

```
switch ( word )
    case value1:
        commands
        breaksw
    case value1:
        commands
        breaksw
    default
        commands
endsw
```

Instead of case, you see a switch statement. (This is one area where the C shell is quite similar to the C programming language.) Each value is specified by a case construct. Each case block ends with a breaksw statement, short for *break switch*. (This mimics the C language break statement.)

A `default` block specifies the action to take if none of the cases matches.

The entire `switch` statement ends with an `endsw` statement, short for *end switch*.

Try It Out   **Casing the C Shell**

The following script provides the operating system quiz from `case_os` in C shell syntax, using the `switch` construct:

```
echo "Please enter your favorite operating system, "
echo -n "linux, macosx, windows, amigados, or beos: "
set os = $<

switch ( $os )
    case linux:
        echo "Way cool, you like Linux."
        breaksw
    case macosx:
        echo "You like Roman numerals."
        breaksw
    case windows:
        echo "Time to check for a virus."
        breaksw
    case amigados:
        echo "AmigaDOS will never die."
        breaksw
    case beos:
        echo "Count yourself lucky."
        breaksw
    default
        echo "Why did you choose $os?"
endsw
```

Enter this script and save it under the name `switch_os`. You can compare this script to the previous example, `case_os`.

When you run this script, you will see the familiar quiz. The output should be the same as the previous example, `case_os`, even if you enter an unexpected value:

```
$ csh switch_os
Please enter your favorite operating system,
linux, macosx, windows, amigados, or beos: wince
Why did you choose wince?
```

How It Works

This script is a conversion, called a *port*, of the `case_os` script to the C shell syntax. The `switch` statement follows the syntax shown previously.

In addition, this script shows how a C shell script reads input from the user. For example:

```
set os = $<
```

This statement serves the same purpose as the Bourne shell syntax using `read`:

```
read os
```

Looping While a Condition Is True

Like the `for` loop, the `while` loop repeats its block of commands a number of times. Unlike the `for` loop, however, the `while` loop iterates until its `while` condition is no longer true. The basic syntax is:

```
while [ test_condition ]
do
    commands...
done
```

The `while` loop is sort of like a combination of an `if` statement and a `for` loop. Use the `while` loop when you don't know in advance how many iterations you need.

Note that the C shell sports a different syntax for a `while` loop:

```
while ( test_condition )
    commands...
end
```

Try It Out   **Looping While a Condition Is True**

With the Bourne shell `while` loop, you can create complex loops, as the following mini command interpreter shows. Enter the following script and save it under the name `while`:

```
command="init"    # Initialization.

while [ "$command" != "exit" ]
do

    echo -n "Enter command or \"exit\" to quit: "
    read command
    echo

    case $command in
    ls)
        echo "Command is ls."
    ;;
    who)
        echo "Command is who."
    ;;
    *)
        if [ $command != "exit" ]
        then
            echo "Why did you enter $command?"
        fi
    ;;
```

```
        esac

    done
```

When you run this script, you will be prompted to enter commands:

```
$ sh while
Enter command or "exit" to quit: ls

Command is ls.
Enter command or "exit" to quit: who

Command is who.
Enter command or "exit" to quit: type

Why did you enter type?
Enter command or "exit" to quit: exit
```

Enter exit to quit the script.

How It Works

This example script manages to combine a while loop, a case statement, an if statement, and the read command. The while loop forms the outer part of a primitive command interpreter.

Each iteration prompts the user to enter a command. The case statement then outputs a different message based on the command. The catch-all case, *, further checks whether the user entered exit and outputs a message only if the user did not enter exit.

The loop then goes to the top and tests the while loop condition. If the user entered exit, the while loop test fails, and the shell jumps over the do-done block to the next statement after the while loop, of which there is none, so the script exits.

Note that this script does not interpret the user input; it merely checks this input for the text exit.

Looping Until a Condition Is True

The until loop is very similar to the while loop. With while, the test must be true to execute the block of commands in the loop. With until, the test must be false. Otherwise, the two loops are the same.

Think of until as "loop until a condition is true" and while as "loop while this condition remains true." In other words, until just reverses the test. The following example shows this test reversal by modifying the previous example to use the until statement.

Try It Out   Looping Until a Condition Is Met

Enter the following script and save it under the name until:

```
command="init"    # Initialization.

until [ "$command" = "exit" ]
do

    echo -n "Enter command or \"exit\" to quit: "
    read command
    echo

    case $command in
    ls)
        echo "Command is ls."
    ;;
    who)
        echo "Command is who."
    ;;
    *)
        if [ $command != "exit" ]
        then
            echo "Why did you enter $command?"
        fi
    ;;
    esac

done
```

When you run this script, you should see the following output:

```
$ sh until
Enter command or "exit" to quit: ls

Command is ls.
Enter command or "exit" to quit: whos

Why did you enter whos?
Enter command or "exit" to quit: who

Command is who.
Enter command or "exit" to quit: exit
```

How It Works

The until script is almost the same as the while script; just the test at the top of the loop changed. Note how the test must be reversed. For example:

```
[ "$command" = "exit" ]
```

This test results in a true value if the value of the variable command equals exit. The while loop, on the other hand, used a different test:

```
[ "$command" != "exit" ]
```

This test results in a true value if the value of the variable command does not equal exit.

Summary

Yow. That is a lot of syntax for one chapter. This chapter includes the basics on how to control which commands in your script get executed. These basics include:

❑ You can use the syntax `${variable}` to access the value of a variable. This syntax is the same as `$variable`, but the curly braces clearly delineate the start and end of the variable name. This means the variable name cannot get merged into adjacent text.

❑ The `for` loop allows your script to iterate a given number of times. A special variant of the `for` loop iterates over files using wildcard syntax, such as `*` and `*.txt`.

❑ The `if` statement executes a command and tests whether the results of the command are true or false.

❑ A special command named `test` provides a zillion command-line options to test different conditions.

❑ You can use `[ ]` in place of the `test` command, placing the `test` command-line options and arguments between square brackets.

❑ The `while` loop iterates while a condition is true. When the condition resolves to false, the `while` loop stops.

❑ The `until` loop reverses the `while` loop test. The `until` loop iterates while the condition is not true.

The next chapter expands the use of shell scripts to the overarching computer environment, discussing operating system issues, how shells start up, and how to turn your shell scripts into executable commands.

Exercises

1. Run the `choose1` example script and enter the imaginary Microsoft product name. Be sure to have your license key ready.

2. Extend the `myls` or `myls2` shell scripts to list the files in a different directory from the current directory, such as /usr/local. The script should still output the name of all the files in the directory.

3. Enhance the script you wrote for Exercise 2 to place the name of the directory in a variable and access the variable in the `for` loop.

4. Enhance the script you wrote for Exercise 3 to ask the user for the name of the directory to list.

5. Enhance the script you wrote for Exercise 4. This new script should ask the user the directory to list and then should output / after directory names and * after executable files. Do not output * if the file is a directory (and has execute permissions on the directory).

Interacting with the Environment

No shell script is an island. Your scripts run within the environment provided by your computer and operating system. For shell scripts, most systems provide a Unix-like environment, which helps a lot because your scripts can query the environment in a consistent manner across systems. This includes Mac OS X, based on Berkeley Unix, and Linux, a Unix work-alike. Even Windows and QNX provide Unix-like environments for shell scripts.

A Unix-like environment provides special settings called *environment variables*, which hold important values for determining where commands are located, as well as the user's home directory.

This chapter covers:

❑   Examining the settings in your system's environment, getting and setting environment variables

❑   Customizing your account, especially how shells start up

❑   Handling command-line arguments and using these arguments to change the way your scripts behave

❑   Making scripts executable so your scripts appear to the end user as operating system commands, no different from commands such as ls and cp

Examining Environment Variables

Environment variables are a type of shell variables.

For the most part, environment variables are the same as other shell variables. There are four main differences, however:

❑   Environment variables are set by the environment, the operating system, during the startup of your shell. (This process is not magic, as you will see in this chapter.)

❑ Shell variables are local to a particular instance of the shell—for example, the shell instance running a script. Environment variables are inherited by any program you start, including another shell.

❑ Environment variables have a special meaning that applies to all scripts.

❑ You must make a special operation to set an environment variable.

The following sections cover these points in depth.

Reading Environment Variables

Environment variables are treated, in most respects, as normal shell variables. That means that if you have an environment variable named *HOME*, you can access the value of this variable by using the dollar sign ($) constructor—for example, $*HOME*. This part is no different than for other variables that you create within your shell scripts.

The most crucial thing about these variables, however, is that they hold settings that presumably reflect the user's environment and wishes. (Sometimes these variables reflect the administrator's wishes instead.)

For example, the *LANG* environment variable, if set, specifies the user's locale, a combination of a code for the user's language, as well as any variants. A user could have a locale of English with a code of en. A user in the United Kingdom would have a variant of English in the UK, en_UK, whereas a user in the United States would have a variant of English in the US, en_US. A spell-checking program can then use the *LANG* environment variable to determine which spelling dictionary to load and thus determine whether *specialization* or *specialisation* is correct, for example.

Thus, your scripts should honor environment variable settings where possible. This is complicated, however, by the fact that not all systems set all variables. Thus, your scripts always have to check whether a variable is set first and then display a default value if necessary.

The following table lists the most commonly available environment variables.

Variable	Usage
COLUMNS	Number of text characters that can fit across one line in the shell window
DISPLAY	Names the graphics display for systems using the X Window System
HISTSIZE	Number of commands to store in the command history (bash and ksh)
HOME	User's home directory
HOSTNAME	Computer's host name
LANG	Specifies user's locale, such as French in France, French in Canada, French in Switzerland

Variable	Usage
LINES	Number of text lines that can fit in the shell window
PATH	List of directories searched for commands
PWD	Current directory
SHELL	Default shell
TERM	Ancient terminal type, if applicable
USER	User name

To see what is defined within your shell, use the set command.

Use setenv instead with csh and tcsh. See below for more on this.

Built into the shell, the set command lists all the variables currently set. If you have access systems running different operating systems, compare the different environments. The following examples show common settings on different operating systems.

Note that set shows more than just the true environment variables. This is explained in more detail later in this chapter.

Try It Out   Listing the Environment on Linux

On a Fedora Core 2 Linux system, you will see an environment like the following:

```
$ set
BASH=/bin/bash
BASH_VERSINFO=([0]="2" [1]="05b" [2]="0" [3]="1" [4]="release"
[5]="i386-redhat-linux-gnu")
BASH_VERSION='2.05b.0(1)-release'
COLORS=/etc/DIR_COLORS.xterm
COLORTERM=gnome-terminal
COLUMNS=73
DESKTOP_SESSION=default
DIRSTACK=()
DISPLAY=:0.0
EUID=500
GDMSESSION=default
GNOME_DESKTOP_SESSION_ID=Default
GNOME_KEYRING_SOCKET=/tmp/keyring-tNORrP/socket
GROUPS=()
GTK_RC_FILES=/etc/gtk/gtkrc:/home2/ericfj/.gtkrc-1.2-gnome2
G_BROKEN_FILENAMES=1
HISTFILE=/home2/ericfj/.bash_history
HISTFILESIZE=1000
HISTSIZE=1000
HOME=/home2/ericfj
HOSTNAME=kirkwall
HOSTTYPE=i386
```

```
IFS=$' \t\n'
INPUTRC=/etc/inputrc
KDEDIR=/usr
LANG=en_US.UTF-8
LESSOPEN='|/usr/bin/lesspipe.sh %s'
LINES=24
LOGNAME=ericfj
LS_COLORS='no=00:fi=00:di=00;34:ln=00;36:pi=40;33:so=00;35:bd=40;33;01:cd=40;33;01:
or=01;05;37;41:mi=01;05;37;41:ex=00;32:*.cmd=00;32:*.exe=00;32:*.com=00;32:
*.btm=00;32:*.bat=00;32:*.sh=00;32:*.csh=00;32:*.tar=00;31:*.tgz=00;31:*.arj=00;31:
*.taz=00;31:*.lzh=00;31:*.zip=00;31:*.z=00;31:*.Z=00;31:*.gz=00;31:*.bz2=00;31:
*.bz=00;31:*.tz=00;31:*.rpm=00;31:*.cpio=00;31:*.jpg=00;35:*.gif=00;35:*.bmp=00;35:
*.xbm=00;35:*.xpm=00;35:*.png=00;35:*.tif=00;35:'
MACHTYPE=i386-redhat-linux-gnu
MAIL=/var/spool/mail/ericfj
MAILCHECK=60
OPTERR=1
OPTIND=1
OSTYPE=linux-gnu
PATH=/usr/kerberos/bin:/usr/local/bin:/usr/bin:/bin:/usr/X11R6/bin:/home2/ericfj/
bin:/usr/java/j2sdk1.4.1_03/bin:/opt/jext/bin
PIPESTATUS=([0]="0")
PPID=19277
PROMPT_COMMAND='echo -ne "\033]0;${USER}@${HOSTNAME%%.*}:${PWD/#$HOME/~}\007"'
PS1='[\u@\h \W]\$ '
PS2='> '
PS4='+ '
PWD=/home2/ericfj/web/local
QTDIR=/usr/lib/qt-3.3
SESSION_MANAGER=local/kirkwall:/tmp/.ICE-unix/19167
SHELL=/bin/bash
SHELLOPTS=braceexpand:emacs:hashall:histexpand:history:interactive-comments:monitor
SHLVL=2
SSH_AGENT_PID=19215
SSH_ASKPASS=/usr/libexec/openssh/gnome-ssh-askpass
SSH_AUTH_SOCK=/tmp/ssh-tke19167/agent.19167
SUPPORTED=en_US.UTF-8:en_US:en
TERM=xterm
UID=500
USER=ericfj
WINDOWID=20971638
XAUTHORITY=/home2/ericfj/.Xauthority
_=env
```

How It Works

As you can see from the listing, there are a lot of environment variables set on Linux. Many of these variables are specific to particular programs or purposes. For example, the *MAILCHECK* and *MAIL* environment variables are used for determining how often to check for new email as well as where to check.

As a best practice, you should define all environment variables to have uppercase names. This follows existing conventions.

The online documentation for each program that uses an environment variable should describe what variables are used as well as how the variables are used. For example, the command to view online documentation, man, uses the *MANPATH* environment variable, if set, to determine which directories to look for online manuals.

Listing the Environment on Mac OS X

On a Mac OS X system, you will see variables similar to the following:

```
$ set
BASH=/bin/bash
BASH_VERSINFO=([0]="2" [1]="05b" [2]="0" [3]="1" [4]="release"
[5]="powerpc-apple-darwin7.0")
BASH_VERSION='2.05b.0(1)-release'
COLUMNS=80
DIRSTACK=()
EUID=501
GROUPS=()
HISTFILE=/Users/ericfj/.bash_history
HISTFILESIZE=500
HISTSIZE=500
HOME=/Users/ericfj
HOSTNAME=Stromness.local
HOSTTYPE=powerpc
IFS=$' \t\n'
LINES=24
LOGNAME=ericfj
MACHTYPE=powerpc-apple-darwin7.0
MAILCHECK=60
OPTERR=1
OPTIND=1
OSTYPE=darwin7.0
PATH=/bin:/sbin:/usr/bin:/usr/sbin
PIPESTATUS=([0]="0")
PPID=524
PS1='\h:\w \u\$ '
PS2='> '
PS4='+ '
PWD=/Users/ericfj
SECURITYSESSIONID=10967b0
SHELL=/bin/bash
SHELLOPTS=braceexpand:emacs:hashall:histexpand:history:interactive-comments:monitor
SHLVL=1
TERM=vt100
TERM_PROGRAM=iTerm.app
UID=501
USER=ericfj
_=/etc/bashrc
__CF_USER_TEXT_ENCODING=0x1F5:0:0
```

How It Works

Note how similar the Mac OS X output is when compared to the Linux output. To a shell script, both operating systems provide an environment that is very similar. Contrast this with the overall operating environments, which differ greatly.

Listing the Environment on Windows XP

On Windows XP under the Cygwin environment, you will see variables like the following:

```
$ set
!::=':::\'
!C:='C:\cygwin\bin'
ALLUSERSPROFILE='C:\Documents and Settings\All Users'
ANT_HOME='C:\ericfj\java\apache-ant-1.5.4'
APPDATA='C:\Documents and Settings\ericfj\Application Data'
BASH=/usr/bin/bash
BASH_VERSINFO=([0]="2" [1]="05b" [2]="0" [3]="1" [4]="release"
[5]="i686-pc-cygwin")
BASH_VERSION='2.05b.0(1)-release'
COLUMNS=80
COMMONPROGRAMFILES='C:\Program Files\Common Files'
COMPUTERNAME=GURNESS
COMSPEC='C:\WINDOWS\system32\cmd.exe'
CVS_RSH=/bin/ssh
DIRSTACK=()
EUID=1006
FP_NO_HOST_CHECK=NO
GROUPS=()
HISTFILE=/home/ericfj/.bash_history
HISTFILESIZE=500
HISTSIZE=500
HOME=/home/ericfj
HOMEDRIVE=C:
HOMEPATH='\Documents and Settings\ericfj'
HOSTNAME=kirkwall
HOSTTYPE=i686
IFS=$' \t\n'
INFOPATH=/usr/local/info:/usr/info:/usr/share/info:/usr/autotool/devel/info:
/usr/autotool/stable/info:
JAVA_HOME='C:\j2sdk1.4.2_01'
LINES=25
LOGONSERVER='\\KIRKWALL'
MACHTYPE=i686-pc-cygwin
MAILCHECK=60
MAKE_MODE=unix
MANPATH=/usr/local/man:/usr/man:/usr/share/man:/usr/autotool/devel/man::
/usr/ssl/man
MAVEN_HOME='C:\ericfj\java\maven-1.0-rc1'
NUMBER_OF_PROCESSORS=1
OLDPWD=/usr/bin
OPTERR=1
OPTIND=1
```

```
OS=Windows_NT
OSTYPE=cygwin
PALMTOPCENTERDIR='C:\Program Files\Sharp Zaurus 2\Qtopia Desktop'
PATH=/usr/local/bin:/usr/bin:/bin:/usr/X11R6/bin:/cygdrive/c/WINDOWS/system32:
/cygdrive/c/WINDOWS:/cygdrive/c/WINDOWS/System32/Wbem:/cygdrive/c/ericfj/apps:/cyg
drive/c/ericfj/java/apache-ant-1.5.4/bin:/cygdrive/c/j2sdk1.4.2_01/bin:/usr/bin:.
PATHEXT='.COM;.EXE;.BAT;.CMD;.VBS;.VBE;.JS;.JSE;.WSF;.WSH'
PIPESTATUS=([0]="0")
PPID=1
PRINTER='HP LaserJet 2100 PCL6'
PROCESSOR_ARCHITECTURE=x86
PROCESSOR_IDENTIFIER='x86 Family 15 Model 2 Stepping 9, GenuineIntel'
PROCESSOR_LEVEL=15
PROCESSOR_REVISION=0209
PROGRAMFILES='C:\Program Files'
PROMPT='$P$G'
PS1=$'\\[\\033]0;\\w\\007\n\\033[32m\\]\\u@\\h \\[\\033[33m\\w\\033[0m\\]\n$ '
PS2='> '
PS4='+ '
PWD=/home/ericfj
SESSIONNAME=Console
SHELL=/bin/bash
SHELLOPTS=braceexpand:emacs:hashall:histexpand:history:interactive-comments:monitor
SHLVL=1
SYSTEMDRIVE=C:
SYSTEMROOT='C:\WINDOWS'
TEMP=/cygdrive/c/DOCUME~1/ericfj/LOCALS~1/Temp
TERM=cygwin
TMP=/cygdrive/c/DOCUME~1/ericfj/LOCALS~1/Temp
UID=1006
USER=ericfj
USERDOMAIN=ORKNEY
USERNAME=ericfj
USERPROFILE='C:\Documents and Settings\ericfj'
WINDIR='C:\WINDOWS'
_=/home/ericfj/.bashrc
f=
```

How It Works

In this example, you can see a lot more of the DOS legacy in the use of drive letters such as C:. The Cygwin package does a good job of merging the Unix assumptions of shell environments with the realities of the Windows system. Thus, you can see both *TMP* (Unix) and *TEMP* (Windows) are set to name temporary directories, as well as both *USER* (Unix) and *USERNAME* (Windows).

Handling Local and Environment Variables

Technically, the set command, used for the previous examples, lists *all* the variables that have a value. This includes environment variables as well as any other variables, called *local variables*. Local variables are variables available within the current shell. *Environment variables* are variables that have been exported. Exported variables are available for subshells. And a *subshell* is a shell launched from within a shell. Confused yet?

The concept of subshells introduces a hierarchy of shells, meaning that your scripts may operate within a subsubshell or a subsubsubshell, and so on. It works like this: When you log in, the system runs an application, typically a shell. This is the ancestor of all further shells you run. This ancestor shell is considered a *login* shell, a shell that gets executed for a user login. The ancestor shell sets up the environment. The ancestor shell then launches a number of applications. For example, in Linux with a graphical desktop, the login shell runs the X Window System server process (traditionally called X). The X server process then launches a number of graphical applications, including any shell windows that appear when you log in. Each of these shell windows is a graphical application. Each of these shell windows, in turn, runs shells. These shells are subshells.

You can then run shells from within these subshells. You've been doing that for each example so far. Every time you use commands such as sh, bash, csh, and so on, you are launching a subshell, or more technically, a subshell of the current subshell. (This is one reason why Unix and Linux systems seem to run so many processes.)

So when you create an environment variable, your script is setting up the value for subshells, children of the shell running your script. Thus, this is really useful when your scripts launch child scripts or programs and want to pass values to the child scripts or programs through environment variables. Your scripts, however, do not set environment variables in the ancestor shell; environment-variable values are exported downward, not upward.

In most cases, you will set up the environment for shells when each shell starts. See the section Customizing Your Account later in this chapter for more on editing the files checked when shells start.

This may seem confusing, but if you use the following guidelines, the situation should make more sense:

❑ Set up the environment for your user account using the standard files defined for that purpose and described in the section Customizing Your Account.

❑ Otherwise, set environment variables within shell scripts only if your scripts are calling scripts or programs and you need to modify the environment for the scripts or programs.

❑ In all other cases, just read environment variables inside your scripts.

Try It Out   Listing Only Environment Variables

You can run the env or printenv commands to just list the exported variables — that is, just the variables considered environment variables. For example:

```
$ printenv
SSH_AGENT_PID=22389
HOSTNAME=kirkwall
SHELL=/bin/bash
TERM=xterm
HISTSIZE=1000
GTK_RC_FILES=/etc/gtk/gtkrc:/home2/ericfj/.gtkrc-1.2-gnome2
WINDOWID=20971679
OLDPWD=/home2/ericfj/writing/beginning_shell_scripting
QTDIR=/usr/lib/qt-3.3
USER=ericfj
LS_COLORS=no=00:fi=00:di=00;34:ln=00;36:pi=40;33:so=00;35:bd=40;33;01:cd=40;33;
01:or=01;05;37;41:mi=01;05;37;41:ex=00;32:*.cmd=00;32:*.exe=00;32:*.com=00;32:
```

```
*.btm=00;32:*.bat=00;32:*.sh=00;32:*.csh=00;32:*.tar=00;31:*.tgz=00;31:*.arj=00;
31:*.taz=00;31:*.lzh=00;31:*.zip=00;31:*.z=00;31:*.Z=00;31:*.gz=00;31:*.bz2=00;
31:*.bz=00;31:*.tz=00;31:*.rpm=00;31:*.cpio=00;31:*.jpg=00;35:*.gif=00;
35:*.bmp=00;35:*.xbm=00;35:*.xpm=00;35:*.png=00;35:*.tif=00;35:
GNOME_KEYRING_SOCKET=/tmp/keyring-Q0LxNA/socket
SSH_AUTH_SOCK=/tmp/ssh-NVH22341/agent.22341
KDEDIR=/usr
SESSION_MANAGER=local/kirkwall:/tmp/.ICE-unix/22341
MAIL=/var/spool/mail/ericfj
DESKTOP_SESSION=default
PATH=/usr/kerberos/bin:/usr/local/bin:/usr/bin:/bin:/usr/X11R6/bin:
/home2/ericfj/bin:/usr/java/j2sdk1.4.1_03/bin:/opt/jext/bin
INPUTRC=/etc/inputrc
PWD=/home2/ericfj/writing/beginning_shell_scripting/scripts
LANG=en_US.UTF-8
GDMSESSION=default
SSH_ASKPASS=/usr/libexec/openssh/gnome-ssh-askpass
HOME=/home2/ericfj
SHLVL=2
GNOME_DESKTOP_SESSION_ID=Default
MY_SHELL=/usr/bin/emacs2
LOGNAME=ericfj
LESSOPEN=|/usr/bin/lesspipe.sh %s
DISPLAY=:0.0
G_BROKEN_FILENAMES=1
COLORTERM=gnome-terminal
XAUTHORITY=/home2/ericfj/.Xauthority
_=/usr/bin/printenv
```

Your output, as usual, will differ based on your system's settings.

How It Works

The `printenv` command lists fewer variables than the `set` command because `set` lists all current variables. The differences follow — that is, the variables reported by `set` but not by `printenv`:

```
BASH=/bin/bash
BASH_VERSINFO=([0]="2"
BASH_VERSION='2.05b.0(1)-release'
COLORS=/etc/DIR_COLORS.xterm
COLUMNS=80
DIRSTACK=()
EUID=500
GROUPS=()
G_BROKEN_FILENAMES=1
HISTFILE=/home2/ericfj/.bash_history
HISTFILESIZE=1000
HOSTTYPE=i386
IFS=$'
LESSOPEN='|/usr/bin/lesspipe.sh
LINES=24
LS_COLORS='no=00:fi=00:di=00;34:ln=00;36:pi=40;33:so=00;35:bd=40;33;01:cd=40;
33;01:or=01;05;37;41:mi=01;05;37;41:ex=00;32:*.cmd=00;32:*.exe=00;32:*.com=00;
32:*.btm=00;32:*.bat=00;32:*.sh=00;32:*.csh=00;32:*.tar=00;31:*.tgz=00;
```

```
31:*.arj=00;31:*.taz=00;31:*.lzh=00;31:*.zip=00;31:*.z=00;31:*.Z=00;31:*.gz=00;
31:*.bz2=00;31:*.bz=00;31:*.tz=00;31:*.rpm=00;31:*.cpio=00;31:*.jpg=00;
35:*.gif=00;35:*.bmp=00;35:*.xbm=00;35:*.xpm=00;35:*.png=00;35:*.tif=00;35:'
MACHTYPE=i386-redhat-linux-gnu
MAILCHECK=60
OPTERR=1
OPTIND=1
OSTYPE=linux-gnu
PIPESTATUS=([0]="0")
PPID=22454
PROMPT COMMAND='echo
PS1='[\u@\h
PS2='>
PS4='+
SHELLOPTS=braceexpand:emacs:hashall:histexpand:history:interactive-comments:monitor
SUPPORTED=en_US.UTF-8:en_US:en
UID=500
_=
```

These variables are considered local to the current shell and not environment variables.

Listing the Environment with the C Shell

The T C shell does support a set command, but it does not output the full environment. For example:

```
$ set
COLORS  /etc/DIR_COLORS.xterm
_       !! | sort

addsuffix
argv    ()
cwd     /home2/ericfj
dirstack        /home2/ericfj
dspmbyte        euc
echo_style      both
edit
file    /home2/ericfj/.i18n
gid     500
group   ericfj
history 100
home    /home2/ericfj
killring        30
owd
path    (/usr/kerberos/bin /usr/local/mozilla /bin /usr/bin /usr/local/bin
/usr/X11R6/bin /home2/ericfj/bin /usr/java/j2sdk1.4.1_03/bin /home2/ericfj/eclipse
/home2/ericfj/apache-ant-1.5.4/bin)
prompt  [%n@%m %c]$
prompt2 %R?
prompt3 CORRECT>%R (y|n|e|a)?
shell   /bin/tcsh
shlvl   2
sourced 1
status  0
```

```
tcsh     6.12.00
term     xterm
tty      pts/19
uid      500
user     ericfj
version tcsh 6.12.00 (Astron) 2002-07-23 (i386-intel-linux) options
8b,nls,dl,al,kan,rh,color,dspm,filec
```

The set command shows internal settings of the C shell, not a list of environment variables. The C shell equivalent of the Bourne shell set command is setenv. When you run setenv from a T C shell on Linux, you will see output similar to the following:

```
$ setenv | sort
COLORTERM=gnome-terminal
CVSROOT=:pserver:ericfj@localhost:/home2/cvsrepos
DESKTOP_SESSION=default
DISPLAY=:0.0
G_BROKEN_FILENAMES=1
GDMSESSION=default
GNOME_DESKTOP_SESSION_ID=Default
GNOME_KEYRING_SOCKET=/tmp/keyring-w8mvQR/socket
GROUP=ericfj
GTK_RC_FILES=/etc/gtk/gtkrc:/home2/ericfj/.gtkrc-1.2-gnome2
HOME=/home2/ericfj
HOST=kirkwall
HOSTNAME=kirkwall
HOSTTYPE=i386-linux
INPUTRC=/etc/inputrc
JAVA_HOME=/usr/java/j2sdk1.4.1_03
KDEDIR=/usr
LANG=en_US.UTF-8
LESSOPEN=|/usr/bin/lesspipe.sh %s
LOGNAME=ericfj
LS_COLORS=no=00:fi=00:di=00;34:ln=00;36:pi=40;33:so=00;35:bd=40;33;01:cd=40;33;
01:or=01;05;37;41:mi=01;05;37;41:ex=00;32:*.cmd=00;32:*.exe=00;32:*.com=00;
32:*.btm=00;32:*.bat=00;32:*.sh=00;32:*.csh=00;32:*.tar=00;31:*.tgz=00;31:*.arj=00;
31:*.taz=00;31:*.lzh=00;31:*.zip=00;31:*.z=00;31:*.Z=00;31:*.gz=00;31:*.bz2=00;
31:*.bz=00;31:*.tz=00;31:*.rpm=00;31:*.cpio=00;31:*.jpg=00;35:*.gif=00;35:*.bmp=00;
35:*.xbm=00;35:*.xpm=00;35:*.png=00;35:*.tif=00;35:
MACHTYPE=i386
MAIL=/var/spool/mail/ericfj
OSTYPE=linux
PATH=/usr/kerberos/bin:/usr/local/mozilla:/bin:/usr/bin:/usr/local/bin:
/usr/X11R6/bin:/home2/ericfj/bin:/usr/java/j2sdk1.4.1_03/bin:/home2/ericfj/eclipse:
/home2/ericfj/apache-ant-1.5.4/bin
PWD=/home2/ericfj
QTDIR=/usr/lib/qt-3.3
SESSION_MANAGER=local/kirkwall:/tmp/.ICE-unix/27573
SHELL=/bin/tcsh
SHLVL=2
SSH_AGENT_PID=27574
SSH_ASKPASS=/usr/libexec/openssh/gnome-ssh-askpass
SSH_AUTH_SOCK=/tmp/ssh-bxy27573/agent.27573
SUPPORTED=en_US.UTF-8:en_US:en
```

```
TERM=xterm
USER=ericfj
USERNAME=ericfj
VENDOR=intel
WINDOWID=23068746
XAUTHORITY=/home2/ericfj/.Xauthority
```

You can also run the `printenv` or `env` commands under the C shell to list the environment variables. For example:

```
$ printenv
COLORTERM=gnome-terminal
CVSROOT=:pserver:ericfj@localhost:/home2/cvsrepos
DESKTOP_SESSION=default
DISPLAY=:0.0
G_BROKEN_FILENAMES=1
GDMSESSION=default
GNOME_DESKTOP_SESSION_ID=Default
GNOME_KEYRING_SOCKET=/tmp/keyring-w8mvQR/socket
GROUP=ericfj
GTK_RC_FILES=/etc/gtk/gtkrc:/home2/ericfj/.gtkrc-1.2-gnome2
HOME=/home2/ericfj
HOST=kirkwall
HOSTNAME=kirkwall
HOSTTYPE=i386-linux
INPUTRC=/etc/inputrc
JAVA_HOME=/usr/java/j2sdk1.4.1_03
KDEDIR=/usr
LANG=en_US.UTF-8
LESSOPEN=|/usr/bin/lesspipe.sh %s
LOGNAME=ericfj
LS_COLORS=no=00:fi=00:di=00;34:ln=00;36:pi=40;33:so=00;35:bd=40;33;01:cd=40;33;
01:or=01;05;37;41:mi=01;05;37;41:ex=00;32:*.cmd=00;32:*.exe=00;32:*.com=00;
32:*.btm=00;32:*.bat=00;32:*.sh=00;32:*.csh=00;32:*.tar=00;31:*.tgz=00;31:*.arj=00;
31:*.taz=00;31:*.lzh=00;31:*.zip=00;31:*.z=00;31:*.Z=00;31:*.gz=00;31:*.bz2=00;
31:*.bz=00;31:*.tz=00;31:*.rpm=00;31:*.cpio=00;31:*.jpg=00;35:*.gif=00;35:*.bmp=00;
35:*.xbm=00;35:*.xpm=00;35:*.png=00;35:*.tif=00;35:
MACHTYPE=i386
MAIL=/var/spool/mail/ericfj
OSTYPE=linux
PATH=/usr/kerberos/bin:/usr/local/mozilla:/bin:/usr/bin:/usr/local/bin:
/usr/X11R6/bin:/home2/ericfj/bin:/usr/java/j2sdk1.4.1_03/bin:/home2/ericfj/eclipse:
/home2/ericfj/apache-ant-1.5.4/bin
PWD=/home2/ericfj
QTDIR=/usr/lib/qt-3.3
SESSION_MANAGER=local/kirkwall:/tmp/.ICE-unix/27573
SHELL=/bin/tcsh
SHLVL=2
SSII_AGENT_PID=27574
SSH_ASKPASS=/usr/libexec/openssh/gnome-ssh-askpass
SSH_AUTH_SOCK=/tmp/ssh-bxy27573/agent.27573
SUPPORTED=en_US.UTF-8:en_US:en
TERM=xterm
USER=ericfj
```

```
USERNAME=ericfj
VENDOR=intel
WINDOWID=23068746
XAUTHORITY=/home2/ericfj/.Xauthority
```

Testing the Environment

As mentioned previously, your scripts should honor environment variable settings. But your scripts also need to handle the case where certain variables are not set. In most cases, you need a fallback strategy to handle such instances.

For example, the *DISPLAY* environment variable names the X Window System display, which represents a combination of monitor, keyboard, and mouse. Graphical X Window programs use the *DISPLAY* setting to know which X display to use. On a multiuser system, this can be very important.

Just about every Linux and Unix system uses the X Window System for graphics. Mac OS X systems can run X as add-on software. You can even run X under Cygwin on Windows.

If the *DISPLAY* environment variable has a value, then X Window programs should use that value. If the *DISPLAY* environment variable is not set, however, a program or script has three choices:

❑   Use the default value for the *DISPLAY*, :0.0 in this case.

❑   Assume the X Window System is not running.

❑   Alert the user that the *DISPLAY* variable is not set, and the script can exit. This is called *die a flaming death* in shell scripting parlance.

There's no magic. Your shell scripts need to make similar decisions if crucial variables are not set. The following Try It Out shows some strategies for handling missing environment variables.

Try It Out   Checking Environment Variables

Enter this script and save it under the name check_env:

```
# Checks for environment variables.

# Uncomment the following line to remove the variable.
#unset DISPLAY

if [ "$DISPLAY" == "" ]
then
    echo "DISPLAY not set, using :0.0 as default."
    DISPLAY=":0.0"
fi


#unset SHELL

if [ "$SHELL" == "" ]
then
```

```
        echo "Using /bin/bash, which is the shell you should use."
        SHELL=/bin/bash
fi



#unset USER

if [ "$USER" == "" ]
then
        echo -n "Please enter your username: "
        read USER
fi



#unset HOME

if [ "$HOME" == "" ]
then
        # Check for Mac OS X home.
        if [ -d "/Users/$USER" ]
        then
                HOME="/Users/$USER"

        # Check for Linux home.
        elif [ -d "/home/$USER" ]
        then
                HOME="/home/$USER"

        else
                echo -n "Please enter your home directory: "
                read HOME
                echo
        fi
fi

# Display all the values.

echo "DISPLAY=$DISPLAY"
echo "SHELL=$SHELL"
echo "USER=$USER"
echo "HOME=$HOME"
```

When you run this script, you will see output like the following:

```
$ sh check_env
DISPLAY-:0.0
SHELL=/bin/bash
USER=ericfj
HOME=/home2/ericfj
```

The output will differ based on your system's values for environment variables. On a Mac OS X system, for example, you will see output like the following:

```
$ sh check_env
DISPLAY not set, using :0.0 as default.
DISPLAY=:0.0
SHELL=/bin/bash
USER=ericfj
HOME=/Users/ericfj
```

Note how this Macintosh does not have the X Window System running.

How It Works

In the check_env script, the general strategy is to try to find a reasonable value for missing variables. If something cannot be guessed, the next step is to ask the user for the information.

If a value isn't set, then the script will try to determine the missing data. For example, if the *HOME* variable isn't set, then the check_env script will check for /Users/*username*, the Mac OS X default home directory, and /home/*username*, the Linux default home directory. If neither of these directories exists, then the check_env script will prompt the user to enter the missing data.

Going through the tests in detail, the script sets the *DISPLAY* variable to :0.0 if *DISPLAY* has no value. This should work on many Unix and Linux systems but not Mac OS X, which by default does not include the X Window System software.

The check_env script will set the *DISPLAY* variable if needed. Note that this script is not exporting the value of the variable (see below), so any setting will be lost when the script ends. This is true of all the other tests as well.

The test of the *SHELL* environment variable sets the shell to /bin/bash if there is no value. The script also outputs a message to alert the user to this fact.

If the *USER* environment variable is not set, the script prompts the user to enter in the username. While you could try to guess the username, this is generally difficult, so the script asks the user to provide this information.

The test for the *HOME* environment variable needs a value for the *USER* environment variable so that it can check for user home directories if needed. If the *HOME* variable has no value, the script first checks for a Mac OS X–type home directory and then a Linux-type home directory.

If neither of these home directories exists, the script asks the user to enter the location of the user's home directory.

At the end of the script, the script outputs all the current values for the four variables.

You can verify how this script works by using the unset command. Prior to each test, the check_env script has an unset line commented out. Uncomment the line to unset the given variable. That way, you force the script to assume the variable is not set and therefore exercise the script logic associated with finding a value.

To uncomment a line, remove the leading # character that marks the line as a comment.

This is a common technique for testing scripts.

Setting Environment Variables

You can read environment variables just like other shell variables. You can also set environment variables just like other shell variables. But you must take extra steps to affix your new values into the environment.

Remember that this environment applies only to programs and shells your script launches. That is, the environment applies only to subshells. You need to modify the environment for shells by editing the files listed in the section Customizing Your Account so that the environment gets properly propagated to subshells.

There are two main reasons to set environment variables:

❑   You want to customize your user account.

❑   Your script needs to set an environment variable that is used by a command or script it calls.

To set an environment variable, you need to export it. To set a variable, you need the following syntax:

```
VARIABLE=VALUE
```

To export a variable into the environment of child processes — that is, to make a plain old shell variable into a super-duper environment variable — use the `export` command:

```
export VARIABLE
```

Thus, you will often see the following pattern used in shell startup scripts:

```
var=value
export var
```

You can combine the two commands onto one line, using the semicolon separator. For example:

```
var=value; export var
```

You can also use a shorthand version with just the `export` command:

```
export var=value
```

The `export` command may export more than one variable at a time. For example:

```
var1=value1
var2=value2
var3=value3
export var1 var2 var3
```

You will find all of these variants used in various shell scripts you encounter, especially in scripts that initialize shells.

In the bash shell, you can also use the set -a command to export all variables set in the shell:

```
$ set -a
```

Your scripts should not assume that a user has run this command, however.

You can see how the export command works, as well as how to create your own environment variables, by running the following example scripts.

Exporting Variables

Enter the following script and save it under the name echo_myvar:

```
echo "inside child script, MY_VAR=$MY_VAR"
```

This script outputs the value of the shell variable *MY_VAR*. The echo_myvar script, however, does not set the variable. That job is for the set_myvar script, following:

```
# Set my_var without exporting.
MY_VAR="Tempest"

echo -n "No export: "
sh echo_myvar

# Now, export and try again.

echo -n "export:    "
export MY_VAR

sh echo_myvar
```

Enter this script and save it under the name set_myvar.

To run these scripts, run the set_myvar script. You should see output like the following:

```
$ sh set_myvar
No export: inside child script, MY_VAR=
export:    inside child script, MY_VAR=Tempest
```

How It Works

The echo_myvar script just outputs the value of the variable *MY_VAR*. This script does not set any value, so the script is utterly dependent on the environment in which it runs. If the environment does not set the variable, the echo_myvar script will display no value. Only if the environment has set a value into the *MY_VAR* variable will the echo_myvar script be able to display any value.

The set_myvar script sets the variable *MY_VAR* to a value and then calls the echo_myvar script. The echo_myvar script, however, does not see any value for this variable. That's because the set_myvar script hasn't exported the value. Thus far, it has just set the variable.

Next, the set_myvar script calls the export command to export the *MY_VAR* variable. It then calls the echo_myvar script. This time, the echo_myvar script sees a value in the *MY_VAR* variable.

Setting Environment Variables in the C Shell

The variable-setting examples so far have used the syntax for the Bourne shell, sh, supported by ksh and bash as well. As you'd expect, the C shell requires a different syntax, using the setenv built-in shell command. The setenv syntax follows:

```
setenv variable value
```

Note that there is no equal sign in this syntax.

For a good source of csh examples, see the system files /etc/csh.login and /etc/csh.cshrc, the system files for initializing the C shell (and tcsh, too), as covered in the section Customizing Your Account. For example:

```
setenv PATH "/bin:/usr/bin:/usr/local/bin:/usr/X11R6/bin"
setenv MAIL "/var/spool/mail/$USER"
```

You do not call export in csh or tcsh.

Reading Values into the Current Environment

When you run a script, your current shell, such as bash, launches a child shell, most often sh, to run the script. You can instead execute a script that modifies the current shell environment using the source command.

The basic syntax is:

```
source script_filename
```

The source command runs the given script in the context of the current shell, not in a child shell. This command is most often used to read in shell startup files to customize the shell.

In addition to the source command, you can use the dot (.) command:

```
.  script_filename
```

This has the same effect as the source command.

Customizing Your Account

When a shell starts up, it reads from a file or files to initialize settings for your system. These files are shell scripts. Some of these files, such as /etc/profile, reside in system directories. Most users cannot modify these files. Other files reside within your home directory. These files are available for you to modify as needed.

Any system files should normally be left alone, as they establish the proper defaults for your system. Administrators might customize these files to allow for sitewide settings.

The files in your home directory, however, are intended for you to modify as needed. You can add any commands you want, using the proper shell syntax, into your personal startup files.

Each shell has a set of files that it looks for, by name. Virtually all personal startup files are located in your home directory, and all but one start with a dot.

> *Remember that files with names that start with a dot are considered hidden files. Hidden files don't appear in file listings without special command-line options and are ignored by most shell globs, such as *.*

The files must have exactly the right name, or the shell will ignore them. For example, for the bash shell, one of the files is `.bashrc`. If you want to use this file to initialize bash, you must name it `.bashrc` (with a leading dot), and the file must reside in your home directory. You must also have read permission for this file.

With a very long history, shells typically support more than one file to hold initial settings. Thus, you may be able to choose from a number of file names, such as `.bash_profile` or `.bash_login`, both of which serve the same purpose.

> **Don't try to set environment variables unless you know how the variable is used. You may end up messing up applications on your system, applications that expect a particular value in an environment variable.**

The following sections describe how each shell starts.

How the Bourne Shell Starts Up

If you run the Bourne shell as a login shell, it looks in your home directory for a file named `.profile`. The shell then sources the commands in this file to read any settings into the current environment.

The Bourne shell does this only if the shell is a login shell — that is, the shell run when you first log in. The Bourne shell does not read the `.profile` file when subsequent shells start.

> *The distinction between login shells and other shells is important to how all the shells start.*

How the Korn Shell Starts Up

When you run ksh as a login shell, it looks for a file in your home directory named `.profile` and sources the commands in that file. This is the same as the Bourne shell.

If you run ksh as a non-login shell, the Korn shell looks for a startup file named by the *ENV* environment variable. This is similar to the C shell's `.cshrc` file.

If *ENV* names a directory, the Korn shell looks for a file named `ksh_env` within that directory. If *ENV* names a file, the Korn shell loads that file.

How the C Shell Starts Up

When you start csh as a login shell, it sources the commands in `/etc/csh.cshrc` and `/etc/csh.login`. Then csh looks for a file in your home directory named `.cshrc` and sources the commands in that file. After that, csh looks for a file in your home directory named `.login` and sources the commands in that file. On logout, a csh login shell sources the commands in `/etc/csh.logout` and the `.logout` file in your home directory.

For non-login shells, csh sources the commands in `/etc/csh.cshrc` and then `.cshrc` in your home directory.

How the T C Shell Starts Up

The T C shell starts up and acts similarly to the C shell. The main difference is that you can name the startup file `.tcshrc` or `.cshrc`. The T C shell will read either file. As with bash, the purpose for supporting the old `.cshrc` file is to make it easier for users to migrate from csh to tcsh.

How Bash Starts Up

Bash combines features of the C shell, the Bourne shell, and the Korn shell. Thus, you will see a number of files that appear similar to the files used by ksh or csh.

When you run bash as a login shell, it first executes the `/etc/profile` file. Then bash looks for files in your home directory. Bash looks for:

- ❑   `.bash_profile`
- ❑   `.bash_login`
- ❑   `.profile`

Bash looks in this order and executes the first file found. The intent is to make it easier to switch from ksh or csh to bash.

When a login shell exits, bash looks for a file named `.bash_logout` in your home directory and sources the commands in the file.

You can launch bash as a login shell using the `--login` option. For example:

```
$ bash --login
```

Use the `--noprofile` option to tell a bash login shell not to read the login files on startup.

When you run bash as a child shell and not as a login shell, bash looks in one of two locations. If the shell is interactive, bash looks for a file named `.bashrc` in your home directory. Otherwise, bash checks for an environment variable named *BASH_ENV*. The *BASH_ENV* variable serves the same purpose and usage as the ksh *ENV* environment variable.

Use the `--norc` to tell bash to not run the `.bashrc` file. Use the `--rcfile` option to tell a noninteractive, non-login bash to use a different file name than `.bashrc` in your home directory.

The following table summarizes the startup, login, and logout files for the main shells.

Shell	Startup File	Login File	Logout File
bash	.bashrc (if not login shell but interactive), $BASH_ENV (if non-interactive and not login)	/etc/profile, then .bash_profile, or .bash_login, or .profile	.bash_logout
csh	/etc/csh.cshrc, then .cshrc	/etc/csh.cshrc, then /etc/csh.login, then .cshrc, then .login	/etc/csh.logout, then .logout
ksh	$ENV	.profile	*None*
sh	*None*	/etc/profile, then .profile	*None*
tcsh	/etc/csh.cshrc, and .tcshrc or .cshrc	/etc/csh.cshrc, then /etc/csh.login, then .tcshrc or .cshrc, then .login	/etc/csh.logout, then .logout

Don't depend on shell customizations. While it is great that you can customize your environment, you should not write your shell scripts to depend on these customizations. That's because once you move to another system, your scripts may fail in unexpected ways.

Because the initialization of the shells is performed while the shell starts up, it is not always apparent what is causing a particular problem. You may spend hours trying to figure out what is wrong in your shell script when the problem lies elsewhere: in the shell initialization files.

Handling Command-Line Arguments

Another area where scripts interact with their environment is the command line. Just as you can pass command-line options and arguments to commands, you can also pass these to shell scripts. Of course, passing items on the command line is the easy part. The hard part comes in what do you do with them inside your scripts.

The first step is to examine all the items passed on the command line to your script.

Reading Command-Line Arguments with the Bourne Shell

When the Bourne shell runs a script, it places the command-line arguments in special variables that you can access within your script. For example, the variable *$1* holds the first item on the command line for your script. This can be a command-line option, such as –v, or a command-line argument, such as the name of a file. The item in the first position is stored in *$1*.

That's why $1 and the like are called positional variables.

The following table lists the special variables set by the Bourne shell for the command-line arguments.

Special Variable	Holds
$0	Name of the script from the command line
$1	First command-line argument
$2	Second command-line argument
$3	Third command-line argument
$4	Fourth command-line argument
$5	Fifth command-line argument
$6	Sixth command-line argument
$7	Seventh command-line argument
$8	Eighth command-line argument
$9	Ninth command-line argument
$#	Number of command-line arguments
$*	All command-line arguments, separated with spaces

The script itself is given the special variable *$0* (zero). The shell sets *$0* with the name of the script, as it appears on the command line.

The command-line arguments are split out into separate variables, *$1* to *$9*. There is no *$10* and above. You are not limited to only nine arguments, however. The special variable *$** holds all the arguments. In addition, *$#* holds a count of the number of arguments.

The Korn shell understands *${10}* for the tenth argument, and so on.

Note that $0 is not counted and not considered part of $.*

Listing Command-Line Arguments

The following script lists command-line arguments:

```
# Checks command-line arguments.

echo "Script: $0"

echo "Number of items on command line: $#"

echo "1st argument: $1"

echo "2nd argument: $2"

echo "All arguments [$*]"
```

Enter this script and save it under the file name `args`. When you run this script with command-line arguments, you will see output like the following:

```
$ sh args arg1 arg2
Script: args
Number of items on command line: 2
1st argument: arg1
2nd argument: arg2
All arguments [arg1 arg2]
```

If you run the script with many arguments, you will see output like the following:

```
$ sh args arg1 2 3 4 5 6 7 8 9 10
Script: args
Number of items on command line: 10
1st argument: arg1
2nd argument: 2
All arguments [arg1 2 3 4 5 6 7 8 9 10]
```

How It Works

The `args` script first lists the value of the `$0` variable, which holds the name of the script. It then lists the number of arguments, as well as the first two arguments, each called out on its own lines of output. Finally, the `args` script outputs all the command-line arguments inside square brackets, [], to show where the arguments start and end.

This should seem fairly easy, but there are a few quirks, as you can see if you run the `args` script with different sets of parameters. For example, run the `args` script with no parameters:

```
$ sh args
Script: args
Number of items on command line: 0
1st argument:
2nd argument:
All arguments []
```

There are zero items, and the arguments are empty.

If you run the script with just one argument, you will see output like the following:

```
$ sh args arg1
Script: args
Number of items on command line: 1
1st argument: arg1
2nd argument:
All arguments [arg1]
```

The value held in $0 is the value of the script file, as passed on the command line. Thus, you may see the full path to a script or other variants of the file name. For example:

```
$ sh /home/ericfj/beginning_shell_scripting/scripts/args arg1 arg2
Script: /home/ericfj/beginning_shell_scripting/scripts/args
Number of items on command line: 2
1st argument: arg1
2nd argument: arg2
All arguments [arg1 arg2]
```

This example calls the args script with the full path to the script file, which the shell dutifully sets into the $0 variable.

In addition, you can pass empty arguments that still count as arguments. For example:

```
$ sh args arg1 "" "                        " arg4
Script: args
Number of items on command line: 4
1st argument: arg1
2nd argument:
All arguments [arg1                        arg4]
```

In this example, the first argument is arg1, a normal-looking argument. The second argument, however, is the empty text string " ". The third argument is a long text string of spaces, and the fourth argument slides back into normalcy with a value of arg4.

When the script shows the value of $* and encloses $* in quotes (with or without extra text, as in the args script), you see all the spaces in $3 in the output.

Because a space acts as a separator on the command line, and an argument can have spaces (or consist entirely of spaces), you can sometimes generate confusing output. For example:

```
$ sh args "1 2 3 4 5 6 7 8 9"
Script: args
Number of items on command line: 1
1st argument: 1 2 3 4 5 6 7 8 9
2nd argument:
All arguments [1 2 3 4 5 6 7 8 9]
```

This script has just one argument, "1 2 3 4 5 6 7 8 9". But because of the spaces in the argument, when the args script outputs the value of $*, it appears as if there were nine command-line arguments.

So your scripts need to be careful when working with command-line arguments.

Command-line arguments can be especially hard on Windows and Mac OS X, where directories with spaces in their names are common, such as the Windows C:\Program Files directory.

Thus far, the example script has just listed the command-line arguments. The next step is to actually make use of them, as in the following Try It Out.

Try It Out   Using Command-Line Arguments

The myls scripts from Chapter 3 created a simple form of the ls command. You can extend the scripts from before to have the user pass the name of the directory to list on the command line. Enter the following script and save it under the name myls3:

```
# Assumes $1, first command-line argument,
# names directory to list.

cd $1
for filename in *
do
    echo $filename
done
```

When you run this script, you will see output like the following, depending on the name of the directory you pass to the script:

```
$ sh myls3 /usr/local
bin
etc
games
include
lib
libexec
man
sbin
share
src
```

How It Works

The myls3 script extends the previous myls script from Chapter 3 and takes the value of the first command-line argument as the name of a directory to list. The myls3 script then changes to that directory and then lists out all the files in that directory, one at a time.

Your scripts will perform similarly, using command-line arguments to define directories and files to work on.

Reading Command-Line Arguments with the C Shell

The C shell and T C shell both support special variables for command-line arguments, similar to sh, bash, and ksh. The main difference with csh and tcsh, however, is the use of *$#argv* in place of *$#*.

With csh and tcsh, the special variable *$#argv* holds a count of the number of command-line arguments.

> *Note that tcsh also supports $# as well as $#argv. Both variables hold the same value.*

Making Scripts Executable

Up to now, all the scripts require you to run a shell, such as sh, and to pass sh the name of the script file to execute. This is very different from running normal commands, such as ls. With ls, you just type in the name of the command, ls. You do not need to pass a script file to ls to generate the output.

As mentioned previously, you can transform your scripts into full-blown executable commands. Users can just type in the name of the command, and they never need know that your new command is really a script.

To transform your script into an executable command, you need to:

❑ Mark the script as executable by giving it execute permissions

❑ Add a line to your script to tell the shell how to execute the script

The following sections describe how to perform these steps.

Marking Files Executable

Under Unix and Unix-like systems, all executable files, be they scripts, commands, or something else, must be marked as executable files. An *executable file* is one that has execute permission. You can change permissions with the chmod command.

Before changing permissions, however, you should check what permissions are already set. To do this, use the ls command with the -1 (ell) option. For example:

```
$ ls -l myls3
-rw-rw-r-- 1 ericfj engineering 124 Oct 12 22:39 myls3
```

Each rw- describes the permissions for the owner of the file (user ericfj in this example), the group the file is associated with (engineering in this example), and the final r-- describes the permissions available to the rest of the world (all other users). The r means read permission. The w means write permission. A dash means no permission.

So rw- means read and write permission, and r-- means read-only permission. There are no execute permissions on this file.

To add an execute permission, use chmod. For example:

```
$ chmod u+x myls3
```

The u+x argument is in a funny form used by chmod. The u means *user* — that is, permissions for the user or owner of the file. The + means *add permission*. The x means *execute permission*.

You can also use octal numbers for permissions, leading to permissions such as 0666. See the online manual for the chmod command for more details.

You can now verify that the script has an execute permission with the ls command:

```
$ ls -l myls3
-rwxrw-r--  1 ericfj engineering 124 Oct 12 22:39 myls3
```

You can now see that the owner of the file has rwx permissions, short for *read, write, and execute*. Our script file is now an executable command.

Note that if you are using csh or tcsh, you must execute the rehash command to rebuild the internal list of executables. For example:

```
$ rehash
```

After making the script file executable, the next step is to tell your shell (as well as any other shell) *how* to execute the file.

Setting the #! Magic Line

Executable files — that is, commands — come from a variety of sources and appear in a variety of formats. Most commands are compiled executable programs. Most commands were written in the C programming language and then compiled into the binary code for your system's processor.

The main sources of commands, however, take one of the following formats.

❑ Compiled executable programs
❑ Java executable archives, called jar files
❑ Scripts in languages such as Python, Perl, Tcl, Ruby, or Lua
❑ Shell scripts

When you try to run an executable command, the first thing the shell must do is determine the type of file and then use the correct method to launch the command. For example, if the file is a compiled executable program, the first few bytes of the file will contain a special code (often called a *magic code* or *magic number* after the file /etc/magic, which holds many such codes). This special code tells the shell that it needs to launch the file as a compiled executable program.

The shell follows the same type of process for running shell scripts. First, the shell needs to determine that the file is a script. This process is helped by the fact that scripts are text files. The first few bytes (as well as all the bytes) of the file must be printable text characters.

Once the shell determines that the file is a script, the next question is what kind of script. The shell needs to determine what program should run the script. For example, if your shell is bash, but you write a Bourne shell script, then bash—your shell—needs to determine which program, sh in this case, to launch to run the script.

By convention, if your script starts with #! (often called a *shebang* because it starts with a hash-exclamation point), then the special comment tells the shell which program should interpret the script. So if the very first line of your script appears as the following, then the shell knows to launch sh to run your script:

```
#!/bin/sh
```

Note that this must be the first line of the file. The # must start on the first column of the file. That is, # must be the first character in the file. Because # starts a comment, if your shell, for some reason, doesn't understand this convention, the #! line will be ignored.

The syntax for the #! line is:

```
#!/full_path_to_interpreter
```

The interpreter is the program that interprets the script and executes the commands in the script. For Bourne shell scripts, the interpreter (or shell) is sh, with a full path of /bin/sh. For shells, the interpreter is the same as the shell program. But for some languages, such as Tcl, you have a choice of two interpreters: tclsh and wish, the latter supporting graphical commands.

Regardless of the interpreter, the shell merely takes the part after the #! and then tries to execute that program.

The following table lists the main locations for shells and interpreters.

Shell or Interpreter	Path
ash	#!/bin/ash
bash	#!/bin/bash
csh	#!/bin/csh
ksh	#!/bin/ksh
perl	#!/usr/bin/perl or #!/usr/local/bin/perl
python	#!/usr/bin/perl or #!/usr/local/bin/perl
sh	#!/bin/sh
tclsh (Tcl)	#!/usr/bin/tclsh or #!/usr/local/bin/tclsh
tcsh	#!/bin/tcsh or #!/usr/local/bin/tcsh
wish (Tcl)	#!/usr/bin/wish or #!/usr/local/bin/wish
zsh	#!/bin/zsh

Scripting languages such as Perl and Python use the same mechanism. For example, a script starting with the following line is clearly a Perl script:

```
#!/usr/bin/perl
```

There is a problem with software add-ons, however. If a given interpreter is not installed with the operating system, the program will likely be installed in /usr/local/bin (for commands added locally) or in some other directory, but not in /bin or /usr/bin. Linux, however, which treats nearly every software package in existence as part of the Linux distribution, almost always places these interpreters in the system directories /bin or /usr/bin. Thus, the #! comment won't always reflect the path to the shell, unfortunately.

Try It Out   Making a Script Executable

Starting with the myls3 script, described previously, you can create a script that uses the #! comment to name the interpreter to run the script. Enter the following and save it under the name myls4:

```
#!/bin/sh

# Assumes $1, first command-line argument,
# names directory to list.

cd $1
for filename in *
do
    echo $filename
done
```

Note that this script is exactly the same as the myls3 script shown previously, with only the first line different. (This line is marked as bold in the preceding code listing.) You can copy the myls3 file to start editing.

Next, mark the file with execute permissions:

```
$ chmod u+x myls4
```

C and T C shell users need to run the rehash command after adding a new command to the command path. Thus, after you call chmod, you should call rehash:

```
$ rehash
```

After calling the chmod command, you can run the script as a command in the current directory:

```
$ ./myls4 /usr/local
bin
etc
games
include
lib
libexec
man
sbin
share
src
```

The output should be the same as for the myls3 script.

How It Works

By making the script executable and by adding the `#!` line, you provide enough information to run your script as an executable command. The `./myls4` in the example tells the shell to run the executable `myls4` in the current directory.

If the current directory is part of the shell's command path, you can run the script as follows:

```
$ myls4 /usr/local
bin
etc
games
include
lib
libexec
man
sbin
share
src
```

You can also copy the script file to one of the directories in your shell's command path. That is, copy the file to one of the directories listed in the *PATH* environment variable. You can now extend your operating system and create new commands.

Summary

Shell scripts are not isolated. Shell scripting was designed specifically to allow users to access their system's environment.

In this chapter, you learned:

❑   Environment variables hold settings specific to your system's environment. This includes the operating system, location of commands, and user settings such as settings for the default shell and a home directory.

❑   Environment variables are regular shell variables. You can access these variables with the dollar sign, $. You can store new values into these variables. But you must export each variable you want to propagate to any subshells.

❑   All the data on the command line, arguments and options, are provided by the shell to your script. The shell stores these values in specially named variables called positional variables, such as *$1* and *$5*. You can access these from within your scripts.

❑   To make a script into an executable command, you need to mark the script with executable permissions and place a specially formatted `#!` comment in the first line of the script.

The next chapter delves into files. Just about every shell script you write will access files in one way or another.

Exercises

1. Write a script that dies a flaming death if the *SHELL* environment variable is not set. Come up with a way to verify both cases, set and not set, to prove your script works.

2. Write a script that goes through all the command-line arguments and lists each one, no matter how many arguments there are. Output only the arguments that are not empty. For example, " " is a valid command-line argument, but it is empty and so should not be listed. Output the total number of command-line arguments as well.

3. Write a script to list out all the command-line arguments, but your script must run under the C shell, bash, ksh, and sh. (Hint: The C shell is the trickiest one.)

4. Write a script that takes any number of directories as command-line arguments and then lists the contents of each of these directories. The script should output each directory name prior to listing the files within that directory.

Scripting with Files

Shells were originally designed to work with files. That's because a huge portion of what you need to do on a Unix system relates to files. Unix, for example, stores most configuration settings in files, and usually text files at that. This is different from Windows, for example, which stores many configuration settings in the Registry.

This means that many simple commands can manipulate the configuration of many applications, especially server applications. All of these commands work with files. In addition to the normal operations of reading from files, writing to files, and so on, shell scripts interact with files in a number of ways, including:

- ❑ Combining files into archives.
- ❑ Testing files with the test command.
- ❑ Dealing with files on Mac OS X, especially for mobile users.
- ❑ Outputting files stored within the scripts. These are called *here* files. You can use here files to drive interactive programs.

Shells provide a number of built-in commands to work with files, but for the most part, your scripts will call non–built-in commands for most work with files. That's because Unix and Unix-like systems offer a rich set of commands for working with files.

You can also use input redirection to read the contents of files. Output redirection allows you to send the output of a command to a file. And command pipelines allow you to feed the results of one command into another. These topics are covered in Chapter 8.

The following sections show all sorts of additional ways to work with files.

Combining Files into Archives

Unix and Unix-like systems include a lot of files as part of the standard operating system. Most anything you do on such a system involves files. This leads to the problem of how to transfer files from one system to another and from one directory to another.

To help with this, you can use the `tar` command. Tar, short for *tape archive,* comes from ancient times as the name suggests. But it remains in heavy use today. With `tar`, you can combine a number of files into one large file, usually called a *tar file.* You can then copy the `tar` file to another system or directory and then extract the files. Tar preserves the original directory structure.

To create a tar archive, use the `cf` command-line options to `tar`. For example:

```
$ tar cf myarchive.tar *.doc
```

This command combines all files with names ending in .doc into a `tar` archive called `myarchive.tar`. (By convention, use a .tar file-name extension for `tar` archives.)

> *Because of its age,* `tar` *does not use a dash with its command-line options. (With some versions of* `tar`, *you can use a dash before the options.)*

The `c` option specifies to create an archive. The `f` option names the archive file.

To extract the files in this archive, use the following format:

```
$ tar xf myarchive.tar
```

The `x` option tells the `tar` command to extract the files.

Following the Unix philosophy of each tool performing one task, `tar` does not compress files. Instead, you can use the `compress` command. Uncompress compressed files with the `uncompress` command. A more modern compression program is called gzip. Gzip compresses to smaller files than `compress` and so is used for almost all compressed files on Unix and Unix-like systems. A newer program called bzip2 also compresses files.

> *The gzip file format is not compatible with the Windows PKZIP format, usually called ZIP files.*

To use gzip, provide `gzip` the name of the file to compress. For example:

```
$ gzip myarchive.tar
```

By default, the gzip program compresses the given file. It then changes the file name to end with a `.gz` extension, indicating that the file is compressed with gzip. The original file is removed. You can verify this with the `ls` command:

```
$ ls myarch*
myarchive.tar.gz
```

Uncompress a gzipped file with gunzip. For example:

```
$ gunzip myarchive.tar.gz
$ ls myarch*
myarchive.tar
```

The gunzip program removes the .gz file and replaces it with an uncompressed version of the original file.

The zip program combines the features of tar and a compression program. Zip creates ZIP file archives that are compatible with the Windows PKZIP and WinZip programs. If you need to go back and forth to Windows systems, zip is a good choice. Java applications use the ZIP file format for Java archive, or *jar*, files. Macintosh systems often use a compression program called StuffIt. StuffIt files typically show a .sit file-name extension.

Working with File Modes

Unix systems use file modes to control which users can access files as well as whether the file is marked executable (covered in Chapter 4). The file modes are divided into three areas that correspond to three classes of people who can potentially access the file: the user or owner of the file, the group associated with the file, and everyone else.

Each file is associated with a group. Files you create will be associated, by default, with your default group. Groups were once very popular, but more recent operating systems tend to make a group for each user, eliminating most of the benefits of group access. (This change was made for security reasons.)

The following table shows the numeric values of the file modes. Note that all the numbers are in octal (base 8) rather than decimal (base 10, like normal numbers).

Value	Meaning
400	Owner has read permission.
200	Owner has write permission.
100	Owner has execute permission.
040	Group has read permission.
020	Group has write permission.
010	Group has execute permission.
004	All other users have read permission.
002	All other users have write permission.
001	All other users have execute permission.

The table shows three-digit values, which control the access for the owner of the file, the group associated with the file, and everyone else, in that order. All these numbers are in octal, which makes it a lot easier to add modes together. For example, 600 means the owner has read and write permission (and no one else has any permissions) because 600 = 200 + 400.

If you ever want evidence that Unix is possessed, note that the mode where all users have read and write permissions is 666.

To change permissions on a file, pass these octal modes to the chmod command. For example:

```
$ ls -l myarchive.tar
-rw-rw-r--  1 ericfj ericfj 266240 Oct 24 21:22 myarchive.tar
$ chmod 600 myarchive.tar
$ ls -l myarchive.tar
-rw-------  1 ericfj ericfj 266240 Oct 24 21:22 myarchive.tar
```

These commands show the file permissions before the change (664) and after the change (600). Note that in the long file listings, r stands for read permission, w for write permission, and x for execute permission. The three sets of letters apply to the owner, the group, and all others.

You can use these letters with the chmod command. This is especially useful if octal math is not your cup of tea, although the alternative is not that easy to understand either. The basic format is u + or - the user permissions, g + or - the group permissions, and o + or - the other users permissions. Use a plus, +, to add permissions, and a minus, -, to remove them.

For example, to set a file to have read and write permissions for the owner and no access to anyone else, use the following as a guide:

```
$ chmod 666 myarchive.tar
$ ls -l myarchive.tar
-rw-rw-rw-  1 ericfj ericfj 266240 Oct 24 21:22 myarchive.tar
$ chmod u+rw,g-rwx,o-rwx myarchive.tar
$ ls -l myarchive.tar
-rw-------  1 ericfj ericfj 266240 Oct 24 21:22 myarchive.tar
```

This example first sets read and write permissions for everyone on the file myarchive.tar. The ls command verifies the new permissions. Then the next chmod command sets the permissions to 600 by adding and removing permissions. Note that you can remove permissions that are not assigned, such as the execute permissions in this example.

You can also perform the permission change using a number of commands. For example:

```
$ chmod u+rw myarchive.tar
```

This command sets up the user permissions for the owner of the file.

```
$ chmod g-rwx myarchive.tar
```

This command removes any permissions from other users in the group associated with the file.

```
$ chmod o-rwx myarchive.tar
```

This command removes any permissions for all other users. Note that you do not have to set all permissions at once. You could, for example, just remove the group and other user permissions.

Testing Files with the test Command

The test command, used with conditionals, includes a number of options to test for file permissions as well as to test the type and size of files.

The following table lists the file options for the test command.

Test	Usage
-d *file name*	Returns true if the file name exists and is a directory
-e *file name*	Returns true if the file name exists
-f *file name*	Returns true if the file name exists and is a regular file
-r *file name*	Returns true if the file name exists and you have read permissions
-s *file name*	Returns true if the file name exists and is not empty (has a size greater than zero)
-w *file name*	Returns true if the file name exists and you have write permissions
-x *file name*	Returns true if the file name exists and you have execute permissions

You can combine the test command with the chmod command, as in the following Try It Out, to lock down permissions on files so that other users cannot access your files. This is very useful in this era of security vulnerabilities.

Try It Out Locking Down File Permissions

Enter the following script and name the file lockdown:

```
# Locks down file permissions.

for filename in *
do
    # Initialize all permissions.
    r=""
    w=""
    x=""

    # Check to preserve existing permissions.
```

```
    if [ -r $filename ]
    then
        r="r"
    fi

    if [ -w $filename ]
    then
        w="w"
    fi

    if [ -x $filename ]
    then
        x="x"
    fi

    # Lock down the file permissions.
    chmod u+$r$w$x,g-rwx,o-rwx $filename

done
```

When you run this script with the following command, there is no output unless there is a problem:

```
$ sh lockdown
```

How It Works

The outer `for` loop in the `lockdown` script loops through each file in the current directory. For each file, the script uses the `test` command (with the `[` shorthand format) to check which permissions are available now. Then the script calls the `chmod` command, using the long letter format. The options to the `chmod` command remove all permissions from the group and other users. The options also preserve any permissions originally available to the user.

> *This script assumes you own all the files in the current directory. If not, see the chown command documentation.*

Dealing with Mac OS X Files

Mac OS X, while Unix-based, is not laid out in what is considered a "standard" Unix layout. This section addresses some differences from Unix-based systems that you should be aware of in dealing with files on a Mac OS X system.

The Legacies of NeXT

Mac OS X's Unix side has its roots in two places, NeXTSTEP and BSD. Most of the differences from Unix-based systems come from NeXT. The biggest distinction is the file system layout. On a standard Mac OS X box, you have a single partition. No swap, no nothing else, just the root partition, /. Swapfiles are discrete files, living in /var/vm. This method of swap has its good and bad points, but it's the generic way of handling swap for Mac OS X, so you don't have a swap partition unless it's been implemented manually.

Another missing item is the /opt directory. It's not a part of the standard OS X setup, and if you assume it's going to be there, you'll have a lot of error messages in your scripts. The /etc, /var, and /tmp directories are all there but actually live inside a directory named /private and are linked to the root level of the boot drive.

User home directories are not in the /Home directory but in /Users, except when they are on a server, and then are in the /Network hierarchy. If your script is going to be running in an elementary/high school environment, then options such as network homes and NetBoot are going to be quite common, and that can change things on you if you aren't prepared for it.

Most nonboot local volumes live in the /Volumes directory, even if they are partitions on the boot drive. The normal exceptions to this are NFS volumes, which still work like they do with most Unix systems, although they can live in /Volumes as well. Volumes in /Volumes typically show up on the user's desktop, and unless you set them otherwise, mount on user login only. So if you need a partition to be visible prior to login, you must manually set up that mount.

Network drives can live in both /Network and /Volumes, depending on the usage and the situation. The important thing to remember is that Mac OS X is not truly Linux or any other kind of Unix. While most things will work the way you expect, if you are going to be dealing with Mac OS X on a regular basis, you should take the time to become familiar with its file system.

Mobile File Systems and Mac OS X

Thanks to the prevalence of FireWire and the ease that the Mac has always had of booting from different partitions, drives, and the like, you will likely work with file systems that are quite dynamic. For the Unix world, Mac OS X users are *extremely* mobile. All those iPod music players can become spare data drives, or even boot drives, without much work. (Install an OS, and select the iPod in System Preferences ➪ Startup Disk.) Because of the way Mac OS X deals with mobile drives, the script that was looking for resources in /usr/local/bin is still going to find that directory, but now it's a totally different /usr/local/bin, and what you want is /Volumes/usr/local/bin. While mobile use is starting to become more common on Linux, the fact is, if you get a room full of Mac users, especially laptop users, together, it's a good bet that at least a third will have some kind of portable FireWire drive with them, and they will be happily using it as a big data shuttle or test boot disk. Many others will be using their iPods. Again, Mac users have *flexible* file system configurations.

> Another fun aspect of FireWire drives and their relatives is that they allow you to ignore permissions. Mac OS X enables the local user to ignore permissions on a locally attached FireWire or USB drive with a click of a button in the Finder's Get Info window. So the Unix permissions on a FireWire or USB drive are only a suggestion, not a rule. *Don't rely solely on Unix file permissions for security*. It takes a Mac OS X power user only about 30 minutes to bypass those, even without using the Terminal.

The message here is don't hardcode paths in your scripts unless you have to, and if you do, try to warn users with read-me files.

Target Disk Mode

Thanks to an Apple feature called Target Disk Mode (TDM), mobile file systems are not limited to just portable hard drives but can also include the computer itself. That's correct — the entire Mac.

As a rule of thumb, any Mac with a G4 can run Target Disk Mode, although some G3 Macs can too. If you aren't sure whether your Mac supports Target Disk Mode, check the list at http://docs.info.apple.com /article.html?artnum=58583.

TDM is ridiculously simple to use. You boot, or restart a Mac, and hold down the *T* key until you see a giant FireWire symbol moving about the screen. (You can't miss it.) You then run a FireWire cable from the machine in Target Disk Mode to another Mac. Wait a few seconds, and *voilà*! You'll see the TDM machine showing up as a big hard drive on the other machine. Not to belabor the point, but again, avoid assumptions about the file system layout wherever possible, and if you can't, give plenty of warning.

Mobile File Systems and Disk Images

Disk images are everywhere. They've become the preferred method of software distribution on the Mac, If you see `.dmg` or `.smi` files, you're dealing with disk images. From a Unix point of view, these are physical disks. For example, here's the result of a `mount` command with a CD, a disk image, and a FireWire drive mounted:

```
$ mount
automount -nsl [291] on /Network (automounted)
automount -fstab [318] on /automount/Servers (automounted)
automount -static [318] on /automount/static (automounted)
/dev/disk1s0 on /Volumes/NWN_XP2 (local, nodev, nosuid, read-only)
/dev/disk2s3 on /Volumes/Untitled 1 (local, nodev, nosuid, journaled)
/dev/disk3 on /Volumes/Casper Suite 2.2 (local, nodev, nosuid, read-only, mounted
by foo)
```

So which line is the disk image? Well, NWN_XP2 is the PC CD of the fantastic game Neverwinter Nights. Untitled 1 is a FireWire drive. Casper Suite 2.2 is a disk image. Note that there's really no way to tell which is which. CD-ROMs are always read-only, but disk images can be read/write, too. The biggest advantages of disk images are that they compress well, they're easy to use, and because they support AES encryption, they can be quite useful as a way to securely send data. (That last feature is a nice way to get around the "ignore permissions" issue on mobile drives, by the way.)

While you may feel you've been beaten about the head regarding the mobility of file systems in a Mac OS X world, there's a reason: You cannot assume that Mac OS X is like every other Unix. It's *mostly* like them at the shell level, but there are some real differences that you are not going to see too many other places, and if you forget that and hardcode everything to reflect a Linux/Solaris/HP-UX/AIX world-view, Mac OS X will make your scripts very sad and unhappy. That's not to say it's all bad. The vast majority of Mac OS X users don't tend to reconfigure their file layouts. They leave things alone. If the OS wants swapfiles in /var/vm instead of a separate swap partition, they're fine with that. If the OS wants to mount things that aren't boot partitions in /Volumes, great! As long as they don't have to dink with it, they're happy. You tend to not see the kind of hardcore customizations at the Unix level that you see on a different platform, so you can avoid most problems by testing to make sure that what you think is the way the world looks is actually the way the world is.

Naming Issues

Before I get into the differences between HFS+ and "normal" Unix physical file systems, there's one more thing to look at, and it's important. It can be summed up as: "Beware the colon and the space" or "Mac users are crazy."

It is fairly uncommon to see volume names with spaces in the rest of the Unix world. The root partition is /, and the others tend to have normal names such as swap, opt, and so on. This is not true in the Mac OS X world. Mac users name their drives, especially portable drives, things that just don't tend to happen in the traditional Unix world. Consider, for example, the person who names all his drives after characters in Herman Melville novels; he mounts drives named Moby Dick, The Pequod, and Quee-Queg.

> *If you assume that spaces are not used, it can bite you back, and it can bite you back hard. It bit Apple on one particularly memorable occasion, wherein a shell script misassumption in the iTunes 2.0 installer caused people with multiple volumes, or spaces in the names of their boot volumes, to suddenly find their drives erased. That would be what those in the IT field call bad.*

As well, while most traditional shell scripters know that the / character is a directory delimiter, on Mac OS X boxes, under the default file system, the colon can do that job as well. So if you use colons in file names, Mac users are going to potentially see some very odd things when they look at those files in the Finder, the file system UI for Mac OS X.

HFS+ Versus UFS: The Mac OS X Holy War

One thing that traditional shell scripters will run into when they start dealing with Mac OS X is the file system. It's not UFS, or EXTFS*. It's normally (at least 95 percent of the time) the Hierarchical File System Extended FS, or more simply HFS+. This was the file system used on the Classic Mac OS starting with Mac OS 8.1, and it's the default file system on every shipping Mac. Luckily, if you sidestep philosophical issues, there are not too many differences between HFS+ and other Unix file systems.

The biggest difference is in the way HFS+ handles case. HFS+ is case insensitive but case preserving. So while it's not going to change the case of any file or directory names, it also doesn't care about it. To HFS+, `filename` and `FILENAME` are the same thing. If you're doing a lot of work with Apache on Mac OS X, you'll want to ensure that the hfs_apple_module is loaded and in use, and the case issue shouldn't cause you problems there either.

> *HFS+'s case insensitivity is going to bite you less than you think because to most Mac users, this is how it's always been, so they don't think that using `filename`, `Filename`, and `FILENAME` is a great way to keep different versions of the same file around. As long as you don't assume case-sensitivity in your scripts (and you shouldn't rely on this as a filing system anyway; it's really a poor way to version data), you should never hit a difference.*

Another difference you'll see, but shouldn't be affected by, is the creation date. In most Unix systems, the only date you use is the modification date. On Mac OS X, HFS+ supports the creation date separately from the modification data as a part of a file's metadata. It's mostly used by users when finding files, and you'd have to explicitly code for it to use it, so it's not something you're going to stumble over.

Because HFS+ doesn't use inodes, it emulates those for the shell environment. It's unlikely you'll ever run into this, because HFS+ emulates hard links and inodes well enough that it should never cause you problems. But if you ask a Mac OS X user about inodes, you're probably going to get a blank look.

While HFS+ emulates hard links and supports symbolic links, it also supports a third lightweight file reference, namely the alias. An alias is like a symbolic link, but with an added feature: with a symbolic link, if you move what the link points to, the link dies. With an alias, if you move what the alias points to, as long as you don't move that file or folder off of the volume, the alias doesn't die; it just gets updated to the new location of the target. An alias appears as a file on disk, but the Finder treats an alias like a link. This dualism can cause problems in your scripts. You're unlikely to create aliases in your scripts. But if your script comes across what appears to be a file, and your script can't use it, it could be an alias.

The Terror of the Resource Fork

The final major difference between HFS+ and UFS file systems involves something that isn't really as much of a concern anymore: the resource fork. In the original versions of the Mac OS file systems, MFS and HFS, each file had two forks: a data fork and a resource fork. The data fork held data and maybe some metadata. The resource fork held things such as icons, code, comments, and so on. The problem was that if you just copied a dual-forked file to something like UFS, the resource fork tended to wither and die, and all you got was the data fork. For documents, this was anything from a nonissue to an annoyance. For applications, it was a death sentence.

However, HFS+ deals with this differently. It certainly supports the resource fork, but it's no longer a hard part of the file. It's just a metadata fork, à la an NTFS file stream that is mostly used by older applications. There are some modern Mac OS X applications that still use resource forks; the biggest example is Microsoft Office. But the vast majority don't do that anymore. They use a single-forked bundle format, which is just a directory that acts like a single file.

The resource fork will not show up directly in listings by the `ls` command. And the `mv` and `cp` commands won't properly copy the resource forks. Thus, you want to use the Finder to move or copy files on a Mac OS X system.

If you want to avoid resource forks, here are some rules of thumb that will keep you out of trouble:

❑ Stay out of /Applications (Mac OS 9) and /System Folder. While old-style apps can live outside of those locations, almost everything in those directories uses a resource fork, and shell scripts have no business in them.

❑ If the application looks like a directory and ends in `.app`, then it's a single-forked app. Otherwise, it's probably a dual-forked app.

For example, here's a directory listing for Microsoft Word (which uses a resource fork) and Adobe Photoshop CS (which doesn't use a resource fork):

```
-rwxrwxr-x   1 jwelch  admin   17069566 Sep 13 12:00 Microsoft Word
drwxrwxrwx   3 jwelch  jwelch       102 Nov 24  2003 Adobe Photoshop CS.app
```

Note that Word is a single file without the `.app` extension, whereas Photoshop is a directory with the .app extension. If you are using non–resource fork–aware shell utilities (almost all of them), and you see the Photoshop structure, you're probably okay. If you see the Word structure on an app, then you should proceed with caution. Unfortunately, it's hard to tell if a file is just a file or a resource-forked application. It's not impossible, but you're not going to do it with standard Unix tools on a Linux system. However, Microsoft Office is one of the last major Mac OS X apps to still use resource forks, so there's one final rule of thumb.

❏ Stay out of any directory whose name contains Microsoft Office in the path or name. There is nothing in there you wish to mess with.

Note that these tips apply to applications. Files are trickier, but they also don't fall apart without a resource fork as often. Nine times out of ten, you just lose an icon. The only notable problem children here are clipping files (which end in .clipping, .textClipping, or .webloc) and old StuffIt Archives (which end in .sit). If you run into a file and aren't sure, make a copy and work on that. If you guess wrong, at least you've just mangled a copy.

At the moment, there aren't a lot of tools that handle resource forks well (although Mac OS X 10.4, aka Tiger, is supposed to fix a lot of this). Apple provides two with its developer tools, namely mvMac and cpMac, which are resource fork–aware versions of mv and cp, respectively. There are some third-party tools, such as hfstar, hfspax, and RsyncX, but they don't ship with the OS, so you can't rely on them. Unfortunately, resource forks are still a way of life on the Mac, so your best bet is to just avoid the places they are likely to be.

Working with Here Files and Interactive Programs

You've seen the mantra again and again in this book: Shell scripts were designed to work with files. You can take advantage of a special feature called here files to embed files within your scripts.

A *here file* or *here document* is a section of text in your shell script that the shell pulls out and treats as a separate file. You can use a here file to create a block of text, for output to the user, or for input to a command such as ftp, telnet, and other interactive applications. The shell runs the command as if you typed in the here file text as input for the command.

You can think of here files as "here is the file." Otherwise, the term sounds very odd.

The basic syntax for a here file is:

```
command <<FileContinuesUntilHere
...text of here file...
FileContinuesUntilHere
```

Use the << operator to signify that the text of the file is embedded within the script. The text FileContinuesUntilHere acts as a marker. The shell treats FileContinuesUntilHere as the end-of-file marker for the here file. (You can choose your own text as the end-of-file marker. You do not have to use FileContinuesUntilHere. Do not use an end-of-file marker that may appear in the text, however. Make your end-of-file markers unique.)

Here files are very similar to input redirection, covered in Chapter 8.

Displaying Messages with Here Files

One of the simplest ways to use here files is to output a message to the user. While the echo command also outputs messages to the user, if you need to output more than three lines, the echo command becomes inconvenient. In this case, a here file works a lot easier for you, the scripter.

In most cases, you can use the cat command to output a here file to the user, as shown in the following Try It Out example.

Try It Out   Displaying Text with Here Files

Enter the following script and save it under the name cat_here:

```
# Uses a here file with the cat command.

cat <<HERE
This is a notice that the official company dress code policy
has changed. All employees are required to follow the new
policy.

We don't want to make a big deal about the policy, which has
been in effect since last September, but it appears that some
people have not been following the new guidelines. Because of
this, we felt it appropriate to introduce the new guidelines
for all employees.

The new policy is available on the company InfoCENTRE. You
will need level 3 security access to view the new company dress
code  policy. All employees should view this policy TODAY. Be
careful, though, not to overload the company InfoCENTRE server.
If you have trouble logging in to the secure company InfoCENTRE
site, please call the 800 number for the internal security
hotline. This number is available on the secure company InfoCENTRE.

You won't be sent home for violating the company dress code policy,
but you will need to work out any issues with your supervisor.
HERE

# Here file has ended, so the shell expects commands.

echo "Please follow this policy immediately."
```

When you run the cat_here script, you see output like the following:

```
$ sh cat_here
This is a notice that the official company dress code policy
has changed. All employees are required to follow the new
policy.

We don't want to make a big deal about the policy, which has
been in effect since last September, but it appears that some
people have not been following the new guidelines. Because of
this, we felt it appropriate to introduce the new guidelines
```

```
for all employees.

The new policy is available on the company InfoCENTRE. You
will need level 3 security access to view the new company dress
code  policy. All employees should view this policy TODAY. Be
careful, though, not to overload the company InfoCENTRE server.
If you have trouble logging in to the secure company InfoCENTRE
site, please call the 800 number for the internal security
hotline. This number is available on the secure company InfoCENTRE.

You won't be sent home for violating the company dress code policy,
but you will need to work out any issues with your supervisor.
Please follow this policy immediately.
```

How It Works

The `cat_here` script outputs enough text to make it inconvenient to use the `echo` command for each line of text. Instead, the `cat_here` script passes a here file to the `cat` command, which outputs all the text. The `echo` command works best for single-line messages, whereas the `cat` command was designed to output the entire contents of a file. The script terminates the here file with the market text HERE.

After the marker HERE, the script continues. You can place any additional commands before and after the here file. In this example, the script calls the `echo` command after the here file ends.

This script does not reflect an actual corporate memo. It is instead a paraphrase of a memo, a secure web site, and an hour long meeting held at a large services firm. It helps to be paid by the minute if you are forced to endure something like this.

Customizing Here Files

Another advantage of here files over input redirection is that you can customize the text in the here file, using shell variables. The shell expands any variables referenced within a here file, just as the shell expands variables within the rest of your scripts. The following Try It Out demonstrates this.

Try It Out   Sending a Message to All Logged-In Users

Enter the following script and name the file `tps_report1`:

```
wall <<EndOfText
Please complete all TPS reports and have them
on my desk by EOB today.

Your cooperation in this matter helps the smooth
flow of our departmental structure.

-Dick
EndOfText

echo "Message sent"
```

179

When you run the `tps_report1` script, you see the following output on the shell window you used to run the script:

```
$ sh tps_report1

Broadcast message from ericfj (Sat Oct 28 12:24:13 2006):

Please complete all TPS reports and have them
on my desk by EOB today.

Your cooperation in this matter helps the smooth
flow of our departmental structure.

-Dick
Message sent
```

All other users see just the message. For example:

```
Broadcast message from ericfj (Sat Oct 28 12:24:13 2006):

Please complete all TPS reports and have them
on my desk by EOB today.

Your cooperation in this matter helps the smooth
flow of our departmental structure.

-Dick
```

How It Works

The `wall` command, short for write (to) all (users), comes from the ancient times when users were logged in to plain ASCII terminals. In this example, `wall` is a handy command to call to test here files. In this more modern era, you can often use instant messaging, or IM, programs to communicate with logged-in users.

This example just sets up the here file; it does not customize the here file with variable values (the subject of the next Try It Out).

> Using a here file as shown in this example is not the most efficient way to pass input to most programs. Instead, you can use input redirection, covered in Chapter 8. Here files provide an advantage, however, if you want to insert variables into the input passed to a program or if the program is normally an interactive program. Interactive programs, such as ftp and telnet, work better for the here file approach.
>
> As with most aspects of shell scripting, you can approach any problem in more than one way. You can use here files or not, depending on your needs. There is no one true way to perform any task.

Try It Out   Changing the Input with Variables

To customize a here file, you merely need to insert variables into the here file in the script. The following example shows this.

```
# Use of variables within a here file.

# If the user forgets to pass the command-line
# arguments, fill in defaults.

if [ $# -lt 1 ]
then
    date_required=today
else
    date_required=$1
fi

if [ $# -lt 2 ]
then
    pithy_statement="Action, urgency, excellence"
else
    pithy_statement=$2
fi



wall <<EndOfText
Please complete all TPS reports and have them
on my desk by EOB $date_required.

Your cooperation in this matter helps the smooth
flow of our departmental structure.

$pithy_statement!
-Dick
EndOfText

echo "Message sent"
```

Enter this script and save it under the file name `tps_report2`. When you run this script, you see output like the following:

```
$ sh tps_report2 Monday Onward

Broadcast message from ericfj (Sat Oct 28 12:45:35 2006):

Please complete all TPS reports and have them
on my desk by EOB Monday.

Your cooperation in this matter helps the smooth
flow of our departmental structure.
```

```
Onward!
-Dick
Message sent
```

How It Works

As before, this script passes the here file to the `wall` command to send a message to all users using shell windows or terminals who are logged into your system. In this case, however, the script places variables at strategic locations within the script.

To promote reuse, the `date_required` variable holds the day the TPS reports are due. With this, you can reuse the script for any time the reports are due. The `pithy_statement` variable holds a pithy statement to end the message.

Both variables set their values from the arguments passed on the command line. The first argument is used for the `date_required` variable and the second for the `pithy_statement`. Note that this script could have used the command-line positional variables *$1* and *$2* directly. Instead, the script checks for the existence of the positional variables. If not set, the script fills in reasonable defaults.

> *Another approach to the same problem of validating input is to output an error message to the user if there are missing arguments.*

If you omit the second argument, you see output like the following:

```
$ sh tps_report2 Monday

Broadcast message from ericfj (Sat Oct 28 12:45:35 2006):

Please complete all TPS reports and have them
on my desk by EOB Monday.

Your cooperation in this matter helps the smooth
flow of our departmental structure.

Action, urgency, excellence!
-Dick
Message sent
```

And if the user omits all the arguments, you see output like the following:

```
$ sh tps_report2

Broadcast message from ericfj (Sat Oct 28 12:45:35 2006):

Please complete all TPS reports and have them
on my desk by EOB today.

Your cooperation in this matter helps the smooth
flow of our departmental structure.

Action, urgency, excellence!
-Dick
Message sent
```

Driving Interactive Programs with Here Files

In addition to placing variables within a here file, another use of here files comes when you need to drive interactive programs from a script.

Driving ftp with a Here File

Enter the following script and name the file ftpget:

```
# Driving an interactive program, ftp.

# Validate number of arguments.
if [ $# -lt 2 ]
then
    echo "Error, usage is:"
    echo "ftpget hostname filename [directory]."
    exit -1
fi

hostname=$1
filename=$2

directory="."  # Default value

if [ $#  ge 3 ]
then
    directory=$3
fi


ftp <<EndOfSession
open $hostname




cd $directory
get $filename
quit

EndOfSession

echo "FTP session ended."
```

You also need to set up something called *auto-login* for the ftp command. See the online documentation for the ftp command for more information on this. The auto-login feature sets up the username and password for the FTP site you attempt to contact. The script needs this feature because the here document does not work well with the ftp command when the ftp command prompts the user for a username and password.

FTP is short for File Transfer Protocol. The example script uses the ftp program, which is a client program designed to access remote FTP servers.

When you run this script (after setting up the `ftp` auto-login feature), you see minimal output like the following or an error if something goes wrong:

```
$ sh ftpget ftp.somehost.yow  index.html WWW
FTP session ended.
```

How It Works

The `ftpget` script is one of the trickiest scripts because of variations in the `ftp` command as well as how the `ftp` command prompts for your login to a remote system.

The basic mode of operation is that the `ftpget` script logs in to a remote site using the `ftp` command. The script then changes to a given directory and downloads the given file name. This seemingly simple task is fraught with error when using a here document because the remote server can output an error, which your script cannot handle. If the session runs well, however, you should see the file on the local system in the current directory.

The here file passes a number of `ftp` commands to the ftp program. The ftp program, designed for interactive use, supports a number of commands within the program itself. The `ftpget` script uses a here file to pass these commands to the `ftp` command, one at a time.

The `ftpget` script starts with the `open` command, to open an FTP session to the remote system. This is where the auto-login feature comes into play. When opening the session to the remote system, the `ftp` command reads in your username and password on the remote system from the `.netrc` file in your home directory. If the `open` fails, the script won't download the file.

The empty space in the here file sends new lines to the remote server because you cannot tell in advance how long it will take for the remote server to be ready for commands.

The script then issues a `cd` command to change directories on the remote system and the `get` command to download a file. The `quit` command ends the FTP session.

If you don't pass enough parameters to the `ftpget` script, you see an error message like the following:

```
$ sh ftpget
Error, usage is:
ftpget hostname filename [directory].
```

Note that there are severe limits to using here files to drive interactive programs. If any part of the interactive program has changed, your here file will no longer work. Furthermore, if any errors occur within the interactive program, your here file–scripted set of commands won't be able to handle the errors.

A package called expect provides greater control over interactive programs. It shines with tasks that are too complex for here files. You can find out more on expect at expect.nist.gov. Also, the wget command was designed for use within scripts.

Try It Out   Driving vi

The `ftpget` script showed an example of how you can use here files to automate interactive programs. A more predictable interactive program is the vi text editor, introduced in Chapter 2.

The following script runs a session with the vi text editor:

```
filename=test.txt

vi $filename <<EndOfCommands
i
This file was created automatically from
a shell script
^[
ZZ
EndOfCommands
```

Save this script under the name run_vi. You can then run the script:

```
$ sh run_vi
```

If you run this script with vim acting as vi, then you will likely see output like the following:

```
$ sh run_vi
Vim: Warning: Input is not from a terminal
```

The file is still edited. The vim command includes more code for detecting whether the editor is run from a terminal. Vim can tell that it is being run from a script or program.

After running the script, you should see the following added to the file test.txt:

```
$ cat test.txt

This file was created automatically from
a shell script
```

If you run the script a second time, it appends to the file. For example:

```
$ sh run_vi
Vim: Warning: Input is not from a terminal
$ cat test.txt

This file was created automatically from
a shell script

This file was created automatically from
a shell script
```

How It Works

The run_vi script provides a file name to the vi command. It then uses a here file to pass text to the vi edit session. The i command places vi in insert mode. The next two lines of text are inserted, as is an extra newline (because the next command appears on a separate line). An Escape character pushes vi out of insert mode and back into command mode. The ZZ command saves the file and exits vi.

The ^[text in the file must be an Escape character. Most text editors won't let you enter an Escape character into the document. One of the easiest ways to enter an Escape is to use vi. In vi, go into insert mode and then press Ctrl-V Ctrl-[, and you get an actual Escape character.

> *Before trying to automate a session in vi to perform scripted edits, take a look at the sed program, covered in Chapter 6.*

Turning Off Variable Substitution

By default, the shell substitutes variable values into the text of any here files. You can turn off this feature by enclosing the end of the here document marker in quotes. For example:

```
cat <<'QuotedEndMarker'
...text...
QuotedEndMarker
```

This allows you to include special formatting in your here file, for example, if you write a script that outputs a script or program source code.

Try It Out   Here with No Substitution

Enter the following script to see how to avoid variable substitution in here files. Save the script under the name here_no:

```
filename="test1"

cat <<'QuotedEndMarker'

With quotes around the here document marker,
you can include variable references such
as $HOME, $filename, and $USER.

QuotedEndMarker
```

When you run this script, you see output like the following:

```
$ sh here_no

With quotes around the here document marker,
you can include variable references such
as $HOME, $filename, and $USER.
```

How It Works

This script uses an ordinary here file, but it turns off the variable substitution. Otherwise, you would see the values of $HOME, $filename, and $USER in the output instead of the literal text.

All of this is done by the magic of enclosing the end marker, QuotedEndMarker, in quotes at the original reference. Do not enclose the marker in quotes at the end of the here file.

Summary

Files. Files. Files. Most shell scripts work with files of some sort. This chapter extends the basic operations on files to include:

- ❏ Combining files into archives with the `tar` command.
- ❏ Compressing files with the `gzip` command.
- ❏ Working with file permissions such as 600 for user read and write but no access to any others.
- ❏ Testing files with the `test` command. This includes testing file permissions.
- ❏ Handling issues on Mac OS X, especially regarding mobile computers and the file system issues that arise as users move from site to site.
- ❏ Using the oddly named here files to output text, even including programs.

The next chapter covers sed, a program you can use to make script-driven modifications to files. You'll find sed to be a powerful command that warrants its own syntax. You'll also find that sed is used in a huge number of shell scripts.

Exercises

1. Modify the lockdown script to remove only the group and other user permissions. *Hint:* The script will then no longer need to check and preserve the existing user permissions.

2. Make the lockdown script an executable script. Show all the necessary steps.

3. Rewrite the `tps_report2` script. Preserve the concept that if the user forgets to pass command-line arguments, the script will fill in useful defaults. But create a more compact way to test the arguments using nested `if` statements.

4. Rewrite the `tps_report2` script using a `case` statement instead of `if` statements.

5. Write a script with a here file that when run outputs a script that, in turn, when run outputs a script. That is, write a script that outputs a script that outputs a script. *Hint:* Start with a script that outputs another script. Then add the additional script.

Processing Text with sed

When you need to edit a file, you typically open up your favorite editor, perform the change, and then save the file and exit. Editors are great for modifying files and seem to be suitable for any type of editing needed. However, imagine you have a web site with a couple of thousand HTML files that need the copyright year at the bottom changed from 2004 to 2005. The interactive nature of editors would require you to type every change that you need to make. You would launch your editor and open each file individually and, like an automaton, make the change, save, exit, repeat. After spending hours performing the same change on thousands of files, you realize you've forgotten about a whole section of the web site and actually have several thousand more, and next year you will need to do this again, with more files. There has to be a better way.

Fortunately, there is. This chapter introduces you to sed, an intelligent text-processing tool that will save you not only time but also, more important, your sanity. The sed command gives you the power to perform these changes on the command line, or in a shell script, with very little headache. Even better, sed will allow you to repeat the advanced batch editing of files simply. Sed can be run on the command line and is a powerful addition to any shell scriptwriter's toolbox. Learning the building blocks of sed will enable you to create tools to solve complex problems automatically and efficiently.

This chapter introduces you to the building blocks of sed by covering the following subjects:

- ❏ Getting and installing sed
- ❏ Methods of invoking sed
- ❏ Selecting lines to operate on
- ❏ Performing substitutions with sed
- ❏ Advanced sed invocation
- ❏ Advanced addressing
- ❏ Common one-line sed scripts

Introducing sed

In this chapter, I give you a gentle introduction to sed and its powerful editing capabilities. Learning sed can take some time, but the investment pays off tenfold in time saved. It can be frustrating to figure out how to use sed to do what you need automatically, and at times you may decide you could do the rote changes interactively in less time. However, as you sharpen your skills, you'll find yourself using sed more frequently and in better ways. Soon you will revel in the divine realm of automation and reach to the programmer's version of nirvana.

The name *sed* means *stream editor*. It's designed to perform edits on a stream of data. Imagine a bubbling stream of cool mountain water filled with rainbow trout. You know that this stream empties into a sewage system a few miles down, and although you aren't a big trout fan you want to save the fish. So you do a little work to reroute the stream through a pipe to drain into a healthy lake. (The process of *piping* is discussed in Chapter 8.) With sed, you can do a little magic while the stream is flowing through the pipe to the lake. With a simple sed statement, the stream and all the trout would flow into the pipe, and out would come the same icy mountain stream, filled with catfish instead of trout. You could also change the cool water into iced tea, but that won't help the fish. Using your traditional text editor is like manually replacing each trout in the stream with catfish by hand; you'd be there forever, fish frustratingly slipping out of your grasp. With sed, it's a relatively simple and efficient task to make global changes to all the data in your stream.

Sed is related to a number of other Unix utilities, and what you learn in this chapter about sed will be useful for performing similar operations using utilities such as vi and grep. Sed is derived originally from the basic line editor ed, an editor you will find on most every Unix system but one that is rarely used because of its difficult user interface. (Although unpopular as an editor, ed continues to be distributed with Unix systems because the requirements to use this editor are very minimal, and thus it is useful in dire recovery scenarios when all other editors may fail because their required libraries are not available.)

Sed is shell independent; it works with whatever shell you want to use it with. Because the default shell on most systems is Bash, the examples here are based on the Bash shell.

Sed can be ugly and frightening, but it is also quite powerful. Maybe you've seen some unintelligible, scary sed, such as the following line, and are wary of learning it because it looks like gibberish:

```
sed '/\n/!G;s/\(.\)\(.*\n\)/&\2\1/;//D;s/.//' myfile.txt
```

Even someone who knows sed well would have to puzzle over this line for a while before they understood that this reversed the order of every character in every line of `myfile.txt`, effectively creating a mirror image of the file. This line makes most people's heads spin. But don't worry. I'll start off with the basics, giving you a strong foundation so that you'll no longer find sed frightening and unintelligible.

sed Versions

Sed is a brick-and-mortar Unix command. It comes standard with nearly every Unix that exists, including Linux and Mac OS X, and it generally does not need to be installed, as it is such an essential shell command. However, it is possible that some systems don't ship with sed or come with a version that doesn't have the same features as others.

In fact, there is a dizzying array of sed implementations. There are free versions, shareware versions, and commercial versions. Different versions may have different options, and some of the examples in this chapter, especially the more advanced ones, may not work as presented with every version.

The most common version is arguably GNU sed, currently at revision 4.1.2. This version is used in the examples throughout this chapter. The GNU sed has a number of extensions that the POSIX sed does not have, making things that used to be difficult much simpler. If you need multibyte support for Japanese characters, there is a BSD implementation that offers those extensions. There is a version of sed called ssed (super-sed) that has more features than GNU sed and is based on the GNU sed code-base. There are versions of sed that are designed for constrained environments so they are small and fast (minised), versions that can be plugged into the Apache web server (mod_sed), and color versions of sed (csed). Most implementations will do the basics of what I cover here, so it is not necessary that you have GNU sed; however, you may find that the extensions that GNU sed offers will make your life easier.

Mac OS X comes with the BSD version of sed; GNU/Linux tends to distribute GNU sed. If your operating system is something else, you will be able to find a version of sed that works for you. The sed Frequently Asked Questions has an entire section devoted to the different versions of sed and where you can find one that works for your operating system (see http://sed.sourceforge.net/sedfaq2.html#s2.2).

Not all sed implementations are without cost. Commercial versions of sed are available, useful because many of them include support or provide sed for an esoteric or outdated operating system. Aside from that reason, they don't offer much more than GNU sed, probably have fewer features, and do not adhere as strictly to POSIX standards.

Sed is generally found at /bin/sed or /usr/bin/sed.

To see what version you have on your system, type the following command:

```
$ sed --version
GNU sed version 4.1.2
Copyright (C) 2003 Free Software Foundation, Inc.
This is free software; see the source for copying conditions.  There is NO
warranty; not even for MERCHANTABILITY or FITNESS FOR A PARTICULAR PURPOSE,
to the extent permitted by law.
```

If this doesn't work, try just typing sed by itself on the command line to see if you get anything at all. You may have to specify /bin/sed or /usr/bin/sed. If the --version argument is not recognized by your system, you are not running GNU sed. In that case, try the following command to get the current version number:

```
$ strings /bin/sed | grep -i ver
```

Installing sed

If you find that you don't have any version of sed installed, I recommend getting a version targeted for your operating system or the one directly from GNU. Mac OS X comes with a BSD version of sed, but you can easily install the GNU version through fink (http://fink.sourceforge.net/). On Debian GNU/Linux you can install sed as root by typing apt-get install sed.

Installing GNU sed by hand is not very difficult. The process is even less difficult if you have a system that already has another version of sed installed, as the GNU sed installation requires some form of sed installed to install itself. This sounds like a chicken-and-egg problem, but the GNU sed provides the necessary bootstrap sed as part of the installation to resolve this. You can get the latest .tar.gz file of GNU sed from ftp://ftp.gnu.org/pub/gnu/sed/. After you have obtained the sed tar, you uncompress it as you would any normal tar file:

```
$ tar -zxf sed-4.1.2.tar.gz
$ cd sed-4.1.2
```

Read the README file that is included with the source for specific instructions.

Bootstrap Installation

If you are building sed on a system that has no preexisting version of sed, you need to follow a bootstrap procedure outlined in README.boot. (If you have the BSD version of sed, you won't need to do this and can skip to the section Configuring and Installing sed.) This is because the process of making sed requires sed itself. The standard GNU autoconf configure script uses sed to determine system-dependent variables and to create Makefiles.

To bootstrap the building of sed, you run the shell script bootstrap.sh. This attempts to build a basic version of sed that works for the configure script. This version of sed is not fully functional and should not be used typically for anything other than bootstrapping the build process.

You should see output like the following when you run bootstrap.sh:

```
$ sh ./bootstrap.sh
Creating basic config.h...
+ rm -f 'lib/*.o' 'sed/*.o' sed/sed
+ cd lib
+ rm -f regex.h
+ cc -DHAVE_CONFIG_H -I.. -I. -c alloca.c
```

It continues building and may report a number of compiler warnings. Don't worry about these; however, if you get errors and the bootstrap version of sed fails to build, you will need to edit the config.h header file that was created for your system. Read the README.boot file and the comments that are contained in the config.h file to determine how to solve this. On most systems, however, this bootstrap version of sed should build fine.

Once the build has completed, you need to install the bootstrapped version of sed somewhere in your $PATH so you can build the full version. To do this, simply copy the sed binary that was built in the sed directory to somewhere in your $PATH. In the following example you create the bin directory in your home directory, append that path to your existing $PATH environment variable, and then copy the sed binary that was created in the bootstrap procedure into your $HOME/bin directory. This will make this version of sed available for the remainder of the build process.

```
$ mkdir $HOME/bin
$ export PATH=$PATH:$HOME/bin
$ cp sed/sed $HOME/bin
```

Configuring and Installing sed

If you already have a version of sed installed on your system, you don't need to bootstrap the installation but can simply use the following command to configure sed:

```
$ sh ./configure
checking for a BSD-compatible install... /usr/bin/install -c
checking whether build environment is sane... yes
checking for gawk... gawk
checking whether make sets $(MAKE)... yes
checking for gcc... gcc
```

This will continue to run through the GNU autoconf configuration, analyzing your system for various utilities, variables, and parameters that need to be set or exist on your system before you can compile sed. This can take some time before it finishes. If this succeeds, you can continue with compiling sed itself. If it doesn't, you will need to resolve the configuration problem before proceeding.

To compile sed, simply issue a make command:

```
$ make
make  all-recursive
make[1]: Entering directory `/home/micah/working/sed-4.1.2'
Making all in intl
make[2]: Entering directory `/home/micah/working/sed-4.1.2/intl'
```

This will continue to compile sed, which shouldn't take too long. On my system the configuration took longer than the compile. If this succeeds, you can install the newly compiled sed simply by issuing the make install command as root:

```
$ su
Password:
# make install
```

Sed will be put in the default locations in your file system. By default, make install installs all the files in /usr/local/bin, /usr/local/lib, and so on. You can specify an installation prefix other than /usr/local using --prefix when running configure; for instance, sh ./configure --prefix=$HOME will make sed so that it will install in your home directory.

> **Warning! Be very careful that you do not overwrite your system-supplied sed, if it exists. Some underlying systems may depend on that version, and replacing it with something other than what the vendor supplied could result in unexpected behavior. Installing into /usr/local or into your personal home directory is perfectly safe.**

How sed Works

Because sed is a *stream* editor, it does its work on a stream of data it receives from stdin, such as through a pipe, writing its results as a stream of data on stdout (often just your screen). You can redirect this output to a file if that is what you want to do (see Chapter 8 for details on redirecting). Sed doesn't typically modify an original input file; instead you send the contents of your file through a pipe to be processed by sed. This means that you don't need to have a file on the disk with the data you want changed; this is particularly useful if you have data coming from another process rather than already written in a file.

Invoking sed

Before you get started with some of the examples that follow, you will need some data to work with. The /etc/passwd file, available on all Unix derivatives, contains some useful data to parse with sed. Everyone will have a slightly different /etc/passwd file, so your results may vary slightly. The output that is shown in the following examples and exercises will be based on the following lines from my /etc/passwd file; you can copy this and save it or download it from the Wrox web site.

If for some reason your system's version of /etc/passwd produces unrecognizably different output from the examples, try using this version instead. If you use this version instead of the file on your system, you will need to change the path in each example from /etc/passwd to the specific location where you put this file.

```
root:x:0:0:root user:/root:/bin/sh
daemon:x:1:1:daemon:/usr/sbin:/bin/sh
bin:x:2:2:bin:/bin:/bin/sh
sys:x:3:3:sys:/dev:/bin/sh
sync:x:4:65534:sync:/bin:/bin/sync
games:x:5:60:games:/usr/games:/bin/sh
man:x:6:12:man:/var/cache/man:/bin/sh
mail:x:8:8:mail:/var/mail:/bin/sh
news:x:9:9:news:/var/spool/news:/bin/sh
backup:x:34:34:backup:/var/backups:/bin/sh
```

As mentioned previously, sed can be invoked by sending data through a pipe to it. Take a look at how this works by piping your password file through sed using the following command. You should see output similar to that shown here, which lists the command usage description for sed:

```
$ cat /etc/passwd | sed
Usage: sed [OPTION]... {script-only-if-no-other-script} [input-file]...

  -n, --quiet, --silent
                 suppress automatic printing of pattern space
  -e script, --expression=script
                 add the script to the commands to be executed
  -f script-file, --file=script-file
                 add the contents of script-file to the commands to be executed
  -i[SUFFIX], --in-place[=SUFFIX]
                 edit files in place (makes backup if extension supplied)
  -l N, --line-length=N
                 specify the desired line-wrap length for the `l' command
  --posix
                 disable all GNU extensions.
  -r, --regexp-extended
                 use extended regular expressions in the script.
  -s, --separate
                 consider files as separate rather than as a single continuous
                 long stream.
```

```
     -u, --unbuffered
                   load minimal amounts of data from the input files and flush
                   the output buffers more often
         --help    display this help and exit
         --version output version information and exit

     If no -e, --expression, -f, or --file option is given, then the first
     non-option argument is taken as the sed script to interpret.  All
     remaining arguments are names of input files; if no input files are
     specified, then the standard input is read.

     E-mail bug reports to: bonzini@gnu.org .
     Be sure to include the word ``sed'' somewhere in the ``Subject:'' field.
```

Many of the different sed options you see here are covered later in this chapter. The important thing to note right now is that because you did not tell sed what to do with the data you sent to it, sed felt that you needed to be reminded about how to use it.

This command dumps the contents of /etc/passwd to sed through the pipe into sed's pattern space. The *pattern space* is the internal work buffer that sed uses to do its work, like a workbench where you lay out what you are going to work on.

Simply putting something on a workbench doesn't do anything at all; you need to know what you are going to do with it. Similarly, dumping data into sed's pattern space doesn't do anything at all; you need to tell sed to do something with it. Sed expects to always do something with its pattern space, and if you don't tell it what to do, it considers that an invocation error. Because you incorrectly invoked sed in this example, you found that it spit out to your screen its command usage.

Editing Commands

Sed expects you to provide an editing command. An editing command is what you want sed to do to the data in the pattern space. The following Try It Out example uses the delete-line editing command, known to sed as d. This command will delete each line in the pattern buffer.

Try It Out   Deleting All Lines with sed

Invoke sed again, but this time tell sed to use the editing command delete line, denoted by the single letter d:

```
$ cat /etc/passwd | sed 'd'
$
```

How It Works

Because sed was invoked properly this time with an editing command, it didn't give the command usage. In fact, it didn't print anything at all. What did happen? This command sent the entire contents of the /etc/passwd file through the pipe to sed. Sed took the first line of /etc/passwd and read it into its pattern buffer. It then performed the delete line editing command on the contents of its pattern buffer and then printed out the pattern buffer. Because the editing command deleted the line in the pattern buffer, the pattern buffer was empty, so when sed printed the pattern buffer, nothing was printed. Sed then read the next line of the /etc/password file and repeated this process until it reached the end of the file. Sed effectively read in each line to the pattern buffer, deleted the line in the buffer, and then printed the empty buffer. This results in printing nothing over and over, not even a new line, so it appears as if nothing happens at all, but internally there is work happening.

Keep in mind that the original /etc/passwd file was not altered at all. Sed only read the contents of the file as input; you did not tell it to write to the file, only read from it. The results of the editing commands on each line are printed to standard output. In this case, nothing was printed to the screen because you used the d editing command to delete every line in the file.

Another important aspect of sed to learn from this example is that it operates line by line. The editing command was not applied to the entire file all at once. Whatever editing command you tell sed to perform will be done to each line in the pattern buffer, in the order that the lines are placed into the buffer.

The editing command was surrounded with single quotes. This was not absolutely necessary, but it is a good habit to get into. This same example could be written without the single quotes and the same output would result (in this case nothing). The singles quotes are useful to explicitly delineate your editing command. Without the single quote, some instances of editing commands might be incorrectly parsed and expanded by the shell. Without the single quotes, the shell may try to change your editing command unexpectedly to something other than you intended, so it's a good habit to add them routinely.

This example piped the contents of the file /etc/passwd to sed. This is a perfectly valid way of using sed, taking input from standard input and sending the output to standard output. However, the next set of examples shows a few different ways that sed can be invoked, to the same effect.

Invoking sed with the -e Flag

Instead of invoking sed by sending a file to it through a pipe, you can instruct sed to read the data from a file, as in the following example.

Try It Out   Reading Data from a File

The following command does exactly the same thing as the previous Try It Out, without the cat command:

```
$ sed -e 'd' /etc/passwd
$
```

How It Works

Invoking sed in this manner explicitly defines the editing command as a sed script to be executed on the input file /etc/passwd. The script is simply a one-character editing command, but it could be much larger, as you'll see in later examples. In this case, input is taken from the file /etc/passwd, and standard output is the screen.

Output from sed is to standard output, which is generally the screen, but you can change this by redirecting the output to a file, using standard output redirection in the shell. Although it is useful to see the output of your sed commands on the screen, often you will want to save the output to a file, rather than simply viewing the results. Because the results of your sed commands are sent to standard output, you simply need to use your shell's I/O redirection capabilities to send standard output to a file. To do this, you use the redirection operator > to place the output into a file, as in the next Try It Out.

Chapter 8 covers redirection of standard output.

Try It Out   Redirection

The following example redirects the standard output from the sed command into the file called new-passwd in the /tmp directory:

```
$ sed -e 'd' /etc/passwd > /tmp/newpasswd
$
```

How It Works

Because this command deletes all the lines in the file, this results in an empty file.

> **Be careful not to redirect the standard out from your sed commands to the original file, or you will cause problems. You may want to actually replace the original file with the results of your sed command, but do not use this command to do so, because the >redirection operator will overwrite the file before adding the results of your sed command. It is important to make sure your sed commands will produce the results you want before you overwrite your original file!**

Typically, what you will do with sed is to redirect your output to a new file. If everything is fine, then you can replace the old file with your new one. GNU sed has an option that allows you to perform your sed operations in-line on the file itself; however, this is dangerous and should be used with care.

The -n, --quiet, and --silent Flags

As you saw in the preceding examples, sed by default prints out the pattern space at the end of processing its editing commands and then repeats that process.

The -n flag disables this automatic printing so that sed will instead print lines only when it is explicitly told to do so with the p command.

The p command simply means to *print* the pattern space. If sed prints out the pattern space by default, why would you want to specify it? The p command is generally used only in conjunction with the -n flag; otherwise, you will end up printing the pattern space twice, as demonstrated in the following Try It Out.

Extra Printing

Type the following command to see what sed will output when you specify the p command without the -n flag:

```
$ cat /etc/passwd | sed 'p' | head -10
root:x:0:0:root user:/root:/bin/sh
root:x:0:0:root user:/root:/bin/sh
daemon:x:1:1:daemon:/usr/sbin:/bin/sh
daemon:x:1:1:daemon:/usr/sbin:/bin/sh
bin:x:2:2:bin:/bin:/bin/sh
bin:x:2:2:bin:/bin:/bin/sh
sys:x:3:3:sys:/dev:/bin/sh
sys:x:3:3:sys:/dev:/bin/sh
sync:x:4:65534:sync:/bin:/bin/sync
sync:x:4:65534:sync:/bin:/bin/sync
games:x:5:60:games:/usr/games:/bin/sh
games:x:5:60:games:/usr/games:/bin/sh
man:x:6:12:man:/var/cache/man:/bin/sh
man:x:6:12:man:/var/cache/man:/bin/sh
mail:x:8:8:mail:/var/mail:/bin/sh
mail:x:8:8:mail:/var/mail:/bin/sh
news:x:9:9:news:/var/spool/news:/bin/sh
news:x:9:9:news:/var/spool/news:/bin/sh
backup:x:34:34:backup:/var/backups:/bin/sh
backup:x:34:34:backup:/var/backups:/bin/sh
```

Type the same command, this time specifying the -n flag:

```
$ cat /etc/passwd | sed -n 'p' | head -10
root:x:0:0:root user:/root:/bin/sh
daemon:x:1:1:daemon:/usr/sbin:/bin/sh
bin:x:2:2:bin:/bin:/bin/sh
sys:x:3:3:sys:/dev:/bin/sh
sync:x:4:65534:sync:/bin:/bin/sync
games:x:5:60:games:/usr/games:/bin/sh
man:x:6:12:man:/var/cache/man:/bin/sh
lp:x:7:7:lp:/var/spool/lpd:/bin/sh
mail:x:8:8:mail:/var/mail:/bin/sh
news:x:9:9:news:/var/spool/news:/bin/sh
backup:x:34:34:backup:/var/backups:/bin/sh
```

How It Works

As you can see in the output from the first command, if you specify the p editing command without the -n flag, duplicate lines are printed. In the second example, however, there are no duplicate lines printed because sed was instructed to be silent and print only the lines you specified (in this case, all of them).

The -n flag has a couple of synonyms; if you find it easier to remember --quiet or --silent, these flags do the same thing.

These are the basic methods for invoking sed. Knowing these will allow you to move forward and use sed in a more practical way. When you are more familiar with some of sed's editing capabilities, you'll be ready for the more advanced methods covered in the Advanced sed Invocation section of this chapter.

sed Errors

It is easy to incorrectly specify your sed editing commands, as the syntax requires attention to detail. If you miss one character, you can produce vastly different results than expected or find yourself faced with a rather cryptic error message.

Sed is not friendly with its error messages, and unfortunately, different versions of sed have different cryptic errors for the same problems. GNU sed tends to be more helpful in indicating what was missing, but it is often very difficult for sed to identify the source of the error, and so it may spit out something that doesn't help much in fixing the problem. I explained in the previous section how GNU sed will output its command usage if you incorrectly invoke it, and you may get other strange errors as well.

Selecting Lines to Operate On

Sed also understands something called addresses. *Addresses* are either particular locations in a file or a range where a particular editing command should be applied. When sed encounters no addresses, it performs its operations on every line in the file.

The following command adds a basic address to the sed command you've been using:

```
$ cat /etc/passwd | sed '1d' |more
daemon:x:1:1:daemon:/usr/sbin:/bin/sh
bin:x:2:2:bin:/bin:/bin/sh
sys:x:3:3:sys:/dev:/bin/sh
sync:x:4:65534:sync:/bin:/bin/sync
games:x:5:60:games:/usr/games:/bin/sh
man:x:6:12:man:/var/cache/man:/bin/sh
mail:x:8:8:mail:/var/mail:/bin/sh
news:x:9:9:news:/var/spool/news:/bin/sh
backup:x:34:34:backup:/var/backups:/bin/sh
```

Notice that the number 1 is added before the delete edit command. This tells sed to perform the editing command on the first line of the file. In this example, sed will delete the first line of /etc/password and print the rest of the file. Because your /etc/passwd file may have so many lines in it that the top of the file scrolls by, you can send the result to the pager more. Notice that the following line is missing from the output:

```
root:x:0:0:root user:/root:/bin/sh
```

Most Unix systems have the root user as the first entry in the password file, but after performing this command you will see the entire password file, with the root user line missing from the top. If you replaced the number 1 with a 2, only the second line is removed.

Address Ranges

So what if you want to remove more than one line from a file? Do you have to tell sed every single line you want to remove? Fortunately not; you can specify a range of lines that you want to be removed by telling sed a starting line and an ending line to perform your editing commands on, as in the following Try It Out.

Address Ranges

Type the following command to see how an address range works with sed:

```
$ cat /etc/passwd | sed '1,5d'
games:x:5:60:games:/usr/games:/bin/sh
man:x:6:12:man:/var/cache/man:/bin/sh
mail:x:8:8:mail:/var/mail:/bin/sh
news:x:9:9:news:/var/spool/news:/bin/sh
backup:x:34:34:backup:/var/backups:/bin/sh
```

How It Works

When you specify two numbers, separated by commas, sed performs the editing command specified on the range that starts with the first number and ends with the second. This example will delete the first five lines of the file.

You do not need to start deleting from the first line of the file but can set an address range for any range within the file, as long as it is in chronological order. `4,10d` will delete the range 4-10, for example.

What happens if you specify a reverse chronological order range?

Try It Out **Reverse Address Ranges**

Try specifying the address range `'10,4d'` to see what happens:

```
$ cat /etc/passwd | sed '10,4d'
root:x:0:0:root user:/root:/bin/sh
daemon:x:1:1:daemon:/usr/sbin:/bin/sh
bin:x:2:2:bin:/bin:/bin/sh
sys:x:3:3:sys:/dev:/bin/sh
sync:x:4:65534:sync:/bin:/bin/sync
games:x:5:60:games:/usr/games:/bin/sh
man:x:6:12:man:/var/cache/man:/bin/sh
mail:x:8:8:mail:/var/mail:/bin/sh
news:x:9:9:news:/var/spool/news:/bin/sh
```

How It Works

In this example, sed reads in each line individually, in order, and applies the editing command to it. Because you've told it to start deleting from line 10, it reads in each line into the pattern buffer until it has counted up to 10, and then it deletes that line. Sed then looks for the range 9-4 to delete, but it won't see those lines after it has reached line 10. Sed does not back up in its processing to look for those lines, so line 10 is deleted, but nothing else.

Now that you have a better understanding of how sed applies its commands to its pattern buffer, what do you think sed does if you specify a line number or range that doesn't exist in the file? Sed dutifully looks for the lines that you specify to apply its command, but it never finds them, so you get the entire file printed out with nothing omitted.

If you forget to complete your address range, you receive an error from sed. The cryptic nature of sed's errors means that sed will tell you something is wrong, but not in a helpful way. For example, if you forgot the number *after* the comma, sed won't understand that you were trying to specify an address range and will complain about the comma:

```
$ cat /etc/passwd | sed '1,d'
sed: -e expression #1, char 3: unexpected `,'
```

If you forgot the number *before* the comma in your address range, sed thinks that you are trying to specify the comma as an editing command and tells you that there is no such command:

```
$ cat /etc/passwd | sed ',10d'
sed: -e expression #1, char 1: unknown command: `,'
```

You can also instruct sed to match an address line and certain numbers following that first match.

Suppose you want to match line 4 and the five lines following line 4. You do this by appending a plus sign before the second address number, as in the following command:

```
$ cat /etc/passwd | sed '4,+5d'
root:x:0:0:root:/root:/bin/sh
daemon:x:1:1:daemon:/usr/sbin:/bin/sh
bin:x:2:2:bin:/bin:/bin/sh
backup:x:34:34:backup:/var/backups:/bin/sh
```

This will match line 4 in the file, delete that line, continue to delete the next five lines, and then cease its deletion and print the rest.

Address Negation

By appending an exclamation mark at the end of any address specification, you negate that address match. To *negate* an address match means to match only those lines that do *not* match the address range.

Try It Out   **Address Negation**

Beginning with the previous example where you specified deleting the first five lines of the /etc/passwd file, you can simply negate that match to say that you want to keep the first ten lines and delete the rest. Type the following command to try this:

```
$ cat /etc/passwd | sed '1,5!d'
root:x:0:0:root user:/root:/bin/sh
daemon:x:1:1:daemon:/usr/sbin:/bin/sh
bin:x:2:2:bin:/bin:/bin/sh
sys:x:3:3:sys:/dev:/bin/sh
sync:x:4:65534:sync:/bin:/bin/sync
```

How It Works

Appending the exclamation mark to the address range 1,5 told sed to match everything *except* the first five lines and perform the deletion. Address negation also works for single-line addresses.

Address Steps

GNU sed has a feature called *address steps* that allows you to do things such as selecting every odd line, every third line, every fifth line, and so on.

Address steps are specified in the same way that you specify a delete range, except instead of using a comma to separate the numbers, you use a tilde (~). The number before the tilde is the number that you want the stepping to begin from. If you want to start stepping from the beginning of the file, you use the number 1. The number that follows the tilde is what is called the *step increment*. The step increment tells sed how many lines to step. The following Try It Outs provide examples of address steps.

Try It Out   Address Stepping

Suppose that you want to delete every third line in your file, beginning with the first line. Run the following command to use an address step to accomplish this:

```
$ cat /etc/passwd | sed '1~3d'
daemon:x:1:1:daemon:/usr/sbin:/bin/sh
bin:x:2:2:bin:/bin:/bin/sh
sync:x:4:65534:sync:/bin:/bin/sync
games:x:5:60:games:/usr/games:/bin/sh
mail:x:8:8:mail:/var/mail:/bin/sh
news:x:9:9:news:/var/spool/news:/bin/sh
```

How It Works

This deletes the first line, steps over the next three lines, and then deletes the fourth line. Sed continues applying this pattern until the end of the file.

Try It Out   More Address Stepping

If you want to start deleting every other line, starting with the second line, you can do so as follows:

```
$ cat /etc/passwd | sed '2~2d'
root:x:0:0:root user:/root:/bin/sh
bin:x:2:2:bin:/bin:/bin/sh
sync:x:4:65534:sync:/bin:/bin/sync
man:x:6:12:man:/var/cache/man:/bin/sh
news:x:9:9:news:/var/spool/news:/bin/sh
```

How It Works

This tells sed to delete the second line, step over the next line, delete the next line, and repeat until the end of the file is reached.

Substitution

This section introduces you to one of the more useful editing commands available in sed, the substitution command. This command is probably the most important command in sed and has a lot of options.

The substitution command, denoted by s, will substitute any string that you specify with any other string that you specify. To substitute one string with another, you need to have some way of telling sed where your first string ends and the substitution string begins. This is traditionally done by bookending the two strings with the forward slash (/) character.

Try It Out   Substitution

Type the following command to perform a basic literal string substitution, replacing the login name root with the reverse:

```
$ cat /etc/passwd | sed 's/root/toor/'
toor:x:0:0:root user:/root:/bin/sh
daemon:x:1:1:daemon:/usr/sbin:/bin/sh
bin:x:2:2:bin:/bin:/bin/sh
sys:x:3:3:sys:/dev:/bin/sh
sync:x:4:65534:sync:/bin:/bin/sync
games:x:5:60:games:/usr/games:/bin/sh
man:x:6:12:man:/var/cache/man:/bin/sh
mail:x:8:8:mail:/var/mail:/bin/sh
news:x:9:9:news:/var/spool/news:/bin/sh
backup:x:34:34:backup:/var/backups:/bin/sh
```

How It Works

This command substitutes the first occurrence on a line of the string root with the string toor. (Notice that this line uses the s editing command and not d.)

If you forget to specify the trailing slash to the sed command, you will get an error. GNU sed will tell you that there is an unterminated s command; other sed implementations will just say that your command is garbled:

```
$ cat /etc/passwd | sed 's/root/toor'
sed: command garbled: s/root/toor
```

It is very important to note that sed substitutes only the *first occurrence on a line*. If the string root occurs more than once on a line (which it does in the example file), only the *first* match will be replaced. Usually you want to replace every string in the file with the new one instead of just the first occurrence. To do this, you must tell sed to make the substitution globally, replacing every occurrence of the string on every line of the file. To tell sed to do a global substitution, add the letter g to the end of the command:

```
$ cat /etc/passwd | sed 's/root/toor/g'
toor:x:0:0:toor user:/toor:/bin/sh
daemon:x:1:1:daemon:/usr/sbin:/bin/sh
bin:x:2:2:bin:/bin:/bin/sh
sys:x:3:3:sys:/dev:/bin/sh
sync:x:4:65534:sync:/bin:/bin/sync
```

```
games:x:5:60:games:/usr/games:/bin/sh
man:x:6:12:man:/var/cache/man:/bin/sh
mail:x:8:8:mail:/var/mail:/bin/sh
news:x:9:9:news:/var/spool/news:/bin/sh
backup:x:34:34:backup:/var/backups:/bin/sh
```

Appending the g at the end of the substitution is passing a *flag* to the substitution command. The following section covers other substitution flags.

Substitution Flags

There are a number of other useful flags that can be passed in addition to the g flag, and you can specify more than one at a time.

The following is a full table of all the flags that can be used with the s substitution command.

Flag	Meaning
g	Replace all matches, not just the first match.
NUMBER	Replace only *NUMBER*th match.
p	If substitution was made, print pattern space.
w *FILENAME*	If substitution was made, write result to *FILENAME*. GNU sed additionally allows writing to /dev/stderr and /dev/stdout.
I or i	Match in a case-insensitive manner.
M or m	In addition to the normal behavior of the special regular expression characters ^ and $, this flag causes ^ to match the empty string after a newline and $ to match the empty string before a newline.

A useful flag to pass to a substitution command is i or its capital incarnation, I. Both indicate to sed to be case insensitive and match either the uppercase or lowercase of the characters you specify. If the /etc/passwd file had both the strings Root and root, the previous sed operation would match only the lowercase version. To get both throughout the entire file, you specify both the i flag and the g flag, as in the following example. Type the following sed substitution command:

```
$ cat /etc/passwd | sed 's/Root/toor/ig'
toor:x:0:0:toor user:/toor:/bin/sh
daemon:x:1:1:daemon:/usr/sbin:/bin/sh
bin:x:2:2:bin:/bin:/bin/sh
sys:x:3:3:sys:/dev:/bin/sh
sync:x:4:65534:sync:/bin:/bin/sync
games:x:5:60:games:/usr/games:/bin/sh
man:x:6:12:man:/var/cache/man:/bin/sh
mail:x:8:8:mail:/var/mail:/bin/sh
news:x:9:9:news:/var/spool/news:/bin/sh
backup:x:34:34:backup:/var/backups:/bin/sh
```

If you specify any number as a flag (NUMBER flag), this tells sed to act on the instance of the string that matched that number. The /etc/passwd file has three instances of the string root in the first line, so if you want to replace only the third match on, add the number 3 at the end of the substitution delimiter, as in the following:

```
$ cat /etc/passwd | sed 's/root/toor/3' |head -2
root:x:0:0:root user:/toor:/bin/sh
daemon:x:1:1:daemon:/usr/sbin:/bin/sh
```

With this command, sed searches for the third instance of the string root in the file /etc/passwd and substitutes the string toor. (I piped the output through the Unix command head with the flag -2 to limit the output to the first two lines for brevity.)

The POSIX standard doesn't specify what should happen when the NUMBER flag is specified with the g flag, and there is no wide agreement on how this should be interpreted amongst the different sed implementations. The GNU implementation of sed ignores the matches before the NUMBER and then matches and replaces all matches from that NUMBER on.

Using an Alternative String Separator

You may find yourself having to do a substitution on a string that includes the forward slash character. In this case, you can specify a different separator by providing the designated character after the s. Suppose you want to change the home directory of the root user in the passwd file. It is currently set to /root, and you want to change it to /toor. To do this, you specify a different separator to sed. I use a colon (:) in this example:

```
$ cat /etc/passwd | sed 's:/root:/toor:' | head -2
root:x:0:0:root user:/toor:/bin/sh
daemon:x:1:1:daemon:/usr/sbin:/bin/sh
```

Notice this is exactly like doing string substitution with the slash character as a separator; the first string to look for is /root; the replacement is /toor.

It is possible to use the string separator character in your string, but sed can get ugly quickly, so you should try to avoid it by using a different string separator if possible. If you find yourself in the situation where you do need to use the string separator, you can do so by escaping the character. To *escape* a character means to put a special character in front of the string separator to indicate that it should be used as part of the string, rather than the separator itself. In sed you escape the string separator by putting a backslash before it, like so:

```
$ cat /etc/passwd | sed 's/\/root/\/toor/' | head -2
root:x:0:0:root user:/toor:/bin/sh
daemon:x:1:1:daemon:/usr/sbin:/bin/sh
```

This performs the exact search and replace as the example before, this time using the slash as a string separator, escaping the slash that appears in the string /root so it is interpreted properly. If you do not escape this slash, you will have an error in your command, because there will be too many slashes presented to sed and it will spit out an error. The error will vary depending on where in the process sed encounters it, but it will be another example of sed's rather cryptic errors:

```
sed: -e expression #1, char 10: unknown option to `s'
```

You can use any separator that you want, but by convention people use the slash separator until they need to use something else, as in this case.

String substitution is not limited to single words. The string you specify is limited only by the string separator that you use, so it is possible to substitute a whole phrase, if you like. The following command replaces the string `root user` with `absolutely power corrupts`:

```
$ cat /etc/passwd | sed 's/:root user/:absolutely power corrupts/g' |head -2
root:x:0:0:absolutely power corrupts:/root:/bin/sh
daemon:x:1:1:daemon:/usr/sbin:/bin/sh
```

It is often useful to replace strings of text with nothing. This is a funny way of saying deleting words or phrases. For example, to remove a word you simply replace it with an empty string, as in the following Try It Out.

Try It Out   Replacing with Empty Space

Use an empty substitution string to delete the `root` string from the `/etc/passwd` file entirely:

```
$ cat /etc/passwd | sed 's/root//g' | head -2
:x:0:0::/:/bin/sh
daemon:x:1:1:daemon:/usr/sbin:/bin/sh
```

How It Works

The `'s/root//g'` tells sed to replace all instances of `root` with the empty replacement string that follows the separator.

The same goes for strings with spaces in them. If you want to remove the `root user` string, you can replace it with an empty string:

```
$ cat /etc/passwd | sed '/root user//g' | head -2
root:x:0:0::/root:/bin/sh
daemon:x:1:1:daemon:/usr/sbin:/bin/sh
```

Address Substitution

As with deletion, it is possible to perform substitution only on specific lines or on a specific range of lines if you specify an address or an address range to the command.

If you want to substitute the string `sh` with the string `quiet` only on line 10, you can specify it as follows:

```
$ cat /etc/passwd | sed '10s/sh/quiet/g'
root:x:0:0:root user:/root:/bin/sh
daemon:x:1:1:daemon:/usr/sbin:/bin/sh
bin:x:2:2:bin:/bin:/bin/sh
```

```
sys:x:3:3:sys:/dev:/bin/sh
sync:x:4:65534:sync:/bin:/bin/sync
games:x:5:60:games:/usr/games:/bin/sh
man:x:6:12:man:/var/cache/man:/bin/sh
mail:x:8:8:mail:/var/mail:/bin/sh
news:x:9:9:news:/var/spool/news:/bin/sh
backup:x:34:34:backup:/var/backups:/bin/quiet
```

This is just like the line-specific delete command, but you are performing a substitution instead of a deletion. As you can see from the output of this command, the substitution replaces the sh string with quiet only on line 10.

Similarly, to do an address range substitution, you could do something like the following:

```
$ cat /etc/passwd | sed '1,5s/sh/quiet/g'
root:x:0:0:root user:/root:/bin/quiet
daemon:x:1:1:daemon:/usr/sbin:/bin/quiet
bin:x:2:2:bin:/bin:/bin/quiet
sys:x:3:3:sys:/dev:/bin/quiet
sync:x:4:65534:sync:/bin:/bin/sync
games:x:5:60:games:/usr/games:/bin/sh
man:x:6:12:man:/var/cache/man:/bin/sh
mail:x:8:8:mail:/var/mail:/bin/sh
news:x:9:9:news:/var/spool/news:/bin/sh
backup:x:34:34:backup:/var/backups:/bin/sh
```

As you can see from the output, the first five lines had the string sh changed to quiet, but the rest of the lines were left untouched.

Advanced sed Invocation

You often want to make more than one substitution or deletion or do more complex editing using sed. To use sed most productively requires knowing how to invoke sed with more than one editing command at a time.

You can specify multiple editing commands on the command line in three different ways, explained in the following Try It Out. The editing commands are concatenated and are executed in the order that they appear. You must specify the commands in appropriate order, or your script will produce unexpected results.

Try It Out   Advanced sed Invocation

This Try It Out shows you three ways to use multiple commands to produce the same output. Create a simple text file called stream.txt, using your favorite editor, and put the following lines in it:

```
Imagine a quaint bubbling stream of cool mountain water filled with rainbow trout
and elephants drinking iced tea.
```

The first way to specify multiple editing commands on the command line is to separate each editing command with a semicolon. To replace the trout with catfish and remove the elephants, try the following command, using semicolons to separate editing commands:

```
$ cat stream.txt | sed 's/trout/catfish/; s/ and elephants//'
```

The second way to specify multiple editing commands on the command line is to specify multiple -e arguments. Try the following command on the stream.txt file:

```
$ cat stream.txt | sed -e 's/trout/catfish/' -e 's/ and elephants//'
```

The third way to specify multiple editing commands on the command line is to use the multiline capability of the Bash shell. Bash knows when you have not terminated a single quote and prompts you for more input until you enter the completing single quote.

To do the example in this way, try typing the following in a Bash shell. After the first single quote, press Enter (Return) as follows:

```
$ cat stream.txt | sed '
> s/trout/catfish/
> s/ and elephants//'
```

How It Works

Each of the three examples in this Try It Out results in the following text:

```
Imagine a quaint bubbling stream of cool mountain water filled with rainbow catfish
drinking iced tea.
```

In the first example, two separate editing commands, separated by semicolons, were specified to one sed command. The first command performed a substitution of the string trout with the replacement catfish, and then a semicolon was placed after the trailing substitution delimiter. The second editing command follows immediately afterward; it replaces the string and elephants with an empty string, effectively deleting that string. The two substitution commands are grouped together, surrounded by the single quotes. Each editing command supplied is performed on each input line in the order they appear; this means that the first substitution is performed, and the resulting text is then provided to the next command for the next substitution. The second command is not run before the first, and the input that the second line receives is always the processed data from the first command. The data progresses in a sequential manner through all the supplied editing commands until it reaches the end.

The second example contains two -e arguments, each individual editing command paired with its own -e flag. Each editing command passed on the command line is performed sequentially on each input line, in the same manner as it is done in the first example.

You can invoke sed using both the semicolon-separated method of the first example and the multiple -e argument of the second example together, as many times as you require. Sed simply concatenates all the commands and script files together in the order they appear. So the first command or commands specified will be executed first, followed by the next, until there are no more commands to execute. The third example, using the multiline capability, results in the exact same output as the previous two examples. It is simply a different way of invoking sed. Korn, Bourne, and zsh all perform in this manner; however, the C shell does not work this way.

These three methods are ways to invoke sed by specifying editing commands on the command line. The other method of invoking sed is to specify a file that contains all the commands that you want sed to run. This is useful when your commands become cumbersome on the command line or if you want to save the commands for use in the future. If you make a mistake on the command line, it can be confusing to try to fix that mistake, but if your commands are specified in a file you can simply re-edit that file to fix your mistake.

To specify the file containing the editing commands you want sed to perform, you simply pass the -f flag followed immediately by the file name containing the editing commands, as in the following Try It Out.

Try It Out   sed Scripts

Create a text file called water.sed with your favorite editor. Place the following text in the file, and then save and exit your editor:

```
s/trout/catfish/
s/ and elephants//
```

As you can see, this file consists of two editing commands and nothing else.

Using the stream.txt file from the previous examples, execute the following command:

```
$ sed -f water.sed stream.txt
Imagine a quaint bubbling stream of cool mountain water filled with rainbow catfish
drinking iced tea.
```

How It Works

This executes the commands you saved in the file water.sed on the stream.txt file. The water.sed file simply contains the editing commands in the order that they should be executed. This produces the same results as the three preceding examples.

As your sed scripts become more complicated, you will find it more and more useful to put them into files and execute them this way.

The comment Command

As in most programming languages, it's useful to include comments in your script to remember what different parts do or to provide information for others who might be trying to decipher your script. To add a comment in a sed script, you do what you do in other shell scripting environments: precede the line with the # character. The comment then continues until the next newline.

There are two caveats with the comment command: the first is that comments are not portable to non-POSIX versions of sed. If someone is running a version of sed that is not POSIX-conformant, their sed may not like comments anywhere in your sed script except on the very first line.

The second caveat with the comment command is that if the first two characters of your sed script are #n, the -n (no auto-print) option is automatically enabled. If you find yourself in the situation where your comment on the first line should start with the n character, simply use a capital N or place a space between the # and the n:

```
# Not going to enable -n
```

```
#Not going to enable -n
```

```
#no doubt, this will enable -n
```

The insert, append, and change Commands

The insert and append commands are almost as harmless as the comment command. Both of these commands simply output the text you provide. Insert (i) outputs the text immediately, before the next command, and append (a) outputs the text immediately afterward.

A classic example that illustrates these commands is converting a standard text file into an HTML file. HTML files have a few tags at the beginning of the files, followed by the body text and then the closing tags at the end. Using i and a, you can create a simple sed script that will add the opening and closing tags to any text file.

Try It Out   Inserting and Appending

Place the following sed program into a file called txt2html.sed:

```
#! /bin/sed -f

1 i\
<html>\
<head><title>Converted with sed</title></head>\
<body bgcolor="#ffffff">\
<pre>\

$ a\
</pre>\
</body>\
</html>
```

Now take a text file (such as stream.txt) and run it through this sed script:

```
$ cat stream.txt | sed -f txt2html.sed
<html>
<head><title>Converted with sed</title></head>
<body bgcolor="#ffffff">
<pre>

Imagine a quaint bubbling stream of cool mountain water filled with rainbow trout
and elephants drinking iced tea.
</pre>
</body>
</html>
```

How It Works

You will see that sed inserted, starting at line 1, the four opening HTML tags that indicate that the file is HTML, and set the `<title>` and the background color. Then your text file is printed, and at the end of your file (denoted by the $), sed appended the closing HTML tags.

The insert and append commands add information only. On the other hand, the change (c) command replaces the current line in the pattern space with the text that you specify. The only difference between the substitute command (s) and the change command (c) is that substitute works on a character-by-character basis, whereas the change command changes the entire line. It works much like substitute but with broader strokes; it completely replaces one thing for another regardless of the context.

To illustrate this, change your `water.sed` script to the following and name it `noelephants.sed`:

```
s/trout/catfish/
/ and elephants/ c\Although you can substitute trout with catfish, there is no
substitute for elephants, so we cannot offer this item.
```

Run this as you did previously in the sed Scripts Try It Out:

```
$ cat stream.txt | sed -f noelephants.sed
Although you can substitute trout with catfish, there is no substitute for
elephants, so we cannot offer this item.
```

Although the first substitution was run, changing the `trout` string to `catfish`, the change command replaces the entire line. When substitute was used in the earlier example, you matched the string `and elephants` and replaced it with an empty string. In this example, you again matched the string `and elephants` but this time used the change command, and instead of substituting, the entire original line was modified.

Advanced Addressing

Knowing exactly where in your file you want to perform your sed operations is not always possible. It's not so easy to know the exact line number or range of numbers you want the command(s) to act upon. Fortunately, sed allows you to apply your knowledge of regular expressions (*regexps*) to make your addressing much more powerful and useful.

In the Selecting Lines to Operate On section, you learned how to specify addresses and address ranges by specifying a line number or range of line numbers. When addresses are specified in this manner, the supplied editing command affects only the lines that you explicitly denoted in the address.

The same behavior is found when you use regular expressions in addresses; only those addresses that match the regular expression will have the editing command applied to them.

Regular Expression Addresses

To specify an address with a regular expression, you enclose the regular expression in slashes. The following example shows the top of my /etc/syslog.conf file as an example (yours may be slightly different):

```
#   /etc/syslog.conf      Configuration file for syslogd.
#
#                          For more information see syslog.conf(5)
#                          manpage.

# First some standard logfiles.  Log by facility.

auth,authpriv.*                  /var/log/auth.log
```

As you can see, a number of comments are in the file, followed by a few spaces and then some lines that are used for syslog. The following Try It Out shows you how to use a simple regular expression to remove all the comments in this file.

Try It Out   Regular Expression Addresses

Take a look at your /etc/syslog.conf file to see the comments and then perform the following command to remove them with a regular expression:

```
$ cat /etc/syslog.conf | sed '/^#/d'


auth,authpriv.*                  /var/log/auth.log
```

Notice how the blank lines are also printed.

How It Works

To understand this command, you need to look at each piece. The first part looks a little bit like a cartoon character swearing, /^#/. This is the address that you are specifying, and in this case it is a regular expression address. (You can tell this because the address is surrounded by slashes.) Directly following the trailing slash is the familiar d editing command that says to delete. The editing command you specify will be applied only to lines that match the pattern you specify in the regular expression.

The ^ character means to match the beginning of the line. Given that, you can extract this regular expression address to mean "match the # character if it is at the beginning of the line." Sed applies the editing command—in this case, the delete command—to every match it finds.

The result of this command is that every line beginning with the # character is deleted and the rest are printed out.

A good way to see exactly what a regular expression will actually match is to do things the other way around. Instead of deleting all the matches, print only the matches, and delete everything else. By using the -n flag to tell sed to not print anything, unless you explicitly tell it to, combined with the p flag, sed prints only the matches it finds and deletes all the other lines:

```
sed -n -e '/regexp/p' /path/to/file
```

or

```
cat /path/to/file | sed -n '/regexp/p'
```

Note the p command is specified after the regular expression, rather than the d.

Try It Out   **Inverted Regular Expression Match**

Try the sed regular expression command from the previous Try It Out, this time printing only the matches and deleting everything else:

```
$ cat /etc/syslog.conf | sed -n '/^#/p'
#  /etc/syslog.conf        Configuration file for syslogd.
#
#                          For more information see syslog.conf(5)
#                          manpage.
#
# First some standard logfiles.  Log by facility.
#
```

How It Works

This command prints to your screen all the comments in the /etc/syslog.conf file and nothing else.

The following table lists four special characters that are very useful in regular expressions.

Character	Description
^	Matches the beginning of lines
$	Matches the end of lines
.	Matches any single character
*	Matches zero or more occurrences of the previous character

In the following Try It Out examples, you use a few of these to get a good feel for how regular expressions work with sed.

Try It Out   **Regular Expression Example 1**

Using a regular expression as an address, try this command. Remember that your output might differ slightly if your input syslog.conf is different from the example used here:

```
$ cat /etc/syslog.conf | sed '/^$/d'
#  /etc/syslog.conf        Configuration file for syslogd.
#
```

```
#                        For more information see syslog.conf(5)
#                        manpage.
#
# First some standard logfiles.  Log by facility.
#
auth,authpriv.*                /var/log/auth.log
```

How It Works

Here, you use two special regular expression characters in your search string. The first special character is the same as that used in the previous example, the ^ character, which matches the beginning of the lines. The second character is the $ character, which matches the end of lines.

This combination means that sed looks through /etc/syslog.conf and matches and then deletes those lines that have nothing between the beginning and end of the line. The result of this sed command is the removal of all blank lines in the file.

> *It is important to note that an empty line in a file does not contain a line full of spaces, tabs, or anything other than a newline.*

If you are concerned that your regular expression might match something that you are not expecting, you can try it with the -n flag and the print command. This tells sed to print all the matches of blank lines and nothing else:

```
$ cat /etc/syslog.conf | sed -n '/^$/p'
```

If the only thing printed is blank lines and nothing else (as is shown in the preceding code), then the regular expression is matching what you expect it to.

Try It Out   Regular Expression Example 2

Here's another example to illustrate the uses of regular expressions with sed. Suppose you want to print only the lines that begin with the letter a, b, or c. Try this command:

```
$ cat /etc/syslog.conf | sed -n '/^[abc]/p'
auth,authpriv.*                /var/log/auth.log
```

How It Works

This combines the regular expression ^ (match at the beginning of the line) with the regular expression [abc] to print only those lines that begin with one of those characters. Notice that it does *not* look for lines that begin with the string abc but instead looks for any one of those characters.

The square brackets denote a range of characters; you can specify [g-t] to get all lowercase characters between *g* and *t* or specify [3-25] to get all numbers between 3 and 25.

Character Class Keywords

Some special keywords are commonly available to regexps, especially GNU utilities that employ regexps. These are very useful for sed regular expressions as they simplify things and enhance readability.

For example, the characters *a* through *z* as well as the characters *A* through *Z* constitute one such class of characters that has the keyword [[:alpha:]], meaning all alphabetic characters. Instead of having to specify every character in a regular expression, you can simply use this keyword instead, as in the following example.

Using the alphabet character class keyword, this command prints only those lines in the /etc/syslog.conf file that start with a letter of the alphabet:

```
$ cat /etc/syslog.conf | sed -n '/^[[:alpha:]]/p'
auth,authpriv.*                 /var/log/auth.log
```

If you instead delete all the lines that start with alphabetic characters, you can see what doesn't fall within the [[:alpha:]] character class keyword:

```
$ cat /etc/syslog.conf | sed '/^[[:alpha:]]/d'
#  /etc/syslog.conf       Configuration file for syslogd.
#
#                         For more information see syslog.conf(5)
#                         manpage.

#
# First some standard logfiles.  Log by facility.
#
```

The following table is a complete list of the available character class keywords in GNU sed.

Character Class Keyword	Description
[[:alnum:]]	Alphanumeric [a-z A-Z 0-9]
[[:alpha:]]	Alphabetic [a-z A-Z]
[[:blank:]]	Blank characters (spaces or tabs)
[[:cntrl:]]	Control characters
[[:digit:]]	Numbers [0-9]
[[:graph:]]	Any visible characters (excludes whitespace)
[[:lower:]]	Lowercase letters [a-z]
[[:print:]]	Printable characters (noncontrol characters)
[[:punct:]]	Punctuation characters
[[:space:]]	Whitespace
[[:upper:]]	Uppercase letters [A-Z]
[[:xdigit:]]	Hex digits [0-9 a-f A-F]

Character classes are very useful and should be used whenever possible. They adapt much better to non-English character sets, such as accented characters.

Regular Expression Address Ranges

I demonstrated in the Address Ranges section that specifying two line numbers, separated by commas, is equivalent to specifying a range of lines over which the editing command will be executed.

The same behavior applies with regular expressions. You can specify two regular expressions, separated by a comma, and sed will match all of the lines from the first line that matches the first regular expression all the way up to, and including, the line that matches the second regular expression. The following Try It Out demonstrates this behavior.

Try It Out   Regular Expression Address Ranges

Create a file called `story.txt` containing the following data:

```
The Elephants and the Rainbow Trout
  - a moral story about robot ethics

Once upon a time, in a land far far away,
there was a stream filled with elephants drinking ice tea
while watching rainbow trout swim by.

The end.

No, really, the story is over, you can go now.
```

Using a simple regular expression address range, you can print specific lines:

```
$ sed -n -e '/Once upon a time/,/The end./p' somefile.txt
Once upon a time, in a land far far away,
there was a stream filled with elephants drinking ice tea
while watching rainbow trout swim by.

The end.
```

How It Works

This regular expression range prints all the lines between the two matching regular expressions, including those lines. It will not print anything before or after those regular expressions.

If `Once upon a time` is not found, no data is printed. However, if `Once upon a time` is found, but not `The end.`, then all subsequent lines are printed. If you specify an address range to sed, it goes through the entire file, printing each line, waiting for the second element of the address range. It has no idea whether `The end.` will appear in the next line it reads or not. The same concept applies when you specify address ranges in terms of line numbers. If you specify a line number that does not exist in the file, sed just prints until it reaches the end of the file, looking for that line number but never finding it. It is perhaps easier to think of the first address as the address where the action will start and the second where it will be stopped. Actions are started as soon as the first match is made, and the action continues on all following lines until the second match stops the action.

Combining Line Addresses with regexps

If you want to use a line address in combination with a regular expression, sed won't stop you. In fact, this is an often-used addressing scheme.

Simply specify the line number in the file where you want the action to start working and then use the regular expression to stop the work.

Try It Out   Line Addresses

Try the following line address, mixed with a regular expression address range using a character class keyword:

```
$ cat /etc/syslog.conf | sed '1,/^$/d'
#
# First some standard logfiles.  Log by facility.
#

auth,authpriv.*                 /var/log/auth.log
```

How It Works

This command starts deleting from the first line in the file and continues to delete up to the first line that is blank.

Advanced Substitution

Doing substitutions with regular expressions is a powerful technique.

Using address ranges with regular expressions simply required taking what you already knew about address ranges and using regular expressions in place of simple line numbers. The same one-to-one mapping works with substitution and regular expressions. You already know that to substitute the string trout with the string catfish throughout the stream.txt file, you simply do the following:

```
$ cat stream.txt | sed 's/trout/catfish/g'
Imagine a quaint bubbling stream of cool mountain water filled with rainbow catfish
and elephants drinking iced tea.
```

To do regular expression substitutions, you simply map a regular expression onto the literal strings as you mapped the regular expression on top of the literal line numbers in the previous section. Suppose you have a text file with a number of paragraphs separated by blank lines. You can change those blank lines into HTML <p> markers, using a regular expression substitution command:

```
sed 's/^$/<p>/g'
```

The first part of the substitution looks for blank lines and replaces them with the HTML <p> paragraph marker.

Add this sed command to the beginning of your `txt2html.sed` file. Now your HTML converter will add all the necessary headers, convert any blank lines into `<p>` markers so that they will be converted better in your browser, and then append the closing HTML tags.

Referencing Matched regexps with &

Matching by regular expression is useful; however, you sometimes want to reuse what you matched in the replacement. That's not hard if you are matching a literal string that you can identify exactly, but when you use regular expressions you don't always know exactly what you matched. To be able to reuse your matched regular expression is very useful when your regular expressions match varies.

The sed metacharacter `&` represents the contents of the pattern that was matched. For instance, say you have a file called `phonenums.txt` full of phone numbers, such as the following:

```
5555551212
5555551213
5555551214
6665551215
6665551216
7775551217
```

You want to make the area code (the first three digits) surrounded by parentheses for easier reading. To do this, you can use the ampersand replacement character, like so:

```
$ sed -e 's/^[[:digit:]][[:digit:]][[:digit:]]/(&)/g' phonenums.txt
(555)5551212
(555)5551213
(555)5551214
(666)5551215
(666)5551216
(777)5551217
```

Let's unpack this; it's a little dense. The easy part is that you are doing this sed operation on the file `phonenums.txt`, which contains the numbers listed. You are doing a regular expression substitution, so the first part of the substitution is what you are looking for, namely `^[[:digit:]][[:digit:]][[:digit:]]`. This says that you are looking for a digit at the beginning of the line and then two more digits. Because an area code in the United States is composed of the first three digits, this construction will match the area code. The second half of the substitution is `(&)`. Here, you are using the replacement ampersand metacharacter and surrounding it by parentheses. This means to put in parentheses whatever was matched in the first half of the command. This will turn all of the phone numbers into what was output previously.

This looks nicer, but it would be even nicer if you also included a dash after the second set of three numbers, so try that out.

Try It Out   Putting It All Together

Using what you know already, you can make these phone numbers look like regular numbers. Put the previous list of numbers in a file, name the file `phonenums.txt`, and try this command:

```
$ sed -e 's/^[[:digit:]]\{3\}/(&)/g' -e 's/)[[:digit:]]\{3\}/&-/g' phonenums.txt >
nums.txt
$ cat nums.txt
(555)555-1212
(555)555-1213
(555)555-1214
(666)555-1215
(666)555-1216
(777)555-1217
```

How It Works

That command is a mouthful! However, it isn't much more than you already did. The first part of the command is the part that puts the parentheses around the first three numbers, exactly as before, with one change. Instead of repeating the character class keyword [[:digit:]] three times, you replaced it with \{3\}, which means to match the preceding regular expression three times.

After that, you append a second pattern to be executed by adding another -e flag. In this second regular expression substitution, you look for a right parenthesis and then three digits, in the same way as before.

Because these commands are concatenated one after another, the first regular expression substitution has happened, and the first three numbers already have parentheses around them, so you are looking for the closing parenthesis and then three numbers. Once sed finds that, it replaces the string by using the ampersand metacharacter to place the numbers where they already were and then adds a hyphen afterward.

At the very end of the command, the output is redirected to a new file called nums.txt. When redirecting to a file, no output is printed to the screen, so you run cat nums.txt to print the output.

Back References

The ampersand metacharacter is useful, but even more useful is the ability to define specific regions in a regular expressions so you can reference them in your replacement strings. By defining specific parts of a regular expression, you can then refer back to those parts with a special reference character.

To do back references, you have to first define a region and then refer back to that region. To define a region you insert backslashed parentheses around each region of interest. The first region that you surround with backslashes is then referenced by \1, the second region by \2, and so on.

Try It Out   Back References

In the previous example you formatted some phone numbers. Now continue with that example to illustrate back references. You now have a file called nums.txt that looks like this:

```
(555)555-1212
(555)555-1213
(555)555-1214
(666)555-1215
(666)555-1216
(777)555-1217
```

With one sed command, you can pick apart each element of these phone numbers by using back references. First, define the three regions in the left side of the sed command. Select the area code, the second set of numbers up to the dash, and then the rest of the numbers.

1. To select the area code, define a regular expression that includes the parenthesis:

```
/.*)/
```

This matches any number of characters up to a right-parenthesis character. Now, if you want to reference this match later, you need to enclose this regular expression in escaped parentheses, like this:

```
/\(.*)\)/
```

Now that this region has been defined, it can be referenced with the \1 character.

2. Next, you want to match the second set of numbers, terminated by the hyphen character. This is very similar to the first match, with the addition of the hyphen:

```
/\(.*-\)/
```

This regular expression is also enclosed in parentheses, and it is the second defined region, so it is referenced by \2.

3. The third set of numbers is specified by matching any character repeating up to the end of the line:

```
/\(.*$\)/
```

This is the third defined region, so it is referred to as \3.

4. Now that you have all your regions defined, put them all together in a search and then use the references in the replacement right side, like so:

```
$ cat nums.txt | sed 's/\(.*)\)\(.*-\)\(.*$\)/Area code: \1 Second: \2 Third: \3/'
Area code: (555) Second: 555- Third: 1212
Area code: (555) Second: 555- Third: 1213
Area code: (555) Second: 555- Third: 1214
Area code: (666) Second: 555- Third: 1215
Area code: (666) Second: 555- Third: 1216
Area code: (777) Second: 555- Third: 1217
```

How It Works

As you see, this command line takes each number and defines the regions that you specified as output.

Hold Space

Like the pattern space, the hold space is another workbench that sed has available. The *hold space* is a temporary space to put things while you do other things, or look for other lines. Lines in the hold space cannot be operated on; you can only put things in the hold space and take things out from it. Any actual work you want to do on lines has to be done in the pattern space. It's the perfect place to put a line that you found from a search, do some other work, and then pull out that line when you need it. In short, it can be thought of as a spare pattern buffer.

There are a couple of sed commands that allow you to copy the contents of the pattern space into the hold space. (Later, you can use other commands to copy what is in the hold space into the pattern space.) The most common use of the hold space is to make a duplicate of the current line while you change the original in the pattern space.

The following table details the three basic commands that are used for operating with the hold space.

Command	Description of Command's Function
h or H	Overwrite (h) or append (H) the hold space with the contents of the pattern space. In other words, it copies the pattern buffer into the hold buffer.
g or G	Overwrite (g) or append (G) the pattern space with the contents of hold space.
x	Exchange the pattern space and the hold space; note that this command is not useful by itself.

Each of these commands can be used with an address or address range.

The classic way of illustrating the use of the hold space is to take a text file and invert each line in the file so that the last line is first and the first is last, as in the following Try It Out.

Try It Out   Using the Hold Space

Run the following sed command on the story.txt file:

```
$ cat story.txt | sed -ne '1!G' -e 'h' -e '$p'
No, really, the story is over, you can go now.

The end.

while watching rainbow trout swim by.
there was a stream filled with elephants drinking ice tea
Once upon a time, in a land far far away,

  - a moral story about robot ethics
The Elephants and the Rainbow Trout
```

How It Works

First, notice that there are actually three separate commands, separated by -e flags. The first command has a negated address (1)and then the command G. This means to apply the G command to every line *except* the first line. (If this address had been written 1G, it would mean to apply the G command *only* to the first line.)

Because the first line read in didn't have the G command applied, sed moved onto the next command, which is h. This tells sed to copy the first line of the file into the hold space.

The third command is then executed. This command says that if this line is the last line, then print it. Because this is not the last line, nothing is printed. Sed is finished processing the first line of the file, and the only thing that has happened is it has been copied into the hold space.

The cycle is repeated by sed reading in the second line of the file. Because the second line does *not* match the address specified in the first command, sed actually executes the G command this time. The G takes the contents of the hold space, which contains the first line because you put it there in the first cycle, and appends this to the end of the pattern space. Now the pattern space contains the second line, followed by the first line.

The second sed command is executed. This takes the contents of the pattern space and overwrites the hold space with it. This means that it is now taking the pattern space, which contains the second line of the file and the first line, and then it places it in the hold space.

The third command is executed, and because sed is not at the end of the file, it doesn't print anything.

This cycle continues until sed reaches the last line of the file, and the third command is finally executed, printing the entire pattern space, which now contains all the lines in reverse order.

More sed Resources

Refer to the following resources to learn even more about sed:

- ❏ You can find the source code for GNU sed at ftp://ftp.gnu.org/pub/gnu/sed.
- ❏ The sed one-liners (see the following section) are fascinating sed commands that are done in one line: http://sed.sourceforge.net/sed1line.txt.
- ❏ The sed FAQ is an invaluable resource: http://sed.sourceforge.net/sedfaq.html.
- ❏ Sed tutorials and other odd things, including a full-color, ASCII breakout game written only in sed, are available at http://sed.sourceforge.net/grabbag/scripts/.
- ❏ The sed-users mailing list is available at http://groups.yahoo.com/group/sed-users/.
- ❏ The man sed and info sed pages have the best information and come with your sed installation.

Common One-Line sed Scripts

The following code contains several common one-line sed commands. These one-liners are widely circulated on the Internet, and there is a more comprehensive list of one-liners available at http://sed.source forge.net/sed1line.txt.

The comments indicate the purpose of each script. Most of these scripts take a specific file name immediately following the script itself, although the input may also come through a pipe or redirection:

```
        # Double space a file
        sed G file

        # Triple space a file
        sed 'G;G' file

        # Under UNIX: convert DOS newlines (CR/LF) to Unix format
        sed 's/.$//' file      # assumes that all lines end with CR/LF
        sed 's/^M$//' file     # in bash/tcsh, press Ctrl-V then Ctrl-M

        # Under DOS: convert Unix newlines (LF) to DOS format
        sed 's/$//' file                    # method 1
        sed -n p file                       # method 2

        # Delete leading whitespace (spaces/tabs) from front of each line
        # (this aligns all text flush left). '^t' represents a true tab
        # character. Under bash or tcsh, press Ctrl-V then Ctrl-I.
        sed 's/^[ ^t]*//' file

        # Delete trailing whitespace (spaces/tabs) from end of each line
        sed 's/[ ^t]*$//' file              # see note on '^t', above

        # Delete BOTH leading and trailing whitespace from each line
        sed 's/^[ ^t]*//;s/[ ^]*$//' file   # see note on '^t', above

        # Substitute "foo" with "bar" on each line
        sed 's/foo/bar/' file       # replaces only 1st instance in a line
        sed 's/foo/bar/4' file      # replaces only 4th instance in a line
        sed 's/foo/bar/g' file      # replaces ALL instances within a line

        # Substitute "foo" with "bar" ONLY for lines which contain "baz"
        sed '/baz/s/foo/bar/g' file

        # Delete all CONSECUTIVE blank lines from file except the first.
        # This method also deletes all blank lines from top and end of file.
        # (emulates "cat -s")
        sed '/./,/^$/!d' file       # this allows 0 blanks at top, 1 at EOF
        sed '/^$/N;/\n$/D' file     # this allows 1 blank at top, 0 at EOF

        # Delete all leading blank lines at top of file (only).
        sed '/./,$!d' file

        # Delete all trailing blank lines at end of file (only).
        sed -e :a -e '/^\n*$/{$d;N;};/\n$/ba' file

        # If a line ends with a backslash, join the next line to it.
        sed -e :a -e '/\\$/N; s/\\\n//; ta' file

        # If a line begins with an equal sign, append it to the previous
        # line (and replace the "=" with a single space).
        sed -e :a -e '$!N;s/\n=/ /;ta' -e 'P;D' file
```

Common sed Commands

In addition to the substitution command, which is used most frequently, the following table lists the most common sed editing commands.

Editing Command	Description of Command's Function
#	Comment. If first two characters of a sed script are #n, then the -n (no auto-print) option is forced.
{ COMMANDS }	A group of COMMANDS may be enclosed in curly braces to be executed together. This is useful when you have a group of commands that you want executed on an address match.
d[address][,address2]]d	Deletes line(s) from pattern space.
n	If auto-print was not disabled (-n), print the pattern space, and then replace the pattern space with the next line of input. If there is no more input, sed exits.

Less Common sed Commands

The remaining list of commands that are available to you in sed are much less frequently used but are still very useful and are outlined in the following table.

Command	Usage
: label	Label a line to reference later for transfer of control via b and t commands.
a[address][,address2]a\ text	Append text after each line matched by address or address range.
b[address][,address2]]b[label]	Branch (transfer control unconditionally) to :label.
c[address][,address2]]\ text	Delete the line(s) matching address and then output the lines of text that follow this command in place of the last line.
D[address][,address2]]D	Delete first part of multiline pattern (created by N command) space up to newline.
g	Replace the contents of the pattern space with the contents of the hold space.
G	Add a newline to the end of the pattern space and then append the contents of the hold space to that of the pattern space.
h	Replace the contents of the hold space with the contents of the pattern space.

Command	Usage
H	Add a newline to the end of the hold space and then append the contents of the pattern space to the end of the pattern space.
i[*address*][,*address2*]\ *text*	Immediately output the lines of text that follow this command; the final line ends with an unprinted "\".
l N	Print the pattern space using N lines as the word-wrap length. Nonprintable characters and the \ character are printed in C-style escaped form. Long lines are split with a trailing "\" to indicate the split; the end of each line is marked with "$".
N	Add a newline to the pattern space and then append the next line of input into the pattern space. If there is no more input, sed exits.
P	Print the pattern space up to the first newline.
r[*address*][,*address2*] *FILENAME*	Read in a line of *FILENAME* and insert it into the output stream at the end of a cycle. If file name cannot be read, or end-of-file is reached, no line is appended. Special file /dcv/stdin can be provided to read a line from standard input.
w[*address*][,*address2*] *FILENAME*	Write to *FILENAME* the pattern space. The special file names /dev/stderr and /dev/stdout are available to GNU sed. The file is created before the first input line is read. All w commands that refer to the same *FILENAME* are output without closing and reopening the file.
x	Exchange the contents of the hold and pattern spaces.

GNU sed-Specific sed Extensions

The following table is a list of the commands specific to GNU sed. They provide enhanced functionality but reduce the portability of your sed scripts. If you are concerned about your scripts working on other platforms, use these commands carefully!

Editing Command	Description of Command's Function
e [*COMMAND*]	Without parameters, executes command found in pattern space, replacing pattern space with its output. With parameter *COMMAND*, interprets *COMMAND* and sends output of command to output stream.
L N	Fills and joins lines in pattern space to produce output lines of N characters (at most). This command will be removed in future releases.

Table continued on following page

Editing Command	Description of Command's Function
Q [EXIT-CODE]	Same as common q command, except that it does not print the pattern space. It provides the ability to return an EXIT-CODE.
R FILENAME	Reads in a line of FILENAME and inserts it into the output stream at the end of a cycle. If file name cannot be read or end-of-file is reached, no line is appended. Special file /dev/stdin can be provided to read a line from standard input
T LABEL	Branch to LABEL if there have been no successful substitutions (s) since last input line was read or branch taken. If LABEL is omitted, the next cycle is started.
v VERSION	This command fails if GNU sed extensions are not supported. You can specify the VERSION of GNU sed required; default is 4.0, as this is the version that first supports this command.
W FILENAME	Write to FILENAME the pattern space up to the first newline. See standard w command regarding file handles.

Summary

As you use sed more and more, you will become more familiar with its quirky syntax and you will be able to dazzle people with your esoteric and cryptic-looking commands, performing very powerful text processing with a minimum of effort.

In this chapter, you learned:

❑ The different available versions of sed.

❑ How to compile and install GNU sed, even on a system that doesn't have a working version.

❑ How to use sed with some of the available editing commands.

❑ Different ways to invoke sed: on the command line with the –e flag, separated by semicolons, with the bash multiline method, and by writing sed scripts.

❑ How to specify addresses and address ranges by specifying the specific line number or specific range of line numbers. You learned address negation and stepping, and regular expression addressing.

❑ The bread and butter of sed, substitution, was introduced, and you learned how to do substitution with flags, change the substitution delimiter, do substitution with addresses and address ranges, and do regular expression substitutions.

❑ Some of the other basic sed commands: the comment, insert, append, and change commands.

❏ What character class keywords are and how to use them.

❏ About the & metacharacter and how to do numerical back references.

❏ How to use the hold space to give you a little breathing room in what you are trying to do in the pattern space.

The next chapter covers how to read and manipulate text from files using awk. Awk was designed for text processing and works well when called from shell scripts.

Exercises

1. Use an address range negation to print only the fifth line of your /etc/passwd file. *Hint:* Use the delete editing command.

2. Use an address step to print every fifth line of your /etc/passwd file, starting with the tenth.

3. Use an address step to delete the tenth line of your /etc/passwd file and no other line.

4. Write a sed command that takes the output from ls -l issued in your home directory and changes the owner of all the files from your username to the reverse. Make sure not to change the group if it is the same as your username.

5. Do the same substitution as Exercise 4, except this time, change only the first ten entries and none of the rest.

6. Add some more sed substitutions to your txt2html.sed script. In HTML you have to escape certain commands in order that they be printed properly. Change any occurrences of the ampersand (&) character into & for proper HTML printing. *Hint:* You will need to escape your replacement. Once you have this working, add a substitution that converts the less than and greater than characters (< and >) to < and > respectively.

7. Change your txt2html.sed script so that any time it encounters the word *trout,* it makes it bold by surrounding it with the HTML bold tags (<b> and the closing </b>). Also make the script insert the HTML paragraph marker (<p>) for any blank space it finds.

8. Come up with a way to remove the dash from the second digit so instead of printing Area code: (555) Second: 555- Third: 1212, you instead print Area code: (555) Second: 555 Third: 1212.

9. Take the line reversal sed script shown in the Hold Space section and re-factor it so it doesn't use the -n flag and is contained in a script file instead of on the command line.

Processing Text with awk

Awk is a programming language that can be used to make your shell scripts more powerful, as well as to write independent scripts completely in awk itself. Awk is typically used to perform text-processing operations on data, either through a shell pipe or through operations on files. It's a convenient and clear language that allows for easy report creation, analysis of data and log files, and the performance of otherwise mundane text-processing tasks. Awk has a relatively easy-to-learn syntax. It is also a utility that has been a standard on Unix systems for years, so is almost certain to be available. If you are a C programmer or have some Perl knowledge, you will find that much of what awk has to offer will be familiar to you. This is not a coincidence, as one of the original authors of awk, Brian Kernighan, was also one of the original creators of the C language. Many programmers would say that Perl owes a lot of its text processing to awk. If programming C scares you, you will find awk to be less daunting, and you will find it easy to accomplish some powerful tasks.

Although there are many complicated awk programs, awk typically isn't used for very long programs but for shorter one-off tasks, such as trimming down the amount of data in a web server's access log to only those entries that you want to count or manipulate, swapping the first two columns in a file, or manipulating comma-separated (CSV) files. This chapter introduces you to the basics of awk, providing an introduction to the following subjects:

- ❑ The different versions of awk and how to install gawk (GNU awk)
- ❑ The basics of how awk works
- ❑ The many ways of invoking awk
- ❑ Different ways to print and format your data
- ❑ Using variables and functions
- ❑ Using control blocks to loop over data

What Is awk (Gawk/Mawk/Nawk/Oawk)?

Awk was first designed by Alfred V. Aho, Peter J. Weinberger, and Brian W. Kernighan at AT&T Bell Laboratories. (If you take the first letter of each of their last names, you see the origin of awk.) They designed awk in 1977, but awk has changed over the years through many different implementations. Because companies competed, rather than cooperated, in their writing of their implementations of the early Unix operating system, different versions of awk were developed for SYSV Unix compared to those for BSD Unix. Eventually, a POSIX standard was developed, and then a GNU Free Software version was created. Because of all these differing implementations of awk, different systems often have different versions installed.

The many different awks have slightly different names; together, they sound like a gaggle of birds squawking. The most influential and widely available version of awk today is GNU awk, known as *gawk* for short. Some systems have the original implementation of awk installed, and it is simply referred to as awk. Some systems may have more than one version of awk installed: the new version of awk, called nawk, and the old version available as oawk (for either old awk or original awk). Some create a symlink from the awk command to gawk, or mawk.

However it is done on your system, it may be confusing and difficult to discern which awk you have. If you don't know which version or implementation you have, it's difficult to know what functionality your awk supports. Writing awk scripts is frustrating if you implement something that is supported in GNU awk, but you have only the old awk installed.

Gawk, the GNU awk

Gawk is commonly considered to be the most popular version of awk available today. Gawk comes from the GNU Foundation, and in true GNU fashion, it has many enhancements that other versions lack.

The enhancements that gawk has over the traditional awks are too numerous to cover here; however, a few of the most notable follow:

- ❑ Gawk tends to provide you with more informative error messages. Most awk implementations try to tell you what line a syntax error occurs, but gawk does one better by telling you where in that line it occurs.

- ❑ Gawk has no built-in limits that people sometimes run into when using the other awks to do large batch processing.

- ❑ Gawk also has a number of predefined variables, functions, and commands that make your awk programming much simpler.

- ❑ Gawk has a number of useful flags that can be passed on invocation, including the very pragmatic options that give you the version of gawk you have installed and provide you with a command summary (`--version` and `--help`, respectively).

- ❑ Gawk allows you to specify line breaks using \ to continue long lines easily.

- ❑ Gawk's regular expression capability is greatly enhanced over the other awks.

❏ Although gawk implements the POSIX awk standard, the GNU extensions it has do not adhere to these standards, but if you require explicit POSIX compatibility this can be enabled with gawk using the invocation flags `--traditional` or `--posix`. For a full discussion of the GNU extensions to the awk language, see the gawk documentation, specifically Appendix A.5 in the latest manual.

If these features are not enough, the gawk project is very active, with a number of people contributing, whereas mawk has not had a release in several years. Gawk has been ported to a dizzying array of architectures, from Atari, Amiga, and BeOS to Vax/VMS. Gawk is the standard awk that is installed on GNU/Linux and BSD machines.

The additional features, the respect that the GNU Foundation has in making quality free (as in freedom) software, the wide deployment on GNU/Linux systems, and the active development in the project are all probable reasons why gawk has become the favorite over time.

What Version Do I Have Installed?

There is no single test to find out what version or implementation of awk you have installed. You can do a few things to deduce it, or you can install it yourself so you know exactly what is installed. Check your documentation, man pages, and info files to see if you can find a mention of which implementation is referenced, looking out for any mention of oawk, nawk, gawk, or mawk. Also, poke around on your system to find where the awk binary is, and see if there are others installed. It is highly unlikely that you have no version installed, but the hard part is figuring out which version you do have.

Gawk takes the standard GNU version flags to determine what version you are running. If you run awk with these flags as shown in the following Try It Out, and it succeeds, you know that you have GNU awk available.

Try It Out   **Checking Which Version of awk You Are Running**

Run awk with the following flags to see if you can determine what implementation you have installed:

```
$ awk --version
GNU Awk 3.1.4
Copyright (C) 1989, 1991-2003 Free Software Foundation.
This program is free software; you can redistribute it and/or modify
it under the terms of the GNU General Public License as published by
the Free Software Foundation; either version 2 of the License, or
(at your option) any later version.

This program is distributed in the hope that it will be useful,
but WITHOUT ANY WARRANTY; without even the implied warranty of
MERCHANTABILITY or FITNESS FOR A PARTICULAR PURPOSE.  See the
GNU General Public License for more details.

You should have received a copy of the GNU General Public License
along with this program; if not, write to the Free Software
Foundation, Inc., 59 Temple Place - Suite 330, Boston, MA  02111-1307, USA.
```

How It Works

The GNU utilities implement a standard library that standardizes some flags, such as `--version` and `--help`, making it easy to determine if the version you have installed is the GNU awk.

This output showed that GNU awk, version 3.1.4, is installed on the system. If you do not have GNU awk, you get an error message. For example, if you have mawk installed, you might get this error:

```
$ awk --version
awk: not an option: --version
```

In this case, you see that it is not GNU awk, or you would have been presented with the version number and the copyright notice. Try the following to see if it is mawk:

```
$ awk -W versions
mawk 1.3.3 Nov 1996, Copyright (C) Michael D. Brennan

compiled limits:
max NF            32767
sprintf buffer     1020
```

Because this flag succeeded, and it shows you what implementation and version (mawk, 1.3.3) is installed, you know that your system has mawk installed.

Installing gawk

By far the most popular awk is the GNU Foundation's implementation, gawk. If you find that your system does not have gawk installed, and you wish to install it, follow these steps. If you have a system that gawk has not been ported to, you may need to install a different awk. The known alternatives and where they can be found are listed in the awk FAQ at www.faqs.org/faqs/computer-lang/awk/faq/.

> **Be careful when putting gawk on your system! Some systems depend on the version of awk that they have installed in /usr/bin, and if you overwrite that with gawk, you may find your system unable to work properly, because some system scripts may have been written for the older implementation. For example, fink for Mac OS X requires the old awk in /usr/bin/awk. If you replace that awk with gawk, fink no longer works properly. The instructions in this section show you how to install gawk without overwriting the existing awk on the system, but you should pay careful attention to this fact!**

By far the easiest way to install gawk is to install a prepackaged version, if your operating system provides it. Installation this way is much simpler and easier to maintain. For example, to install gawk on the Debian GNU/Linux OS, type this command:

```
apt-get install gawk
```

Mac OS X has gawk available through fink. Fink is a command-line program that you can use to fetch and easily install some useful software that has been ported to OS X. If you don't have fink installed on your system, you can get it at http://fink.sourceforge.net/download/index.php.

If your system does not have packages, or if you want to install gawk on your own, follow these steps:

1. Obtain the gawk software. The home page for GNU gawk is www.gnu.org/software/gawk/. You can find the latest version of the software at http://ftp.gnu.org/gnu/gawk/. Get the latest .tar.gz from there, and then uncompress and untar it as you would any normal tar:

```
$ tar -zxf gawk-3.1.4.tar.gz
$ cd gawk-3.1.4
```

2. Review the README file that is included in the source. Additionally, you need to read the OS-specific README file in the directory README_d for any notes on installing gawk on your specific system.

3. To configure awk, type the following command:

```
$ sh ./configure
checking for a BSD-compatible install... /usr/bin/install -c
checking whether build environment is sane... yes
checking for gawk... gawk
checking whether make sets $(MAKE)... yes
checking for gcc... gcc
```

This continues to run through the GNU autoconf configuration, analyzing your system for various utilities, variables, and parameters that need to be set or exist on your system before you can compile awk. This can take some time before it finishes. If this succeeds, you can continue with compiling awk itself. If it doesn't, you need to resolve the configuration problem(s) that are presented before proceeding. Autoconf indicates if there is a significant problem with your configuration and requires you to resolve it and rerun ./configure before it can continue. It is not uncommon for autoconf to look for a utility and not find it and then proceed. This does not mean it has failed; it exits with an error if it fails.

4. To compile awk, issue a make command:

```
$ make
        make 'CFLAGS=-g -O2' 'LDFLAGS=-export-dynamic' all-recursive
make[1]: Entering directory `/home/micah/working/gawk-3.1.4'
Making all in intl
make[2]: Entering directory `/home/micah/working/gawk-3.1.4/intl'
make[2]: Nothing to be done for `all'.
make[2]: Leaving directory `/home/micah/working/gawk-3.1.4/intl'
Making all in .
```

This command continues to compile awk. It may take a few minutes to compile, depending on your system.

5. If everything goes as expected, you can install the newly compiled awk simply by issuing the make install command as root:

```
$ su
Password:
# make install
```

Awk is placed in the default locations in your file system. By default, `make install` installs all the files in /usr/local/bin, /usr/local/lib, and so on. You can specify an installation prefix other than `/usr/local` using `--prefix` when running `configure`; for instance, `sh ./config-ure --prefix=$HOME` will `make` awk so that it installs in your home directory. However, please heed the warning about replacing your system's installed awk, if it has one!

How awk Works

Awk has some basic functionality similarities with sed (see Chapter 6). At its most basic level, awk simply looks at lines that are sent to it, searching them for a pattern that you have specified. If it finds a line that matches the pattern that you have specified, awk does something to that line. That "something" is the action that you specify by your commands. Awk then continues processing the remaining lines until it reaches the end. Sed acts in the same way: It searches for lines and then performs editing commands on the lines that match. The input comes from standard in and is sent to standard out. In this way, awk is stream-oriented, just like sed.

In fact, there are a number of things about awk that are similar to sed. The syntax for using awk is very similar to sed; both are invoked using similar syntax; both use regular expressions for matching patterns.

Although the similarities exist, there are syntactic differences. When you run awk, you specify the pattern, followed by an action contained in curly braces. A very basic awk program looks like this:

```
awk '/somedata/ { print $0 }' filename
```

The rest of this brief section provides just an overview of the basic steps awk follows in processing the command. The following sections fill in the details of each step.

In this example, the expression that awk looks for is *somedata*. This is enclosed in slashes, and the action to be performed, indicated within the curly braces, is `print $0`. Awk works by stepping through three stages. The first is what happens before any data is processed; the second is what happens during the data processing loop; and the third is what happens after the data is finished processing. Before any lines are read in to awk and then processed, awk does some preinitialization, which is configurable in your script, by specifying a `BEGIN` clause. At the end of processing, you can perform any final actions by using an `END` clause.

Invoking awk

You can invoke awk in one of several ways, depending on what you are doing with it. When you become more familiar with awk, you will want to do quick things on the command line, and as things become more complex, you will turn them into awk programs.

The simplest method is to invoke awk on the command line. This is useful if what you are doing is relatively simple, and you just need to do it quickly. Awk can also be invoked this way within small shell scripts. You run an awk program on the command line by typing awk and then the program, followed by the files you want to run the program on:

```
awk 'program' filename1 filename2
```

The `filename1` and `filename2` are not required. You can specify only one input file, or two or more, and awk can even be run without any input files. Or you can pipe the data to awk instead of specifying any input files:

```
cat filename1 | sed 'program'
```

The *program* is enclosed in single quotes to keep the shell from interpreting special characters and to make the *program* a single argument to awk. The contents of *program* are the pattern to match, followed by the curly braces, which enclose the action to take on the pattern. The following Try It Out gives you some practice running basic awk programs.

Try It Out   **A Simple Command-Line awk Program**

Try this simple awk program, which runs without any input files at all:

```
$ awk '{ print "Hi Mom!" }'
```

If you run this as written, you will see that nothing happens. Because no file name was specified, awk is waiting for input from the terminal. If you hit the Enter key, you see the string `"Hi Mom!"` printed on the terminal. You need to issue an end-of-file to get out of this input; do this by pressing Ctrl-D.

Awk can also be invoked using bash's multiline capability. Bash is smart enough to know when you have not terminated a quote or a brace and prompts you for more input until you close the open quote or brace.

To do the preceding example in this way, type the following in a bash shell. After the first curly brace, press the Enter key to move to the next line:

```
$ awk '{
> print "Hi Mom!"
> }'
```

Once you have typed these three lines, hit the Enter key, and you will see again the string `"Hi Mom!"` printed on the terminal. Again you will need to issue an end-of-file by pressing Ctrl-D to get out of this input.

How It Works

The result of this command is the same output from the preceding command, just invoked in a different manner. The Korn, Bourne, and Z shell all look for closing single quotes and curly braces, and prompt you when you haven't closed them properly.

Note, however, that the C shell does not work this way.

Your awk commands will soon become longer and longer, and it will be cumbersome to type them on the command line. At some point you will find putting all your commands into a file to be a more useful way of invoking awk. You do this by putting all the awk commands into a file and then invoking awk with the `-f` flag followed by the file that contains your commands. The following Try It Out demonstrates this way of invoking awk.

Try It Out   **Running awk Scripts with awk -f**

In this Try It Out, you take the simple program from the previous Try It Out, place it into a file, and use the -f flag to invoke this program. First, take the text that follows and place it into a file called hello.awk:

```
{ print "Hi Mom!" }
```

Notice that you do not need to place single quotes around this text, as you did when you were invoking awk on the command line. When the program is contained in a file, this is not necessary.

Adding .awk at the end of the file is not necessary but is a useful convention to remember what files contain what types of programs.

Next, invoke sed using the -f flag to point it to the file that contains the program to execute:

```
$ awk -f hello.awk
```

This outputs the exact same output as the previous two examples did:

```
"Hi Mom!"
```

How It Works

Awk takes the -f flag, reads the awk program that is specified immediately afterward, and executes it. This outputs exactly the same way as the example showing you how to invoke awk on the command line.

You can also write full awk shell scripts by adding a magic file handle at the top of the file, as in the following Try It Out.

Try It Out   **Creating Self-Contained awk Programs**

Type the following script, including the { print "Hi Mom!" } from the preceding example, into a file called mom.awk:

```
#!/usr/bin/awk -f
# This is my first awk script!
# I will add more as I learn some more awk

{ print "Hi Mom!" } # This prints my greeting
```

If the awk on your system is located somewhere other than /usr/bin/awk, you need to change that path accordingly.

Now make the mom.awk script executable by typing the following on the command line:

```
$ chmod +x mom.awk
```

Now you can run this new shell script on the command line as follows:

```
$ ./hello.awk
Hi Mom!
```

This command tells the shell to execute the file hello.awk located in the current working directory. If you are not currently in the same directory as the script is located, this will not work. You need to type the full path of the script.

How It Works

Because the execute bit was set on the program, the shell knows that it should be able to run this file, rather than it simply containing data. It sees the magic file marker at the beginning, denoted by the shebang (#!), and uses the command that immediately follows to execute the script.

You may have noticed the comments that were snuck into the awk script. It is very common in shell scripting to add comments by placing the # symbol and then your comment text. In awk, the comments are treated as beginning with this character and ending at the end of the line. Each new line that you want to have a comment on requires another # symbol.

The print Command

Earlier, in the section How awk Works, you saw the basic method of using awk to search for a string and then print it. In this section, you learn exactly how that `print` command works and some more advanced useful incarnations of it.

First, you need some sample data to work with. Say you have a file called `countries.txt`, and each line in the file contains the following information:

Country	Internet domain	Area in sq. km	Population	Land lines	Cell phones

The beginning of the file has the following contents:

```
Afghanistan    .af    647500     28513677      33100      12000
Albania        .al    28748      3544808       255000     1100000
Algeria        .dz    2381740    32129324      2199600    1447310
Andorra        .ad    468        69865         35000      23500
Angola         .ao    1246700    10978552      96300      130000
```

The following command searches the file `countries.txt` for the string Al and then uses the `print` command to print the results:

```
$ awk '/Al/ { print $0 }' countries.txt
Albania        .al    28748    3544808       255000     1100000
Algeria        .dz    2381740  32129324      2199600    1447310
```

As you can see from this example, the regular expression surrounds the string to be searched for, in this case Al, and this matches two lines. The lines that are matched then have the command specified within the curly braces acted on it; in this case `print $0` is executed, printing the lines.

This isn't very interesting, because you can do this with grep or sed. This is where awk starts to become interesting, because you can very easily say that you want to print only the matching countries' landline and cell phone usage:

```
$ awk '/Al/ { print $5,$6 }' countries.txt
255000 1100000
2199600   1447310
```

In this example, the same search pattern was supplied, and for each line that is matched, awk performs the specified actions, in this case, printing the fifth and sixth field. Awk automatically stores each field in its numerical sequential order. By default, awk defines the fields as any string of printing characters separated by spaces. The first field is the $0 field, which represents the entire line; this is why when you specified the action print $0, the entire line was printed for each match. Field $1 represents the first field (in our example, Country), the $2 represents the second field (Internet Domain), and so on.

By default, awk's behavior is to print the entire line, so each of the following lines results in the same output:

```
awk '/Al/' countries.txt
awk '/Al/ { print $0 }' countries.txt
awk '/Al/ { print }' countries.txt
```

Although explicitly writing print $0 is not necessary, it does make for good programming practice because you are making it very clear that this is your action instead of using a shortcut.

It is perfectly legal to omit a search pattern from your awk statement. When there is no search pattern provided, awk by default matches all the lines of your input file and performs the action on each line.

For example, the following command prints the number of cell phones in each country:

```
$ awk '{ print $6 }' countries.txt
12000
1100000
1447310
23500
130000
```

It prints each line because I did not specify a search pattern.

You can also insert text anywhere in the command action, as demonstrated in the following Try It Out.

Try It Out   Inserting Text

Type the following awk command to see the number of cell phones in use in each of the countries included:

```
$ awk '{ print "Number of cell phones in use in",$1":",$6 }' countries.txt
Number of cell phones in use in Afghanistan: 12000
Number of cell phones in use in Albania: 1100000
Number of cell phones in use in Algeria: 1447310
Number of cell phones in use in Andorra: 23500
Number of cell phones in use in Angola: 130000
```

How It Works

The `print` command is used only one time, not multiple times for each field. A comma separates the print elements in most cases, except after the `$1` in this example. The comma inserts a space between the element printed before and after itself. (Try putting a comma after the `$1` in the preceding command to see how it changes the output.)

For each line in the file, awk prints the string `Number of cell phones in use in`, and then it prints a space (because of the comma). Then it prints field number 1 (the country), followed by the simple string `:` (colon), and then another comma puts in a space, and finally field number 6 (cell phones) is inserted.

`Print` is a simple command; all by itself it just prints the input line. With one argument it prints the argument; with multiple arguments it prints all the arguments, separated by spaces when the arguments are separated by commas or together without spaces when the arguments are not comma delineated.

If you want to print a newline as part of your `print` command, just include the standard newline sequence as part of the string, as in the following Try It Out.

Try It Out   Printing Newlines

Write a quick letter to Mom that puts the strings on separate lines, so it looks nicer:

```
$ awk 'BEGIN { print "Hi Mom,\n\nCamp is fun.\n\nLove,\nSon" }'
Hi Mom,

Camp is fun.

Love,
Son
```

How It Works

In this example, you put the entire awk program into a `BEGIN` block by placing the word `BEGIN` right before the first opening curly brace. Whatever is contained in a `BEGIN` block is executed one time immediately, before the first line of input is read (similarly, the `END` construct is executed once after all input lines have been read). Previously, you were putting your awk programs into the main execution block, and the `BEGIN` was empty and was not specified. Commands that are contained in the main block are executed on lines of input that come from a file or from the terminal. If you recall, the previous Try It Out sections required that you hit the Enter key for the output to be printed to the screen; this was the input that awk needed to execute its main block. In this example, all your commands are contained in the `BEGIN` block, which requires no input, so it prints right away without your needing to provide input with the Enter key.

Awk uses the common two-character designation `\n` to mean *newline*. Whenever awk encounters this construct in a print command, it actually prints a newline rather than the string `\n`.

Using Field Separators

The default field separator in awk is a blank space. When you insert a blank space by pressing the space-bar or Tab key, awk delineates each word in a line as a different field. However, if the data that you are working with includes spaces within the text itself, you may encounter difficulties.

For example, if you add more countries to your `countries.txt` file to include some that have spaces in them (such as Dominican Republic), you end up with problems. The following command prints the area of each country in the file:

```
$ awk '{ print $3 }' countries.txt
647500
28748
2381740
.do
468
1246700
```

Why is the `.do` included in the output? Because one of the lines of this file contains this text:

```
Dominican Republic  .do  8833634    48730  901800  2120400
```

The country Dominican Republic counts as two fields because it has a space within its name. You need to be very careful that your fields are uniform, or you will end up with ambiguous data like this. There are a number of ways to get around this problem; one of the easiest methods is to specify a unique field separator and format your data accordingly. In this case, you need to format your `countries.txt` file so that any country that has spaces in its name instead had underscores, so Dominican Republic becomes Dominican_Republic.

Unfortunately, it isn't always practical or possible to change your input data file. In this case, you can invoke awk with the `-F` flag to specify an alternative field separator character instead of the space. A very common field separator is the comma, so to instruct awk to use a comma as the character that separates fields, invoke awk using `-F,` to indicate the comma should be used instead. Most databases are able to export their data into CSV (Comma Separated Values) files. If your data is formatted using commas to separate each field, you can specify that field separator to awk on the command line, as the following Try It Out section demonstrates.

Try It Out   Alternative Field Separators

Reformat your `countries.txt` file so the fields are separated by commas instead of spaces, and save it in a file called `countries.csv`, so it looks like the following:

```
Afghanistan,.af,647500,28513677,33100,12000
Albania,.al,28748,3544808,255000,1100000
Algeria,.dz,2381740,32129324,2199600,1447310
Andorra,.ad,468,69865,35000,23500
Angola,.ao,1246700,10978552,96300,130000
Dominican Republic,.do,8833634,48730,901800,2120400
```

Then run the following on the command line:

```
$ awk -F, '{ print $3 }' countries.csv
647500
28748
2381740
8833634
468
1246700
```

As with spaces, make sure that the new field separator that you specify isn't being used in the data as well. For example, if the numbers in your data are specified using commas, as in 647,500, the numbers before and after the commas will be interpreted as two separate fields.

How It Works

Awk processes each line using the comma as the character that separates fields instead of a space. It reads each line of your `countries.csv` file, looks for the third field, and then prints it. This makes entries such as Dominican Republic, which has a space in its name, to be processed as you expect and not as two separate fields.

Using the printf Command

The `printf` (formatted print) command is a more flexible version of `print`. If you are familiar with C, you will find the `printf` command very familiar; it was borrowed from that language. Printf is used to specify the width of each item printed. It also can be used to change the output base to use for numbers, to determine how many digits to print after the decimal point, and more. Printf is different from `print` only because of the format string, which controls how to output the other arguments. One main difference between `print` and `printf` is that `printf` does not include a newline at the end. Another difference is that with `printf` you specify how you want to format your string. The `printf` command works in this format:

```
printf(<string>,<format string>)
```

The parentheses are optional, but otherwise, the basic `print` command that you have been using so far is almost identical:

```
printf("Hi Mom!\n")
```

The string is the same with the exception of the added `\n` character, which adds a newline to the end of the string. This doesn't seem very useful, because now you have to add a newline when you didn't before. However, `printf` has more flexibility because you can specify format codes to control the results of the expressions, as shown in the following Try It Out examples.

Try It Out   The printf Command

Try the following `printf` command:

```
$ awk '{ printf "Number of cell phones in use in %s: %d\n", $1, $6 }' countries.txt
Afghanistan    .af    647500     28513677    33100     12000
Albania        .al    28748      3544808     255000    1100000
Algeria        .dz    2381740    32129324    2199600   1447310
Andorra        .ad    468        69865       35000     23500
Angola         .ao    1246700    10978552    96300     130000
```

How It Works

As you see, this prints the output in exactly the same format as the command that used `print` instead of `printf`.

The `printf` command prints the string that is enclosed in quotes until it encounters the *format specifier*, the percent symbol followed by a format control letter. (See the table following the next Try It Out for a list of format control characters and their meanings.) The first instance, `%s`, tells awk to substitute a string, which is the first argument (in this case, `$1`), so it puts the `$1` string in place of the `%s`. It then prints the colon and a space, and then encounters the second format specifier, `%d`, which tells awk to substitute a digit, the second argument. The second argument is `$6`, so it pulls that information in and replaces the `%d` with what `$6` holds. After that, it prints a newline.

Try It Out   printf Format Codes

Try the following command to print the number of cell phones in each country in decimal, hex, and octal format:

```
$ awk '{ printf "Decimal: %d, Hex: %x, Octal: %o\n", $6, $6, $6 }' countries.txt
Decimal: 12000, Hex: 2ee0, Octal: 27340
Decimal: 1100000, Hex: 10c8e0, Octal: 4144340
Decimal: 1447310, Hex: 16158e, Octal: 5412616
Decimal: 23500, Hex: 5bcc, Octal: 55714
Decimal: 130000, Hex: 1fbd0, Octal: 375720
```

How It Works

In this example, the same number is being referenced three times by the `$6`, formatted in decimal format, hexadecimal format, and octal format, depending on the format control character specified.

The following table lists the format control characters and what kind of values they print:

Format Control Character	Kind of Value Printed
%c	Prints a number in ASCII format. *awk '{ printf "%c", 65 }'* outputs the letter *A*.
%d %i	Either character prints a decimal integer.
%e %E	Prints number in exponential format. awk '{ *printf " %3.2e\n", 2134 }'* prints *2.13e+03*.

Format Control Character	Kind of Value Printed
%f	Prints number in floating-point notation. awk '{ printf " %3.2f\n", 2134 }' prints 213.40.
%g %G	Prints a number in scientific notation or in floating-point notation, depending on which uses the least characters.
%o	Prints an unsigned octal integer.
%s	Prints a string.
%u	Prints an unsigned decimal integer.
%x %X	Prints an unsigned hexadecimal integer; using %X prints capital letters.
%%	Outputs a % character.

Using printf Format Modifiers

These printf format characters are useful for representing your strings and numbers in the way that you expect. You can also add a modifier to your printf format characters to specify how much of the value to print or to format the value with a specified number of spaces.

You can provide an integer before the format character to specify a width that the output would use, as in the following example:

```
$ awk '{ printf "|%16s|\n", $6 }' countries.txt
|      Afghanistan|
|          Albania|
|          Algeria|
```

Here, the width 16 was passed to the format modifier %s to make the string the same length in each line of the output. You can left-justify this text by placing a minus sign in front of the number, as follows:

```
$ awk '{ printf "|%-16s|\n", $1 }' countries.txt
|Afghanistan     |
|Albania         |
|Algeria         |
```

Use a fractional number to specify the maximum number of characters to print in a string or the number of digits to print to the right of the decimal point for a floating-point number:

```
$ awk '{ printf "|%-.4s|\n", $1 }' countries.txt
|Afgh|
|Alba|
|Alge|
```

Try It Out   **Using printf Format Modifiers**

In this example, you use printf to create headings for each of the columns in the countries.txt file and print the data underneath each column. Put the following into a file called format.awk:

```
BEGIN { printf "%-15s %20s\n\n", "Country", "Cell phones" }
      { printf "%-15s %20d\n", $1, $6 }
```

Then call this script, using the countries.txt file as input:

```
$ awk -f format.awk countries.txt
Country                     Cell phones

Afghanistan                       12000
Albania                         1100000
Algeria                         1447310
Andorra                           23500
```

How It Works

The first block is contained within a BEGIN statement, so it is executed initially and only one time. This allows the header to be printed, and then the main execution block is run over the input data.

Printf format specifiers are used to left-justify the first string and specify that the column width be 15 characters wide; the second string has 20 characters specified as the format string. Because you used the same format string specifiers for the headers, they line up above the data.

Using the sprintf Command

The sprintf function operates exactly like printf, with the same syntax. The only difference is that it assigns its output to a variable (variables are discussed in the next section), rather than printing it to standard out. The following example shows how this works:

```
$ awk '{ variable = sprintf("[%-.4s]", $1); print variable}' countries.txt
|Afgh|
|Alba|
|Alge|
```

This assigns the output from the sprintf function to the variable *variable* and then prints that variable, which results in the same output as if you had used printf.

Using Variables in awk

In Chapter 2, variables were introduced as a mechanism to store values that can be manipulated or read later, and in many ways they operate the same in awk, with some differences in syntax and particular built-in variables. The last section introduced the sprintf command, which assigns its output to a variable. The example in that section was a *user-defined* variable. Awk also has some predefined, or *built-in,* variables that can be referenced. The following sections provide more detail on using these two types of variables with awk.

User-Defined Variables

User-defined variables have a few rules associated with them. They must not start with a digit and are case sensitive. Besides these rules, your variables can consist of alphanumeric characters and underscores. A user-defined variable must not conflict with awk's reserved built-in variables or commands. For example, you may not create a user-defined variable called `print`, because this is an awk command. Unlike some programming languages, variables in awk do not need to be initialized or declared. The first time you use a variable, it is set to an empty string (`" "`) and assigned 0 as its numerical value. However, relying on default values is a bad programming practice and should be avoided. If your awk script is long, define the variables you will be using in the BEGIN block, with the values that you want set as defaults.

Variables are assigned values simply by writing the variable, followed by an equal sign and then the value. Because awk is a "weak-typed" language, you can assign numbers or strings to variables:

```
myvariable = 3.141592654
myvariable = "some string"
```

When you perform a numeric operation on a variable, awk gives you a numerical result; if a string operation is performed, a string will be the result.

In the earlier section on `printf`, the Try It Out example used format string modifiers to specify columnar widths so that the column header lined up with the data. This format string modifier could be set in a variable instead of having to type it each time, as in the following code:

```
BEGIN { colfmt="%-15s %20s\n"; printf colfmt, "Country", "Cell phones\n" }
      { printf colfmt, $1, $6 }
```

In this example, a user-defined variable called `colfmt` is set, containing the format string specifiers that you want to use in the rest of the script. Once it is defined, you can reference it simply by using the variable; in this case it is referenced twice in the two `printf` statements.

Built-in Variables

Built-in variables are very useful if you know what they are used for. The following subsections introduce you to some of the most commonly used built-in variables.

Remember, you should not create a user-defined variable that conflicts with any of awk's built-in variables.

The FS Variable

`FS` is awk's built-in variable that contains the character used to denote separate fields. In the section Using Field Separators you modified this variable on the command line by passing the `-F` argument to awk with a new field separator value (in that case, you replaced the default field separator value with a comma to parse CSV files). It is actually more convenient to put the field separator into your script using awk's built-in `FS` variable rather than setting it on the command line. This is more useful when the awk script is in a file, rather on the command line where specifying flags to awk is not difficult.

To change the field separator within a script you use the special built-in awk variable, `FS`. To change the field separator variable, you need to assign a new value to it at the beginning of the script. It must be done before any input lines are read, or it will not be effective on every line, so you should set the field separator value in an action controlled by the BEGIN rule, as in the following Try It Out.

Try It Out   Using the Field Separator Variable

Type the following into a file called `countries.awk`:

```
# Awk script to print the number of cell phones in use in each country

BEGIN { FS = "," } # Our data is separated by commas

{ print "Number of cell phones in use in",$1":",$6 }
```

Note that there are double quotes around the comma and that there are no single quotes around the curly braces, as there would be on the command line.

This script can be invoked using the `-f` flag. Use it against the CSV version of the `countries.csv` file that contains each field separated by a comma:

```
$ awk -f countries.awk countries.csv
```

Note the difference between the -F flag and the -f flag. You use the -f flag here to execute the specified countries.awk script. This script sets the field separator (FS) variable to use a comma as the field separator, rather than setting the field separator using the -F flag on the command line, as in a previous example.

How It Works

In the BEGIN block of the awk script, the *FS* built-in variable is set to the comma character. It remains set to this throughout the script (as long as it doesn't get redefined later). Awk then uses this to determine what separates fields, just like it did when the `-F` flag was used on the command line.

FS Regular Expressions

The *FS* variable can contain more than a single character, and when it does, it is interpreted as a regular expression. If you use a regular expression for a field separator, you then have the ability to specify several characters to be used as delimiters, instead of just one, as in the following Try It Out.

Try It Out   Field Separator Regular Expressions

The following assignment of the *FS* variable identifies a comma followed by any number of spaces as the field separator:

```
$ echo "a,,,   b,,,,, c,,   d, e,, f,   g" | awk 'BEGIN {FS="[,]+[ ]+"} {print $2}'
b
```

How It Works

The *FS* variable is set to match the regular expression that says any number of commas and any number of spaces. Notice that no matter how many spaces or commas there are between fields, the regular expression matches the fields as expected.

The NR Variable

The built-in variable *NR* is automatically incremented by awk on each new line it processes. It always contains the number of the current record. This is a useful variable because you can use it to count how many lines are in your data, as in the following Try It Out.

Using the NR Variable

Try using the *NR* variable to print the number of lines in your countries.txt file:

```
$ awk 'END { print "Number of countries:", NR }' countries.txt
Number of countries: 5
```

How It Works

Each line is read into awk and processed, but because there is no BEGIN or main code block, nothing happens until all of the lines have been read in and processed. After all of the lines have been processed (the processing is nothing, but awk still reads each line in individually and does nothing to them), the END block is executed. The *NR* variable has been automatically incremented internally for each line read in, so at the END the variable has the total of all the lines that have been read in from the file, giving you a count of the lines in a file.

Of course, you could use the much easier Unix utility wc to get the same output.

Try It Out **Putting It All Together**

In this Try It Out, you add line numbers to the output that you created in the earlier columnar display example by adding the *NR* variable to the output. Edit the format.awk script so it looks like the following:

```
BEGIN { colfmt="%-15s %20s\n"; printf colfmt, "Country", "Cell phones\n" }
      { printf "%d. " colfmt, NR, $1, $6 }
```

And then run it:

```
$ awk -f format.awk countries.txt
Country                  Cell phones

1. Afghanistan                 12000
2. Albania                   1100000
3. Algeria                   1447310
4. Andorra                     23500
5. Angola                     130000
```

How It Works

You set the *colfmt* variable to have the printf format specifier in the BEGIN block, as you did in the User-Defined Variables section, and then print the headers. The second line, which contains the main code block, has a printf command with the format character %d. This specifies that a digit will be put in this position, followed by a period and then a space. The *colfmt* format specifier variable is set, and then the elements of the printf command are specified. The first is the *NR* variable; because this is a digit and is the first element, it gets put into the %d. position. The first line read in will have *NR* set to the number 1, so the first line prints 1. followed by the formatting and field 1 and field 6. When the next line is read in, *NR* gets set to 2, and so on.

The following table contains the basic built-in awk variables and what they contain. You will find these very useful as you make awk scripts and you need to make decisions about how your script runs depending on what is happening internally.

Built-in Variable	Contents
ARGC, ARGV	Contains a count and an array of the command-line arguments.
CONVFMT	Controls conversions of numbers to strings; default value is set to %.6g.
ENVIRON	Contains an associative array of the current environment. Array indices are set to environment variable names.
FILENAME	The name of the file that awk is currently reading. Set to - if reading from STDIN; is empty in a BEGIN block.
FNR	Current record number in the current file, incremented for each line read. Set to 0 each time a new file is read.
FS	Input field separator; default value is " ", a string containing a single space. Set on command line with flag -F.
NF	Number of fields in the current input line. NF is set every time a new line is read.
NR	Number of records processed since the beginning of execution. It is incremented with each new record read.
OFS	Output field separator; default value is a single space. The contents of this variable are output between fields printed by the print statement.
ORS	Output record specifier; the contents of this variable are output at the end of every print statement. Default value is \n, a newline.
PROCINFO	An array containing information about the running program. Elements such as "gid", "uid", "pid", and "version" are available.
RS	Input record separator; default value is a string containing a newline, so an input record is a single line of text.

Control Statements

Control statements are statements that control the flow of execution of your awk program. Awk control statements are modeled after similar statements in C, and the looping and iteration concepts are the same as were introduced in Chapter 3. This means you have your standard if, while, for, do, and similar statements.

All control statements contain a control statement keyword, such as if, and then what actions to perform on the different results of the control statement.

if Statements

One of the most important awk decision making statements is the if statement. It follows a standard *if (condition) then-action [else else-action]* format, as in the following Try It Out.

Try It Out   Using if Statements

Type the following command to perform an if statement on the countries.txt file:

```
$ awk '{ if ($3 < 1000) print }'
Andorra .ad 468 69865 35000 23500
```

How It Works

Awk reads in each line of the file, looks at field number 3, and then does a check to see if that field's contents are less than the number 1,000, performing a comparative operation on the field. (*Comparative operations* are tests that you can perform to see if something is equal to, greater than, less than, true/false, and so on.) With this file, only the Andorra line has a third field containing a number that is less than 1,000.

Notice that the if conditional does not use a then, it just assumes that whatever statement follows the condition (in this case, print) is what should be done if the condition is evaluated to be true.

If statements often have else statements as well. The else statements define what to do with the data that does not match the condition, as in this Try It Out.

Try It Out   Using else

Type the following into a file called ifelse.awk to see how an else statement enhances an if:

```
{ if ($3 < 1000)
        printf "%s has only %d people!\n", $1, $3
  else
        printf "%s has a population larger than 1000\n", $1 }
```

Notice how the script has been formatted with whitespace to make it easier to read and understand how the flow of the condition works. This is not required but is good programming practice!

Then run the script:

```
$ awf -f ifelse.awk countries.txt
Afghanistan has a population larger than 1000
Albania has a population larger than 1000
Algeria has a population larger than 1000
Andorra has only 468 people!
Angola has a population larger than 1000
```

How It Works

The condition if ($3 < 1000) is tested. If it is true for a country, the first printf command is executed; otherwise, the second printf command is executed.

An else statement can include additional if statements to make the logic fulfill all conditions that you require. For example:

```
{ if ( $1 == "cat" )
     print "meow";
  else if ( $1 == "dog" )
     print "woof";
  else if ( $1 == "bird" )
     print "caw";
  else
     print "I do not know what kind of noise " $1 " makes!" }
```

Each condition is tested in the order it appears, on each line in succession. Awk reads in a line, tests the first field to see if it is cat and if so, prints meow. Otherwise, awk goes on to test whether the first field is instead dog and, if so, prints woof. This process continues until awk reaches a condition that tests to be true or runs out of conditions. If $1 isn't cat, dog, or bird, then awk admits it doesn't know what kind of noise the animal that is in $1 makes.

Comparison Operators

These examples use the *less than* operation, but there are many other operators available for making conditional statements powerful. Another example is the *equal* comparison operator, which checks to see if something is equal to another thing. For example, the following command looks in the first field on each line for the string Andorra and, if it finds it, prints it:

```
awk '{ if ($1 == "Andorra") print }'
```

Unlike some languages, relational expressions in awk do not return a value; they evaluate to a true condition or a false condition only.

The following table lists the comparison operators available in awk.

Comparison Operator	Description
<	Less than
<=	Less than or equal to
>	Greater than
>=	Greater than or equal to
!=	Not equal
==	Equal

It is also possible to combine as many comparison operators in one statement as you require by using AND (&&) as well as OR (| |) operators. This allows you to test for more than one thing before your control statement is evaluated to be true.

For example:

```
$ awk '{ if ((($1 == "Andorra") && ($3 <= 500)) || ($1 == "Angola")) print }'
Andorra .ad 468 69865 35000 23500
Angola .ao 1246700 10978552 96300 130000
```

This prints any line whose first field contains the string Andorra and whose third field contains a number that is less than or equal to 500, or any line whose first field contains the string Angola.

As this example illustrates, each condition that you are testing must be surrounded by parentheses. Because the first and second condition are together (the first field has to match Andorra *and* the third field must be less than or equal to 500), the two are enclosed together in additional parentheses. There are also opening and closing parentheses that surround the entire conditional.

Arithmetic Functions

The comparison operators are useful for making comparisons, but you often will want to make changes to variables. Awk is able to perform all the standard arithmetic functions on numbers (addition, subtraction, multiplication, and division), as well as modulo (remainder) division, and does so in floating point. The following Try It Out demonstrates some arithmetic functions.

Try It Out   Using awk as a Calculator

Type the following commands on the command line:

```
$ awk 'BEGIN {myvar=10; print myvar+myvar}'
20
$ awk 'BEGIN {myvar=10; myvar=myvar+1; print myvar}'
11
```

How It Works

In these examples, you start off setting the variable myvar to have the value of 10. The first example does a simple addition operation to print the result of adding the value of myvar to myvar, resulting in adding 10 + 10. The second example adds 1 to myvar, puts that value into myvar, and then prints it. In the first example, myvar was not changed from its value of 10, so after the print statement, it still contains the value 10, but in the second example, the result is added to the variable, so myvar changed to the new value.

In the second example, you used an arithmetic operation to increase the value of the variable by one. There is actually a shorter way of doing this in awk, and it has some additional functionality. You can use the operator ++ to add 1 to a variable, and the operator -- to subtract 1. The position of these operators makes the increase or decrease happen at different points.

Try It Out   Increment and Decrement Operators

To get a good understanding of how this works, try typing the following examples on the command line:

```
$ awk 'BEGIN {myvar=10; print ++myvar; print myvar}'
11
11
$ awk 'BEGIN {myvar=10; print myvar++; print myvar}'
10
11
```

How It Works

In these two examples, the variable myvar is initialized with the value of 10. In the first example, a print is done on ++myvar that instructs awk to increment the value of myvar by 1 and then print it; this results in the printing of the first 11. Then you print myvar a second time to illustrate that the variable has actually been set to the new incremented value of 11. This is the same process shown in the previous section using myvar=myvar+1.

The second command is an example of a postincrement operation. The value of myvar is *first* printed and then it is incremented. The new value of myvar is then printed to illustrate that the variable was actually incremented.

A third set of increment operator shortcuts are the += and the -= operators. These allow you to add to or subtract from the variable.

Try It Out   Using the Add-to Operator

For example, you can use the += operator to add up all the cell phone users in your countries.txt file:

```
$ awk 'BEGIN {celltotal = 0}
>{celltotal += $6}
>END { print celltotal }' /tmp/countries.txt
2712810
```

How It Works

This example uses the += operator to add to the celltotal variable the contents of field number 6. The first line of the file is read in, and celltotal gets the value of the sixth field added to it (the variable starts initialized as 0 in the BEGIN block). It then reads the next line of the file, taking the sixth field and adding it to the contents of the celltotal variable. This continues until the end, where the value of that variable is printed.

Output Redirection

Be careful when using comparison operators, because some of them double as shell output variables in different contexts. For example the > character can be used in an awk statement to send the output from a command or a function into the file specified. For example, if you do the following:

```
$ awk 'BEGIN { print 4+5 > "result" }'
```

you create a file called `result` in your current working directory and then print the result of the sum of 4 + 5 into the file. If the file `result` already exists, it will be overwritten, unless you use the shell append operator, as follows:

```
$ awk 'BEGIN { print 5+5 >> "result" }'
```

This appends the summation of 5 + 5 to the end of the `result` file. If that file doesn't exist, it will be created.

Output from commands can also be piped into other system commands in the same way that this can be done on the shell command line.

While Loops

`While` statements in awk implement basic looping logic, using the same concepts introduced in Chapter 3. Loops continually execute statements until a condition is met. A `while` loop executes the statements that you specify *while* the condition specified evaluates to true.

`While` statements have a condition and an action. The condition is the same as the conditions used in `if` statements. The action is performed as long as the condition tests to be true. The condition is tested; if it is true, the action happens, and then awk loops back and tests the condition again. At some point, unless you have an infinite loop, the condition evaluates to be false, and then the action is not performed and the next statement in your awk program is executed.

Try It Out — Using while Loops

Try this basic `while` loop to print the numbers 1 through 10:

```
$ awk 'BEGIN { while (++myvar <= 10 ) print myvar }'
```

How It Works

The variable `myvar` starts off with the value of 0. Awk then uses the variable increment operators to increment `myvar` by 1 to have the value of 1. The `while` condition is tested, "Is `myvar` less than or equal to 10?" The answer is that myvar is 1, and 1 is less than 10, so print the value of `myvar`. The loop repeats, the `myvar` variable is incremented by 1, the condition is tested, it passes, and the value of the variable is printed (2).

For Loops

`For` loops are more flexible and provide a syntax that is easier to use, although they may seem more complex. They achieve the same results as a `while` loop but are often a better way of expressing it. Check out this example.

Try It Out — Using for Loops

This `for` loop prints every number between 1 and 10:

```
$ awk 'BEGIN { for ( myvar = 1; myvar <= 10; myvar++ ) print myvar }'
```

How It Works

For loops have three pieces. The first piece of the `for` loop does an initial action; in this case, it sets the variable `myvar` to 1. The second thing it does is set a condition; in this case, as long as `myvar` is less than or equal to 10, continue looping. The last part of this `for` loop is an increment; in this example, you increment the variable by 2. So in English, you could read this a, "For every number between 1 and 1-, print the number."

Functions

Awk has some built-in functions that make life as an awk programmer easier. These functions are always available; you don't need to define them or bring in any extra libraries to make them work. A function is called with arguments and returns the results. Functions are useful for things such as performing numeric conversions, finding the length of strings, changing the case of a string, running system commands, printing the current time, and the like.

Different functions have different requirements for how many arguments must be passed in order for them to work. Many have optional arguments that do not need to be included or have defaults that can be set if you desire. If you provide too many arguments to a function, gawk gives you a fatal error, while some awk implementations just ignore the extra arguments.

Functions are called in a standard way: the function name, an opening parenthesis, and then before the final parenthesis the arguments to the function. For example, `sin($3)` is calling the `sin` function and passing the argument `$3`. This function returns the mathematical sine value of whatever argument is sent to it.

Function arguments that are expressions, such as x+y, are evaluated before the function is passed those arguments. The result of x+y is what is passed to the function, rather than "x+y" itself.

Try It Out   Function Examples

Try these functions to see how they work:

```
$ awk 'BEGIN {print length("dog")}'
3
$ awk 'BEGIN {x=6; y=10; print sqrt(x+y)}'
4
```

How It Works

The first function in the example is the length function. It takes a string and tells you how many characters are in it. You pass the argument `do`, and it returns the length of that string.

The second sets two variables and then calls the square root function, using the additive of those two variables as the function argument. Because the expression is evaluated before the function is passed the argument, x+y is evaluated to be 16 and then `sqrt(16)` is called.

Awk has a number of predefined, built-in functions, and gawk has even more extensive ones available. The number of functions available are too many to list here, but you should look through the manual pages to see what functions are available, especially before you struggle to try to do something that may be implemented already in a built-in function.

The following table provides a list of some of the more common functions and what they do.

Function	Description of Function
atan(x,y)	Returns arctangent of y/x in radians
cos(x)	Returns the cosine of x
exp()	Returns the exponential e^x
index(*in, find*)	Searches string *in* for the first occurrence of *find* and returns its character position
int(x)	Returns nearest integer to x
length(*[string]*)	Returns number of characters in *string*
log(x)	Returns the logarithm of x
rand()	Returns a random number between 0 (zero) and 1
sin(x)	Returns the radial sine of x
sqrt(x)	Returns the square root of x
strftime(*format*)	Returns the time in the *format* specified, similar to the C function strftime().
tolower(*string*), toupper(*string*)	Changes the case of *string*
system(*command*)	Executes *command* and returns the exit code of that command
systime()	Returns the current seconds since the system epoch

Resources

The following are some good resources on the awk language:

❏   You can find the sources to awk at ftp://ftp.gnu.org/pub/gnu/awk.

❏   The Awk FAQ has many useful answers to some of the most commonly asked questions. It is available at www.faqs.org/faqs/computer-lang/awk/faq/.

❏   The GNU Gawk manual is a very clear and easy-to-understand guide through the language: www.gnu.org/software/gawk/manual/gawk.html.

❏   The newsgroup for awk is comp.lang.awk.

Summary

Awk can be complex and overwhelming, but the key to any scripting language is to learn some of the basics and start writing some simple scripts. As you practice, you will become more proficient and faster with writing your scripts. Now that you have a basic understanding of awk, you can dive further into the complexities of the language and use what you know to accomplish whatever it is you need to do in your shell scripts.

In this chapter:

- ❑ You learned what awk is and how it works, all the different versions that are available, and how to tell what version you have installed on your system. You also learned how to compile and install gawk, the most frequently used awk implementation.

- ❑ You learned how awk programs flow, from BEGIN to END, and the many different ways that awk can be invoked: from the command line or by creating independent awk scripts.

- ❑ You learned the basic awk print command and the more advanced printf and sprintf.

- ❑ You learned about different fields, the field separator variable, and different ways to change this to what you need according to your data.

- ❑ You learned about string formatting and format modifier characters, and now you can make nice-looking reports easily.

- ❑ You learned how to create your own variables and about the different built-in variables that are available to query throughout your programs.

- ❑ Control blocks were introduced, and you learned how to do if, for, and do loops.

- ❑ Arithmetic operators and comparison operators were introduced, as well as different ways to increment and decrement variables.

- ❑ You were briefly introduced to some of awk's standard built-in functions.

Exercises

1. Pipe your /etc/passwd file to awk, and print out the home directory of each user.

2. Change the following awk line so that it prints exactly the same but doesn't make use of commas:

```
awk '{ print "Number of cell phones in use in",$1":",$6 }' countries.txt
```

3. Print nicely formatted column headings for each of the fields in the countries.txt file, using a variable to store your format specifier.

4. Using the data from the countries.txt file, print the total ratio of cell phones to all the land-lines in the world.

5. Provide a total of all the fields in the countries.txt at the bottom of the output.

Creating Command Pipelines

The designers of Unix created an operating system with a philosophy that remains valid to this day. The Unix designers established the following:

- ❑ Everything is a file. Devices are represented as special files, as are networking connections and plain old normal files.

- ❑ Each process runs in an environment. This environment includes standard files for input, output, and errors.

- ❑ Unix has many small commands, each of which was designed to perform one task and to do that task well. This saves on memory and processor usage. It also leads to a more elegant system.

- ❑ These small commands were designed to accept input from the standard input file and send output to the standard output files.

- ❑ You can combine these small commands into more complex commands by creating command pipelines.

This chapter delves into these concepts from the perspective of shell scripts. Because shell scripts were designed to call commands, the ability to create command pipelines, thereby making new, complex commands from the simple primitive commands, provides you with extraordinary power. (Be sure to laugh like a mad scientist here.)

This chapter covers how you can combine commands and redirect the standard input, output, and errors, as well as pipe commands together.

Working with Standard Input and Output

Every process on Unix or a Unix-like system is provided with three open files (usually called file descriptors). These files are the standard input, output, and error files. By default:

❑ **Standard input** is the keyboard, abstracted as a file to make it easier to write scripts and programs.

❑ **Standard output** is the shell window or terminal from which the script runs, abstracted as a file to again make writing scripts and programs easier.

❑ **Standard error** is the same as standard output: the shell window or terminal from which the script runs.

When your script calls the `read` command, for example, it reads data from the standard input file. When your script calls the `echo` command, it sends data to the standard output file.

A *file descriptor* is simply a number that refers to an open file. By default, file descriptor 0 (zero) refers to standard input and is often abbreviated as stdin. File descriptor 1 refers to stdout, and file descriptor 2 refers to stderr. These numbers are important when you need to access a particular file, especially when you want to redirect these files to other locations. File descriptor numbers go up from zero.

Redirecting Standard Input and Output

Because the keyboard and shell window are treated as files, it's easier to redirect a script's output or input. That is, you can send the output of a script or a command to a file instead of to the shell window. Similarly, you can change the input of a script or command to come from a file instead of the keyboard. To do this, you create commands with a special > or < syntax.

To review, the basic syntax for a command is:

```
command options_and_arguments
```

The options are items such as -l for a long file listing (for the `ls` command). Arguments are items such as file names.

To redirect the output of a command to a file, use the following syntax:

```
command options_and_arguments > output_file
```

To redirect the input of a command to come from a file, use the following syntax:

```
command options_and_arguments < input_file
```

You can combine both redirections with the following syntax:

```
command options_and_arguments < input_file > output_file
```

You can use this syntax within your scripts or at the command line.

Try It Out   **Redirecting Command Output**

To try this, type in the following command at the prompt:

```
$ ls /usr/bin > commands.txt
```

You can then see the data that would have gone to the screen with the `more` command:

```
$ more commands.txt
[
411toppm
a2p
a2ps
ab
abiword
AbiWord-2.0
ac
access
```

The output will continue for quite a while. The commands you see will differ based on your system, but you should see commands such as [, covered in Chapter 3.

How It Works

The > operator tells the shell to redirect the output of the command to the given file. If the file exists, the shell deletes the old contents of the file and replaces it with the output of the command, `ls` in this case. Each line in the file `commands.txt` will contain the name of a file from /usr/bin, where many system commands reside.

The `more` command sends the contents of the file to the shell window, one window at a time.

Note that if your system does not have the more command, try the less command. Cygwin on Windows, for example, does not include the more command by default.

Try It Out   Redirecting a Command's Input

Use the < operator to redirect the input for a command. For example:

```
$ wc -l < commands.txt
2291
```

How It Works

The `wc` command, short for *word count*, counts the number of bytes, words, and lines in a file. The -1 (*ell*) option tells the `wc` command to output only the number of lines. This gives you a rough estimate as to the number of commands in /usr/bin.

In this example, the input to the `wc` command comes from the file named `commands.txt`. The shell sends the contents of the file `commands.txt` as the standard input for the `wc` command. You'll find input redirection very useful for programs that cannot open files on their own, such as the `mail` command.

Redirecting Standard Error

In addition to redirecting the standard input and output for a script or command, you can redirect standard error. Even though standard error by default goes to the same place as standard output — the shell window or terminal — there are good reasons why stdout and stderr are treated separately. The main reason is that you can redirect the output of a command or commands to a file, but you have no way of knowing whether an error occurred. Separating stderr from stdout allows the error messages to appear on your screen while the output still goes to the file.

To redirect stderr from a command to a file, use the following syntax:

```
command options_and_arguments 2> output_file
```

The 2 in 2> refers to file descriptor 2, the descriptor number for stderr.

The C shell uses a different syntax for redirecting standard error. See the next section for more on this.

Redirecting Both Standard Output and Standard Error

In the Bourne shell (as well as Bourne-shell derivatives such as bash and ksh), you can redirect stderr to the same location as stdout in a number of ways. You can also redirect standard error to a separate file. As part of this, you need to remember that the file descriptors for the standard files are 0 for stdin, 1 for stdout, and 2 for stderr.

Try It Out   Sending stderr to the Same Place as stdout

If you redirect stdout to a file, you can use the 2>&1 syntax to redirect stderr to the same location as stdout:

```
$ ls /usr/bin > commands.txt 2>&1
```

How It Works

The example command has three parts.

❑   ls /usr/bin is the command run — that is, ls with its argument, /usr/bin.

❑   > commands.txt redirects the output of the ls command — that is, stdout — to the file named commands.txt.

❑   2>&1 sends the output of file descriptor 2, stderr, to the same location as file descriptor 1, stdout. Because you already redirected stdout, any errors will also go into the file commands.txt.

You can see this if you try the ls command with a directory that does not exist. For example:

```
$ ls /usr2222/bin > commands.txt 2>&1
$ more commands.txt
ls: /usr2222/bin: No such file or directory
```

Note that this example assumes that your system has no directory named /usr2222/bin.

> **You have to be very careful entering in 2>&1 because an ampersand (&) alone means to run a command in the background. Do not place any spaces around 2>&1.**

Try It Out   **Redirecting Both stderr and stdout at Once**

You can redirect both stdout and stderr to the same location with the &> syntax. For example:

```
$ ls /usr2222/bin &> commands.txt
$ more commands.txt
ls: /usr2222/bin: No such file or directory
```

How It Works

In this example, ls is the command, /usr2222/bin is the argument to the ls command, and &> commands.txt redirects both stdout and stderr to the file named commands.txt.

If you do not redirect both file descriptors, then errors will be sent to the shell window or terminal. For example:

```
$ ls /usr2222/bin > commands.txt
ls: /usr2222/bin: No such file or directory
```

In this case, errors go to the screen, and any output would go to the file named commands.txt. (There will be no output in the case of an error like this one.)

> The C shell equivalent to redirect both stdout and stderr to the same place is >&. For example:
>
> ```
> ls >& output.txt
> ```
>
> There is no easy way to redirect stderr to one place and then stdout to another. See the note on Csh Programming Considered Harmful at www.faqs.org/faqs/unix-faq /shell/csh-whynot/ for more on why you may not want to use the C shell for scripting.

Appending to Files

The > operator can be quite destructive. Each time you run a command redirecting stdout to a file with >, the file will be truncated and replaced by any new output. In many cases, you'll want this behavior because the file will contain just the output of the command. But if you write a script that outputs to a log file, you typically don't want to destroy the log each time. This defeats the whole purpose of creating a log.

To get around this problem, you can use the >> operator to redirect the output of a command, but append to the file, if it exists. The syntax follows:

```
command >> file_to_append
```

The shell will create the file to append if the file does not exist.

Try It Out   Appending to a File

Enter the following commands:

```
$ uptime >> sysload.txt
$ uptime >> sysload.txt
$ uptime >> sysload.txt
$ more sysload.txt
 20:45:09 up 23 days,  1:54, 78 users,  load average: 0.23, 0.13, 0.05
 20:45:21 up 23 days,  1:54, 78 users,  load average: 0.20, 0.13, 0.05
 20:45:24 up 23 days,  1:54, 78 users,  load average: 0.18, 0.12, 0.05
```

How It Works

The `uptime` command lists how long your system has been up—that is, the time since the last reboot. It also lists a system load average. By using the >> append operator, you can view the output of the `uptime` command over time.

Use the >> operator any time you want to preserve the original contents of a file but still want to write additional data to the file.

Use the > operator when there is no need to preserve the contents of a file or where you explicitly want to overwrite the file.

Truncating Files

You can use a shorthand syntax for truncating files by omitting the command before the > operator. The syntax follows:

```
> filename
```

You can also use an alternate format with a colon:

```
: > filename
```

Note that : > predates the use of smiley faces in email messages.

Both of these command-less commands will create the file if it does not exist and truncate the file to zero bytes if the file does exist.

Try It Out   Truncating Files

Try the following commands to see file truncating in operation:

```
$ ls /usr/bin > commands.txt
$ ls -l
total 5
-rw-r--r--   1 ericfj    None         3370 Nov  1 07:25 commands.txt
drwxr-xr-x+  2 ericfj    None            0 Oct 13 12:30 scripts
-rw-r--r--   1 ericfj    None          232 Sep 27 10:09 var
```

```
$ : > commands.txt
$ ls -l
total 1
-rw-r--r--    1 ericfj   None             0 Nov  1 07:25 commands.txt
drwxr-xr-x+   2 ericfj   None             0 Oct 13 12:30 scripts
-rw-r--r--    1 ericfj   None           232 Sep 27 10:09 var
```

How It Works

The original command redirects the output of `ls` to a file named `commands.txt`. You can then perform a long listing on the file to see how many bytes are in the file, `3370` in this example (your results should differ).

Next, the `: >` operator truncates the file to a length of zero bytes. Again, use a long listing to verify the size.

Sending Output to Nowhere Fast

On occasion, you not only want to redirect the output of a command, you want to throw the output away. This is most useful if:

❑　A command creates a lot of unnecessary output.

❑　You want to see error messages only, if there are any.

❑　You are interested only in whether the command succeeded or failed. You do not need to see the command's output. This is most useful if you are using the command as a condition in an `if` or `while` statement.

Continuing in the Unix tradition of treating everything as a file, you can redirect a command's output to the null file, `/dev/null`. The null file consumes all output sent to it, as if `/dev/null` is a black hole star.

The file /dev/null is often called a bit bucket.

To use this handy file, simply redirect the output of a command to the file. For example:

```
$ ls /usr/bin > /dev/null
```

The Cygwin environment for Windows includes a /dev/null to better support Unix shell scripts.

Redirecting input and output is merely the first step. The next step is to combine commands into command pipelines.

Piping Commands

Command pipelines extend the idea of redirecting the input and output for a program. If you can redirect the output of one command and also redirect the input of another, why not connect the output of one command as the input of another? That's exactly what command pipelines do.

The basic syntax is:

```
command options_and_arguments | command2 options_and_arguments
```

The pipe character, |, acts to connect the two commands. The shell redirects the output of the first command to the input of the second command.

Note that command pipelines are often redundant to the normal redirection. For example, you can pass a file as input to the wc command, and the wc command will count the characters in the file:

```
$ wc < filename
```

You can also pass the name of the file as a command-line argument to the wc command:

```
$ wc filename
```

Or you can pipe the output of the cat command to the wc command:

```
$ cat filename | wc
```

Not all commands accept file names as arguments, so you still need pipes or input redirection. In addition, you can place as many commands as needed on the pipeline. For example:

```
command1 options_and_arguments | command2 | command3 | command4 > output.txt
```

Each of the commands in the pipeline can have as many arguments and options as needed. Because of this, you will often need to use the shell line-continuation marker, \, at the end of a line. For example:

```
command1 options_and_arguments | \
    command2 | \
    command3 | \
    command4 > output.txt
```

You can use the line-continuation marker, \, with any long command, but it is especially useful when you pipe together a number of commands.

Note that in your scripts, you don't need to use the line-continuation marker.

Piping with Unix Commands

Unix commands were designed with pipes in mind, as each command performs one task. The designers of Unix expected you to pipe commands together to get any useful work done.

For example, the spell command outputs all the words it does not recognize from a given file. (This is sort of a backward way to check the spelling of words in a file.) The sort command sorts text files, line by line. The uniq command removes duplicate lines. You can combine these commands into a primitive spell-checking command.

Try It Out   Checking Spelling the Primitive Way

Imagine you are living in a cave. Saber-toothed tigers roam outside. Mammoths taste bad. Try the following command line:

```
$ spell filename.txt | sort | uniq > suspect_words.txt
```

Choose a text file and pass it as the file name to the spell command. This is the file that will be checked. Any file with a lot of words will do. Running this command on an outline for this book generates a number of suspect words:

```
$ more suspect_words.txt
AppleScript
arg
Awk
backticks
basename
bashrc
BBEdit
bc
builtin
CDE
commnads
csh
Csh
CSH
CVS
drive's
dtedit
elif
eq
expr
fc
--More--(28%)
```

At least one of these words, *commnads,* is misspelled.

How It Works

The spell command goes through the file named by the command-line argument and outputs every word that is not in its internal word list. The assumption is that these words must be misspelled. As you can see from the example, virtually all computer and shell scripting terms are considered errors.

> Note that modern programs such as the OpenOffice.org office suite contain much better spell-checking packages. The spell command is a really old Unix command but very useful for testing pipelines.

The spell command outputs these words to stdout, one word per line. This one-per-line style is common among many Unix commands because this style makes it so easy to process the data. The command pipeline then pipes the output of the spell command to the input of the sort command. The sort command sorts the lines. (Modern versions of the spell command may sort as well, making this step unnecessary.)

The output of the sort command is a list of words, one per line, in sorted order. The command line pipes this output to the uniq command (another command always used in examples like this). The uniq command, short for *unique*, removes duplicate adjacent lines. Thus, the input must be sorted before calling uniq.

Finally, the command pipeline sends the data to the file named suspect_words.txt. You can then check this file to see a list of all the words that spell flagged as errors.

As you can see, the invention of word processing software really made life easier. The buildup of print-out paper forced people out of caves and into suburbia.

The concepts here work the same for any pipelines you need to create.

Creating Pipelines

Creating command pipelines can be difficult. It's best to approach this step by step, making sure each part of the pipeline works before going on to the next part.

For example, you can create a series of commands to determine which of many user accounts on a Unix or Linux system are for real users. Many background services, such as database servers, are given user accounts. This is mostly for the sake of file permissions. The postgres user can then own the files associated with the Postgres database service, for example. So the task is to separate these pseudo user accounts from real live people who have accounts on a system.

On Unix and Linux, user accounts are traditionally stored in /etc/passwd, a specially formatted text file with one line per user account.

Mac OS X supports a /etc/passwd file, but in most cases, user accounts are accessed from DirectoryServices or lookup. You can still experiment with the following commands to process formatted text in the /etc/passwd file, however. In addition, many systems do not use /etc/passwd to store all user accounts. Again, you can run the examples to see how to process formatted text.

An /etc/passwd file from a Linux system follows:

```
$ more /etc/passwd
root:x:0:0:root:/root:/bin/bash
bin:x:1:1:bin:/bin:/sbin/nologin
daemon:x:2:2:daemon:/sbin:/sbin/nologin
adm:x:3:4:adm:/var/adm:/sbin/nologin
lp:x:4:7:lp:/var/spool/lpd:/sbin/nologin
sync:x:5:0:sync:/sbin:/bin/sync
shutdown:x:6:0:shutdown:/sbin:/sbin/shutdown
halt:x:7:0:halt:/sbin:/sbin/halt
mail:x:8:12:mail:/var/spool/mail:/sbin/nologin
news:x:9:13:news:/etc/news:
uucp:x:10:14:uucp:/var/spool/uucp:/sbin/nologin
operator:x:11:0:operator:/root:/sbin/nologin
games:x:12:100:games:/usr/games:/sbin/nologin
gopher:x:13:30:gopher:/var/gopher:/sbin/nologin
ftp:x:14:50:FTP User:/var/ftp:/sbin/nologin
nobody:x:99:99:Nobody:/:/sbin/nologin
```

```
rpm:x:37:37:::/var/lib/rpm:/sbin/nologin
vcsa:x:69:69:virtual console memory owner:/dev:/sbin/nologin
nscd:x:28:28:NSCD Daemon:/:/sbin/nologin
sshd:x:74:74:Privilege-separated SSH:/var/empty/sshd:/sbin/nologin
rpc:x:32:32:Portmapper RPC user:/:/sbin/nologin
rpcuser:x:29:29:RPC Service User:/var/lib/nfs:/sbin/nologin
nfsnobody:x:65534:65534:Anonymous NFS User:/var/lib/nfs:/sbin/nologin
pcap:x:77:77::/var/arpwatch:/sbin/nologin
mailnull:x:47:47:::/var/spool/mqueue:/sbin/nologin
smmsp:x:51:51::/var/spool/mqueue:/sbin/nologin
apache:x:48:48:Apache:/var/www:/sbin/nologin
squid:x:23:23:::/var/spool/squid:/sbin/nologin
webalizer:x:67:67:Webalizer:/var/www/usage:/sbin/nologin
dbus:x:81:81:System message bus:/:/sbin/nologin
xfs:x:43:43:X Font Server:/etc/X11/fs:/sbin/nologin
named:x:25:25:Named:/var/named:/sbin/nologin
ntp:x:38:38::/etc/ntp:/sbin/nologin
gdm:x:42:42::/var/gdm:/sbin/nologin
postgres:x:26:26:PostgreSQL Server:/var/lib/pgsql:/bin/bash
ericfj:x:500:500:Eric Foster-Johnson:/home2/ericfj:/bin/bash
bobmarley:x:501:501:Bob Marley:/home/bobmarley:/bin/bash
```

The /etc/passwd file uses the following format for each user account:

```
username:password:userID:groupID:Real Name:home_directory:starting_shell
```

Each field is separated by a colon. So you can parse the information for an individual user:

```
bobmarley:x:501:501:Bob Marley:/home/bobmarley:/bin/bash
```

In this case, the user name is bobmarley. The password, x, is a placeholder. This commonly means that another system handles login authentication. The user ID is 501. So is the user's default group ID. (Linux systems often create a group for each user, a group of one, for security reasons.) The user's real name is Bob Marley. His home directory is /home/bobmarley. His starting shell is bash. (Good choice.)

Like the ancient spell command used previously, making broad assumptions is fun, although not always accurate. For this example, a real user account is a user account that runs a shell (or what the script thinks is a shell) on login and does not run a program in /sbin or /usr/sbin, locations for system administration commands. As with the spell command, this is not fully accurate but good enough to start processing the /etc/passwd file.

You can combine all this information and start extracting data from the /etc/passwd file one step at a time.

Try It Out   Processing User Names

The cut command extracts, or cuts, pieces of text from formatted text files. The following command tells cut to extract the username, real name, and starting shell fields from the /etc/passwd file:

```
$ cut -d: -f1,5,7 /etc/passwd
root:root:/bin/bash
bin:bin:/sbin/nologin
```

```
daemon:daemon:/sbin/nologin
adm:adm:/sbin/nologin
lp:lp:/sbin/nologin
sync:sync:/bin/sync
shutdown:shutdown:/sbin/shutdown
halt:halt:/sbin/halt
mail:mail:/sbin/nologin
news:news:
uucp:uucp:/sbin/nologin
operator:operator:/sbin/nologin
games:games:/sbin/nologin
gopher:gopher:/sbin/nologin
ftp:FTP User:/sbin/nologin
nobody:Nobody:/sbin/nologin
rpm::/sbin/nologin
vcsa:virtual console memory owner:/sbin/nologin
nscd:NSCD Daemon:/sbin/nologin
sshd:Privilege-separated SSH:/sbin/nologin
rpc:Portmapper RPC user:/sbin/nologin
rpcuser:RPC Service User:/sbin/nologin
nfsnobody:Anonymous NFS User:/sbin/nologin
pcap::/sbin/nologin
mailnull::/sbin/nologin
smmsp::/sbin/nologin
apache:Apache:/sbin/nologin
squid::/sbin/nologin
webalizer:Webalizer:/sbin/nologin
dbus:System message bus:/sbin/nologin
xfs:X Font Server:/sbin/nologin
named:Named:/sbin/nologin
ntp::/sbin/nologin
gdm::/sbin/nologin
postgres:PostgreSQL Server:/bin/bash
ericfj:Eric Foster-Johnson:/bin/bash
bobmarley:Bob Marley:/bin/bash
```

With the cut command, you have narrowed the data, removing extraneous fields, which makes it easier to filter the entries.

Note that cut starts counting with 1. Many Unix-related commands start at 0.

The next step is to filter out all the items with starting programs in the /sbin directory, especially the aptly named /sbin/nologin, which implies an account where the user is not allowed to log in. To do this, you can pipe the results to the grep command:

```
$ cut -d: -f1,5,7 /etc/passwd | grep -v sbin
root:root:/bin/bash
sync:sync:/bin/sync
news:news:
postgres:PostgreSQL Server:/bin/bash
ericfj:Eric Foster-Johnson:/bin/bash
bobmarley:Bob Marley:/bin/bash
```

The `-v` option tells `grep` to output all lines that do not match the expression. This is very useful for shell scripts.

You now have a lot less data. The next filter should focus on keeping only those user accounts that run a shell. Because all shells have *sh* in their names, you can use `grep` again:

```
$ cut -d: -f1,5,7 /etc/passwd | grep -v sbin | grep sh
root:root:/bin/bash
postgres:PostgreSQL Server:/bin/bash
ericfj:Eric Foster-Johnson:/bin/bash
bobmarley:Bob Marley:/bin/bash
```

Note that not all shells are required to have sh in their names. This is an assumption used for simplicity.

The data looks good — well, mostly good. You still have a false positive with the `postgres` account because it is listed as having bash for its shell. (Exercise 3 in the exercises at the end of the chapter aims to get you to solve this issue.)

The next step is to display the data in a way that looks better than the previous output. To display the data, you can go back to the `awk` command. The following awk program will format the data better:

```
awk -F':' ' { printf( "%-12s %-40s\n", $1, $2 )   } ' users.txt
```

See Chapter 7 for more on the awk command.

This command tells `awk` to process the data in the file named `users.txt`. To create this file, you can redirect the output of the previous command:

```
cut -d: -f1,5,7 /etc/passwd | grep -v sbin | grep sh | sort > users.txt
```

For example:

```
$ cut -d: -f1,5,7 /etc/passwd | grep -v sbin | grep sh > users.txt
$ more users.txt
root:root:/bin/bash
postgres:PostgreSQL Server:/bin/bash
ericfj:Eric Foster-Johnson:/bin/bash
bobmarley:Bob Marley:/bin/bash
```

The data now appears in the file named `users.txt`, ready for the `awk` command. To make for a better display, the `sort` command rearranges the output in alphabetical order:

```
$ cut -d: -f1,5,7 /etc/passwd | grep -v sbin | grep sh | sort > users.txt
$ more users.txt
bobmarley:Bob Marley:/bin/bash
ericfj:Eric Foster-Johnson:/bin/bash
postgres:PostgreSQL Server:/bin/bash
root:root:/bin/bash
```

Putting this all together, enter the following script and save it under the name `listusers`:

```
cut -d: -f1,5,7 /etc/passwd | grep -v sbin | grep sh | sort > users.txt

awk -F':' ' { printf( "%-12s %-40s\n", $1, $2 )   } ' users.txt

# Clean up the temporary file.
/bin/rm -rf users.txt
```

When you run this script, you should see output like the following:

```
$ sh listusers
bobmarley    Bob Marley
ericfj       Eric Foster-Johnson
postgres     PostgreSQL Server
root         root
```

Your output will differ based on the user accounts listed in `/etc/passwd` on your system.

How It Works

Yow. That is a lot of work for a very short script. Note how you build up the piped command line slowly, one step at a time. You'll often need to follow this approach when creating a complicated command line.

> *Also note that there are a lot of commands available on your system, just waiting for you to use them in shell scripts.*

The `listusers` script makes a lot of assumptions. Each of these assumptions can break down and cause the script to miss a user or, more likely, include false positives in the list of user accounts. The `postgres` account in the example output shows a false positive. Furthermore, someone with a real name of *Linusbinsky* would fail the *sbin* `grep` test. You probably don't have a user with this name, but it shows that people's names often make filtering rules very hard to create.

In addition to piping between commands, you can pipe data to and from your shell scripts, as in the following Try It Out.

Try It Out   **Piping with Scripts**

Enter the following script and save it under the name `echodata`:

```
#!/bin/sh
echo -n "When is the project due? "
read DUE
echo
echo "Due $DUE."
```

Mark the script file as executable:

```
$ chmod a+x echodata
```

This is a very simple script that prompts the user to enter data and a due date, and then repeats the data. The purpose of the script is just to experiment with pipes.

Enter the following piped command:

```
$ echo today | ./echodata
When is the project due?
Due today.
```

How It Works

The echodata script prompts the user with the echo command and then uses the read command to read input from stdin, normally the keyboard. You can pipe the output of the echo command to the echodata script. With that, the script has the data it needs from stdin, so the script will complete right away. It will not wait for you to type in any data.

Using tee to Send the Output to More Than One Process

The tee command sends output to two locations: a file as well as stdout. The tee command copies all input to both locations. This proves useful, for example, if you need to redirect the output of a command to a file and yet still want to see it on the screen. The basic syntax is:

```
original_command | tee filename.txt | next_command
```

In this example, the tee command sends all the output of the original_command to both the next_command and to the file filename.txt. This allows you to extract data from the command without modifying the result. You get a copy of the data, written to a file, as well as the normal command pipeline.

Try It Out   Tee Time

To see the tee command in action, try the following commands:

```
$ ls -1 /usr/bin | tee usr_bin.txt | wc -1
2291
$ more usr_bin.txt
[
411toppm
a2p
a2ps
ab
abiword
AbiWord-2.0
ac
access
aclocal
aclocal-1.4
aclocal-1.5
aclocal-1.6
```

```
aclocal-1.7
aclocal-1.8
aconnect
activation-client
addftinfo
addr2line
addr2name.awk
addresses
allcm
--More--(0%)
```

How It Works

This command counts the number of files in the directory /usr/bin. The -1 (one) option tells the ls command to output each file name one to a line. The -1 (ell) option tells the wc command to report just the number of lines in the data.

Note how the wc command consumes the data. With the wc command, you have a count, but the data itself is gone. That's where the tee command comes into play. The tee command feeds all the data to the wc command, but it also makes a copy to the file usr_bin.txt.

Summary

You can get a lot of work done by combining simple commands. Unix systems (and Unix-like systems) are packed full of these types of commands. Many in the programming community liken scripting to the glue that ties commands together. You can think of the operating system as a toolbox and the shell as a way to access these tools. This philosophy will make it a lot easier to write shell scripts that you can use again and again.

This chapter covers redirecting input, output, and errors, as well as creating command pipelines.

❑   You can redirect the output of commands to files using the > operator. The > operator will truncate a file if it already exists. Use >> in place of > if you want to append to the file.

❑   You can redirect the error output of commands using &>, or 2>&1 to send the error output to the same location as the normal output.

❑   You can redirect the input of commands to come from files using the < operator.

❑   Redirect the output of one command to the input of another using the pipe character, |. You can pipe together as many commands as you need.

❑   The tee command will copy its input to both stdout and to any files listed on the command line.

The next chapter shows how to control processes, capture the output of commands into variables, and mercilessly kill processes.

Exercises

1. Discuss the ways commands can generate output. Focus particularly on commands called from shell scripts.

2. Use pipes or redirection to create an infinite feedback loop, where the final output becomes the input again to the command line. Be sure to stop this command before it fills your hard disk. (If you are having trouble, look at the documentation for the `tail` command.)

3. Modify the `listusers` script so that it does not generate a false positive for the `postgres` user and other, similar accounts that are for background processes, not users. You may want to go back to the original data, `/etc/passwd`, to come up with a way to filter out the `postgres` account.

Controlling Processes

Shell scripts were designed to run commands. Up to this point, all the scripts in the book have launched various commands, but all in isolation. The most you've seen so far is piping commands to connect the output of one command to the input of another. But the commands run from the scripts do not provide data back to the scripts, other than through writing data to a file. To make processes better fit into shell scripts, you need the capability to start and stop processes, as well as capture the output of processes into shell variables.

This chapter delves into processes and shows how you can launch and control processes from your scripts, including:

- ❑   Exploring the processes running on your system
- ❑   Launching processes in the foreground and the background
- ❑   Using command substitution to set variables from commands
- ❑   Checking the return codes of processes

Exploring Processes

There is a lot of terminology associated with processes. Don't be daunted; it's easier to understand when you see it in action than to explain.

Simply put, a *process* is a running program. A *program* is a file on disk (or other storage) that can be executed. Most programs are compiled into the binary format required by the processor chip and operating system. For example, the ls command is a program, compiled for a particular system. An ls program compiled for Linux on a Pentium system will not run in Windows, even on the same computer and processor chip. That's because the operating system defines the format of executable binary files.

A *command* is a program that is part of the operating system. For example, ls is a command in Linux and Windows systems, while format.exe is a command in Windows.

The act of making a program stored on disk into a process is called *launching* or running. The operating system reads the program file on disk, creates a new process, and loads the program into that process. Some operating systems allow for multiple processes to run from the same program. Other operating systems impose a limit, such as allowing only one instance of a program to run at any given time.

There are a lot of differences between operating systems and how they handle processes. Luckily, shells abstract a lot of the details, making for a more consistent view.

Checking Process IDs

When the operating system launches a process, it gives the process and ID. You can view this ID if you list the running processes with the ps command on Unix and Linux systems, or use the Task Manager in Windows. Figure 9-1 shows the Windows XP Task Manager.

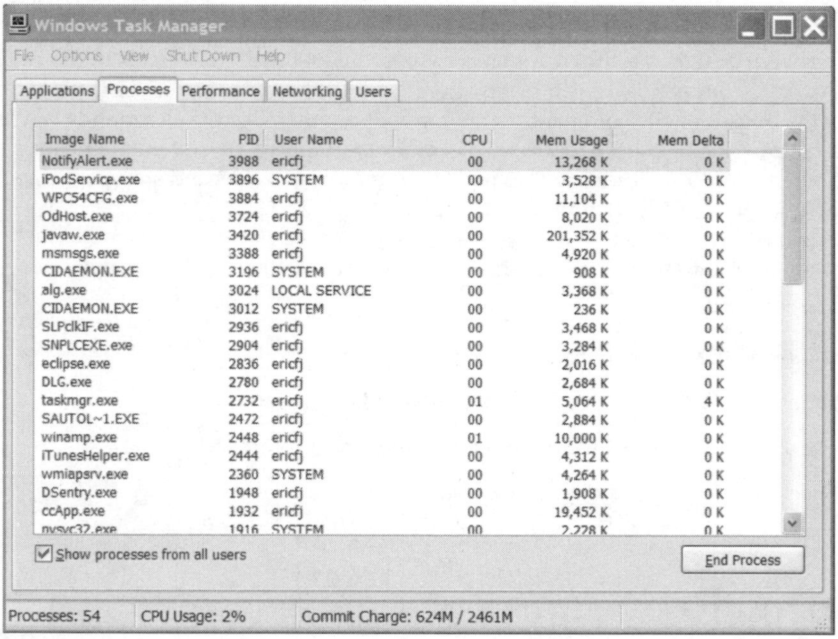

Figure 9-1

In Figure 9-1, each process has a process ID, or PID. Each process ID uniquely identifies one process. The process ID is the number you need if you want to control or terminate the process.

Isn't it odd that the main way you interact with a running process is to terminate it?

The ps command lists the active processes. For example:

```
$ ps -ef
UID         PID  PPID  C STIME TTY          TIME CMD
root          1     0  0 Oct08 ?        00:00:05 init [5]
root          2     1  0 Oct08 ?        00:00:00 [ksoftirqd/0]
```

```
root         3     1   0 Oct08 ?        00:00:02 [events/0]
root         4     3   0 Oct08 ?        00:00:00 [kblockd/0]
root         6     3   0 Oct08 ?        00:00:00 [khelper]
root         5     1   0 Oct08 ?        00:00:00 [khubd]
root         7     3   0 Oct08 ?        00:00:10 [pdflush]
root        10     3   0 Oct08 ?        00:00:00 [aio/0]
root         9     1   0 Oct08 ?        00:00:10 [kswapd0]
root       117     1   0 Oct08 ?        00:00:00 [kseriod]
root       153     1   0 Oct08 ?        00:00:04 [kjournald]
root      1141     1   0 Oct08 ?        00:00:00 [kjournald]
root      1142     1   0 Oct08 ?        00:00:08 [kjournald]
root      1473     1   0 Oct08 ?        00:00:00 syslogd -m 0
root      1477     1   0 Oct08 ?        00:00:00 klogd -x
rpc       1505     1   0 Oct08 ?        00:00:00 portmap
rpcuser   1525     1   0 Oct08 ?        00:00:00 rpc.statd
root      1552     1   0 Oct08 ?        00:00:00 rpc.idmapd
root      1647     1   0 Oct08 ?        00:00:00 /usr/sbin/smartd
root      1657     1   0 Oct08 ?        00:00:00 /usr/sbin/acpid
root      1858     1   0 Oct08 ?        00:00:00 /usr/sbin/sshd
root      1873     1   0 Oct08 ?        00:00:00 xinetd -stayalive -pidfile /var
root      1892     1   0 Oct08 ?        00:00:01 sendmail: accepting connections
smmsp     1901     1   0 Oct08 ?        00:00:00 sendmail: Queue runner@01:00:00
root      1912     1   0 Oct08 ?        00:00:00 gpm -m /dev/input/mice -t imps2
root      1923     1   0 Oct08 ?        00:00:00 crond
xfs       1945     1   0 Oct08 ?        00:00:01 xfs -droppriv -daemon
daemon    1964     1   0 Oct08 ?        00:00:00 /usr/sbin/atd
dbus      1983     1   0 Oct08 ?        00:00:00 dbus-daemon-1 --system
root      1999     1   0 Oct08 ?        00:00:00 mdadm --monitor --scan
root      2017     1   0 Oct08 tty1     00:00:00 /sbin/mingetty tty1
root      2018     1   0 Oct08 tty2     00:00:00 /sbin/mingetty tty2
root      2024     1   0 Oct08 tty3     00:00:00 /sbin/mingetty tty3
root      2030     1   0 Oct08 tty4     00:00:00 /sbin/mingetty tty4
root      2036     1   0 Oct08 tty5     00:00:00 /sbin/mingetty tty5
root      2042     1   0 Oct08 tty6     00:00:00 /sbin/mingetty tty6
root      2043     1   0 Oct08 ?        00:00:00 /usr/bin/gdm-binary -nodaemon
root      2220  2043   0 Oct08 ?        00:00:25 /usr/bin/gdm-binary -nodaemon
root      2231  2220   0 Oct08 ?        05:52:20 /usr/X11R6/bin/X :0 -audit 0 -au
root      2805     1   0 Oct08 ?        00:00:00 /sbin/dhclient -1 -q -lf /var/li
root     18567     3   0 Oct18 ?        00:00:09 [pdflush]
root     20689     1   0 Nov03 ?        00:00:00 /usr/libexec/bonobo-activation-s
ericfj   22282     1   0 Nov04 ?        00:00:00 /usr/libexec/bonobo-activation-s
ericfj   25801  2220   0 Nov06 ?        00:00:02 /usr/bin/gnome-session
ericfj   25849 25801   0 Nov06 ?        00:00:00 /usr/bin/ssh-agent /etc/X11/xinit
ericfj   25853     1   0 Nov06 ?        00:00:01 /usr/libexec/gconfd-2 5
ericfj   25856     1   0 Nov06 ?        00:00:00 /usr/bin/gnome-keyring-daemon
ericfj   25858     1   0 Nov06 ?        00:02:12 metacity --sm-save-file 10940799
ericfj   25860     1   0 Nov06 ?        00:00:03 /usr/libexec/gnome-settings-daem
ericfj   25865  1873   0 Nov06 ?        00:00:08 fam
ericfj   25879     1   0 Nov06 ?        00:00:04 xscreensaver -nosplash
ericfj   25888     1   0 Nov06 ?        00:00:13 gnome-panel --sm-config-prefix
/ericfj  25890     1   0 Nov06 ?        00:00:28 magicdev --sm-config-prefix /mag
ericfj   25895     1   0 Nov06 ?        00:00:39 nautilus --sm-config-prefix /nau
ericfj   25909     1   0 Nov06 ?        00:00:03 eggcups --sm-config-prefix /eggc
ericfj   25912     1   0 Nov06 ?        00:00:00 /usr/libexec/gnome-vfs-daemon -
ericfj   25914     1   0 Nov06 ?        00:00:10 gnome-terminal --sm-config-prefi
```

```
ericfj    25939     1   0 Nov06 ?        00:00:01 /usr/bin/pam-panel-icon --sm-cli
root      25944 25939   0 Nov06 ?        00:00:00 /sbin/pam_timestamp_check -d roo
ericfj    25946     1   0 Nov06 ?        00:00:00 /usr/libexec/mapping-daemon
ericfj    25948     1   0 Nov06 ?        00:00:04 /usr/libexec/nautilus-throbber
ericfj    25949 25914   0 Nov06 ?        00:00:00 gnome-pty-helper
ericfj    25950 25914   0 Nov06 pts/92   00:00:00 bash
ericfj    25959 25914   0 Nov06 pts/93   00:00:00 bash
ericfj    25962 25914   0 Nov06 pts/94   00:00:00 bash
ericfj    26007     1   0 Nov06 ?        00:00:02 /usr/libexec/clock-applet --oaf-
ericfj    26009     1   0 Nov06 ?        00:00:01 /usr/libexec/notification-area-a
ericfj    26011     1   0 Nov06 ?        00:00:01 /usr/libexec/mixer_applet2 --oaf
ericfj    26018     1   0 Nov06 ?        00:00:28 /usr/libexec/wnck-applet --oaf-a
ericfj    26020     1   0 Nov06 ?        00:00:04 /usr/libexec/wireless-applet --o
ericfj    26022     1   0 Nov06 ?        00:00:02 /usr/libexec/gweather-applet-2
ericfj    26025 25950   0 Nov06 pts/92   00:00:00 /bin/sh /home2/ericfj/bin/favs
ericfj    26026 26025   0 Nov06 pts/92   00:00:32 xmms /home2/ericfj/multi/mp3/fav
root      26068     1   0 Nov06 ?        00:00:00 [usb-storage]
root      26069     1   0 Nov06 ?        00:00:00 [scsi_eh_12]
ericfj    26178     1   0 Nov06 ?        00:00:00 /bin/sh /usr/lib/firefox-0.9.3/f
ericfj    26188 26178   0 Nov06 ?        00:00:00 /bin/sh /usr/lib/firefox-0.9.3/r
ericfj    26193 26188   0 Nov06 ?        00:07:47 /usr/lib/firefox-0.9.3/firefox-b
root      26232 25950   0 Nov06 pts/92   00:00:00 su
root      26235 26232   0 Nov06 pts/92   00:00:00 bash
ericfj    27112     1   0 Nov06 ?        00:00:00 /usr/bin/artsd -F 10 -S 4096 -s
root      27742     1   0 04:08 ?        00:00:00 cupsd
ericfj     8585     1   0 07:51 ?        00:01:03 /usr/lib/ooo-1.1/program/soffice
ericfj     8604  8585   0 07:51 ?        00:00:00 /usr/lib/ooo-1.1/program/getstyl
ericfj     8615     1   0 07:53 ?        00:00:09 gedit file:///home2/ericfj/writi
ericfj     9582     1   0 19:22 ?        00:00:03 /usr/bin/esd -terminate -nobeeps
ericfj     9621 25962   0 19:37 pts/94   00:00:00 ps -ef
```

On most modern operating systems, you will find a lot of processes running at any given time.

Note that the options to the ps command to view all processes are either -ef or -aux, depending on the version of Unix. Berkeley-derived versions of Unix such as Mac OS X tend to use -aux, and System V–based versions of Unix tend to use -ef.

Linux systems support both types of options.

With Bourne shell scripts, a special variable, $$, holds the process ID, or PID, of the current process — that is, the process running your script. Note that this process is most likely a running instance of /bin/sh.

Another special variable, $!, holds the PID of the last command executed in the background. If your script has not launched any processes in the background, then $! will be empty.

Try It Out   Reading Process IDs

Enter the following script. Save it under the file name process_id:

```
echo "The current process ID is $$."

if [ "$!" != "" ]
```

```
then
    echo "The ID of the last-run background process is $!."
else
    echo "No background process ID stored in" '$!'
fi

# Now, run something in the background.
ls > /dev/null &
if [ "$!" != "" ]
then
    echo "The ID of the last-run background process is $!."
else
    echo "No background process ID stored in" '$!'
fi
```

When you run this script, you'll see output like the following:

```
$ sh process_id
The current process ID is 9652.
No background process ID stored in $!
The ID of the last-run background process is 9653.
```

It is very likely that the process ID numbers will differ on your system, however. Each operating system assigns process IDs to each new process. Operating systems differ in how they choose the numbers to assign. In addition, if one system has run a lot of processes, it will have used up more process IDs than another system that may have run only a few processes. Just assume that each process has an ID number.

How It Works

The process_id script first outputs the value of $$. The shell fills in $$ with the ID of its process. Next, the process_id script checks if the special variable $! has a value. If set, $! holds the ID of the last-run background process — that is, the background process last run from your script. Because the script has not launched any processes in the background, you should expect this to be empty.

Notice how the if statement test places the variable $! within quotes. That's so there actually is an argument for the test command, [, even if the variable $! is empty. This is important, or the if statement will not operate properly.

Next, the process_id script launches a process, ls in this case, in the background. Now the special variable $! should have a value.

Reading the /proc File System

In addition to the normal process listings, Linux systems support a special file system called /proc. The /proc file system holds information on each running process as well as hardware-related information on your system. The /proc file system started out holding just process information. Now it holds all sorts of operating system and hardware data.

The neat thing about the /proc file system is that it appears to be a normal directory on disk. Inside /proc, you'll find more directories and plain text files, making it easy to write scripts. Each process, for example, has a directory under /proc. The directory name is the process ID number.

The /proc file system holds more than information on processes. It also contains information on devices connected on USB ports, system interrupts, and other hardware-related statuses.

Listing Files in /proc

Concentrating on processes, you can use the standard file-related commands to view the contents of the /proc file system. For example:

```
$ ls -CF /proc
1/        11234/   11572/   1892/    2231/    dma          mounts@
10/       11237/   11575/   1901/    27112/   driver/      mtrr
11087/    11238/   11594/   1912/    27742/   execdomains  net/
11135/    11248/   11623/   1923/    2805/    fb           partitions
11139/    11293/   11632/   1945/    3/       filesystems  pci
11142/    11295/   117/     1964/    4/       fs/          scsi/
11144/    11297/   11751/   1983/    5/       ide/         self@
11146/    11304/   12032/   1999/    6/       interrupts   slabinfo
11151/    11306/   1473/    2/       7/       iomem        stat
11165/    11308/   1477/    2017/    9/       ioports      swaps
11174/    11312/   1505/    2018/    acpi/    irq/         sys/
11179/    11322/   1525/    2024/    asound/  kcore        sysrq-trigger
11181/    11327/   153/     2030/    buddyinfo kmsg        sysvipc/
11195/    11379/   1552/    2036/    bus/     loadavg      tty/
11198/    11380/   1647/    2042/    cmdline  locks        uptime
11200/    1141/    1657/    2043/    cpuinfo  mdstat       version
11225/    1142/    18567/   20689/   crypto   meminfo      vmstat
11230/    11564/   1858/    2220/    devices  misc
11232/    11565/   1873/    22282/   diskstats modules
```

Note all the numbered directories. These represent the processes in the system. Inside each process-specific directory, you'll find information about the particular process. For example:

```
$ ls -CF /proc/12032
attr/   cmdline  environ  fd/    mem    root@  statm   task/
auxv    cwd@     exe@     maps   mounts stat   status  wchan
```

How It Works

The /proc file system isn't really a directory on disk. Instead, it is a virtual file system, where the Linux kernel maps internal kernel data structures to what looks like files and directories on disk. This is really handy because so many Linux commands are designed to work with files.

The first ls command lists the contents of /proc at a given time. This means your output will differ but should still appear similar to the example.

The -CF option to the ls command appends / on directories, * on executable files, and @ on symbolic links.

Next, select a running process. In this example, the next ls command views the contents of the /proc/12032 directory. Note that your process numbers will very likely differ.

You can guess what some of the files in this directory hold. For example, the cmdline file holds the command-line parameters to the process. The environ file holds the environment variables and their values under which the process was launched. The fd subdirectory lists the open file descriptors. A long listing of the fd subdirectory can be the most interesting. For example:

```
$ ls -CFl /proc/12032/fd
total 4
lrwx------  1 ericfj ericfj 64 Nov  8 20:08 0 -> /dev/pts/97
lrwx------  1 ericfj ericfj 64 Nov  8 20:08 1 -> /dev/pts/97
lrwx------  1 ericfj ericfj 64 Nov  8 20:08 2 -> /dev/pts/97
lr-x------  1 ericfj ericfj 64 Nov  8 20:08 255 ->
/home2/ericfj/writing/beginning_shell_scripting/scripts/exercise_09_01
```

Note the three open file descriptors 0, 1, and 2. These correspond to stdin, stdout, and stderr, respectively. There is also file descriptor 255.

A more interesting process has more open file descriptors. For example:

```
$ ls -CFl /proc/11751/fd
total 25
lr-x------  1 ericfj ericfj 64 Nov  8 20:09 0 -> /dev/null
l-wx------  1 ericfj ericfj 64 Nov  8 20:09 1 -> pipe:[9645622]
lr-x------  1 ericfj ericfj 64 Nov  8 20:09 10 -> pipe:[9710243]
l-wx------  1 ericfj ericfj 64 Nov  8 20:09 11 -> pipe:[9710243]
lrwx------  1 ericfj ericfj 64 Nov  8 20:09 12 -> socket:[9710244]
lrwx------  1 ericfj ericfj 64 Nov  8 20:09 13 -> socket:[9710250]
lrwx------  1 ericfj ericfj 64 Nov  8 20:09 14 -> socket:[9710252]
lrwx------  1 ericfj ericfj 64 Nov  8 20:09 15 -> socket:[9710255]
lrwx------  1 ericfj ericfj 64 Nov  8 20:09 16 -> socket:[9710260]
lrwx------  1 ericfj ericfj 64 Nov  8 20:09 17 -> socket:[9710256]
lr-x------  1 ericfj ericfj 64 Nov  8 20:09 18 -> pipe:[9710402]
lrwx------  1 ericfj ericfj 64 Nov  8 20:09 19 -> socket:[9710284]
l-wx------  1 ericfj ericfj 64 Nov  8 20:09 2 -> pipe:[9645622]
l-wx------  1 ericfj ericfj 64 Nov  8 20:09 20 -> pipe:[9710402]
lr-x------  1 ericfj ericfj 64 Nov  8 20:09 21 -> pipe:[9710403]
l-wx------  1 ericfj ericfj 64 Nov  8 20:09 22 -> pipe:[9710403]
lrwx------  1 ericfj ericfj 64 Nov  8 20:09 23 -> socket:[9710404]
lrwx------  1 ericfj ericfj 64 Nov  8 20:09 24 -> socket:[9710407]
lrwx------  1 ericfj ericfj 64 Nov  8 20:09 3 -> socket:[9710237]
lr-x------  1 ericfj ericfj 64 Nov  8 20:09 4 -> pipe:[9710240]
l-wx------  1 ericfj ericfj 64 Nov  8 20:09 5 -> pipe:[9710240]
lr-x------  1 ericfj ericfj 64 Nov  8 20:09 6 -> pipe:[9710241]
l-wx------  1 ericfj ericfj 64 Nov  8 20:09 7 -> pipe:[9710241]
lr-x------  1 ericfj ericfj 64 Nov  8 20:09 8 -> pipe:[9710242]
l-wx------  1 ericfj ericfj 64 Nov  8 20:09 9 -> pipe:[9710242]
```

This process is using quite a number of network sockets and pipes. This is for a GNOME text editor, gedit.

Explore the /proc file system to see what you can find. Once you find some interesting files, you can use the cat command to view the file contents. For example:

```
$ cat /proc/11751/environ
SSH_AGENT_PID=11135HOSTNAME=kirkwallTERM=dumbSHELL=/bin/bashHISTSIZE=1000QTDIR=/u
sr/lib/qt3.3USER=ericfjLS_COLORS=SSH_AUTH_SOCK=/tmp/sshPwg11087/agent.110
87KDEDIR=/usrPATH=/usr/kerberos/bin:/usr/local/bin:/usr/bin:/bin:/usr/X11R6/b
```

```
in:/home2/ericfj/bin:/usr/java/j2sdk1.4.1_03/bin:/opt/jext/binDESKTOP_S
ESSION=defaultMAIL=/var/spool/mail/ericfjPWD=/home2/ericfjINPUTRC=/etc/in
putrcLANG=en_US.UTF-8GDMSESSION=defaultSSH_ASKPASS=/usr/libexec/openssh/gn
ome-ssh-askpassSHLVL=1HOME=/home2/ericfjLOGNAME=ericfjLESSOPEN=|usr/bin/less
pipe.sh%sDISPLAY=:.0.0G_BROKEN_FILENAMES=1XAUTHORITY=/home2/ericfj/.Xau
thorityGTK_RC_FILES=/etc/gtk/gtkrc:/home2/ericfj/.gtkrc-1.2-
gnome2SESSION_MANAGER=local/kirkwall:/tmp/.ICE-unix/11087GNOME_KEYRI
NG_SOCKET=/tmp/keyring-9XCKKR/socketGNOME_DESKTOP_SESSION_ID=Default
```

If you stare at this output long enough (with your eyes in a slight squint), you can see a set of environment variables. The problem is that the output is all mashed together.

Try It Out   Viewing Process Data from /proc

To see what is going on in the preceding code block, you can use the od command, short for *octal dump*. The od command dumps the file contents as a set of octal characters. With the -a option, it also prints out ASCII text for all printable characters.

For example:

```
$ od -a /proc/11751/environ
0000000    S    S    H    _    A    G    E    N    T    _    P    I    D    =    1    1
0000020    1    3    5  nul    H    O    S    T    N    A    M    E    =    k    i    r
0000040    k    w    a    l    l  nul    T    E    R    M    =    d    u    m    b  nul
0000060    S    H    E    L    L    =    /    b    i    n    /    b    a    s    h  nul
0000100    H    I    S    T    S    I    Z    E    =    1    0    0    0  nul    Q    T
0000120    D    I    R    =    /    u    s    r    /    l    i    b    /    q    t    -
0000140    3    .    3  nul    U    S    E    R    =    e    r    i    c    f    j  nul
0000160    L    S    _    C    O    L    O    R    S    = nul    S    S    H    _    A
0000200    U    T    H    _    S    O    C    K    =    /    t    m    p    /    s    s
0000220    h    -    P    w    g    1    1    0    8    7    /    a    g    e    n    t
0000240    .    1    1    0    8    7  nul    K    D    E    D    I    R    =    /    u
0000260    s    r  nul    P    A    T    H    =    /    u    s    r    /    k    e    r
0000300    b    e    r    o    s    /    b    i    n    :    /    u    s    r    /    l
0000320    o    c    a    l    /    b    i    n    :    /    u    s    r    /    b    i
0000340    n    :    /    b    i    n    :    /    u    s    r    /    X    1    1    R
0000360    6    /    b    i    n    :    /    h    o    m    e    2    /    e    r    i
0000400    c    f    j    /    b    i    n    :    /    u    s    r    /    j    a    v
0000420    a    /    j    2    s    d    k    1    .    4    .    1    _    0    3    /
0000440    b    i    n    :    /    o    p    t    /    j    e    x    t    /    b    i
0000460    n  nul    D    E    S    K    T    O    P    _    S    E    S    S    I    O
0000500    N    =    d    e    f    a    u    l    t  nul    M    A    I    L    =    /
0000520    v    a    r    /    s    p    o    o    l    /    m    a    i    l    /    e
0000540    r    i    c    f    j  nul    P    W    D    =    /    h    o    m    e    2
0000560    /    e    r    i    c    f    j  nul    I    N    P    U    T    R    C    =
0000600    /    e    t    c    /    i    n    p    u    t    r    c  nul    L    A    N
0000620    G    =    e    n    _    U    S    .    U    T    F    -    8  nul    G    D
0000640    M    S    E    S    S    I    O    N    =    d    e    f    a    u    l    t
0000660  nul    S    S    H    _    A    S    K    P    A    S    S    =    /    u    s
0000700    r    /    l    i    b    e    x    e    c    /    o    p    e    n    s    s
0000720    h    /    g    n    o    m    e    -    s    s    h    -    a    s    k    p
0000740    a    s    s  nul    S    H    L    V    L    =    1  nul    H    O    M    E
0000760    =    /    h    o    m    e    2    /    e    r    i    c    f    j  nul    L
0001000    O    G    N    A    M    E    =    e    r    i    c    f    j  nul    L    E
```

```
0001020    S    S    O    P    E    N    =    |    /    u    s    r    /    b    i    n
0001040    /    l    e    s    s    p    i    p    e    .    s    h   sp    %    s  nul
0001060    D    I    S    P    L    A    Y    =    :    0    .    0  nul    G    _    B
0001100    R    O    K    E    N    _    F    I    L    E    N    A    M    E    S    =
0001120    1  nul    X    A    U    T    H    O    R    I    T    Y    =    /    h    o
0001140    m    e    2    /    e    r    i    c    f    j    /    .    X    a    u    t
0001160    h    o    r    i    t    y  nul    G    T    K    _    R    C    _    F    I
0001200    L    E    S    =    /    e    t    c    /    g    t    k    /    g    t    k
0001220    r    c    :    /    h    o    m    e    2    /    e    r    i    c    f    j
0001240    /    .    g    t    k    r    c    -    1    .    2    -    g    n    o    m
0001260    e    2  nul    S    E    S    S    I    O    N    _    M    A    N    A    G
0001300    E    R    =    l    o    c    a    l    /    k    i    r    k    w    a    l
0001320    l    :    /    t    m    p    /    .    I    C    E    -    u    n    i    x
0001340    /    1    1    0    8    7  nul    G    N    O    M    E    _    K    E    Y
0001360    R    I    N    G    _    S    O    C    K    E    T    =    /    t    m    p
0001400    /    k    e    y    r    i    n    g    -    9    X    C    K    K    R    /
0001420    s    o    c    k    e    t  nul    G    N    O    M    E    _    D    E    S
0001440    K    T    O    P    _    S    E    S    S    I    O    N    _    I    D    =
0001460    D    e    f    a    u    l    t  nul
0001470
```

Now you can see that this file uses a null (ASCII 0) character, displayed as nul, to separate each entry. The null character doesn't work well with normal Unix and Linux tools for working with text files, unfortunately. Hence, the mashed-looking output.

To get around this, use the tr command:

```
$ tr "\000" "\n" < /proc/11751/environ | sort
DESKTOP_SESSION=default
DISPLAY=:0.0
G_BROKEN_FILENAMES=1
GDMSESSION=default
GNOME_DESKTOP_SESSION_ID=Default
GNOME_KEYRING_SOCKET=/tmp/keyring-9XCKKR/socket
GTK_RC_FILES=/etc/gtk/gtkrc:/home2/ericfj/.gtkrc-1.2-gnome2
HISTSIZE=1000
HOME=/home2/ericfj
HOSTNAME=kirkwall
INPUTRC=/etc/inputrc
KDEDIR=/usr
LANG=en_US.UTF-8
LESSOPEN=|/usr/bin/lesspipe.sh %s
LOGNAME=ericfj
LS_COLORS=
MAIL=/var/spool/mail/ericfj
PATH=/usr/kerberos/bin:/usr/local/bin:/usr/bin:/bin:/usr/X11R6/bin:/home2/ericfj/
bin:/usr/java/j2sdk1.4.1_03/bin:/opt/jext/bin
PWD=/home2/ericfj
QTDIR=/usr/lib/qt-3.3
SESSION_MANAGER=local/kirkwall:/tmp/.ICE-unix/11087
SHELL=/bin/bash
SHLVL=1
SSH_AGENT_PID=11135
SSH_ASKPASS=/usr/libexec/openssh/gnome-ssh-askpass
```

```
SSH_AUTH_SOCK=/tmp/ssh-Pwg11087/agent.11087
TERM=dumb
USER=ericfj
XAUTHORITY=/home2/ericfj/.Xauthority
```

Now you can see the environment variables in all their glory.

How It Works

The `tr` command, short for *translate,* translates one pattern of text for another in its input, outputting the translated text. In this case, `tr` converts \000, the null character (ASCII 0), to \n, a newline. Most Unix and Linux tools work much better with newlines as the delimiter between entries, as opposed to a null character as the delimiter.

The double quotes around the \000 and \n are essential, as you want the shell to interpret these characters and substitute the two actual characters, ASCII 0 and ASCII 10, in place of \000 and \n, respectively. The \000 entry is formatted as an octal number.

Killing Processes

Armed with a process ID, you can kill a process. Typically, processes end when they are good and ready. For example, the `ls` command performs a directory listing, outputs the results, and then exits. Other processes, particularly server processes, remain around for some time. And you may see a process that remains running when it no longer should. This often happens with processes that get stuck for some reason and fail to exit at the expected time.

> *Stuck is a technical term for when something weird happens in software, and the program won't do what it should or stop doing what it shouldn't. This is the software equivalent of when your mom says to you that "I put the thing in the thing and now it won't come out," referring to a CD-ROM lovingly shoved into the gap between two optical drives, and the CD-ROM would apparently not eject.*

Ironically, in Unix and Linux systems, the `kill` command merely sends a signal to a process. The process typically decides to exit, or commit suicide, when it receives a signal. Thus, `kill` doesn't really kill anything. It is more of an accessory to the crime. Think of this as a "Manchurian Candidate" kind of event, as most commands are programmed to commit suicide on a signal.

The `kill` command needs the process ID of the process to signal as a command-line argument. You can use command-line options to determine which kind of signal to send. In most cases, you want to use the -9 option, which sends a kill signal (known as SIGKILL) to the process. For example, to kill a process with the ID of 11198, use the following command:

```
$ kill -9 11198
```

You need to own the process or be logged in as the root user to kill a process. The online documentation for the `kill` command can tell you other signals. Not all commands support all signals.

Launching Processes

Most often, your scripts will launch processes instead of kill them. With the rich command set available, your scripts can perform a lot of work by running one command after another.

The actual task of launching processes differs by operating system. For example, in Windows, you need to call `CreateProcess`, a Win32 API call. In Unix and Linux, you can call `fork` and `exec`. The `fork` call clones your current process, and `exec` launches a process in a special way, covered following.

Fortunately, the shell hides some of these details for you. Even so, you still need to make a number of choices regarding how you want to launch processes.

The following sections describe four such ways:

- ❑ Running commands in the foreground
- ❑ Running commands in the background
- ❑ Running commands in subshells
- ❑ Running commands with the `exec` command

Running Commands in the Foreground

To run a command from within your scripts, simply place the command in your script. For example:

```
ls
```

This tells the script to execute the command and wait for the command to end. This is called running the command in the *foreground*. You've been doing this since Chapter 2.

The shell treats any extra elements on the same line as the command as options and arguments for the command. For example:

```
ls -l /usr/local
```

Again, this is what you have been adding to your scripts since Chapter 2. The key point is that the shell runs the command in the foreground, waiting for the command to exit before going on.

Running Commands in the Background

Place an ampersand character, &, after a command to run that command in the background. This works on the command line. You can also use this technique in your shell scripts.

This can work for any command, but commands don't work well if run in the background if:

- ❑ They send output to stdout, unless you redirect stdout for the command.

❑   They need to read from stdin to get input from the user, unless you redirect stdin for the command.

❑   Your script needs to interact with the command.

Running Commands in Subshells

Placing a set of commands inside parentheses runs those commands in a *subshell*, a child shell of the current shell. For example:

```
( cd /usr/local/data; tar cf ../backup.tar . )
```

In this case, the subshell runs the cd command to change to a different directory and then the tar command to create an archive from a number of files.)

See Chapter 4 for more on using subshells.

Running Commands with the exec Command

The exec command runs a command or shell script and does not return to your original script. Short for *execute*, exec runs any script or command, replacing your current script with the process you execute. In other words, the exec command overlays your script with another process, a script, or a command.

This is based on the C language exec call.

The basic syntax for exec follows:

```
exec command options arguments
```

To use exec, all you really need to do is prefix a command and all its options and arguments with exec. For example:

```
$ exec echo "Hello from exec."
```

This command uses exec to launch the echo command. The effects of exec, however, are more apparent when you call exec in a script, as in the following example.

Try It Out   Calling exec from a Script

Enter the following script and save it under the name exec1:

```
# Test of exec.

exec echo "Hello from exec. Goodbye."

echo "This line will not get output."
```

When you run this script, you will see only the first line of output. For example:

```
$ sh exec1
Hello from exec. Goodbye.
```

How It Works

This script outputs only one of two commands. The first command uses exec to launch the echo command. The output of this command appears. Then the script exits. The shell never encounters the second echo command and so never runs it.

Launching a process from exec is a handy way to start processes, but you always need to keep in mind that exec does not return. Instead, the new process runs in place of the old. This means your script exits, or more precisely, the exec command overlays the shell running your script with the command exec launches.

Using exec is more efficient than merely launching a process because you free up all the resources used by your script. Note that while your scripts may be small, the shell that runs them, such as /bin/sh, is not a trivial program, so it uses system resources, especially memory.

Typically, scripts call exec near the end. For example, a script may determine which device driver to load based on the operating system or hardware capabilities. Then the script can call exec to run the process that loads the device driver. Whenever you have a similar need for a script that makes some decisions and then launches a process, exec is the call for you.

Don't limit your use of exec to just scripts that decide which program to run. You can find exec useful for scripts that need to set up the environment or locate files for another program to use. In this case, your script needs to find the necessary items, set up the environment using the export command, and then call exec to launch the process.

Capturing the Output of Processes

In addition to being able to launch commands from your scripts, you can run commands and capture the output of those commands. You can set variables from the output of commands or even read whole files into variables. You can also check on the return codes from processes. Return codes are another way processes can output information.

Using Backticks for Command Substitution

Surround a command with backtick characters, `` ` ``, to execute a command in place. The shell runs the command within the backticks and then replaces the backtick section of the script with the output of the command. This format, often called *command substitution,* fills in the output from a command. This is similar to variable substitution, where the shell replaces $variable with the value of the variable.

The ` character is often called a backtick. That's because an apostrophe, ', is called a tick, so ` is a backtick. This is similar to /, a slash, and \, a backslash.

The basic syntax follows:

```
`command`
```

If the command requires options or arguments, place these inside the backtick characters, too. For example:

```
`command option argument argument2`
```

You can also use variables as arguments or options to the command. For example:

```
`command $1 $2 $3`
```

This backtick syntax proves very, very useful for building up text messages and values in your scripts. For example, you can use the output of the date command in a message output by the echo command. For example:

```
$ echo "The date is `date`"
The date is Sun Nov 12 16:01:23 CST 2006
```

You can also use the backtick syntax in for loops, as in the following Try It Out.

Try It Out   Using Backticks in for Loops

Enter the following script and name the file tick_for:

```
echo "Using backticks in a for loop."

for filename in `ls -1 /usr/local`
do
      echo $filename
done
```

When you run this script, you will see output like the following, depending on what is in your /usr/local directory:

```
$ sh tick_for
Using backticks in a for loop.
bin
etc
games
include
lib
libexec
man
sbin
share
src
```

How It Works

This script uses command substitution to create a list that the for loop can use for iteration. The script creates the list from the files in the /usr/local directory, using the ls command. On each iteration through the loop, the script outputs one file name.

This is very similar to the myls example scripts in Chapter 3.

This example shows how you can use the backtick syntax to execute commands within control structures such as a `for` loop. In most cases, however, you'll want to set variables to hold the results of commands.

Using Parentheses in Place of Backticks

The backtick syntax has been around a long, long time. Newer shell scripts, however, may use an alternate format using parentheses:

```
$(command)
```

This syntax is very similar to the syntax for subshells, used in a previous example and described in Chapter 4.

You can also pass arguments and options to the command:

```
$(command options argument1 argument2)
```

The two formats, backticks or `$( )`, are both acceptable for command substitution. The parenthesis format is preferred for the future, but most old scripts use the older backtick format.

Setting Variables from Commands

The basic format for using command substitution with variable settings follows:

```
variable=`command`
```

For example:

```
today=`date`
```

As you'd expect, you can also pass options or arguments to the command. For example:

```
scriptname=`basename $0`
```

The `basename` command returns the base file name, removing any path information and any file-name extension. For example, the `basename` command transforms `/usr/local/report.txt` to `report.txt`:

```
$ basename /usr/local/report.txt
report.txt
```

You can also have `basename` strip a suffix or file-name extension:

```
$ basename /usr/local/report.txt .txt
report
```

In this example, you need to pass the suffix to remove, `.txt`, as a separate command-line argument.

Many scripts use the `basename` command as a handy way to get the base name of the script. For example, if `$0`, the special variable holding the script name, holds /usr/local/bin/backup, you may want to display messages with just the name `backup`.

Of course, you can place the name inside your script. This is called *hard-coding* the value. You can also use the `basename` command with the *$0* variable to return the base name of your script.

Performing Math with Commands

Another common use for command substitution is to perform math operations and then set variables to the results. Shell scripts weren't made for performing computations. The moment you try to calculate anything, you see the truth of this. To help get around this problem, you can call on a number of math-related commands, including `expr` and `bc`.

The `expr` command, short for *expression evaluator*, provides an all-purpose evaluator for various types of expressions, including math expressions.

Try It Out   Using the expr Command

Try entering the following commands to get an idea for how `expr` works:

```
$ expr 40 + 2
42
$ expr 40 / 10
4
$ expr 42 % 10
2
$ expr 4 * 10
expr: syntax error
$ expr "4 * 10"
4 * 10
$ expr 4 \* 10
40
$ expr 42 - 2
40
```

How It Works

In most cases, you can merely pass a math expression to `expr`. For example, the following command adds the numbers 40 and 2:

```
$ expr 40 + 2
42
```

In addition, the percent sign, %, provides the remainder in a division operation, while / divides.

The hardest math expression, however, is multiplication. The `expr` command, as do many programming languages, uses an asterisk, *, as the multiplication sign. Unfortunately, the shell also uses the asterisk in wildcard globs. So the following command passes far more than three arguments to the `expr` command:

```
$ expr 4 * 10
expr: syntax error
```

The * in this command gets interpreted by the shell first, not `expr`. The shell assumes that you wanted a listing of all the files in the current directory, passing all of these to the `expr` command. This is what causes the syntax error in this example.

The following command passes a text string to `expr`, which gets you no closer to performing multiplication:

```
$ expr "4 * 10"
4 * 10
```

This command passes one argument, a text string, to `expr`. Because there is nothing to evaluate, `expr` outputs the text string itself.

It's these types of things that make many people leave Unix and Linux in total frustration.

What you need to do is escape the asterisk. The shell uses a backslash to escape characters. For example:

```
$ expr 4 \* 10
40
```

You can also use `expr` with shell variables, as shown in the following Try It Out.

Try It Out   **Using Variables with expr**

Enter the following commands to see how `expr` uses shell variables:

```
$ x=10
$ expr $x + 10
20
$ x=`expr $x + 10`
$ echo $x
20
$ x=`expr $x + 10`
$ echo $x
30
```

How It Works

In this example, `expr` works with a variable, x. In the first command, you set x to 10. The `expr` command then gets 10 + 10 and, as you'd expect, outputs 20. Note that you did not change the value of x, which remains 10.

Next, you set x to the results of the expression $x + 10. Because the value of x remains 10, this command again passes 10 + 10 to `expr`, which outputs 20. In this case, however, you set the value of x to 20. Also note how no output appears. That's because the backticks sent the output of the `expr` command to the shell, which used that output to set the variable x. To see the value of x, use the `echo` command, as shown in this example. The value of x is now 20.

Run the same two commands again, and the shell sets x to 30.

You can nest backticks within a backtick expression by escaping the interior backticks. To do this, use a backslash prior to the interior backticks, as in the following example.

Try It Out   Nesting Backticks

Enter the following script and save it under the name `ticktick`:

```
# Nested backticks.

tock=`tick=\`expr 5 \* 10\`; expr $tick + 10`

echo "tock = $tock."
```

When you run this script, you'll see output like the following:

```
$ sh ticktick
tock = 60.
```

How It Works

In this example, the `ticktick` script sets the *tock* variable, using command substitution. Inside the backticks for the command substitution, however, the script also sets the *tick* variable, also using command substitution. When the script sets the *tick* variable, however, it needs to use the backslash backtick format, `\'`. In addition, and just to make things more complicated, the multiplication operator, `*`, requires a backslash as well.

> *See the online documentation on the expr command for more on how it can evaluate logical expressions, much like the test command, as well as string expressions.*

Reading Files into Variables

You can take advantage of command substitution to read in files into variables. For example, you can use the output of the `cat` command with command substitution, as shown following:

```
file_contents=`cat filename`
```

In addition, you can use the shorthand method by redirecting stdin with no command. For example:

```
file_contents=`<filename`
```

Both these constructs will have the same results.

> Be careful with this construct. Do not load a huge file into a shell variable. And never load a binary file into a shell variable. Evaluating such a variable can lead to unexpected results, depending on the data in the file. The shell gives you awesome power. Don't use that power to hurt yourself.

Using `expr` is far easier than most alternatives, but the `expr` command works best for small expressions. If you have a complicated set of calculations to perform, or you need to work with decimal numbers (often called *real* or *floating-point* numbers), your best bet is to use the `bc` command.

The bc command provides a mini programming language, and you can pass it a number of commands in its special language. To use the bc command, you typically pipe a set of bc commands to the program.

The bc syntax is similar to that of the C language. The most crucial difference from shell scripts is that you do not use a dollar sign, $, in front of variables when you want to access their values. This will create an error in bc.

Try It Out   Running bc Interactively

You can run bc interactively or from scripts. To run bc interactively, run the bc command from the shell prompt. For example:

```
$ bc
bc 1.06
Copyright 1991-1994, 1997, 1998, 2000 Free Software Foundation, Inc.
This is free software with ABSOLUTELY NO WARRANTY.
For details type `warranty'.
scale=2
x=10
x + 10
20
x
10
tax=100*7/100
tax
7.00
x = x + tax
x
17.00
print x
17.00
quit
```

How It Works

Once you run the bc command, you're in the world of bc (in more ways than one). By default, bc doesn't display a prompt. Instead, you simply type in expressions and commands for bc to evaluate. You set variables similar to how the shell does it.

The scale command sets the amount of decimal precision to two decimal places. (Within bc, *scale* is a special variable.) The next bc command sets the variable x to 10. You can create an expression such as $x + 10$. The bc command outputs the result but does not change the variable x. You can enter the name of the variable alone, such as x, to output its value. But as mentioned previously, do not use a $ when accessing the value of a variable.

The example sets the variable *tax* to 100 times 7 divided by 100. The bc command will evaluate these operators in a defined order. As in math class, you can use parentheses to define the way to evaluate the expression. In this case, the default order suffices.

Note how once x is set to a decimal value, it always appears with two decimal places (the result of the earlier *scale* setting).

The print command outputs a variable or a text string. In this example, you need to press the Enter key to continue.

If running interactively, you need to use the quit command to exit from bc. You do not need this if calling bc from a script.

You can pass these same commands to bc to perform calculations for you, as in the following Try It Out.

Try It Out   Running bc from Scripts

Enter the following script and save it under the name math1:

```
# Using bc for math.
# Calculates sales tax.

echo -n "Please enter the amount of purchase: "
read amount
echo

echo -n "Please enter the total sales tax: "
read rate
echo

result=$( echo "
scale=2; tax=$amount*$rate/100.00;total=$amount+tax;print total" | bc )

echo "The total with sales tax is: \$ $result."
```

When you run this script, you will see output like the following:

```
$ sh math1
Please enter the amount of purchase: 100.0

Please enter the total sales tax: 7

The total with sales tax is: $ 107.00.
```

How It Works

This script calculates sales tax on purchases. It asks the user to input an amount of purchase and then a tax rate, in percent.

For those readers not in the United States, sales tax is similar to a VAT but charged only at the point of final sale to a customer.

The math1 script calls the bc command using command substitution with the parenthesis format. The echo command outputs a number of bc commands, which the script pipes to the bc command. The echo command is important because it converts the text in the script, the bc commands, to stdout. The pipe then connects the echo command's stdout to the bc command's stdin. If you just put the bc commands without the echo command, the shell will try to interpret these commands.

This pattern of using echo to output commands to the bc command is very common. You can also store the bc commands in a file and redirect bc's stdin to that file. Or you can use a here document in your script, shown in the next example.

You can enter the numbers with as much decimal precision as desired. The bc command won't care. The first command passed to bc is *scale*, which sets the decimal precision to two decimal places for this example.

The final bc command prints the variable you are interested in, *total*. The shell will set the *result* variable to the value of this variable.

If you have a lot of commands, the echo approach will not be convenient. Instead, you can place the commands inside a here document, covered in Chapter 5. Enter the following script and save it under the name math2:

```
# Using bc for math with a here document.
# Calculates sales tax.

echo -n "Please enter the amount of purchase: "
read amount
echo

echo -n "Please enter the total sales tax: "
read rate
echo

result=$(bc << EndOfCommands
scale=2    /* two decimal places */

tax = ( $amount * $rate ) / 100
total=$amount+tax

print total

EndOfCommands
)

echo "The total with sales tax is: \$ $result."
```

When you run this script, you will see output like the following:

```
$ sh math2
Please enter the amount of purchase: 100.00

Please enter the total sales tax: 7

The total with sales tax is: $ 107.00.
```

Another useful math command is dc, the desktop calculator. Despite its name, dc is a command-line tool.

Capturing Program Return Codes

The Bourne shell supports a special variable, *$?*. The shell sets this variable to the return code of the last process executed. A value of zero means the command was successful—that is, the command exited with a nonerror status. Any other value means the command exited with an error.

You can check the value of $? in your scripts to see whether commands succeeded or not. You can also place commands in if statements as described in Chapter 3.

Enter the following script and save it under the name return_codes:

```
DIR=/
ls $DIR > /dev/null
echo "Return code from [ls $DIR] was $?."

DIR=/foobar
ls $DIR > /dev/null 2>&1
echo "Return code from [ls $DIR] was $?."
```

When you run this script, you should see the following output:

```
$ sh return_codes
Return code from [ls /] was 0.
Return code from [ls /foobar] was 1.
```

Your output will differ if you actually have a directory named /foobar.

How It Works

This script runs a command, ls /, that should work. The return code is 0 because the ls command exited normally. The second ls command, however, should fail, because most systems do not have a directory named /foobar. Trying to list a nonexistent directory results in an error. The ls command returns a nonzero, and therefore nonsuccess, status.

If the script did not redirect stdout and stderr, then you would see an error message like the following:

```
$ ls /foobar
ls: /foobar: No such file or directory
```

Summary

You now have a number of ways to run programs and scripts from within your scripts, listed in the following table.

Method	Usage
sh script_file	Runs script_file with the Bourne shell in a separate process.
. script_file	Runs script_file from within the current process.
script_file	Runs script_file if it has execute permissions and is in the command path, the PATH environment variable, or if you provide the full path to the script.
command	Runs command, assumed to be a program, if it has execute permissions and is in the command path, the PATH environment variable, or if you provide the full path to the command executable.

Method	Usage
exec script_or_command	Launches the given script or command in place of the current script. This does not return to the original script.
$(script_or_command)	Runs script or command and replaces the construct with the output of the script or command.
`script_or_command`	Runs script or command and replaces the construct with the output of the script or command.

You can add all these methods to your scripting toolbox. More important, when you look at system shell scripts, you'll be able to decipher these constructs.

This chapter covers how to:

❑ Find which processes are running on your system using the Windows Task Manager or the Unix and Linux ps command.

❑ Determine the process IDs for these processes from the lists of running processes.

❑ Query information about processes. In Linux, you can access the special /proc file system to get detailed information on running processes.

❑ Kill processes with the kill command.

❑ Run a process and check its return value to see if the process succeeded or not.

Shells provide a special variable that holds the process ID, $$. Another special variable, $!, holds the process ID of the last-run process. The special variable $? holds the return code of the last-run process. A value of zero indicates success. Any other value indicates a failure.

The next chapter shows how to create blocks within your scripts, called *functions*, so that you can reuse common blocks of scripting commands. Functions also allow you to hide a lot of the complexity of scripting.

Exercises

1. Write a short script that outputs its process number and waits, allowing you to view the contents of the Linux /proc in another shell window. That is, this script should remain at rest long enough that you can view the contents of the process-specific directory for that process.

2. The tick_for example of using the ls command within a for loop appears, at least at first glance, to be a bit clumsy. Rewrite the tick_for script using a wildcard glob, such as *.txt. Make the output appear the same. Discuss at least one major difference between these scripts.

3. Rewrite the math1 or math2 script using the expr command instead of the bc command. Note that expr will not work well with floating-point, or decimal, numbers.

Shell Scripting Functions

In writing shell scripts, you will often find yourself repeating the same code over and over again. Repeatedly typing the same code can be tiring and can lead to errors. This is where shell scripting functions should be used. Shell functions are used to simplify your shell scripts, making them easier to read and maintain.

Shell functions are like a magic box: You throw some things into it, it begins to shake and glow with a holy aura, and then out pops your data, magically changed. The magic that is performed on your data is a set of common operations that you have encapsulated into the function and given a name. A function is simply a way of taking a group of commands and putting a name on them. The bash man page describes functions as storing "a series of commands for later execution. When the name of a shell function is used as a simple command name, the list of commands associated with that function name is executed."

Other programming languages call functions *subroutines*. In essence they are atomic shell scripts, having their own exit codes and arguments. The main difference is that they run within your current shell script. This means that you have one instantiation of the shell, rather than spawning a new instance of the shell for each function. Instead of defining functions, you can put your functions into separate shell scripts, in separate files, and then run those scripts from within your shell script. However, this means you have to maintain a number of individual files, and that can get messy.

This chapter covers the following topics:

- ❑ Defining and using functions
- ❑ Using arguments and returning data from functions
- ❑ Function variable scope
- ❑ Understanding recursion

Defining Functions

The syntax for defining functions is not complex. Functions just need to be named and have a list of commands defined in the body. Choose function names that are clear descriptions of what the function does and short enough that they are useful. In bash, a function is defined as follows:

```
name () { commandlist; }
```

This function is very dry, but it illustrates the syntax of the most basic function definition. The name of the function is `name`. It is followed by a required set of parentheses that indicates this to be a function. Then a set of commands follows, enclosed in curly braces, each command separated by semicolons. The space immediately following the first curly brace is mandatory, or a syntax error will be generated.

The curly braces surround what is known as a *block of code*, sometimes referred to as the *body* of the function. A block of code combines several different commands into one unit. Anything that is contained in a block of code is executed as one unit. Blocks of code are valid shell scripting constructs outside of functions.

For example, the following is valid bash syntax defining two distinct blocks of code:

```
$ { ls -l; df -h; } ; { df -h; ls -l; }
```

If you were to type this rather useless bit of shell code into the shell and run it, you would find that the first block of code has both its commands executed in order, and then the second block of code has its two commands executed in order.

Blocks of code behave like anonymous functions; they have no name, and unlike functions, variables used in blocks of code are visible outside of the function. So if you set a value to a variable in a block of code, it can be referenced outside of that block of code:

```
$ { a=1; }
$ echo $a
1
```

Blocks of code are not functions because they have no names and because their variables are visible outside of the block. They are useful for combining sequences of commands, but they cannot be replicated without retyping the block of code.

Adding Names to Blocks of Code

A function is simply a block of code with a name. When you give a name to a block of code, you can then call that name in your script, and that block of code will be executed.

You can see how functions work by defining a basic function in the shell.

Try It Out   A Basic Function

Type the following in a bash shell:

```
$ diskusage() { df -h; }
```

How It Works

After you type this line and press Enter, you are returned to the shell prompt, and nothing is printed to the screen unless there was an error in your syntax. You've just defined your first simple function. The name of the function is `diskusage`, and the function runs the command `df -h` when it is referenced.

You can see the function that you have just declared by using the built-in bash command `declare` with the `-f` flag:

```
$ declare -f diskusage
diskusage ()
{
    df -h
}
```

Notice that the shell has reformatted the function. It's actually more readable like this, and when you write functions in shell scripts, it is good programming practice to format your functions like this for legibility.

If you put more than one command in your function's block of code, separate each command with a semicolon, and end the list of commands with a final semicolon. For example, the following function places three separate commands in the code block:

```
$ diskusage () { df; df -h ; du -sch ; }
$
```

When you print out the function in the shell using the `declare` shell built-in command, you will see how multiple commands look when they have been formatted:

```
$ declare -f diskusage
diskusage ()
{
    df;
    df -h;
    du -sch
}
```

You can declare a function on the command line using the shell's multiline input capability.

Try It Out   Multiline bash Function Declaration

Type `diskusage ()` and then press the Enter key to begin declaring this function:

```
$ diskusage ()
> {
> df
> df -h
> }
$
```

Note how the commands that are placed within the command block do not have a semicolon after them. It is perfectly legal to omit the semicolon in a multiline function declaration, as the newline is inter-preted as the end of the command. You must include a semicolon in single-line declarations because without it the shell does not know when one command ends and another begins.

How It Works

The shell's multiline input capability kicks in after you enter the first line by prompting you with the > character. The shell knows that there is more to the function that you are inputting and so is prompting you to continue. When the shell encounters the } character, it knows that the function has been fully entered, and it returns you to the standard shell prompt.

Function Declaration Errors

It is easy to incorrectly declare and use functions. Because everyone does it, it is good to know what the most common syntax mistakes and their resulting errors are so you can recognize them and fix them.

If you forget to include the parentheses in your function declaration, the error you receive will not tell you that; it will instead be confused by the unexpected curly braces.

Try It Out   Function Declaration Errors

Incorrectly define the function diskusage without using parentheses:

```
$ diskusage { df -h ; }
bash: syntax error near unexpected token `}'
```

How It Works

Bash attempts to parse this and does not have any idea that you are trying to declare a function, so its error message is a little cryptic. Watch out for this; it means that you forgot to include the required parentheses in your function declaration.

Another common error is encountered when specifying the contents of the code block. If you do not put the proper spaces between the curly braces and the commands, bash will be confused about what you are trying to do.

Try It Out   Function Formatting Errors

Use bad formatting to declare the diskusage format, omitting the required spaces within the curly braces:

```
$ diskusage () {df -h;}
bash: syntax error near unexpected token `{df'
$ diskusage () { df -h;}
$
```

How It Works

The first attempted function declaration neglects to include the required space that must immediately follow the first curly brace. Without that space, bash gives you an error because it isn't expecting what it finds. The second command puts the initial space after the opening curly brace but does not include a space immediately before the closing curly brace; because this is valid syntax, bash does not complain, and the declaration works. You do not need that final space, but it makes your functions more readable and is a good standard to adopt.

Using Functions

To use a function that you have declared is as simple as executing a command in the shell, using the name of the function as the command.

Using Functions

You can execute the `diskusage` function that you declared in the shell in the previous section by simply typing the command in the shell in which you declared the function:

```
$ diskusage
Filesystem              1K-blocks       Used Available Use% Mounted on
/dev/hdb3                  474474     235204    214771  53% /
...
```

How It Works

Calling the function that you declared causes the shell to execute the commands enclosed in the code block of the function. In this case, disk usage commands were placed in the code block, so the output of the `df` command specified is printed to the screen.

This function has been defined in the currently running shell, and it is available there only. After you have defined a function, it is known in the shell you defined it in, as well as any subshell started by that shell. Additionally, a function is available only in the shell *script* that you define it in and not in any others, unless you define it there as well. See how this works in this Try It Out.

Function Availability

Open a new shell, different from the one you defined the `diskusage` function in from the previous Try It Out, either in another window or by simply typing **bash** in your current shell. Now attempt to call the `diskusage` function you defined in the other shell:

```
$ diskusage
bash: diskusage: command not found
```

How It Works

You get an error about the command not being found because the `diskusage` function was declared in the other shell, and it is not available in this new shell — only in the shell instance where you defined it. This is covered later in the chapter under the discussion of function scope.

Declaring before Use

When you define a function, the commands that are in the block of code are *not* executed. The shell does parse the list of commands to verify that the syntax is valid, and if so, it stores the name of the function as a valid command.

As demonstrated in the previous section, the shell must have the function name stored before it can be called, or there will be an error. This means that a function must be known by a shell script before it can be used; otherwise, it is an unknown command. You should always make sure that your functions are declared early in your shell scripts so that they are useful throughout the rest of your scripts. The following Try It Out shows what happens when you try to call a function before declaring it.

Try It Out   Calling Functions before Declaring Them

Put the following basic script into a file and call it `functiondisorder.sh`:

```
#!/bin/sh

diskusage

diskusage() {
  df -h
}
```

Now make this script executable by running the following command:

```
$ chmod +x functiondisorder.sh
```

Finally, run the script:

```
$ ./functiondisorder.sh
./functiondisorder.sh: line 3: diskusage: command not found
```

How It Works

As you can see from the output of running this script, the function `diskusage` was not known before it was used, so it generated an error. If the function is moved to the beginning of the script, before it is referenced, it will run properly.

The order of your function declarations does not matter as long as they are declared before they are called, as demonstrated in the following Try It Out.

Try It Out   Proper Function Order

Put the following text into a file called `functionorder.sh`:

```
#!/bin/sh

quit () {
  exit 0
}

greetings () {
  echo "Greetings! Thanks for running this function!"
}

greetings
quit
echo "The secret message is: You will never see this line."
```

Now make this script executable by changing the mode to have the execute bit set:

```
$ chmod +x functionorder.sh
```

And finally, run the script to see what it outputs:

```
$ ./functionorder.sh
Greetings! Thanks for running this function!
```

How It Works

The shell parses the shell script and loads the functions that are defined at the beginning. It does not care in what order you are going to call them, so putting one before the other causes no errors. Once the functions have been loaded, they are called in the script, causing the first echo line to be printed and then the script to exit with a zero exit code. Notice that the second echo line is not printed.

It is good practice to declare all of your functions at the beginning of your shell script so that they are all in one central place and can be found easily later. If you realize halfway through a long shell script that you need a function and declare it there, and then use it afterward throughout the script, it will not cause any technical problem, but this practice makes for code that tends toward tangled spaghetti. Such code is hard to understand, hard to maintain, and more likely to contain bugs than the corresponding cleaner code.

It is instructive to note that if you try to declare a function within the declaration of another function, the second function will not be defined until the first function is called. It is better to avoid this headache and keep each function as an entirely separate unit.

Although you do not want to define functions inside of functions, it is not uncommon to call a function from within another function, as in the following example.

Try It Out   Calling Functions from within Other Functions

Put the following into a file called functioncall.sh:

```
#!/bin/bash

puerto_rico () {
  echo "Calling from Puerto Rico"
  haiti
}
haiti () {
  echo "Answering from Haiti"
}

puerto_rico
```

Notice that the haiti() function is being called before it is defined.

Now make the file executable:

```
$ chmod +x functioncall.sh
```

And finally, run the script:

```
$ ./functioncall.sh
"Calling from Puerto Rico"
"Answering from Haiti"
```

How It Works

Calling a function before it is defined seems contrary to the previous dictum regarding declaring functions before you use them. However, if you ran this script, you would see that it works. The puerto_rico function is called; it echoes Calling from Puerto Rico, and then it calls the second function, which simply echoes Answering from Haiti.

This script doesn't fail because of how bash works. Namely, it loads the two functions, but it does *not* execute any commands until it reaches the part of the script that actually calls the puerto_rico function. By the time it calls the function to actually execute it, it already has loaded into memory both the puerto_rico function and the haiti function.

Function Files

If you are writing a shell script that is long, I hope you will find yourself abstracting many aspects of your script into functions so that you may reuse your code rather than rewrite your code. Putting your functions at the beginning of your script is good practice; however, if the number of functions that you have defined becomes so large that your actual script doesn't start for pages and pages, you should consider putting all your functions into a function file.

A function file simply contains all of your functions, rather than putting them in your main script. To create a function file, remove your functions from your main script, and put them in a separate file. You must also add a line into your main script to load these functions; otherwise, they will not be known to the main script. To load these functions from your function file, you would replace the functions in your main script with the following line:

```
source function_file
```

The bash command source reads in and executes whatever file you specify; in this case, the file you are specifying is function_file. The name of this file is up to you. Because function_file contains only functions, bash simply loads all of these into memory and makes them available to the main script. (If you have commands outside of functions in this file, they are also run.) If you want to decrease the legibility of your shell script by taking a shortcut, you can substitute a period (.) for the bash command source; the period does the same thing as source but is much harder to notice. It is better to explicitly spell out that this is what you are doing by using source to keep your code readable.

When abstracting your functions into a function file, you should consider a number of things. One important consideration is where in the file system your function file is located. In the preceding example, no path was specified, so function_file has to exist in the directory where the main script is located. It must be located here every time this script is run. If you wish to put your functions in another location, you simply need to specify the path locating the function_file. This brings up another consideration: namely, that now you must manage multiple files associated with your one script. If these are worthy tradeoffs, then it makes sense to put your functions into a separate file; otherwise, it may be wise to leave them in the script itself.

Putting your functions into a function file makes these functions available to other scripts. You can write useful functions that you may want to reuse in the future, and instead of copying and pasting the functions from one script to another, you can simply reference the appropriate function files. Functions do not have to be associated with a particular script; they can be written to be completely atomic so that they are useful for as many scripts as possible.

Common Usage Errors

A common problem when invoking functions is including the parentheses when you shouldn't. You include the parentheses only when you are defining the function itself, not when you are using it. In the following Try It Out, you see what happens when you try to invoke a function using parentheses.

Try It Out   Incorrect Invocation

If you still have the diskusage function defined in your shell, try invoking it with parentheses:

```
$ diskusage ()
>
```

How It Works

It doesn't work! In fact, it gives you a bash continuation prompt; why is that? This will not work because the shell interprets it as a redefinition of the function diskusage. Typically, such an incorrect invocation results in a prompt similar to what you see in the preceding code. This is because the shell is interpreting what you thought was an invocation as a declaration of the function. This is no different from the multiline shell declaration example earlier on. If you try to invoke a function with parentheses within a script, you may get various different errors, usually of the form syntax error near unexpected token: and then the next line in your script. It can get confusing trying to figure out what went wrong, so try to remember that the parentheses are required for declaring a function only and must be omitted when using a function.

Undeclaring Functions

If you have defined a function, but you no longer want to have that function defined, you can undeclare the function using the unset command, as in the following example.

Try It Out   Undeclaring Functions

If you still have the diskusage function defined, you can unset it as follows:

```
$ declare -f diskusage
diskusage ()
{
    df -h
}
$ unset diskusage
$ declare -f diskusage
$ diskusage
bash: diskusage: command not found
```

How It Works

The first command shows that the `diskusage` function is still defined. Then you unset that function with the second command so it is not printed when you run the `declare -f` command the second time. The last command attempts to invoke the function, but the shell gives an error because the function is no longer defined. When a function is undefined, it is unknown to the shell as a valid command and cannot be used any longer.

Using Arguments with Functions

After functions have been declared, you effectively use them as if they were regular commands. Most regular Unix commands can take various arguments to change their behavior or to pass specific data to the command. In the same way that you can pass arguments to commands, you can use arguments when you execute functions. When you pass arguments to a function, the shell treats them in the same way that positional parameter arguments are treated when they are passed to commands or to shell scripts.

The individual arguments that are passed to functions are referenced as the numerical variables, $1, $2, and so on. The number of arguments is known as $#, and the set of variables available as $@. This is no different from how shell scripts themselves handle arguments.

Try It Out   Having Arguments

Put the following into a file called `arguments.sh`:

```
#!/bin/sh

arg ()
{
        echo "Number of arguments: $#"
        echo "Name of script: $0"
        echo "First argument: $1"
        echo "Second argument: $2"
        echo "Third argument: $3"
        echo "All the arguments: $@"
}

arg no yes maybe
```

Then make the script executable:

```
$ chmod +x arguments.sh
```

Then execute the `argument.sh` script:

```
$ ./arguments.sh
Number of arguments: 3
Name of script: ./arguments.sh
First argument: no
Second argument: yes
Third argument: maybe
All the arguments: no yes maybe
```

How It Works

The $# argument is expanded to print the number of arguments passed to the function. This does not include the $0 argument, or the $@ argument; the $0 argument is still set to the name of the script, not to the name of the function, as is apparent from the output; the first, second, and third arguments are all printed, and then the set of arguments is printed when $@ is echoed.

Using Return Codes with Functions

Every command you run in Unix returns an exit code, indicating the success or various failures that could occur. This exit code is not output on the screen after every command you type, but it is set into a shell variable, $?. Every time you run a command, this variable is set to the new exit code of that command. It is common in shell scripting to test this variable to see if something you ran succeeded the way you expect. Typically, if you run a command and it succeeds, an exit code of 0 is set into the $? variable; if the command doesn't succeed, the exit code will be set to a nonzero status. The different nonzero numbers that can be used for an exit code that fails depend solely on the program itself; generally, what they mean is documented in the man page of the command under the EXIT STATUS section of the man page. You can see the exit code at any point in the shell simply by running echo $?, which prints the exit code of the last command run, as you can see in the following Try It Out.

Try It Out   Shell Exit Codes

Run the following command in the shell:

```
$ nonexistant
bash: nonexistant: command not found
```

Then, before you type anything else, test the exit code:

```
$ echo $?
127
```

Compare the result with a valid command:

```
$ pwd
/tmp
$ echo $?
0
```

How It Works

The first command was a nonexistent Unix command, and bash gave an error indicating this. An exit code is also set, and in the first case, a nonexistent command exit code (127) is visible when you run echo $? immediately after running the command. The second example shows that when you run a valid command, the exit code is set to zero.

In the same way that commands in Unix return exit codes, shell scripts are often written to exit with different codes depending on the relative success or failure of the last command executed in the script, or if you explicitly specify an exit code with the exit command.

Within shell scripts themselves, functions are also designed to be able to return an exit code, although because the shell script isn't actually exiting when a function is finished, it is instead called a *return code*. Using return codes enables you to communicate outside of your function to the main script the relative success or failure of what happened within the function. In the same way that you can specify in your shell script exit with the exit code, you can specify return with a return code in a function. Analogous to exit codes, return codes are by convention a success if they are zero and a failure if they are nonzero. Additionally, in the same manner that exit codes work, if no return code is specified in a function, the success or failure of the last command in the function is returned by default.

Try It Out   **Returning from Functions**

Put the following into a text file called return.sh:

```
#!/bin/sh

implicit_good_return ()
{
        echo
}

explicit_good_return ()
{
        echo
        return
        this wont ever be executed
}

implicit_bad_return ()
{
        nosuchcommand
}

explicit_bad_return ()
{
        nosuchcommand
        return 127
}

implicit_good_return
echo "Return value from implicit_good_return function: $?"

explicit_good_return
echo "Return value from explicit_good_return function: $?"

implicit_bad_return
echo "Return value from implicit_bad_return_function: $?"

explicit_bad_return
echo "Return value from explicit_bad_return function: $?"
```

Then make it executable:

```
$ chmod +x return.sh
```

Finally, run it to see what it outputs:

```
$ ./return.sh
Return value from implicit_good_return function: 0

Return value from explicit_good_return function: 0
./return.sh: line 17: nosuchcommand: command not found
Return value from implicit_bad_return_function: 127
./return.sh: line 22: nosuchcommand: command not found
Return value from explicit_bad_return function: 127
```

How It Works

There are four functions defined at the top of the script, each one demonstrating different aspects of using return in functions. After the declaration of each function, they are invoked in turn, and their return codes are echoed to the screen.

The first function, implicit_good_return, simply runs the command echo when invoked (this is why there is the first empty line in the output). This function does not explicitly issue a return, but it is implicitly defined as the result code of the last command in the function that was executed. In this function's case, it is the result code of the echo command. This command executes successfully, and the $? exit code variable is set to zero, so the return value from this function is implicitly set to zero.

The second function explicitly issues a return call after it is finished executing its commands. It runs the echo command, as the first function did, and then it explicitly issues a return. The return has no numeric value provided in this example, so bash returns the value of the last command, in this case the result code of running echo. When the return is encountered, the function immediately exits and proceeds no further. It is for this reason the line after the return is never executed. When the return is encountered, the function is completed.

The third function deliberately executes a command that doesn't exist and implicitly returns, as the first example did, with no explicit return specified. Because of this, it returns the exit code of the last command run; in this case, the last command run fails because of error 127, so it returns this value. Error 127 is bash's error code for *no such command*.

In the final example, the same command as the third function is attempted, but in this case an explicit return is specified, this time with a result code, 127. This is a little redundant, because this result code is set already, but it shows that you can specify your own return value; it does not have to be the default shell built-in error codes. In fact, you may wish to return values from functions in situations where there is no error, but you want to know which way a function went.

Variable Scope: Think Globally, Act Locally

Functions are often written to perform work and produce a result. That result is something that you usually want to use in your shell script, so it needs to be available outside the context of the function where it is set. In many programming languages, variables in functions and subroutines are available only within the functions themselves. These variables are said to have *local scope* because they are local only to the function. However, in bash shell scripts, variables are available everywhere in the script; hence, they are referred to as having *global scope* and are called *global variables*.

Programmers who fancy themselves to have style will recognize global variables as the path that leads to sloppy code. Throwing the scope wide open allows for mistakes and carelessness, because there are no formal restrictions keeping you from doing something that obfuscates or redefines a variable without your knowing it. Programs are generally easier to read, understand, and hence maintain when global variables are restricted. If you can read and modify a variable anywhere in your script, it becomes difficult to remember every place that you have used it and hard to reason through all the potential uses and changes it might undergo. It is easy to end up with unexpected results if you are not careful. You may even forget that you used a variable in some function and then use it again, thinking it has never been used.

However, you can still write good, clean code by being careful. Keeping your variable names unique to avoid namespace pollution is a good first step. In the same way that your function names should be named clearly, so should your variables. It is bad practice to use variables such as *a* or *b*; instead use something descriptive so you aren't likely to use it again unless you are using it for the exact purpose it was meant for.

Try It Out   Variable Scope

The following shell script, called `chaos.sh`, provides a good illustration of how variable scope works:

```
#!/bin/bash

chaos () {
 if [ "$1" = "begin" ]
 then
        butterfly_wings="flapping"
        location="Brazil"
        return 0
 else
        return 1
 fi
}

theorize () {

 chaos_result=$?
 if [ "$butterfly_wings" = "flapping" ]
 then
        tornado="Texas"
 fi

 if [ $chaos_result -eq 0 ]
 then
        echo -n "If a butterfly flaps its wings in $location, a tornado"
        echo " is caused in $tornado."
 else
        echo -n "When a butterfly rests at night in $location, the"
        echo " stars are big and bright in $tornado."
 fi
}

# Begin the chaos
chaos yes

# What happens when we instigate chaos?
```

```
theorize

# Stop the madness
chaos no

# What happens when there is no chaos?
theorize
```

How It Works

This script illustrates not only how variables are available in a global scope but also bad scripting practice involving global variables and, as a bonus, a mixed metaphor. Let's go over it from the beginning to fully understand what is going on.

In the beginning, the function chaos is defined. It tests the first positional argument to see if it is set to yes; if it is, the function sets the butterfly wings flapping, sets the location to Brazil, and finally returns a zero. If the first positional argument is not set to yes, then the function returns a 1 and sets no variables.

The second function is then defined. This function looks at the result returned from the first function. (This implicitly makes the theorize function useful only if it is called after the chaos function; this can be improved so that if a mistake is made and you theorize before calling chaos, you will have an expected result, preferably an error.) It then looks to see if the butterfly wings are flapping, and if they are, it starts up a tornado in Texas. Here, you see an example of global variables: The value of the butterfly_wings variable in the chaos function is available in this theorize function. If the variable scope were limited, you would not have this variable available. The next thing that happens in the function is that the chaos_result variable is tested. If it equals 0, it prints out the first message; otherwise, it prints out the second message.

After the two functions have been defined, they are called at the end of the script, first by passing the variable yes to the chaos function and then calling the theorize function to see what happens when chaos has been passed the yes variable. It then calls the chaos function again with no and then theorizes what happens when there is no chaos.

If you run this script, it prints the first echo line, followed by the second echo line. This seems to be the correct behavior. However, because of sloppy programming, I am using global variables in ways that I think work, and they appear to work in this way, but you will soon discover that this approach has problems with some cases. If you change the script slightly so that chaos is called with the no variable first and with the yes variable second, and then run the script, unplanned results occur:

```
When a butterfly rests at night in , the stars are are big and bright in .
If a butterfly flaps its wings in Brazil, a tornado is caused in Texas.
```

Some locations are missing in this output. You might argue that you would never call the functions in this order, but trying to remember this is not the solution; the code should be written so you don't have to remember this.

Using the global variable $tornado sloppily in the output to stand for a location is not the right way to do things (nor is theorizing like this). When you typed the line in the script that said:

```
echo " stars are big and bright in $tornado"
```

it did seem odd that stars would be big and bright in a tornado, didn't it? It sometimes requires more code to be less sloppy, but lines of code should be saved by using functions, rather than by cutting corners.

Understanding Recursion

Recursion has been humorously defined as follows: "When a function calls itself, either directly or indirectly. If this isn't clear, refer to the definition of recursion." Recursion can be very powerful when used in functions to get work done in a beautifully simple manner. You have seen how it is possible to call a function from within another function. To perform recursion, you simply have a function call itself, rather than calling another function. Variables in functions need to change every time they are recursed; otherwise, you end up with an infinite loop scenario, so your program, infinitely recursing over itself without ever finishing, will never end. The beauty of recursion is to loop just the right number of times and not infinitely. Recursion allows you to loop as many times as necessary without having to define the number of times. The following Try It Out shows you how to perform simple recursion.

Try It Out   Recursion

Type the following script into a file called `recursion.sh`:

```bash
#!/bin/bash

countdown() {

        if [ $1 -lt 0 ]
        then
          echo "Blast off!"
          return 0
        fi

        current_value=$1
        echo $current_value
        current_value=`expr $1 - 1`
        countdown $current_value
}

countdown 10

if [ $? -eq 0 ]
then
 echo "We have lift-off!"
 exit 0
fi
```

Make the script executable:

```
$ chmod +x recursion.sh
```

Then run it:

```
$ ./recursion.sh
10
9
```

```
8
7
6
5
4
3
2
1
0
"Blast off!"
"We have lift-off!"
```

How It Works

This shell script contains only one function, countdown, and when it is called with a numerical argument, it counts down from that number to 0. This works through function recursion.

The function first tests to see if the positional argument $1 is less than 0. If it is, the rocket blasts off, and the function returns 0. This is an important element of a recursive function; it stops an endless loop from happening. If you would like to see what an endless loop looks like, remove this if block, and run the script again. You will need to interrupt the endless loop with Ctrl-C, otherwise, it will run forever.

In the first pass through this function, the positional argument $1 is set to the number 10. The if block tests and finds that 10 is not less than 0, so it does not exit and instead continues with the rest of the code block.

The next step in the process is for the value of the positional argument $1 to be put into the variable current _value; then this value is echoed to the screen. Then the current_value variable has 1 subtracted from it, and the result of this subtraction is placed into the value itself.

The next and last command in this code block is to call the function itself, passing the variable current_value to the function. This is where the recursion happens. Because prior to this, the current_value variable had 1 subtracted from it, the second iteration of the function will be called with the number 9, rather than 10 again.

This recursion happens until the test at the beginning of the function has found that the value of $1 is less than 0. When it is, it launches the rocket and then returns a success value. The script continues by testing the result of the countdown function, and if it finds that the result was good, it announces to the world, We have lift-off!

This example shows that recursion requires two things. The first is that something must change in the function each time it is iterated over; otherwise, it will do the same thing over and over until eternity. The thing that is changed each time can be a variable, an array, a string, or the like. The second thing that must be in place to keep recursion from happening infinitely is that there must be a test of the thing that changes in order to determine when the recursion should end.

Summary

Functions are an essential aspect of shell scripting. They allow you to organize your scripts into modular elements that are easier to maintain and to enhance. Although you do not need to use functions, they often help you save time and typing by defining something once and using it over and over again. Because the syntax for defining functions is very simple, you are encouraged to use them whenever you can. Functions can be understood, both conceptually as well as syntactically, as shell scripts within shell scripts. This concept is extended even more powerfully when you use functions recursively.

In this chapter, you learned:

- ❏ What functions are and how they are useful in saving time and typing
- ❏ What makes a function: the function name and the associated code block
- ❏ How to declare functions in a single line, on multiple lines, in shell scripts, and in separate function files
- ❏ How to show what a function is defined as, how to test if a function is defined, and how to undefine a function
- ❏ Some common function declaration missteps and how to avoid them
- ❏ How numerical positional variables can be used as function arguments as well as the standard shell arguments
- ❏ How to define and use exit status and return values in functions
- ❏ Variable scope, global variables, and problematic aspects to global variables
- ❏ And finally, how to use recursion in functions to perform powerful operations

Tracking down difficult bugs in your scripts can sometimes be the most time-consuming process of shell scripting, especially when the error messages you get are not very helpful. The next chapter covers techniques for debugging your shell scripts that will make this process easier.

Exercises

1. Experiment with defining functions: See what happens when you fail to include a semicolon on the command line between commands or when you forget to close the function with the final curly brace. Become familiar with what happens when functions are defined incorrectly so you will know how to debug them when you use them practically.

2. What is wrong with creating a function called `ls` that replaces the existing command with a shortcut to your favorite switches to the `ls` command?

3. What is the difference between defining a shell function and setting a shell alias?

4. Write an alarm clock script that sleeps for a set number of seconds and then beeps repeatedly after that time has elapsed.

5. Use a recursive function to print each argument passed to the function, regardless of how many arguments are passed. You are allowed to echo only the first positional argument (`echo $1`).

Debugging Shell Scripts

According to legend, the first computer bug was a real insect, a moth that caused problems for the inner workings of an early computer. Since that time, problems in computer software have been termed *bugs*. Debugging is the glorified act of removing errors from your scripts.

Let's face it, scripts aren't always perfect. Even so, almost everything surrounding bugs remains controversial. Whether a particular behavior in a program or script is a bug or a feature can inspire great debate. Many companies consider the term *bug* itself to be pejorative, so they mandate more innocent-sounding terms. For example, Microsoft uses *issue* instead of *bug*. Apparently, using the term *bug* or *defect* could imply that their software isn't perfect.

> *Calling a behavior a bug can hurt people's feelings. For your own scripting efforts, however, consider debugging to simply be the act of making your scripts work the way you'd like and leave it at that.*

Scripts can create a lot of havoc on your system. For example, your script may remove files necessary for the system to properly function. Or, worse yet, your scripts might accidentally copy a file on top of a crucial system file. The act of changing file permissions may inflict your system with a security hole. For example, a malicious script was discovered as one of the first attacks on Mac OS X systems. Therefore, numerous issues demand your attention.

In most cases, though, you simply need to do the following:

1. Determine what has gone wrong.

2. Correct the problem.

Sounds simple, doesn't it? Unfortunately, this is not always the case. However, several techniques can help, including the following:

❑ If the shell outputs an error message, you need to decipher the message to determine the real error that caused problems for the shell.

❑ Whether or not you see an error message, you can use several general techniques to track down bugs.

❑　The shell can help, too. You can run your scripts in a special debugging mode to get a better idea of what is going on and where the problem occurs.

❑　You can often avoid bugs in the first place by thoroughly testing your scripts prior to using them in a production environment. Furthermore, following good scripting practices will help avoid bugs.

This chapter covers general debugging techniques, as well as specific ways to track down and correct problems in scripts, whether in your scripts or scripts created by someone else. Most of these techniques are, by their nature, general-purpose techniques. Despite over 50 years of software development, on the earliest computers to modern PCs, the industry still faces problems with bugs. No magic techniques have appeared, despite any claims to the contrary. Although you can follow many practices to help find bugs and avoid them in the first place, you should expect bugs.

One of the first steps you need to take is to decipher any error messages.

Deciphering Error Messages

When the shell outputs an error message, it does so with a reason. This reason isn't always readily apparent, but when the shell outputs an error, there is likely some problem with your script. The error message may not always indicate the true nature of the problem or the real location within your script, but the message indicates that the shell has detected an error.

What you need to do, of course, is the following:

1.　Decipher the error message to figure out what the shell is complaining about.

2.　Track down the error to the real location of the problem in your script.

3.　Fix the error.

All of these are easier said than done, and much of the difficulty results from how the shell processes your script.

The shell processes your scripts sequentially, starting with the first command and working its way down to the end, or an `exit` statement, which may terminate the script prior to the end of the file. The shell doesn't know in advance what the values of all variables will be, so it cannot determine in advance whether the script will function or not.

For example, consider the following script from Chapter 2:

```
DIRECTORY=/usr/local
LS=ls
CMD="$LS $DIRECTORY"
$CMD
```

This script builds a command in a variable and then executes the value of the variable as a command with arguments. Any similar constructs in your scripts make it hard for the shell to determine in advance if the script is correct, at least as far as syntax is concerned.

In this particular example, all variables are set from within the script. This means that prior analysis could work. However, if the script used the read command to read in a value from the user, or if the script used an environment variable, then there is no way the shell can know in advance of running the script whether all variables have values that will make the script operate correctly.

The following sections work through some examples that show different types of errors you are likely to encounter and provide tips for deciphering the messages and tracking down the problems.

Finding Missing Syntax

One of the most common problems when writing shell scripts is following the often-cryptic syntax requirements. If you miss just one little thing, then the shell will fail to run your script.

Try It Out   Detecting Syntax Errors

Enter the following script and name the file debug_done:

```
# Has an error in a for loop.
#

for filename in *.doc
do
    echo "Copying $filename to $filename.bak"
    cp $filename $filename.bak
# done

echo "Completed backup operation on `date`."
```

Can you find the error? When you run this script, you'll see output like the following:

```
$ sh debug_done
debug_done: line 11: syntax error: unexpected end of file
```

How It Works

This script makes it easy to find the error, as the correct syntax appears commented out. A for loop must have a do-done block. In the debug_done script, the done is missing, at least as far as the shell is concerned.

The shell here is not very helpful. It tells you that the error appears at line 11, which is an empty line at the end of the script file. The shell doesn't detect the error until the end of the file because the for loop could continue for an arbitrarily long time. The fact that some lines are indented and others are not makes no difference to the shell. The shell cannot tell your intent. The shell can only look at the existing syntax. (The indenting, though, should help you find the problem.)

That said, it would be nicer if the shell output an error message such as the following:

```
for loop started at line 4 without a done statement.
```

This is indeed the error, but, alas, the shell outputs a cryptic message:

```
debug_done: line 11: syntax error: unexpected end of file
```

To help decipher this, think of `unexpected end of file` as shell-speak for *something started but didn't end and now I am at the end of the file.*

When you see such an error, work backward from the end of the file back to the beginning. Look for block constructs, such as `if` statements and `for` loops. Look for a missing ending element, such as the `done` statement in the preceding example.

The next example shows a case where the shell is a bit more forthcoming about the detected problem.

Try It Out   Tracking Errors to the Right Location

Enter the following script and name the file `debug_quotes`:

```
# Shows an error.

echo "USER=$USER
echo "HOME=$HOME"
echo "OSNAME=$OSNAME"
```

When you run this script, you'll see twice the shell's output as the last script:

```
$ sh debug_quotes
debug_quotes: line 6: unexpected EOF while looking for matching `"'
debug_quotes: line 8: syntax error: unexpected end of file
```

How It Works

Wow. The shell messages have increased 100 percent. Aren't you lucky? Actually, this time you are lucky. From these error messages, you know two things:

❏   There is a missing double quote.

❏   Something in the script started but did not properly end.

Combining these two, you can guess, just from the error message, that the problem is a missing double quote, `"`, at the *end* of an item. The shell detected the start of a double-quoted text sequence but never the end of the sequence.

Because this script is so short, it isn't that hard to track down the error to the first `echo` statement:

```
echo "USER=$USER
```

This statement is clearly missing the ending double-quote character.

If the script were longer, it might be harder to track down the missing double quote. Knowing what to look for really helps.

If you choose a text editor that performs syntax highlighting, you can often use the highlight colors to help track down problems. That's because syntax errors will often cause the highlight colors to go awry or appear to be missing something. For example, in this case with the missing ending double quote, the editor will likely show the text message as continuing to the next line. The colors should then look wrong for this type of construct, alerting you to a potential problem. Editors such as jEdit (www.jedit.org) and others described in Chapter 2 perform syntax highlighting.

Finding Syntax Errors

Another common source of scripting errors lies in simple typos — errors of some kind in the script. For example, forgetting something as simple as a space can create a lot of problems.

Try It Out   Missing Spaces

Enter the following script and save it under the name debug_sp:

```
# Shows an error.
echo -n "Please enter the amount of purchase: "
read amount
echo

echo -n "Please enter the total sales tax: "
read rate
echo

if [$rate -lt 3 ]
then
    echo "Sales tax rate is too small."
fi
```

When you run this script, you'll see the following error:

```
$ sh debug_sp
Please enter the amount of purchase: 100

Please enter the total sales tax: 7

debug_sp: line 11: [7: command not found
```

How It Works

This example shows how picky the shell can be. All the necessary syntax elements are present. The script looks correct for all intents and purposes. However, one little problem exists: a missing space on line 11, as shown in the following:

```
if [$rate -lt 3 ]
```

> This statement is wrong because of the way in which the if statement works. With if, the next element is assumed to be a command. Remember that [is a command, a shorthand for the test command. The] is really just a command-line argument for the [command. In other programming languages, [and] would be considered part of the syntax, but with shell scripts, [is a command. The if statement runs the next element as a command. With this error, [$rate should resolve to a command. It does not, so the shell outputs an error.

In this example, the shell correctly identifies the line with the error. This is good because the sequence [7, identified as the error, does not appear in the file. The [7 comes from the [$rate construct. The 7 comes from the value entered by the user and stored in the variable *rate*. The [comes from the if statement.

To solve this problem, you need to perform a bit of detective work. The strange value 7 appears nowhere in the script. You need to somehow associate the 7 with the value entered for the *rate* variable. When corrected, the line should read as follows:

```
if [ $rate -lt 3 ]
```

The error was a missing space between the [and the variable value specified by *$rate*.

Notice that in this case, the shell ran the script up to the point where the error occurs. You will often not see an error until the shell has executed part of the script.

The next example shows one of the errors most difficult to track down: a syntax error in a command, which the shell will not detect.

Try It Out   Errors in Calling Programs

Enter the following script and save the file under the name debug_call:

```
# Shows another error, harder to find.

# Using bc for math.
# Calculates sales tax.

echo -n "Please enter the amount of purchase: "
read amount
echo

echo -n "Please enter the total sales tax: "
read rate
echo

result=$( echo "
scale=2; tax=$amount\*$rate/100.00;total=$amount+tax;print total" | bc )

echo "The total with sales tax is: \$ $result."
```

When you run this script, you'll see the following output:

```
$ sh debug_call
Please enter the amount of purchase: 100

Please enter the total sales tax: 7

(standard_in) 2: illegal character: \
The total with sales tax is: $ .
```

How It Works

This example is tough. The shell doesn't stop the script until it detects an error. That means quite a few commands could have run before that time. If these commands involve removing or modifying files, you could experience trouble when the script dies prematurely.

The shell outputs useful errors in this case, because it indicates that the backslash character is an illegal character. Therefore, now you just need to find the backslash character. Luckily, this script only has two backslash characters.

All of these examples are fairly simple. You can find the errors without a lot of work. That won't always be true when you are working with a larger shell script, especially a script that was written a while ago and is no longer fresh in anyone's memory. In addition, if someone else wrote the script, you have an even larger burden to decipher someone else's scripting style. To help solve script problems, you can try the following general-purpose techniques.

Tracking Down Problems with Debugging Techniques

Because computers have been plagued by bugs since the very beginning, techniques for foiling bugs have been around almost as long.

> *Learn these techniques and you'll become an excellent programmer. These techniques apply to shell scripts and programming in any computer language.*

If you can, try to track the errors to the actual commands in the script that appear to be causing the errors. This is easier said than done, of course; otherwise, this book wouldn't need a chapter on the subject of debugging.

In general, you want to isolate the problem area of the script and then, of course, fix the problem. The larger the script, the more you need to isolate the problem area. Fixing the problem isn't always easy either, especially if you can only isolate the area where the bug occurs and not the actual cause of the bug.

Use the following points as a set of guidelines to help track down and solve scripting problems.

Look Backward

Start with the line number that the shell outputs for the error and work backward, toward the beginning of the script file. As shown previously, the line number reported by the shell often fails to locate the problem. That's because the shell cannot always track errors back to their sources. Therefore, you need to start with the reported error line and work backward, trying to find an error.

Typically, the shell detects an error, such as a missing double quote or ending statement for an `if`, `for`, `while`, or other construct. The shell's error message tells you where the shell detected the problem, often at the end of the file. You need to traverse backward toward the beginning of the file, looking for the missing item.

In many cases, the shell will help out by telling you what kind of item is missing, which can narrow the search considerably.

Look for Obvious Mistakes

Look for syntax errors, typos, and other obvious mistakes. These types of errors are usually the easiest to find and fix.

For example, a typo in a variable name will likely not get flagged as an error by the shell but may well be problematic. In most cases, this will mean a variable is accessed (read) but never set to a value. The following script illustrates this problem:

```
echo -n "Please enter the amount of purchase: "
read amount
echo

echo -n "Please enter the total sales tax: "
read rate
echo

if [ $tax_rate -lt 3 ]
then
    echo "Sales tax rate is too small."
fi
```

The variable read in is *rate*, but the variable accessed is *tax_rate*. Both are valid variable names, but the *tax_rate* variable is never set.

Look for Weird Things

No, this is not another front in the culture wars between conservative pundits and the rest of us. Instead, the goal is to focus your energies on any part of a script that looks strange. It doesn't matter what appears strange or whether the strangeness can be justified. Look for any part of the script that appears weird for any reason.

> *What you are doing is trying to find likely places for an error. The assumption here is that anything that looks weird is a good candidate for the error.*

Of course, *weird* is another one of those technical terms sporting a nonprecise definition. All that can be said is that you'll know it when you see it. Moreover, as your experience with scripts grows, you'll be better able to separate the normal from the strange.

To help determine what is weird and what is not, use the following guidelines:

❑   Any use of command substitution, especially when several items are piped to a command, as shown in the previous examples with the bc command.

❑   Any here document. These are just weird. Very useful, but weird.

❑ Any statement calling a command you do not recognize.

❑ Any `if` statement with a complex test, such as an AND or OR operation combining two or more test conditions.

❑ Any use of `awk` if it looks like the output is not correct.

❑ Any use of `sed` if the script is modifying a number of files and the files are not modified correctly.

❑ Any redirection of `stderr`.

❑ Any statement that looks too clever for its own good.

These guidelines may seem a bit strict, but they've proved useful in practice. Again, you're trying to identify areas of the script you should examine more closely, areas with a higher potential for holding the error or errors.

Look for Hidden Assumptions

For example, not all Unix systems include a compiler for programs written in the C programming language. Sun's Solaris is rather well known for the lack of a general-purpose C compiler with its standard operating system. Scripts that assume all systems contain a C compiler are making an unjustified assumption. Such an assumption may be buried within the script, making it even harder to find.

Windows systems rarely include a C compiler either, but if you have loaded the Cygwin environment for scripting on Windows, you can use the C compiler that is part of Cygwin.

Common assumptions include the following:

❑ That a certain command exists on the given system. Or, that the command has a certain name. For example, the C compiler command name has traditionally been `cc`, but you can find names such as `lpicc`, or `gcc` for C compilers. With `gcc`, however, there is usually a shell script called `cc` that calls `gcc`.

❑ That a command takes a certain type of option. For example, the `ps` command options to list all processes may be `aux` or `ef`, depending on the system.

❑ That a command will actually run. This may sound hilarious, but such a problem may occur on purpose or by silly oversight. For example, Fedora Core 3 Linux ships with a shell script named `/usr/bin/java`. This script outputs an error message that is a placeholder for the real `java` command. Unfortunately, however, if you install the latest version of the `java` command from Sun Microsystems, you'll find the `java` command under `/usr/java`. The Sun java package does not overwrite the `/usr/bin/java` script. Therefore, even if the `java` command is installed, you may get the wrong version, depending on your command path.

❑ That files are located in a certain place on the hard disk. This is especially true of device files. For example, SUSE Linux normally mounts the CD-ROM drive at `/cdrom`. Older versions of Red Hat Linux mounted the CD-ROM drive at `/mnt/cdrom` by default. Newer versions of Fedora Core Linux mount the CD-ROM drive at `/media/cdrom`. In addition, these are all very similar versions of Linux.

Divide and Conquer

This technique worked for the ancient Romans; why not make it work for you? The divide-and-conquer technique is a last resort when you cannot narrow down the location of a problem. You'll use this most often when debugging long shell scripts written by others.

You start by choosing a location about halfway into the script file. You do not have to be exact. Stop the script at the halfway point with an `exit` statement. Run the script. Does the error occur? If so, you know the problem lies within the first half of the script. If not, then you know the problem lies within the last half of the script.

Next, you repeat the process in whichever half of the script appears to have the error. In this case, you divide the relevant half of the script in half again (into one-fourth of the entire script). Keep going until you find the line with the error.

You should not have to divide the script more than 10 times. Any book on computer algorithms should be able to explain why.

This technique is simple, but it doesn't always work. Some scripts simply aren't appropriate for stopping at some arbitrary location. Nor is this technique appropriate if running part of the script will leave your system in an uncertain state—for example, starting a backup without completing the backup.

In this case, you can try a less aggressive approach. Instead of stopping the script at a dividing point, put in a `read` statement, as shown in the following example:

```
echo "Press enter to continue."
read ignored
```

This example requires the user to press the Enter key. The variable read in, *ignored*, is, you guessed it, ignored. The point of this snippet of a script is to pause the script. You can extend this technique by accessing the values of variables in the message passed to the `echo` command. This way, you can track the value of key variables through the script.

Break the Script into Pieces

This technique is analogous to the divide-and-conquer method. See if you can break the script into small pieces. You want the pieces to be small enough that you can test each one independently of the others. By making each piece work, you can then make the entire script work, at least in theory.

In many cases, if you can break each piece of the script into a function, then you can test each function separately. (See Chapter 10 for more information about writing functions.) Otherwise, you need to extract a section of script commands into a separate script file.

In either case, you want to verify that the scripted commands work as expected. To test this, you need to provide the expected input and verify that the script section or function produces the required output. This can be tedious, so you may want to do this only for areas you've identified as likely error areas (using the other techniques in this section, of course).

Once you verify that all of the pieces work, or you fix them to work, you can start assembling the pieces. Again, take a step-by-step approach. You want to assemble just two pieces first and then add another, and another, and so on. The idea is to ensure that you always have a working script as you assemble the pieces back together. When finished, you should have a working version of the original script. Your script may now look a lot different from the original, but it should work.

Trace the Execution

This technique is a lot like a Dilbert cartoon with a tagline of "You be the computer now." You need to pretend to be the computer and step through the script. Start at the beginning, examining each statement. Essentially, you pretend you are the shell executing the script. For each statement, determine what the statement does and how that affects the script. You need to work through the script step by step.

Look over all the commands, especially each `if` statement, `for` loop, `case` statement, and so on. What you want to do is see how the script will really function. Often, this will show you where the error or errors are located. For example, you'll see a statement that calls the wrong command, or an `if` statement with a reversed condition, or something similar. This process is tedious, but usually, with time, you can track down problems.

While you step through the code, statement by statement, keep in mind the other techniques, especially the ones about looking for hidden assumptions and detecting weird things. If any statement or group of statements stands out, perform more investigation. For example, look up the online documentation for the commands. You can see if the script is calling the commands properly.

Another good technique is to replace commands in the script with echo. That way, you see the command that would be executed but avoid the problematic commands.

Get Another Set of Eyes

Following this advice literally may help you defeat biometric security, but actually you want more than the eyes. Ask another person to look at the script.

Start by describing the problem and then explain how you narrowed down the search to the area in which you think the error occurs. Then ask the person to look at the script. The goal of this technique is obvious: Often, another person can see what you have overlooked. This is especially true if you have been working at the problem for a while.

Don't feel embarrassed doing this, as top-level software developers use this technique all the time.

All of these techniques are manual techniques, however. You must perform all of the work yourself. While primitive, the shell does offer some help for debugging your scripts through the use of special command-line options.

Running Scripts in Debugging Mode

What's missing from all these attempts to track down bugs is a good debugger. A *debugger* is a tool that can run a program or script that enables you to examine the internals of the program as it runs. In most debuggers, you can run a script and stop it at a certain point, called a *breakpoint*. You can also examine the value of variables at any given point and watch for when a variable changes values.

Most other programming languages support several debuggers. Shells don't, however. With shell scripting, you're stuck with the next best thing: the ability to ask the shell to output more information.

The following sections describe the three main command-line options to help with debugging, -n, -v, and -x.

Disabling the Shell

The -n option, short for *noexec* (as in no execution), tells the shell to not run the commands. Instead, the shell just checks for syntax errors. This option will not convince the shell to perform any more checks. Instead, the shell just performs the normal syntax check. With the -n option, the shell does not execute your commands, so you have a safe way to test your scripts to see if they contain syntax errors.

The following example shows how to use the -n option.

Try It Out   Checking for Syntax Only

Run the example debug_quotes script, previously shown, with the -n option:

```
$ sh -n debug_quotes
debug_quotes: line 6: unexpected EOF while looking for matching `"'
debug_quotes: line 8: syntax error: unexpected end of file
```

How It Works

This example doesn't do any more than try to run the script, except for one crucial thing: The shell does not execute the commands. This allows for a much safer way to test a script.

This option is safer because the shell is not executing potentially error-ridden commands. When a script dies due to an error, it usually does not die at the end of the code. Instead, it dies somewhere in the middle. This means all the ending commands, which are presumably needed for proper operation, are never run. Thus, the script may leave your system in an undetermined state, causing all sorts of problems—not only now but some time later as well.

Displaying the Script Commands

The -v option tells the shell to run in *verbose* mode. In practice, this means that the shell will echo each command prior to executing the command. This is very useful in that it can often help you find errors.

Try It Out   Listing Users Verbosely

Run the listusers script from Chapter 8 as follows:

```
$ sh -v listusers

cut -d: -f1,5,7 /etc/passwd | grep -v sbin | grep sh | sort > users.txt

awk -F':' ' { printf( "%-12s %-40s\n", $1, $2 )    } ' users.txt
ericfj        Eric Foster-Johnson
netdump       Network Crash Dump user
root          root

# Clean up the temporary file.
/bin/rm -rf users.txt
```

If the listusers script is not handy, you can try this with any valid script that produces some output.

How It Works

Notice how the output of the script gets mixed in with the commands of the script. It's rather hard to tell them apart. For example, the following lines are the script's output:

```
ericfj       Eric Foster-Johnson
netdump      Network Crash Dump user
root         root
```

These lines appear right after the awk command in the script—naturally so, as the awk command produces the output. However, with the -v option, at least you get a better view of what the shell is doing as it runs your script.

Note that if you specify the -v option by itself, the shell will execute every line in the script.

Combining the -n and -v Options

You can combine the shell command-line options. Of these, the -n and -v options make a good combination because you can check the syntax of a script while seeing the script output.

The following example shows this combination.

Try It Out   Combining Options

This example uses the previously-shown debug_quotes script. Run the script as follows:

```
$ sh -nv debug_quotes

# Shows an error.

echo "USER=$USER
echo "HOME=$HOME"
echo "OSNAME=$OSNAME"

debug_quotes: line 6: unexpected EOF while looking for matching `"'
debug_quotes: line 8: syntax error: unexpected end of file
```

How It Works

This example shows the lines of the script as the shell checks the syntax. Again, the shell does not execute the commands in the script. The shell does, however, output two errors.

Tracing Script Execution

The -x option, short for *xtrace* or *execution trace*, tells the shell to echo each command after performing the substitution steps. Thus, you'll see the value of variables and commands. Often, this alone will help diagnose a problem.

In most cases, the -x option provides the most useful information about a script, but it can lead to a lot of output. The following examples show this option in action.

Try It Out   Tracing a User List

Run the listusers script with the following command:

```
$ sh -x listusers
+ cut -d: -f1,5,7 /etc/passwd
+ grep -v sbin
+ grep sh
+ sort
+ awk -F: ' { printf( "%-12s %-40s\n", $1, $2 )   } ' users.txt
ericfj       Eric Foster-Johnson
netdump      Network Crash Dump user
root         root
+ /bin/rm -rf users.txt
```

How It Works

Note how the shell outputs a + to start each line that holds a command. With this output, you can better separate the script's commands from the script's output.

The preceding example shows a relatively straightforward script. The following examples show slightly more complicated scripts.

Try It Out   Tracing through Nested Statements

Enter the following script and name the file nested_if:

```
if [ "$MYHOME" == "" ]
then
    # Check for Mac OS X home.
    if [ -d "/Users/$USER" ]
    then
        HOME="/Users/$USER"

    # Check for Linux home.
    elif [ -e "/home/$USER" ]
    then
        if [ -d "/home/$USER" ]
        then
            HOME="/home/$USER"
        fi
    else
        echo -n "Please enter your home directory: "
        read HOME
        echo
    fi
fi
```

When you trace this script, you'll see the following output, depending on your home directory:

```
$ sh -x nested_if
+ '[' '' == '' ']'
+ '[' -d /Users/ericfj ']'
+ '[' -e /home/ericfj ']'
+ '[' -d /home/ericfj ']'
+ HOME=/home/ericfj
```

Note that everyone should choose ericfj as their user name.

How It Works

This example shows how the shell steps through a set of nested `if` statements. This particular example runs on a Linux system, or at least a system that places user home directories under /home.

Note that testing for the existence of the user's home directory and testing whether the user's home directory is a directory is redundant. You could simply use the test, or [, -d option to check whether the item is a directory. The -d option will fail if the item does not exist.

With the tracing, you can see each `if` statement that gets executed, but note how the output does not include the `if`. Instead, the output shows the `if` condition with the [shorthand for the `test` command.

Try It Out   **Tracing with Command Substitution**

Enter the following script and save it under the name `trace_here`:

```
# Using bc for math with a here document.
# Calculates sales tax.

echo -n "Please enter the amount of purchase: "
read amount
echo

echo -n "Please enter the total sales tax: "
read rate
echo

result=$(bc << EndOfCommands
scale=2   /* two decimal places */

tax = ( $amount * $rate ) / 100
total=$amount+tax

print total

EndOfCommands
)

echo "The total with sales tax is: \$ $result on `date`."
```

When you run this script, you'll see the following output, depending on the values you enter:

```
$ sh -x trace_here
+ echo -n 'Please enter the amount of purchase: '
Please enter the amount of purchase: + read amount
100
+ echo

+ echo -n 'Please enter the total sales tax: '
Please enter the total sales tax: + read rate
7
+ echo

++ bc
+ result=107.00
++ date
+ echo 'The total with sales tax is: $ 107.00 on Thu Nov 25 07:51:36 CST 2004.'
The total with sales tax is: $ 107.00 on Thu Nov 25 07:51:36 CST 2004.
```

How It Works

You can see the shell's output includes lines with two plus signs, ++. This shows where the shell performs command substitution.

In the next example, you can see how the -x option tells the shell to output information about each iteration in a for loop. This is very useful if the loop itself contains a problem. The -x option enables you to better see how the script looks from the shell's point of view.

Try It Out   Tracing a for Loop

Enter the following script, the myls3 script from Chapter 4:

```
# Assumes $1, first command-line argument,
# names directory to list.

cd $1
for filename in *
do
    echo $filename
done
```

When you trace this script, you will see the following output, depending on the contents of your /usr/local directory:

```
$ sh -x myls3 /usr/local
+ cd /usr/local
+ for filename in '*'
+ echo bin
bin
+ for filename in '*'
+ echo etc
etc
```

```
+ for filename in '*'
+ echo games
games
+ for filename in '*'
+ echo include
include
+ for filename in '*'
+ echo lib
lib
+ for filename in '*'
+ echo libexec
libexec
+ for filename in '*'
+ echo man
man
+ for filename in '*'
+ echo sbin
sbin
+ for filename in '*'
+ echo share
share
+ for filename in '*'
+ echo src
src
```

How It Works

Note the huge amount of output for such a small script. The shell traces each iteration through the `for` loop.

Avoiding Errors with Good Scripting

After all this work, you can see that tracking down errors can be difficult and time-consuming. Most script writers want to avoid this. While there is no magical way to never experience errors, you can follow a few best practices that will help you avoid problems.

The basic idea is to write scripts so that errors are unlikely to occur; and if they do occur, the errors are easier to find. The following sections provide some tips to help you reduce the chance of errors.

Tidy Up Your Scripts

Because many script errors are caused by typos, you can format your script to make the syntax clearer. The following guidelines will not only make it easier to understand your scripts, but also help you see if they contain syntax errors:

❑ Don't jam all the commands together. You can place blank lines between sections of your script.

❑ Indent all blocks inside `if` statements, `for` loops, and so on. This makes the script clearer, as shown in the following example:

```
if [ $rate -lt 3 ]
then
    echo "Sales tax rate is too small."
fi
```

Note how the `echo` statement is indented.

❑ Use descriptive variable names. For example, use *rate* or, better yet, *tax_rate* instead of *r* or, worse, *r2*.

❑ Store file and directory names in variables. Set the variables once and then access the values of the variables in the rest of your script, as shown in the following example:

```
CONFIG_DIR=$HOME/config
if [ -e $CONFIG_DIR ]
then
    # Do something....
fi
```

This way, if the value of the directory ever changes, you have only one place in your script to change. Furthermore, your script is now less susceptible to typos. If you repeatedly type a long directory name, you may make a mistake. If you type the name just once, you are less likely to make a mistake.

Comment Your Scripts

The shell supports comments for a reason. Every script you write should have at least one line of comments explaining what the script is supposed to do.

In addition, you should comment all the command-line options and arguments, if the script supports any. For each option or argument, explain the valid forms and how the script will use the data.

These comments don't have to be long. Overly verbose comments aren't much help. However, don't use this as an excuse to avoid commenting altogether. The comments serve to help you, and others, figure out what the script does. Right now, your scripts are probably fresh in your memory, but six months from now you'll be glad you commented them.

Any part of your script that appears odd, could create an error, or contains some tricky commands merits extra comments. Your goal in these places should be to explain the rationale for the complex section of commands.

Create Informative Error Messages

If the cryptic error messages from the shell impede your ability to debug scripts, then you shouldn't contribute to the problem. Instead, fight the Man and be a part of the solution. Create useful, helpful error messages in your scripts.

One of the most interesting, and perhaps confusing, error messages from a commercial application was "Pre-Newtonian degeneracy discovered." The error was a math error, not a commentary about the moral values of old England.

Error messages should clearly state the problem discovered, in terms the user is likely to understand, along with any corrective actions the user can take.

You may find that the error messages are longer than the rest of your script. That's okay. Error messages are really a part of your script's user interface. A user-friendly interface often requires a lot of commands.

Simplify Yourself Out of the Box

Clever commands in your scripts show how clever you are, right? Not always, especially if one of your scripts doesn't work right. When faced with a script that's too clever for itself, you can focus on simplifying the script. Start with the most complicated areas, which are also likely to be the areas that aren't working. Then try to make simpler commands, `if` statements, `for` loops, `case` statements, and so on.

Often, you can extract script commands from one section into a function or two to further clarify the situation. The idea is to end up with a script that is easier to maintain over the long run. Experience has shown that simpler scripts are far easier to maintain than overly complicated ones.

Test, Test, and Test Again

Test your scripts. Test your scripts. Yep, test your scripts. If you don't test your scripts, then they will become examples for others of problematic debugging.

In many cases, especially for larger scripts, you may need to follow the techniques described in the section on breaking scripts into pieces. This concept works well for the scripts you write as well. If you can build your scripts from small, tested pieces, then the resulting whole is more likely to work (and more likely to be testable).

The only way you can determine whether your scripts work is to try them out.

Summary

Scripts can experience problems. Usually, it isn't the script suffering from a bad hair day. Instead, there is usually some sort of problem in the script or a faulty assumption that caused the problem. When a problem occurs, the shell should output some sort of error message. When this happens, you need to remember the following:

❑ One of the first things you have to do is decipher the error messages from the shell, if there are any.

❑ Error messages may not always refer to the right location. Sometimes you have to look around in the script to find the error.

❑ The script may contain more than one error.

❑ The shell -v command-line option runs a script in verbose mode.

❑ The shell -n command-line option runs a script in no-execute mode. The shell will not run any of the commands. Instead, it will just check the syntax of your script.

❏ The shell –x command-line option runs the shell in an extended trace mode. The shell will print out information on each command, including command substitution, prior to executing the command.

❏ Always test your scripts prior to using them in a production environment.

This chapter ends the part of the book that covers the beginning steps of shell scripting. The next chapter begins by showing you how to use scripts — in this case, how to use scripts to graph system performance data, along with any other data you desire. With the next chapter, you'll use the techniques introduced so far in real-world situations.

Exercises

1. What is wrong with the following script? What is the script supposed to do? At least, what does it look like it is supposed to do? Write a corrected version of the script.

```
# Assumes $1, first command-line argument,
# names directory to list.

directory=$1

if [ -e $directory ]
then
    directroy="/usr/local"
fi

cd $directroy
for filename in *
do
    echo -n $filename

    if [ -d $filename ]
    then
        echo "/"
    elif [ ! -x $filename ]
    then
        echo "*"
    else
        echo
    fi
done
```

2. What is wrong with this script? What is the script supposed to do? At least, what does it look like it is supposed to do? Write a corrected script.

```
#!/bin/sh

# Using bc for math,
# calculates sales tax.

echo -n Please enter the amount of purchase: "
read amount
```

```
echo

echo -n "Please enter the total sales tax rate: "
read rate
echo

result=$( echo "
scale=2; tax=$amount*$rate/100.00;total=$amount+tax;print total" | bc )

if [ $( expr "$result > 200" ) ]
then
    echo You could qualify for a special free shipping rate.
    echo -n Do you want to? "(yes or no) "
    read shipping_response
    if [ $shipping_response -eq "yes" ]
    then
        echo "Free shipping selected.
    fi
fi

echo "The total with sales tax = \$ $result."
echo "Thank you for shopping with the Bourne Shell."
```

Graphing Data with MRTG

System administrators use scripts every day. Quite a lot of this activity involves using scripts to verify that systems continue to run properly, as well as to gather performance information.

MRTG, short for the *Multi Router Traffic Grapher,* was originally designed to monitor the network traffic from one or more routers. MRTG takes a very useful approach to network monitoring: It outputs web pages showing the network traffic data. The actual graphs are image files in PNG format. Thus, you need no special software to view the network statistics. In addition, you can view the data remotely if you have a web server running on the system on which MRTG runs.

One of the most useful aspects of MRTG is that the package can monitor just about anything. In addition, anything it can monitor, it can graph. Furthermore, MRTG uses a fixed amount of disk space for storing its statistics. (Older data get replaced by averages.) This means MRTG won't fill your hard disks with data files over time.

MRTG proves useful for all of the following purposes:

- ❏ Monitoring network throughput, the purpose for which MRTG was originally designed
- ❏ Monitoring CPU usage
- ❏ Tracking disk usage
- ❏ Watching for spikes in allocated memory
- ❏ Ensuring that applications such as web servers, database managers, and network firewalls remain functioning

This chapter covers using MRTG to graph system, network, and application data. Using MRTG is fun, as you can get immediate visual feedback about your scripts. As you'll see, however, this chapter covers far more than just MRTG. Along the way, you'll learn how to use scripts to monitor your system's CPU, disk, memory, networks, and applications. These techniques are useful even if you never run MRTG.

Working with MRTG

MRTG is an application that, when run, checks a configuration file. MRTG then monitors all of the items defined in the configuration file, called *targets*. A target is a system or network router to monitor or, more important, a script to run. You configure which targets MRTG should graph by editing a text file. MRTG then runs the configured script for each target. MRTG stores the data in special MRTG data files. At the end of its run, MRTG generates graphs for all of the configured items. By default, MRTG generates daily, weekly, monthly, and yearly graphs of the monitored data. Figure 12-1 shows an example web page created by MRTG.

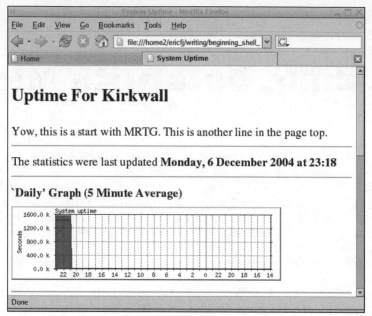

Figure 12-1

To graph data over time, you need to run MRTG periodically. By default, you should run MRTG every five minutes. On Unix and Linux systems, use a utility called `cron` to run MRTG every five minutes. On Windows, you can set up MRTG as a scheduled task.

For example, MRTG includes code to monitor the traffic going through network routers. Running MRTG every five minutes enables you to see the network throughput in terms of input and output packets, over time. You can use MRTG's graphs to identify times of the day when your servers face the heaviest load and also help to track down network problems.

> *cron enables you to run applications or scripts in the background at scheduled intervals. For example, you may want to run a backup every night.*

MRTG uses SNMP, the Simple Network Management Protocol, to monitor network routers. If your routers support SNMP, you can use MRTG out of the box to monitor the router traffic. If you run SNMP on other systems, you can configure MRTG to monitor any values provided by SNMP.

> SNMP includes a network protocol for gathering data from remote network devices. Most routers support SNMP to report statistics on packets sent and received, errors encountered, and so on. With SNMP client software, included in MRTG, you can query the remote device for whatever data it provides. (The remote device may be protected by security to prevent unwanted access.)
>
> Because so many routers support SNMP, MRTG is enabled to read data via SNMP.
>
> Many server systems also provide information via SNMP. If this is the case, you can use SNMP to query for available disk space, memory usage, and a full listing of every running process. SNMP-enabled printers can even report when they run out of paper. You can configure MRTG to monitor any of this data.

Monitoring Other Data with MRTG

MRTG works by polling for values during every specified time period—that is, every time you run MRTG. By default, MRTG expects to poll for data every five minutes. The data MRTG acquires every five minutes is merely two values per item, or target, MRTG monitors. In addition, because MRTG only needs two values (numbers) per target it monitors, you can set up all sorts of interesting monitoring scripts.

In addition to supporting SNMP-accessible data, MRTG can graph literally anything that can provide two values over time. It is this factor that makes MRTG so interesting. See the section Writing Scripts for MRTG, later in this chapter, for more on this topic.

Installing MRTG

MRTG is written in Perl, another scripting language, with performance-intensive parts written in C. The C parts must be compiled for each platform. This means you need to either build MRTG from the source code or download MRTG prebuilt for your system.

Download MRTG from the MRTG home page at http://people.ee.ethz.ch/~oetiker/webtools/mrtg/. MRTG is free under an open-source license.

For Linux systems, you can download an RPM package file of MRTG. Or you can use a tool such as apt, yum, or up2date, shown in the following example, to download and install MRTG:

```
# up2date mrtg
```

In this example, the up2date command will download the package named mrtg and then install the package, if there are no conflicts with existing packages.

See Red Hat RPM Guide (Wiley, 2002) for more on RPM package management on Linux and other operating systems.

> Part of MRTG's success is due to its use of a fixed amount of disk space to store its statistics. By compressing past data to averages, MRTG dramatically cuts the amount of space it requires. In addition, by sticking to a fixed amount of space, you don't have to worry about MRTG filling your hard disk over time. The last thing you want from a monitoring tool is the tool itself crashing your system.
>
> The fixed-size database of statistics is available separately from MRTG. It's called *RRD*, for *round-robin database*, and you can download this package from http://people.ee.ethz.ch/~oetiker/webtools/rrdtool/.
>
> You can script the `rrdtool` program to store statistics and later retrieve them. You can also use `rrdtool` to generate images on the fly, creating graphs of the data on demand.

Writing Scripts for MRTG

Each time you run the `mrtg` command, MRTG either uses SNMP to gather data or executes a script or program for each configured target.

MRTG runs a script or program that MRTG expects to output four values. Each value should appear on a separate line. MRTG then collects the data. Each run of the script provides one data point. The format required is listed in the following table.

Line	Holds
Line 1	Value of the first variable
Line 2	Value of the second variable
Line 3	Uptime of the system, as a human-readable text string
Line 4	Name of the system or target

In normal usage, the first variable holds the count of incoming bytes or packets. The second variable holds the count of outgoing bytes or packets.

You can set the third line to either the output of the `uptime` command or to dummy text (such as `dummy`). This value is only used in the HTML web output. If you remove that section from the output, you can output dummy text. Otherwise, you want to output text that states how long the system has been up, or running, since its last shutdown or crash.

The fourth name should be the system or target name. This name, again, is just used for the display. In practice, it usually works well to pass this name on the command line to your script. This approach enables your script to monitor several targets. For example, a script that tracks disk usage could be applied to monitor any system at your organization. By passing the hostname of the system, you can make a more generic script.

For a script to work with MRTG, you must mark the script with execute permission, and you must insert the magic first-line comment that specifies the shell that should run the script. The following first-line comment, for example, specifies that the Bourne shell should run the script:

```
#!/bin/sh
```

See Chapter 4 for more information about the magic first-line comment.

You can test this out by writing a script to read from the Linux /proc file system, as in the following example. The Linux /proc file system holds special pseudo-files that contain system information. Your scripts can read directly from these pseudo-files as if they were real files. The files in /proc contain information on memory usage, disk consumption, and network statistics, along with detailed information on each running process.

Try It Out   Monitoring System Uptime

Enter the following script and name the file up2mrtg:

```
#!/bin/sh
# Gets system uptime. $1 is the host name.
upt=`</proc/uptime`

for line in $upt dummy $1
do
    echo "$line"
done
```

You must mark this script with execute permission. Use the following command as a guide:

```
$ chmod a+x up2mrtg
```

This command adds execute permission for all users, making the script executable.

When you run this script, you need to pass the hostname of the system. For example, on a system named kirkwall, use a command like the following:

```
$ ./up2mrtg kirkwall
1488565.42
1348929.42
dummy
kirkwall
```

How It Works

The Linux file /proc/uptime contains two values: the number of seconds the system has been running and the number of seconds spent idle. The lower the second number in relation to the first, the more busy your system is. You can view this file with the following command:

```
$ more /proc/uptime
1488765.25 1349093.59
```

Note that the /proc filesystem is specific to Linux.

The up2mrtg script outputs the four values as required by MRTG. You must remember, however, to pass the system hostname on the command line.

It is vitally important that you test your scripts prior to running them from MRTG. Because MRTG runs in the background, you may never know something has gone wrong until you have lost a lot of valuable data.

Writing a More Complete Script

To expand on the previous example, enter the following script and name the file up2mrtg2:

```
#!/bin/sh
# Gets system uptime.
upt=`</proc/uptime`

for line in $upt
do
    echo "$line"
done
echo `uptime`
echo `hostname`
```

Again, mark the file as executable:

```
$ chmod a+x up2mrtg2
```

When you run this script, you'll see output like the following:

```
$ ./up2mrtg2
1489021.22
1349304.98
21:07:31 up 17 days, 5:37, 5 users, load average: 0.06, 0.09, 0.18
kirkwall
```

How It Works

This script extends the previous script to actually output the system uptime, as all MRTG scripts should do. You can decide whether or not to include this information in your scripts. Note how this script changes the handy for loop. The last two lines now appear separately. This enables you to better see the last two data items.

The third line uses the echo command to output the value of the uptime command. The fourth line uses the echo command to output the value of the hostname command.

Note that you could also skip the echo command and call the uptime and hostname commands directly. Each command outputs one line of text.

Remember to test your scripts before you try to use MRTG to run them. Luckily, because your scripts are supposed to output four lines, you can easily test these scripts to determine whether they work properly. Chapter 11 has more on the whys and wherefores of testing.

Once you have a script and you've tested it, you're ready to start working on MRTG.

Configuring MRTG

The most difficult aspect of using MRTG is writing the configuration file. Once you've done this, though, you can simply copy a configuration file and edit just a few values. Furthermore, if you have an example configuration file from which to work, configuring MRTG will be a lot easier.

On Linux, the default MRTG configuration file is located at /etc/mrtg/mrtg.cfg. Because you pass the name of the configuration file to the mrtg command, you can store this file anywhere. If you use MRTG to monitor routers or other SNMP devices, store the configuration file in a secure directory that other users cannot read, because the MRTG configuration file will hold SNMP community names and passwords.

MRTG comes with good documentation, but expect to attempt to run MRTG a few times before everything works to your satisfaction. You'll usually need to edit the MRTG configuration file, run the `mrtg` command, and then view the output a few times before everything works right. Expect to repeat this cycle until it all works. The following sections show you how to configure MRTG and create the configuration file needed by this program.

Each time you run MRTG, the `mrtg` command loads in its configuration file. This file defines which targets to monitor. The configuration file also defines output options for customized HTML and other aspects of a single MRTG run.

To configure MRTG, you need to do the following:

❑   Configure the `mrtg` command to run your scripts by editing the MRTG configuration file.

❑   Customize the output, again by editing the MRTG configuration file.

The first step in configuring MRTG is to define the directories it should work in and use to store data.

Configuring the Global Values

To run MRTG, you first need to name a number of directories. You need to define output directories in which MRTG finds images used in HTML files and where MRTG should store the HTML files it produces. Normally, MRTG should create one HTML file per target you define.

For example, to define the output directories, you can use the following:

```
HtmlDir: /var/www/mrtg
ImageDir: /var/www/mrtg
```

You also need to define at least two directories in which MRTG will log data and alert you if data crosses thresholds, as shown here:

```
LogDir: /var/lib/mrtg
ThreshDir: /var/lib/mrtg
```

You can define several threshold settings. See the MRTG documentation for more information.

You can also set the WorkDir directory to define one top-level directory, as shown in the following example:

```
WorkDir: /opt/mrtg
```

All other directories will then be located underneath the work directory. In many cases, you need to separate the HTML output to a set of directories that can be accessed by your web server (such as Apache). Thus, the output directories need to be in a more public location. The internal working files used by MRTG, and the logs and alerts it generates, should reside in a less public directory. Because of this, all the examples define the HtmlDir, ImageDir, LogDir, and ThreshDir separately. None of the examples use the WorkDir setting.

After you set up the MRTG directory settings, you can optionally tell MRTG to run forever in daemon mode. (A *daemon* is a process that runs in the background as a server. The term is essentially equivalent to a Windows *service*.)

If you run MRTG in daemon mode, then the `mrtg` command will run forever (until killed). The `mrtg` command will handle all scheduling tasks, such as gathering data every five minutes. If you tell MRTG to run as a daemon, you should also define the data-gathering interval, such as five minutes:

```
RunAsDaemon: Yes
 Interval:    5
```

> **Even if you plan to run MRTG in daemon mode, don't set this up yet. You'll want to run the `mrtg` command repeatedly as you wring out all the configuration and script issues. Only when everything works fine should you set up daemon mode or run MRTG under `cron` or another scheduler.**

When you have verified that MRTG works properly with your configuration, you can define MRTG either as a daemon or to run from `cron`. If you define MRTG as a daemon, you need to edit your system startup scripts to launch MRTG each time your system reboots.

After filling in the global values, the next step is to configure MRTG to run your scripts.

Configuring MRTG Targets for Your Scripts

You need to configure MRTG to call your scripts. Do this by setting up a target for each script you want MRTG to run.

You must define at least two parameters per target: the target itself, which defines the script to run, and the maximum number of bytes. The syntax follows:

```
Target[target_name]: `script_to_run`
MaxBytes[target_name]: value
```

Replace the `target_name` with the name of your target. You must be consistent with the name over all the settings for that target. For example, if the target name is `uptime`, you could define a target as follows:

```
Target[uptime]: `/usr/local/bin/up2mrtg kirkwall`
MaxBytes[uptime]: 10001010
```

Be sure to place the script to run, with all its needed parameters, inside the backticks. (This is similar to how you define command substitution in a shell script.) Note how the example passes the command-line argument kirkwall to the script. In addition, note how you need to include the full path to your script. You may want to copy your scripts to a common system directory, such as /usr/local/bin, as used in this example.

Set the MaxBytes to some large setting (this is most useful for SNMP-related targets).

You can define additional targets, all of which require the Target and MaxBytes settings. These two settings are all you really need to define a shell script as a target.

Customizing MRTG Output

After defining the basics for a target, you most likely will want to customize the HTML output, along with the graphs. If you don't, you'll see graph legends appropriate for router traffic, which is probably not what you want. The next two sections elaborate on how you can customize the HTML produced by MRTG, along with the graphs, which are generated as image files.

Configuring Target HTML Outputs

The Title option sets the title of the generated HTML document:

```
Title[uptime]: System Uptime
```

As shown previously, you must use a consistent name for the target, here referenced as uptime. You can define HTML codes for the top of the output page using the PageTop option, as shown here:

```
PageTop[uptime]: <H2>Uptime For Kirkwall</H2>
  Yow, this is a start with MRTG.
  This is another line in the page top.
```

This shows an example of a multi-line value. With MRTG, you must indent each following line by a few spaces. If you don't, MRTG won't know that you want a longer value.

You can also define several HTML configuration options, as shown in the following table.

Option	Holds
PageTop	HTML codes added to the beginning of the document body.
PageFoot	HTML codes added to the end of the document body.
AddHead	Adds text between the end of the title tag and prior to the end of the head tag. This is mostly useful for linking to external Cascading Style Sheets (CSS files).
BodyTag	Defines the HTML document body tag. You can define a background image, margins, and so on.

By default, MRTG generates a graph for the current day, as well as averages over the last week, month, and year. You can turn off, or *suppress,* any of these graphs. For example, if the average over the last year isn't helpful, you can suppress the output of the graph, as shown in the following example:

```
Suppress[uptime]: y
```

Generating images files is one of the more expensive operations performed by MRTG. Suppressing one or more images for a target can help reduce the burden of monitoring.

In addition to customizing the HTML output, you can customize the graphs.

Configuring Graphs

To be as portable as possible, and to enable you to view the data in normal web browsers, such as Firefox, Safari, or Internet Explorer, MRTG outputs graphs as image files in PNG format. This is really one of the cleverest features of MRTG. You can view these images in web pages as well as in other applications that can display images.

You can define several configuration options to control how the graph images are made.

The PNGTitle option defines the text to appear immediately above the graph (still within the generated image). You likely don't want a router-based title. Change the title by setting the following option:

```
PNGTitle[uptime]: System uptime
```

The YLegend similarly controls the text displayed with the y axis, as shown here:

```
YLegend[uptime]: Seconds
```

You want to ensure that you do not define a lot of text for this option, as the text is drawn vertically.

MRTG normally draws a legend at the bottom of the HTML output that shows what the colors on each graph depict. The default text is not appropriate for uptime measurements. You can turn this off by setting the LegendI and LegendO (oh) options to empty text, as shown in the following example:

```
LegendI[uptime]:
# Legend-"Oh" not zero
LegendO[uptime]:
```

The Options option provides the most complicated setting. You can define a comma-delimited list of options to set for the graphs for the given target:

```
Options[uptime]: noinfo, gauge, nopercent, transparent
```

This example sets the noinfo, gauge, nopercent, and transparent options. The noinfo option suppresses the text near the start of the HTML document that lists the system name and uptime. If you suppress this, you do not have to output the system uptime from your scripts, enabling the MRTG task to use less system resources.

The gauge option tells MRTG that each reading holds the current status of the device or system. For example, when monitoring disk usage, the current reading is the value of disk space used. MRTG should not add this value to previous readings. In other words, the gauge option tells MRTG that this target is not a counter. (Many network routers act as counters.)

The nopercent option tells MRTG not to print usage percentages. Again, when monitoring something other than a network router, you probably want to turn off the percentages.

The `transparent` option tells MRTG to make the PNG images have a transparent background color. This enables the images to appear better against a variety of background colors.

The following complete example in the Try It Out section enables you to work with MRTG yourself.

Try It Out   Verifying Your MRTG Configuration

Create the following MRTG configuration file (save the file under the name `mrtg_uptime.cfg`):

```
HtmlDir: /var/www/mrtg
ImageDir: /var/www/mrtg
LogDir: /var/lib/mrtg
ThreshDir: /var/lib/mrtg

Target[uptime]: `/usr/local/bin/up2mrtg kirkwall`
MaxBytes[uptime]: 10001010

# HTML output settings.
Title[uptime]: System Uptime
PageTop[uptime]: <H2>Uptime For Kirkwall</H2>
  Yow, this is a start with MRTG.
  This is another line in the page top.

Suppress[uptime]: y


# Graph output settings.

Options[uptime]: noinfo, gauge, nopercent, transparent

PNGTitle[uptime]: System uptime
YLegend[uptime]: Seconds
LegendI[uptime]:
# Legend-"Oh" not zero
LegendO[uptime]:
```

Once you have a configuration file ready, try the `mrtg` command with the `--check` option. This option tells the `mrtg` command to verify the configuration file.

On many Linux systems, you will see output like the following the first time you run the `mrtg` command:

```
$ mrtg --check mrtg_uptime.cfg
----------------------------------------------------------------------
ERROR: Mrtg will most likely not work properly when the environment
       variable LANG is set to UTF-8. Please run mrtg in an environment
       where this is not the case. Try the following command to start:

       env LANG=C /usr/bin/mrtg --check mrtg_uptime.cfg
----------------------------------------------------------------------
```

This complaint results from the default value of the LANG environment variable for Fedora Core 3 Linux (in the United States). You can view this value with the `echo` command, as described in Chapter 4:

```
$ echo $LANG
en_US.UTF-8
```

The suggested command changes the environment and then runs the command. You can try this command as follows:

```
$ env LANG=C /usr/bin/mrtg --check mrtg_uptime.cfg
$
```

Unless you see some output, you can assume that the file appears okay to the `mrtg` command.

How It Works

The `--check` option tells the `mrtg` command to just check your configuration file. Because so much of the behavior of the command depends on the configuration file, this is a good starting point.

You can add blank lines in your configuration file to make the file easier to understand. In addition, as with shell scripts, # indicates a comment.

If you have a typo in your configuration file, you may see output like the following:

```
$ env LANG=C /usr/bin/mrtg --check mrtg_uptime.cfg
WARNING: "MaxBytes[uptime]" not specified
ERROR: Please fix the error(s) in your config file
```

If you see this type of output, you need to fix an error in your configuration file.

Running MRTG

The basic syntax for running the `mrtg` command is as follows:

```
mrtg /full/path/to/config/file
```

You may also need to prepend an environment setting, as shown here:

```
env LANG=C /usr/bin/mrtg /full/path/to/config/file
```

Try It Out   **Running MRTG**

You can then run the `mrtg` command as follows:

```
$ env LANG=C /usr/bin/mrtg  mrtg_uptime.cfg
/usr/bin//rateup: Permission denied
Rateup ERROR: Can't open uptime.tmp for write
ERROR: Skipping webupdates because rateup did not return anything sensible
WARNING: rateup died from Signal 0
 with Exit Value 1 when doing router 'uptime'
 Signal was 0, Returncode was 1
```

If you see an error like this, the likely problem is that the user trying to run the `mrtg` command (that is, you) does not have permissions to modify the MRTG working or output directories, as defined in the MRTG configuration file. You can change permissions on the directories or change the configuration to name directories for which you have the necessary permissions.

You may also see some warnings the first few times you run the `mrtg` command. Just try it a few times until you either know you have a real problem or `mrtg` stops complaining. A normal run should generate no output to the shell:

```
$ env LANG=C /usr/bin/mrtg  mrtg_uptime.cfg
```

How It Works

Run in the nondaemon mode, the `mrtg` command will start up, parse the configuration file, and then run your script. When complete, you should see image files and an HTML file, named `uptime.html` in this example (the base name comes from the target name defined in the configuration file). The `mrtg` command will write out these files to the directory you configured for images.

Viewing Your First MRTG Output

The HTML output created by this first example should look something like what is shown in Figure 12-2.

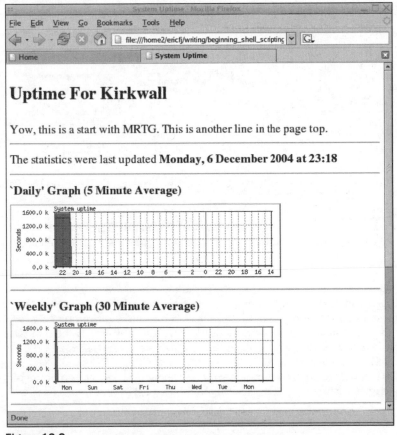

Figure 12-2

Note that at the beginning, you won't see a lot of data. You have to run `mrtg` a number of times until it gathers enough data to create meaningful graphs.

Now you should have `mrtg` ready to run whenever you want. You can then set up `cron` or some other program to run the `mrtg` command every five minutes or so. Alternatively, you can run the `mrtg` command in daemon mode.

Configuring cron

`cron` enables you to run applications or scripts in the background at scheduled intervals. In most cases, you'll want to run MRTG every five minutes.

> **Don't set up `cron` to run MRTG until you have fully configured and tested your MRTG setup.**

To set up a periodic task with `cron`, you need to create a `crontab` file. A `crontab` file tells `cron` when to run your task, as well as the command to run. The `crontab` file defines one task to run periodically per line. Each line has six fields, as shown in the following table.

Field	Holds
1	Minutes after the hour
2	Hour, in 24-hour format
3	Day of the month
4	Month
5	Day of the week
6	Command to run

The first five fields specify the times to run the command. The last field defines the actual command to run.

> **Remember to include the full paths in your commands. The pseudo-user running the `cron` scheduler will probably not have as extensive a path setting as you do.**

You can use an asterisk, `*`, to indicate that the command should be run for every value for that field. That is, run the command for the range of the first possible value of the field to the last. For example, if you place an asterisk for the month field, this tells `cron` to run your command every month, at the times specified by the other fields. Similarly, an asterisk in the day of the week field tells `cron` to run your command every day. Most `crontab` entries, therefore, have several asterisks.

The day of the week starts at 0, for Sunday. Minutes range from 0 to 59, and hours of the day from 0 to 23. You can use ranges, such as `10-15`, or a comma-delimited list of times, such as `5,10,15,20`.

A special asterisk syntax of fractions enables you to define running a task every two hours, or every five minutes. (The latter time is most useful for MRTG.) Use */2 for the hours field to specify every two hours and */5 in the minutes field to specify every five minutes.

For example, to run the mrtg command every five minutes, you would create a crontab entry like the following:

```
*/5 * * * * env LANG=C /usr/bin/mrtg  /path/to/mrtg_uptime.cfg
```

See the online documentation on the crontab file format, the crontab command, and the cron scheduler for more information about setting up cron to run mrtg.

Maximizing MRTG Performance

Performance is a big consideration when using MRTG. Normally, you'd think that a process that runs every five minutes should not take up too much processing resources. However, if you monitor several systems, MRTG can start to slow your system. Some steps you can take to improve the performance of MRTG include the following:

❑ Reduce the use of awk. Awk was designed to create reports, and if you use awk to generate just four lines of data, this tends to be overkill. Often, the smaller cut program will suffice for generating data for MRTG.

❑ Simplify your data-gathering scripts. Every command in your scripts is one more thing that must be run every time MRTG gathers data.

❑ Reduce the number of graphs generated. Do you really need to see the averages over the last year? In many cases, a monthly average is sufficient.

❑ Increase the interval time. Can you run MRTG every ten minutes instead of every five?

❑ Try running the mrtg command in daemon mode instead of running mrtg with cron. In this mode, you remove the time required to start the Perl interpreter with each mrtg run.

❑ Use rrdtool to store the MRTG data. Often, users integrate rrdtool along with generating images only on demand. Normally, MRTG generates images for each target each time MRTG is run. With rrdtool, however, you can generate images only when a user (typically an administrator) wants to see the data. This avoids a huge amount of work normally done by MRTG. See the MRTG documentation for more information about this.

Now you should be able to set up and run MRTG to graph any sort of data you desire. The following sections show you how to write scripts to monitor your computer, your network, and your applications with MRTG, with a special emphasis on writing MRTG scripts.

Monitoring Your Computer with MRTG

Unix and Linux systems support several commands that your scripts can call to monitor aspects of the computer and its resources. In all cases, though, the steps are essentially the same:

1. Try the commands you think will provide the data points you need.

2. Write a script to monitor the data points you need.

3. Test your script.

4. Configure MRTG to run your script and produce the output you want.

5. Test MRTG running your script.

You may need to repeat some of the steps as you tweak how your script or MRTG should run.

The following sections show examples for monitoring the memory, CPU, and disk usage on a given system.

Graphing Memory Usage

Memory usage provides one of the most important measurements for enterprise systems, especially for application servers, which are often bound by memory more than anything else. (Java applications tend to use a lot of memory.)

The first step is to determine a command that reports the needed data. Surprisingly, this can be hard to come by, at least in a convenient format.

The vmstat program reports on the usage of virtual memory. With the -s option, it provides a rather long listing, as shown in the following example:

```
$ vmstat -s
     1003428  total memory
      994764  used memory
      541292  active memory
      357064  inactive memory
        8664  free memory
      219024  buffer memory
      445344  swap cache
     4096564  total swap
         132  used swap
     4096432  free swap
     7454093 non-nice user cpu ticks
        9889 nice user cpu ticks
      334778 system cpu ticks
    89245397 idle cpu ticks
      187902 IO-wait cpu ticks
      175440 IRQ cpu ticks
           0 softirq cpu ticks
     9668006 pages paged in
    12105535 pages paged out
          14 pages swapped in
          45 pages swapped out
   996496185 interrupts
   167392215 CPU context switches
  1100813430 boot time
      114917 forks
```

All the values you want are here, but the output covers more than one line, which can prove harder to create a script to monitor.

The command is vm_stat on Mac OS X.

In addition, the `vmstat` command-line options differ on Solaris, Linux, and other systems. Therefore, you need to determine which options are available on your system and then test the most promising ones to see how the data appears.

Without any options, the `vmstat` command provides a briefer report:

```
$ vmstat
procs -----------memory---------- ---swap-- -----io---- --system-- ----cpu----
 r  b   swpd   free   buff  cache   si   so    bi    bo   in   cs us sy id wa
 2  0    132  12056 220112 441864    0    0    10    12    9   40  8  1 92  0
```

An even better report uses the `-a` option, to show active memory:

```
$ vmstat -a
procs -----------memory---------- ---swap-- -----io---- --system-- ----cpu----
 r  b   swpd   free  inact active   si   so    bi    bo   in   cs us sy id wa
 2  0    464  11048 235860 568736    0    0     9    11   15    3  9  0 90  0
```

You can refine the output to filter out the header information by using the `tail` command. By default, the `tail` command prints the last ten lines of a file. With the `-1` (one) option, however, you can ask `tail` to print the last line. Combine `tail` with `vmstat`, and you have output that's easier to parse, as shown here:

```
$ vmstat -a | tail -1
 1  0    464   8880 237840 568908    0    0     9    11   15    3  9  0 90  0
```

This is the command that the example script uses, but you may want to explore other interesting commands. As before, the commands may not be available on all systems; and the options may differ, too, even where the commands are available.

The `free` command lists the amount of free memory, as shown in the following example:

```
$ free
             total       used       free     shared    buffers     cached
Mem:       1003428     994984       8444          0     219072     446128
-/+ buffers/cache:     329784     673644
Swap:      4096564        132    4096432
```

You can also access the Linux pseudo-file, `/proc/meminfo`:

```
$ more meminfo
MemTotal:      1003428 kB
MemFree:         15640 kB
Buffers:        219988 kB
Cached:         439816 kB
```

There are many more lines of output. The first two lines, though, are enough to track memory usage. As you can see, a wealth of information is available.

Using the `vmstat -a` command, you can create an MRTG monitoring script, as shown in the following example. You can actually create a monitoring script from any of these commands.

Graphing Memory Usage with MRTG

Enter the following script and name the file mem2mrtg:

```
#!/bin/sh
# Gets system memory usage.
# Active memory, free memory.
stats=`vmstat -a | tail -1`

set $stats  ; echo $6
set $stats  ; echo $4

echo `uptime`
echo `hostname`
```

As with all the examples, you need to mark the file with execute permission. When you run this script, you'll see output like the following:

```
$ ./mem2mrtg
568228
39736
22:21:40 up 19 days, 6:51, 5 users, load average: 0.13, 0.35, 0.34
kirkwall
```

How It Works

This script takes advantage of a side effect of calling the built-in set command. The set command normally expects a variable to set. With no command-line arguments, set prints out the current environment. However, if you have command-line arguments that are not variable settings, then the set command will extract the values into the positional variables $1, $2, $3, and so on (just like the command-line positional variables). Thus, the script can call set with a complex output line and then use the positional variables to hold the numeric values the script deems interesting. Tricky, but very useful.

In this script, the variable *stats* holds the results of the command, vmstat -a | tail -1. The set command then extracts the values into the positional parameters, $1, $2, and so on. The echo command outputs the sixth parameter, the active memory usage.

The next line repeats the set command, extracting the fourth parameter. This is technically unnecessary. You can simply add another echo command, as shown here:

```
set $stats  ; echo $6 ; echo $4
```

This approach would be more efficient. For clarity, though, the script separates the lines.

After you have created the script to monitor memory usage, you need to configure MRTG to run your script, as well as define the output options for the graph. The following Try It Out example shows how to set this up.

Configuring MRTG to Monitor Memory Usage

You can define an MRTG configuration for this target as follows:

```
# Memory usage.
Target[kirkwall.memory.usage]: `/usr/local/bin/mem2mrtg`
MaxBytes[kirkwall.memory.usage]: 10001010

# HTML output settings.
Title[kirkwall.memory.usage]: Kirkwall Memory Usage
PageTop[kirkwall.memory.usage]: <H2>Memory Usage For Kirkwall</H2>

Suppress[kirkwall.memory.usage]: ym

# Graph output settings.
Options[kirkwall.memory.usage]: gauge, nopercent, transparent, growright

PNGTitle[kirkwall.memory.usage]: kirkwall vm

YLegend[kirkwall.memory.usage]: Memory
ShortLegend[kirkwall.memory.usage]:b
kMG[kirkwall.memory.usage]: k,m
Legend1[kirkwall.memory.usage]: Active Memory
Legend2[kirkwall.memory.usage]: Free Memory
Legend3[kirkwall.memory.usage]: Max Active Memory
Legend4[kirkwall.memory.usage]: Max Free Memory
LegendI[kirkwall.memory.usage]:  Active:
LegendO[kirkwall.memory.usage]:  Free:
```

Note that this example holds just the part of the MRTG configuration file that works with the memory target. Place this example into your MRTG configuration file. You may want to change the target name, shown here as `kirkwall.memory.usage`.

How It Works

This configuration example defines an MRTG target named `kirkwall.memory.usage` (for a system with a hostname of *kirkwall*). The target tells MRTG to run the `mem2mrtg` script, located in /usr/local/bin.

> *Remember to copy the script to the proper directory location.*

The `Options` setting introduces the `growright` option, which tells MRTG to generate a graph going to the right, instead of to the left. This changes where the history appears on the graph.

The `ShortLegend` defines the units, here listed as `b` for bytes. The oddly named `kMG` setting sets the prefix to `m`, short for *mega*, as in *megabytes*, and `k`, short for *kilo*.

> *The best way to get the hang of these types of settings is to play around with different values, run mrtg, and see what results you get. The MRTG documentation describes each option, but the effect of changes is not readily apparent until you can see the resulting HTML page and graphs. In addition, remember that you won't have much of a graph until about 20 minutes have elapsed.*

The legend settings define the graph's legend and are shown here for an example from which to work.

When you use this configuration, you'll see output similar to that in Figure 12-3.

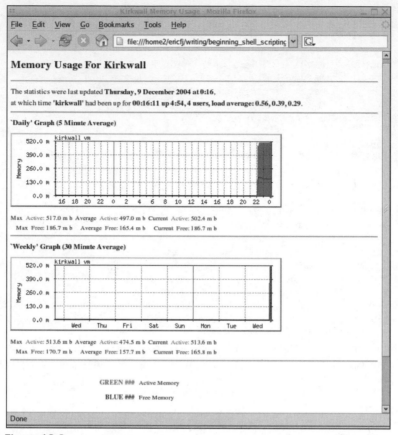

Figure 12-3

Graphing CPU Usage

The `up2mrtg` script, shown previously, provides an example for monitoring CPU usage. This script, how-ever, works on Linux only, as the /proc file system is available only on Linux. A more general approach can be achieved with the `uptime` command, which includes a system load average, along with the number of active users.

> *The number of active users is often wrong. A single user may appear to the system to be many users when the user is running a graphical desktop.*

The basic format provided by the `uptime` command follows:

```
$ uptime
 22:07:29 up 11 days,  6:36,  5 users,  load average: 0.03, 0.15, 0.27
```

Two useful values from this output include the number of users and the load average. The `uptime` com-mand outputs the load average for the last minute, the last 5 minutes, and the last 15 minutes. Because MRTG already averages, the best value to use is the number from the last minute.

Note how this follows the first step listed previously. You need to first try the command or commands you think will provide the necessary data.

Try It Out   Graphing CPU Usage with MRTG

Enter the following script and name the file `load2mrtg`:

```
#!/bin/sh
# Gets system load average.

stats=`uptime | cut -d',' -f2,3`

set $stats  ; load=$5
users=$1

echo $load
echo $users

echo `uptime`
echo `hostname`
```

When you run this command, you'll see output like the following:

```
$ ./load2mrtg
0.30
4
20:23:39 up 1:02, 4 users, load average: 0.30, 0.37, 0.64
kirkwall
```

How It Works

This example pipes the output of the `uptime` command to the `cut` command. The `cut` command, using a comma as a separator, pulls out the user's number and the system load averages. The `set` command again places the extracted text into the positional variables *$1*, *$2*, and so on. From there, you can extract the two desired numbers.

The `load2mrtg` script outputs both the user count and the average CPU load. You can optionally turn off one or more values, as these two points don't graph together well.

Try It Out   Configuring MRTG to Monitor CPU Usage

Enter the following configuration to your MRTG configuration file:

```
Target[kirkwall.cpu.load]: `/usr/local/bin/load2mrtg`
MaxBytes[kirkwall.cpu.load]: 10001010

# HTML output settings.
Title[kirkwall.cpu.load]: Kirkwall CPU Load
PageTop[kirkwall.cpu.load]: <H2>CPU Load For Kirkwall</H2>
Suppress[kirkwall.cpu.load]: ym


# Graph output settings.
```

```
Options[kirkwall.cpu.load]: gauge, nopercent, transparent, growright

PNGTitle[kirkwall.cpu.load]: kirkwall CPU

YLegend[kirkwall.cpu.load]: Load avg.
ShortLegend[kirkwall.cpu.load]: avg.
Legend1[kirkwall.cpu.load]: Average CPU load
Legend2[kirkwall.cpu.load]: Number of users
Legend3[kirkwall.cpu.load]: Max CPU load
Legend4[kirkwall.cpu.load]: Max users
LegendI[kirkwall.cpu.load]:  Load:
LegendO[kirkwall.cpu.load]:  Users:
```

How It Works

This configuration example defines an MRTG target named `kirkwall.cpu.load` (again for a system with a hostname of *kirkwall*). The target tells MRTG to run the `load2mrtg` script, located in /usr/local/bin. You need to add this example to your MRTG configuration file.

The options are the same as for the previous configuration. When you use this configuration, you'll see output similar to what is shown in Figure 12-4.

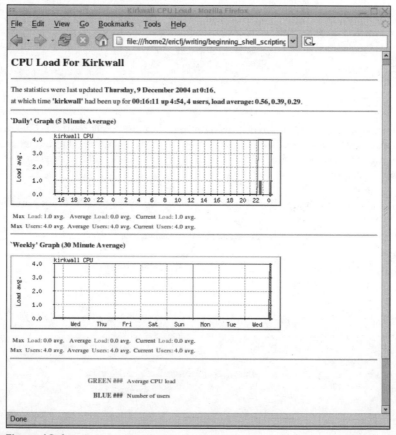

Figure 12-4

Graphing Disk Usage

The df command, short for *disk free*, displays the amount of free disk space, along with used and total space. Without any command-line arguments or options, df generates output on all mounted file systems, as shown in the following example:

```
$ df
Filesystem           1K-blocks     Used Available Use% Mounted on
/dev/hda2            24193540  3908604  19055964  18% /
/dev/hda1              101086     8384     87483   9% /boot
none                  501712        0    501712   0% /dev/shm
/dev/hda5            48592392 24888852  21235156  54% /home2
/dev/sda1             499968   373056    126912  75% /media/CRUZER
```

Due to boneheaded defaults on Unix, you should pass the -k option to the df command. The -k option tells the df command to output values in kilobytes, rather than 512-byte blocks (or half-kilobytes). On Linux, as shown in this example, the default output of df is in kilobytes. However, for many Unix systems this is not true, so you should always pass the -k option to df.

> HP-UX was historically particularly annoying in this regard.

If you pass a file system, or its mount point, the df command will output data for only that file system, as shown in the following example:

```
$ df -k /media/CRUZER/
Filesystem           1K-blocks     Used Available Use% Mounted on
/dev/sda1             499968   373056    126912  75% /media/CRUZER
```

This example shows the disk usage of a 512 MB USB flash, or thumb, drive on a Linux system.

With this example, you can see that you're close to extracting the data to be monitored. If you pipe the output of the df command to the tail command, as shown in the mem2mrtg script, then you will eliminate the clutter and have one line of output, as shown in this example:

```
$ df -k /media/CRUZER/ | tail -1
/dev/sda1             499968   373056    126912  75% /media/CRUZER
```

With this, you should have enough information to create a script.

Try It Out   **Graphing Disk Usage with MRTG**

Enter the following script and name the file df2mrtg:

```
#!/bin/sh
# Gets system disk usage.
# Pass file system, such as / as $1

# Save argument before we overwrite it.
```

```
filesystem=$1

stats=`df -k $filesystem | tail -1`

set $stats

echo $3    # Used
echo $4    # Available

echo `uptime`
echo `hostname`
```

When you run this script, you need to pass the name of the file system to be monitored or a mount point, such as / or /boot. When you run this script, you should see output like the following:

```
$ ./df2mrtg /
3908608
19055960
22:13:55 up 2:52, 4 users, load average: 0.35, 0.45, 0.63
kirkwall
```

How It Works

This script is very similar to the previous scripts. By now, you should be seeing a pattern to the scripts. The main difference here is that this script requires a command-line argument of the file system to monitor. It also calls the df command to acquire the data.

Try It Out   Configuring MRTG to Monitor Disk Usage

Enter the following MRTG configuration for this target:

```
Target[kirkwall.disk.slash]: `/usr/local/bin/df2mrtg /`
MaxBytes[kirkwall.disk.slash]: 10001010

# HTML output settings.
Title[kirkwall.disk.slash]: / Disk Usage
PageTop[kirkwall.disk.slash]: <h2>Disk usage for /</h2>
Suppress[kirkwall.disk.slash]: ym

Options[kirkwall.disk.slash]: gauge, nopercent, transparent, growright

PNGTitle[kirkwall.disk.slash]: Disk usage
YLegend[kirkwall.disk.slash]: Kilobytes

ShortLegend[kirkwall.disk.slash]: b
Legend1[kirkwall.disk.slash]: Used space
Legend2[kirkwall.disk.slash]: Available space
Legend3[kirkwall.disk.slash]: Max Used
Legend4[kirkwall.disk.slash]: Max Available
LegendI[kirkwall.disk.slash]:  Used:
LegendO[kirkwall.disk.slash]:  Available:
```

How It Works

Again, by now you should recognize the pattern to these configurations. Add this configuration to your MRTG configuration file. You can copy this configuration and change the title and the command-line argument passed to the df2mrtg script to monitor another file system, as shown in the following example:

```
# Monitor another file system.

Target[kirkwall.disk.home]: `/usr/local/bin/df2mrtg /home2`
MaxBytes[kirkwall.disk.home]: 10001010

# HTML output settings.
Title[kirkwall.disk.home]: /home2 Disk Usage
PageTop[kirkwall.disk.home]: <h2>Disk usage for /home2</h2>
Suppress[kirkwall.disk.home]: ym

# Graph output settings.
Options[kirkwall.disk.home]: gauge, nopercent, transparent, growright

PNGTitle[kirkwall.disk.home]: Disk usage
YLegend[kirkwall.disk.home]: Kilobytes

ShortLegend[kirkwall.disk.home]: b
Legend1[kirkwall.disk.home]: Used space
Legend2[kirkwall.disk.home]: Available space
Legend3[kirkwall.disk.home]: Max Used
Legend4[kirkwall.disk.home]: Max Available
LegendI[kirkwall.disk.home]:  Used:
LegendO[kirkwall.disk.home]:  Available:
```

This example monitors a /home2 file system.

Once you've established a means to monitor a system, you can expand it to monitor other systems. The next step is to monitor the connections, especially network connections, between systems.

Monitoring Networks with MRTG

Probably the simplest command to start with is ping. Named after the echoing sound made by old submarine radar systems, ping sends out network packets to a remote host. On the remote side, the host should send those same packets back. The ping command then times the response or times out if there is a network problem.

Here is an example:

```
$ ping -c 1 stromness
PING stromness (127.0.0.1) 56(84) bytes of data.
64 bytes from stromness (127.0.0.1): icmp_seq=0 ttl=64 time=0.089 ms

--- stromness ping statistics ---
1 packets transmitted, 1 received, 0% packet loss, time 0ms
rtt min/avg/max/mdev = 0.089/0.089/0.089/0.000 ms, pipe 2
```

By default, the ping command runs forever. You normally need to use Ctrl-C to stop, or kill, the ping command. The -c 1 (one) option shown here tells ping to send out one block of data and then stop. You'll need to use options like this if you use ping in a script.

Unfortunately, ping suffers from two main problems:

1. Most firewalls block ping requests.

2. Some network hardware responds to ping requests on its own. This means you can get a false positive result from ping, whereby ping thinks the connection is working, but the remote computer may have crashed.

Another handy command is netstat, short for network status. With the -i option, netstat returns information about all of the available network interfaces, as shown here:

```
$ netstat -i
Kernel Interface table
Iface    MTU Met    RX-OK RX-ERR RX-DRP RX-OVR    TX-OK TX-ERR TX-DRP TX-OVR Flg
eth0    1500   0  1564596      0      0      0   865349    664      0      0 BMRU
lo      6436   0     5800      0      0      0     5800      0      0      0 LRU
```

In this example, the eth0 interface is the normal Ethernet port. The lo interface is the software-only loopback interface. To filter for a particular interface, you can pipe the output of the netstat command to the grep command, as shown in the following example:

```
$ netstat -i | grep eth0
eth0    1500   0    65798      0      0      0    47099     28      0      0 BMRU
```

On a Mac OS X system, the typical name for the first (and usually only) Ethernet interface is en0. On Linux, the default name is eth0.

Also on Mac OS X, the netstat command returns more than one line per network interface. Because of this, you can pipe the results to the tail -1 (one) command, as shown in the following:

```
$ netstat -i | grep eth0 | tail -1
eth0    1500   0    65798      0      0      0    47099     28      0      0 BMRU
```

The netstat command outputs several values for each network interface. The normal values to check are the count of packets sent and received okay — TX-OK and RX-OK in the example shown previously.

Armed with the netstat command, you can create a shell script to check a network interface that can be called by MRTG, as shown in the following example.

Try It Out   **Graphing Network Connectivity with MRTG**

Enter the following script and name the file net2mrtg:

```
#!/bin/sh
# Network status.
# Pass name of network interface, such as eth0, as $1.
```

```
interface=$1    # Save value, because we overwrite $1

stats=`netstat -i | grep $interface | tail -1`

set $stats
echo $4
echo $8

echo `uptime`
echo `hostname`
```

When you run this script, you need to pass the name of a network interface, such as eth0, en0, and so on:

```
$ ./net2mrtg eth0
65798
47099
22:45:56 up 3:24, 4 users, load average: 0.65, 0.34, 0.31
kirkwall
```

How It Works

As with the previous examples, this script makes use of the handy set command. You then need to configure MRTG to use this script, as shown in the following example.

Try It Out   **Configuring MRTG to Monitor Network Throughput**

Add the following to your MRTG configuration file:

```
Target[kirkwall.net.eth0]: `/usr/local/bin/net2mrtg eth0`
MaxBytes[kirkwall.net.eth0]: 10001010

# HTML output settings.
Title[kirkwall.net.eth0]: Net Stats for eth0
PageTop[kirkwall.net.eth0]: <h2>Net Stats for eth0</h2>
Suppress[kirkwall.net.eth0]: y

# Graph output settings.
Options[kirkwall.net.eth0]: gauge, nopercent, transparent, growright

PNGTitle[kirkwall.net.eth0]: Net Throughput
YLegend[kirkwall.net.eth0]: Packets
```

How It Works

This example follows most of the previous patterns, but because the net2mrtg script monitors network throughput, you can acccept a number of MRTG defaults for the legends on the graphs.

To graph data from routers, servers, and other systems, see http://people.ee.ethz.ch/~oetiker/webtools/ mrtg/links.html.

Up to now, you've only examined how to monitor your system-level computing infrastructure. Taking this up one level, you may need to monitor several applications.

Monitoring Applications with MRTG

One of the most commonly used applications, especially on Unix and Unix-like systems, is some form of web server. Many systems run the Apache web server, but it really shouldn't matter. Because web servers support a known and very simple network protocol, you can attempt to monitor a web server from any system on the network.

There are some things you cannot monitor remotely, of course, but this example focuses on the techniques needed to monitor applications remotely.

When you monitor a remote application, you may want to time how long it takes to get the data, perform some known operation and verify that you got the expected amount of data, or both. You may additionally try to verify the content of the data, but that's going far beyond the purpose for which MRTG was designed.

To test a web server, one of the commands you would likely try is the wget command, a command-line program that downloads web pages.

A good web page to download is the root document, as this should be available on just about every web server. For example, to download the root document from a book publisher's site, try a command like the following:

```
$ wget http://www.wiley.com/
--23:26:57--  http://www.wiley.com/
           => `index.html'
Resolving www.wiley.com...  xxx.xxx.xxx.xxx
Connecting to www.wiley.com[xxx.xxx.xxx.xxx]:80... connected.
HTTP request sent, awaiting response... 301
Location: /WileyCDA/ [following]
--23:26:57--  http://www.wiley.com/WileyCDA/
           => `index.html'
Connecting to www.wiley.com[xxx.xxx.xxx.xxx]:80... connected.
HTTP request sent, awaiting response... 200 OK
Length: unspecified [text/html]

    [ <=>                                   ] 42,840        141.31K/s

23:26:58 (140.88 KB/s) - `index.html' saved [42,840]
```

In this example (which has the network IP address blocked out), you can see that the wget command downloaded index.html, and the file downloaded is 42,840 bytes. The file is important, as wget actually saves the file to disk. Any script for MRTG should then delete the file when done. In addition, the number of bytes has an annoying comma, which you'll want to filter out.

Furthermore, there are too many lines of output. Luckily, wget helps reduce the output. The -nv command-line option, short for *not verbose,* reduces the output (and the -q, or quiet, option eliminates the output). For example:

```
$ wget -nv http://www.wiley.com/
23:32:14 URL:http://www.wiley.com/WileyCDA/ [42,840] -> "index.html.2" [1]
```

Now you can see one line of output. But notice how wget creates a new file, index.html.2, to avoid overwriting the first file. Any command that will be called repeatedly, as MRTG will do with your scripts, should not fill up the system's hard disk. Therefore, you need some way to change the output options.

The -O (oh) option tells wget to output to a given file instead of outputting to names that match the remote file names. A special file name, -, tells wget to send the output to stdout. You can then cheat and redirect stdout to /dev/null, to throw away the output, as shown in the following example:

```
$ wget -nv -O - http://www.wiley.com/ > /dev/null
23:37:16 URL:http://www.wiley.com/WileyCDA/ [42,840] -> "-" [1]
```

Notice that the wget summary output remains. You can see why with the following command:

```
$ wget -nv -O - http://www.wiley.com/ > /dev/null 2> /dev/null
$
```

The summary output is sent to stderr, not stdout.

The next step is to filter out the number of bytes from the summary output. You can use the cut command for this.

Try It Out   Retrieving a Document from a Web Server

Try the following command:

```
$ wget -nv  -O - http://www.wiley.com/ 2>&1 > /dev/null | \
cut -d' ' -f3 | tr "\[\]" " " | tr -d ","
 42840
```

Note that your byte count may differ the next time this book publisher changes its home page.

How It Works

This example command finally cleans up the output to one number, without the superfluous comma. Breaking this complex command into pieces, you can see the following:

```
wget -nv  -O - http://www.wiley.com/ 2>&1 > /dev/null | \
cut -d' ' -f3 | \
tr "\[\]" " " | \
tr -d ","
```

The wget command downloads the web document. The -nv option turns on *not-verbose* mode. The -O (oh) option tells wget to output the document to a file, and the dash, -, sets the file to stdout. The next step is pretty tricky. The 2>&1 redirects stderr to stdout. This must occur before the > /dev/null, because that redirects stdout to the null device. If you reverse the two, you'll get no output.

The cut command splits the output on spaces and extracts the third field. That leaves just the number in square brackets, as shown in this example:

```
$ wget -nv  -O - http://www.wiley.com/ 2>&1 > /dev/null | \
cut -d' ' -f3
 [42,840]
```

The next command, `tr`, translates the square brackets into blank spaces:

```
$ wget -nv  -O - http://www.wiley.com/ 2>&1 > /dev/null | \
cut -d' ' -f3 | \
tr "\[\]" " "
42,840
```

The pattern passed to the `tr` command, `"\[\]"`, uses the backslash characters to escape the square brackets, as brackets are used in regular expressions.

The output of this command line gets tantalizingly closer to the desired output. The second `tr` command removes the yucky comma, as shown in this example:

```
$ wget -nv  -O - http://www.wiley.com/ 2>&1 > /dev/null | \
cut -d' ' -f3 | \
tr "\[\]" " " | \
tr -d ","
42840
```

Note how this example successively cleans up the output for usage in a script. You'll often need to follow a similar process to gradually make the output more usable.

You can then write a script to graph the data retrieved from a remote web server. The assumption is that if the graph dips, there is a problem.

Try It Out   Monitoring a Web Server

Enter the following script and name the file `web2mrtg`:

```
#!/bin/sh
# Retrieves a document from a web server.
# You need to pass the URL to test.
# Data output is ONE value: the number of bytes
# downloaded.

stats=`wget -nv "$url" 2>&1 | cut -d' ' -f3,5 | tr "\[\"]" " " | tr -d ","`

stats=`wget -nv  -O - "$1" 2>&1 > /dev/null | \
    cut -d' ' -f3 | \
    tr "\[\]" " " | \
    tr -d ","
`

set $stats

bytes=$1

echo $bytes
echo 0

echo `uptime`
echo `hostname`
```

When you run this script, you'll see output like the following:

```
$ ./web2mrtg http://www.wiley.com/
42840
0
00:07:46 up 4:46, 4 users, load average: 0.16, 0.28, 0.25
kirkwall
```

How It Works

After delving into the complex command line, the rest of the script follows the pattern used so far.

Of course, there are several other ways you can monitor web servers and other network server applications. This example should get you started and open up a whole range of possibilities.

Try It Out   **Configuring MRTG to Monitor Web Servers**

The following example shows an MRTG configuration for this target:

```
# Application monitoring.
Target[web.download.bytes]: `/usr/local/bin/web2mrtg http://www.wiley.com/`
MaxBytes[web.download.bytes]: 10001010

# HTML output settings.
Title[web.download.bytes]: Web Page Download
PageTop[web.download.bytes]: <H2>Web Page Download</H2>
    Dips in the graph indicate problems.

Suppress[web.download.bytes]: ym

# Graph output settings.
Options[web.download.bytes]: gauge, nopercent, transparent, growright, noo

PNGTitle[web.download.bytes]: Web

YLegend[web.download.bytes]: Bytes
ShortLegend[web.download.bytes]:b

Legend1[web.download.bytes]: Downloaded
Legend3[web.download.bytes]: Max Downloaded Memory
LegendI[web.download.bytes]:  Downloaded:
```

How It Works

This example follows most of the previous patterns. It introduces the noo option, which tells mrtg not to graph the second variable (the output variable if you were monitoring a network router — hence, no-o or no-output). This means you only have to set up half the legends.

The web2mrtg script, shown previously, takes in the URL to download. Thus, you can monitor any web page, not just the root document of a particular server.

For reference, the following example shows a full MRTG configuration file, named `mrtg_sys.cfg`:

```
HtmlDir: /var/www/mrtg
ImageDir: /var/www/mrtg
LogDir: /var/lib/mrtg
ThreshDir: /var/lib/mrtg

Target[kirkwall.net.eth0]: `/usr/local/bin/net2mrtg eth0`
MaxBytes[kirkwall.net.eth0]: 10001010

# HTML output settings.
Title[kirkwall.net.eth0]: Net Stats for eth0
PageTop[kirkwall.net.eth0]: <h2>Net Stats for eth0</h2>
Suppress[kirkwall.net.eth0]: y

# Graph output settings.
Options[kirkwall.net.eth0]: gauge, nopercent, transparent, growright

PNGTitle[kirkwall.net.eth0]: Net Throughput
YLegend[kirkwall.net.eth0]: Packets


Target[kirkwall.disk.slash]: `/usr/local/bin/df2mrtg /`
MaxBytes[kirkwall.disk.slash]: 10001010

# HTML output settings.
Title[kirkwall.disk.slash]: / Disk Usage
PageTop[kirkwall.disk.slash]: <h2>Disk usage for /</h2>
Suppress[kirkwall.disk.slash]: ym

Options[kirkwall.disk.slash]: gauge, nopercent, transparent, growright

PNGTitle[kirkwall.disk.slash]: Disk usage
YLegend[kirkwall.disk.slash]: Kilobytes

ShortLegend[kirkwall.disk.slash]: b
Legend1[kirkwall.disk.slash]: Used space
Legend2[kirkwall.disk.slash]: Available space
Legend3[kirkwall.disk.slash]: Max Used
Legend4[kirkwall.disk.slash]: Max Available
LegendI[kirkwall.disk.slash]:  Used:
LegendO[kirkwall.disk.slash]:  Available:


# Monitor another file system.
Target[kirkwall.disk.home]: `/usr/local/bin/df2mrtg /home2`
MaxBytes[kirkwall.disk.home]: 10001010

# HTML output settings.
Title[kirkwall.disk.home]: /home2 Disk Usage
PageTop[kirkwall.disk.home]: <h2>Disk usage for /home2</h2>
Suppress[kirkwall.disk.home]: ym

# Graph output settings.
```

```
Options[kirkwall.disk.home]: gauge, nopercent, transparent, growright

PNGTitle[kirkwall.disk.home]: Disk usage
YLegend[kirkwall.disk.home]: Kilobytes

ShortLegend[kirkwall.disk.home]: b
Legend1[kirkwall.disk.home]: Used space
Legend2[kirkwall.disk.home]: Available space
Legend3[kirkwall.disk.home]: Max Used
Legend4[kirkwall.disk.home]: Max Available
LegendI[kirkwall.disk.home]:  Used:
LegendO[kirkwall.disk.home]:  Available:


Target[kirkwall.cpu.load]: `/usr/local/bin/load2mrtg`
MaxBytes[kirkwall.cpu.load]: 10001010

# HTML output settings.
Title[kirkwall.cpu.load]: Kirkwall CPU Load
PageTop[kirkwall.cpu.load]: <H2>CPU Load For Kirkwall</H2>

Suppress[kirkwall.cpu.load]: ym


# Graph output settings.
Options[kirkwall.cpu.load]: gauge, nopercent, transparent, growright

PNGTitle[kirkwall.cpu.load]: kirkwall CPU

YLegend[kirkwall.cpu.load]: Load avg.
ShortLegend[kirkwall.cpu.load]: avg.
Legend1[kirkwall.cpu.load]: Average CPU load
Legend2[kirkwall.cpu.load]: Number of users
Legend3[kirkwall.cpu.load]: Max CPU load
Legend4[kirkwall.cpu.load]: Max users
LegendI[kirkwall.cpu.load]:  Load:
LegendO[kirkwall.cpu.load]:  Users:



# Memory usage.
Target[kirkwall.memory.usage]: `/usr/local/bin/mem2mrtg`
MaxBytes[kirkwall.memory.usage]: 10001010

# HTML output settings.
Title[kirkwall.memory.usage]: Kirkwall Memory Usage
PageTop[kirkwall.memory.usage]: <H2>Memory Usage For Kirkwall</H2>

Suppress[kirkwall.memory.usage]: ym

# Graph output settings.
```

```
Options[kirkwall.memory.usage]: gauge, nopercent, transparent, growright

PNGTitle[kirkwall.memory.usage]: kirkwall vm

YLegend[kirkwall.memory.usage]: Memory
ShortLegend[kirkwall.memory.usage]:b
kMG[kirkwall.memory.usage]: k,m
Legend1[kirkwall.memory.usage]: Active Memory
Legend2[kirkwall.memory.usage]: Free Memory
Legend3[kirkwall.memory.usage]: Max Active Memory
Legend4[kirkwall.memory.usage]: Max Free Memory
LegendI[kirkwall.memory.usage]:  Active:
LegendO[kirkwall.memory.usage]:  Free:


# Application monitoring.
Target[web.download.bytes]: `/usr/local/bin/web2mrtg http://www.wiley.com/`
MaxBytes[web.download.bytes]: 10001010

# HTML output settings.
Title[web.download.bytes]: Web Page Download
PageTop[web.download.bytes]: <H2>Web Page Download</H2>
    Dips in the graph indicate problems.

Suppress[web.download.bytes]: ym

# Graph output settings.
Options[web.download.bytes]: gauge, nopercent, transparent, growright, noo

PNGTitle[web.download.bytes]: Web

YLegend[web.download.bytes]: Bytes
ShortLegend[web.download.bytes]:b

Legend1[web.download.bytes]: Downloaded
Legend3[web.download.bytes]: Max Downloaded Memory
LegendI[web.download.bytes]:  Downloaded:
```

Yow. MRTG configurations can grow large, and this example monitors only a few items.

You can do a lot more with MRTG. If you have any data available via SNMP, consult the MRTG documentation for information on how to configure MRTG to monitor data via SNMP. In addition, look for the webalizer command to find a utility similar to MRTG but designed to work with web server log files.

One drawback to MRTG, however, is that you need to reconfigure MRTG each time you change a router or system.

Summary

MRTG provides a handy tool for monitoring anything on your system, which is why this tool has stood the test of time and been adopted in major corporations. You can write scripts to monitor disk and memory usage, network throughput, and so on.

This chapter doesn't cover every MRTG option. For more details, refer to the MRTG documentation. Instead, this chapter has focused on how to get started with MRTG. Armed with these techniques, you should be able to configure MRTG to suit your needs.

MRTG enables you to do all of the following:

❑   Generate graphs that show the values output by your scripts over time.

❑   View detailed information for the current day.

❑   View summary information for the last week, month, and year.

❑   Monitor systems without filling your hard disk. The fact that MRTG uses a fixed amount of disk space really helps.

The next chapter extends the discussion to using shell scripts to help administer your systems.

Exercises

1.   What are some types of things that you could monitor the same way, whether you were working on Windows, Mac OS X, Unix, or Linux?

2.   How would you go about graphing data on a database such as Oracle, Postgres, SQL Server, or DB2?

3.   Look up some other monitoring packages, such as mon or Big Brother. (Both are available free on the Internet.) You can also try commercial packages such as HP OpenView and CA Unicenter.

Scripting for Administrators

The last chapter covered a major use of scripts for administrators: monitoring the systems you administer. Using MRTG, you can monitor CPU usage, available disk space, and network router throughput, among other things, but scripts come in handy in quite a few other areas. This chapter won't show you magical ways to run all of your systems. Instead, it describes how you can use scripts to improve your daily life and manage your systems with less work, including the following:

- ❑ Deciding when and where to write scripts
- ❑ Creating scripts in an organized fashion
- ❑ Scripting complicated commands
- ❑ Troubleshooting with scripts
- ❑ Removing annoyances with scripts
- ❑ Cleaning up yucky data formats
- ❑ Automating your daily work with scripts

This chapter contains some very simple scripts and some complicated scripts. In all cases, though, the goal is to show techniques, not cleverness, and to focus on generating ideas for making your work easier.

Why Write Scripts?

From an administrator's point of view, scripts enable you to do the following:

- ❑ Automate frequently run tasks
- ❑ Remember complicated command-line options and file paths
- ❑ Filter through data and respond with just the crucial items that require your attention

In these cases, scripts come in handy and, best of all, generally do not require a long time to write.

Scripting is fun. In about three minutes, you can create a useful script. The problem is that if you write all of your scripts in a totally ad hoc manner, you will end up with a confusing mess. If you approach your administration scripts with even a small amount of discipline, you will create a script library that will save you hours and hours of time.

Following a few simple guidelines will help you avoid ending up with a confusing mess:

❑ Use a consistent style. Indent your scripts to make them easier to read. (Use any indenting style you prefer; you're not limited to the style shown by the examples in this book.)

❑ Store your scripts in a common location. For example, store your scripts in /usr/local/bin or the bin subdirectory of your home directory, $HOME/bin. You might also want to separate your administrative scripts into a directory of their own.

❑ Document your scripts. Comment liberally. You want to especially document why you wrote the script or what problem it helps to solve. In addition, specify how to call the script, the command-line arguments and options, and so on.

None of these guidelines should require much work or restrict your creativity.

Note that some very sick people have even gone so far as to write poetry in scripts, usually in another scripting language called Perl. Avoid these people. They are the first who will become zombies when the big meteor hits the Earth. Remember, you were warned.

You've probably noticed the focus on not spending a lot of time. In today's IT environments, administrators typically manage too many systems with too few resources. Spend your time going after the proverbial low-hanging fruit, the easy ones, first. Tackle the harder stuff later.

Scripting Complicated Commands

Computers can remember things very well. People can't always do the same. If you have commands you need to run, but you tend to forget the command-line arguments or options, you can solve the problem by storing the command in a script. For example, the following script has only one actual command.

Try It Out   Turning on Networking over USB

Enter the script and name the file yopy:

```
#!/bin/sh

# Starts networking over a USB port for a connected device.
# Turn the device on, plug in the Yopy PDA, and then run this
# script.

/sbin/ifconfig usb0 192.168.1.1
echo "Yopy is on 192.168.1.1"
```

When you run this script, you'll see the following output:

```
$ yopy
Yopy is on 192.168.1.1
```

If the USB port cannot be configured for networking, you'll see an error like the following:

```
$ yopy
SIOCSIFADDR: Permission denied
usb0: unknown interface: No such device
Yopy is on 192.168.1.1
```

How It Works

In this script, the comments are longer than the commands. Don't worry about that, though. Enter as many comments as you think you need in your scripts, regardless of the length. These small scripts are not going to fill up your hard drive.

See the section on Commenting Your Scripts in Chapter 2 for more information on the importance of comments.

This script calls the `ifconfig` command to turn on TCP/IP networking over a USB link. The real purpose of the script is to enable a network link to a Yopy PDA over a USB cable. The Yopy runs Linux, the popular MySQL database, and the minimalist Boa web server.

See www.yopy.com for more information about this cool PDA.

While the script was written to establish a network link to a PDA, from a scripting point of view, this script remembers things for the poor, overworked administrator:

❑ The `ifconfig` command resides in /sbin on this Linux system, not /bin, /usr/bin, nor /usr/sbin.

❑ The USB networking device is usb0, although this is usually easy to figure out.

❑ The IP address to talk to the Yopy is statically configured to 192.168.1.1. This is important for the Yopy's MySQL database security.

Any time you face a similar situation, turn to scripts to keep crucial data for you. Even a one-line script is worth creating if it saves you time and frustration.

The next example shows a few more lines of scripting commands but is similarly short.

Try It Out   Monitoring HTTP Data

Enter the following script and name the file `tcpmon`:

```
#!/bin/sh

# Runs the Apache Axis TCP monitor as a proxy between
# a web client and server. The tcpmon program then
# displays all the HTTP traffic between the client
# and server.
#
AXIS=$HOME/java/xml/axis-1_2RC2/lib ; export AXIS

CLASSPATH=$AXIS/axis.jar:$AXIS/log4j-1.2.8.jar ; export CLASSPATH

# java org.apache.axis.utils.tcpmon [listenPort targetHost targetPort]
java -Xmx400m org.apache.axis.utils.tcpmon 28080 vodka.liquor.vod 85
```

Run this script as shown here:

```
$ ./tcpmon
```

This script generates no output. Instead, it creates a window for monitoring network traffic.

How It Works

This script runs the Apache Axis TCP monitor program. Axis is a package for accessing web services from Java applications. The `tcpmon` program is a utility program in the Axis package.

> *See ws.apache.org/axis/ for more information about Apache Axis.*

The `tcpmon` program displays a window showing each HTTP request to a remote web server and the full contents of the corresponding response. With web servers, the data sent to the remote server, along with the response, are encoded in XML and usually not visible to the user. Thus, a tool such as `tcpmon` can shed some light on any problems that might develop when calling on remote web services.

Because Axis requires a Java runtime engine, you must have the `java` command available on your system. Prior to calling the `java` command, you need to set up the *classpath*, the set of directories that hold compiled Java code that the program requires.

This script sets the `CLASSPATH` environment variable, used by the `java` command, to hold two files: `axis.jar` and `log4j-1.2.8.jar`. Both of these files reside inside the Axis distribution. The script sets the `AXIS` environment variable to this directory, which makes it easier to change the name of the directory if Axis is installed in another location or upgraded to a new version. Using the `AXIS` environment variable also shortens the line that sets the `CLASSPATH` environment variable.

The `tcpmon` script, therefore, remembers the following:

❑ Where on disk the Axis package was installed. Because the installation directory has the version number, this can be hard to remember.

❑ Which Java libraries, called *jar files*, are required by the `tcpmon` program.

❑ The Java class name of the `tcpmon` program, `org.apache.axis.utils.tcpmon`. The class name is needed to launch the application.

❑ That the `tcpmon` program can use a lot of memory. The `-Xmx400m` sets the program to use a maximum of 400 megabytes of memory for Java objects.

❑ The command-line arguments needed for the `tcpmon` program, as well as the required order for the command-line arguments.

❑ The hostname and port number of the remote server.

❑ The local port number used as a proxy for the remote server.

As you can see, even with a short script, you can save a lot of useful information in a script.

> *The preceding script was instrumental in testing a web site designed for a vodka promotion. The web site shown, vodka.liquor.vod, is fake, to protect the innocent.*

While the scripting of complicated commands usually results in fairly small scripts, troubleshooting enables you to create more detailed scripts. Creating larger scripts does not necessarily show your scripting prowess. The goal, as always, is to solve problems.

Troubleshooting Your Systems

Just as writing larger scripts is not an end in itself, it is very important when troubleshooting that you don't end up reporting too much information. Therefore, when you create your troubleshooting scripts, focus on reporting only problems or essential information.

One of the most common problems on systems, especially those with minimal attention, is filling disks. To see how much space is used on a given disk or on all your system's disks, you can use the df command, as shown here:

```
$ df -k
Filesystem          1K-blocks      Used Available Use% Mounted on
/dev/hda2            24193540   3980000  18984568  18% /
/dev/hda1              101086     10933     84934  12% /boot
none                  501696         0    501696   0% /dev/shm
/dev/hda5            48592392  25049972  21074036  55% /home2
/dev/sda1             507104    147936    359168  30% /media/TITAN
```

This example shows all the disks mounted on a particular system. The -k command-line option tells the df command to return the results in 1K blocks. You can then interpret the results to determine whether any of the disks requires further attention. Alternatively, you could write a script to perform the interpretation for you.

Try It Out   Checking Disk Space

Enter the following script and name the file diskcheck:

```
#!/bin/sh

# Output warnings if disks are too full (in percentage
# terms) or have too little space available.

# This script goes through all the mounted file systems
# and checks each to see if the disk is nearly full,
# reporting only on those disks that warrant more attention.


# Set thresholds
min_free=4000

max_in_use=90


# Get a list of all file systems.
filesystems=`df -k | grep -v Use | grep -v none | awk '{ print $6 }'`

for filesystem in $filesystems
do
    # Cache results for this file system.
```

```
        entry=`df -k $filesystem | tail -1`

        # Split out the amount of space free as well as in-use percentage.
        free=`echo $entry | cut -d' ' -f4`
        in_use=`echo $entry | cut -d' ' -f5 | cut -d'%' -f1 `

        # Check the file system percent in use.
        if [ $(expr "$in_use > $max_in_use" ) ]
        then
            echo "$filesystem has only $free KB free at $in_use%."
        else
            # Check the available space against threshold.
            # Only make this check if the in use is OK.

            result=$( echo "
                scale=2    /* two decimal places */
                print $free < $min_free" | bc)


            if [ $(expr "$result != 0" ) ]
            then
                echo "$filesystem has only $free KB free."
            fi
        fi
    done
```

When you run this script, and if everything is okay, you'll see no output:

```
$ sh diskcheck
$
```

Conversely, if you have a disk or disks that are nearly filled up, you'll see output like the following:

```
$ sh diskcheck
/home2 has only 200768 KB free at 91%.
```

How It Works

This script introduces no new concepts, so you should be able to read the script and determine what it does.

This script uses two threshold values to check disk space: a percentage full value and an amount free. If the disk is more than the threshold amount full, in percentage terms, the script considers this a problem. Furthermore, if the disk has only a minimal amount of space left, the script considers this a problem. These two thresholds enable the script to work for most any disk, large or small.

The thresholds appear at the top of the script to make it easier to change the values. Feel free to modify the values to whatever makes sense in your environment.

After setting the thresholds, the first major command extracts the name of each mounted file system using the df command:

```
filesystems=`df -k | grep -v Use | grep -v none | awk '{ print $6 }'`
```

Breaking this command line into pieces, the first command, df -k, lists the amount of disk space in kilobytes (-k). Most modern versions of df use kilobytes by default, but even so, using this option is safe and harmless. If you come across a system that uses the 512-byte blocks instead, the -k option will fix up the results.

The grep -v command looks for all lines that do not match the given pattern. The grep -v Use command removes the first header line. The second grep command, grep -v none, removes the special /dev/shm entry on Linux systems. You can add other grep commands to remove any extraneous devices.

The last command on this line, awk, prints the sixth field in the output. This is the name of the mount point where the file system is mounted. Use $1 instead of $6 if you want the device entry for the file system instead. In most cases, the mount point, such as /, /tmp, or /home, proves more meaningful than the device entry, such as /dev/hda5 or /dev/sdb1.

The next step is to loop over all the file systems, using a for loop:

```
for filesystem in $filesystems
do
    # ...
done
```

In each iteration of the loop, the first step is to call the df command again with just the name of the specific file system:

```
entry=`df -k $filesystem | tail -1`
```

This is not very efficient, as the script just called the df command previously, but this format makes it easier to extract the data. The script pipes the results of the df command to the tail command to remove the header line.

Once the script has the data on a file system, it can retrieve the most interesting values. In this case, these values are the percent used and the amount of free space:

```
# Split out the amount of space free as well as in-use percentage.
    free=`echo $entry | cut -d' ' -f4`
    in_use=`echo $entry | cut -d' ' -f5 | cut -d'%' -f1 `
```

The script sets the *free* variable to the amount of free space, held in the fourth field of the data. The cut command extracts the necessary field.

You should always pass a field delimiter to the cut command. Set this using the -d option.

The script sets the *in_use* variable to the percentage of the disk that is used. In this case, the script calls the cut command twice. The first call to cut extracts the value, such as 51%. The second cut command removes the percent sign and leaves just the number, so the script can perform comparisons on the percentage.

The most important comparison is to check whether the disk is too full, percentagewise:

```
if [ $(expr "$in_use > $max_in_use" ) ]
then
    echo "$filesystem has only $free KB free at $in_use%."
else
    # ...
fi
```

The `if` statement contains a lot of syntax. You must put the value passed to the `expr` command in quotes; otherwise, the shell will interpret > as redirecting `stdout` and, similarly, < as redirecting `stdin`.

If the first check passes, then the script verifies that at least a certain minimal amount of disk space is available. This test does not make sense if the script is already displaying a warning about the disk, so the script only performs this check if the first check passes.

This check uses the `bc` command:

```
result=$( echo "
    scale=2    /* two decimal places */
    print $free < $min_free" | bc)

if [ $(expr "$result != 0" ) ]
then
    echo "$filesystem has only $free KB free."
fi
```

An earlier version of this script used the `expr` command, similar to the first check:

```
if [ $(expr "$free < $min_free" ) ]
then
    echo "$filesystem has only $free KB free."
fi
```

This did not work, surprisingly. The numbers reported by the `df` command are all whole numbers (integers), so no floating-point math is required. Previously, we needed the `bc` command to handle floating-point math. The numbers, while integers, were too big for the poor old `expr` command. Any disks with gigabytes of space will overload `expr`, hence the use of the `bc` command.

Another important task when troubleshooting a system is verifying that the necessary processes are running, such as a web server or a database, as shown in the following Try It Out.

Try It Out   Checking for Processes

As shown in a number of previous examples, you can use the `ps` command to list processes:

```
$ ps -e
  PID TTY          TIME CMD
    1 ?        00:00:00 init
    2 ?        00:00:00 ksoftirqd/0
    3 ?        00:00:00 events/0
    4 ?        00:00:00 khelper
    5 ?        00:00:00 kacpid
   27 ?        00:00:00 kblockd/0
   28 ?        00:00:00 khubd
   37 ?        00:00:00 pdflush
   38 ?        00:00:00 pdflush
   40 ?        00:00:00 aio/0
   39 ?        00:00:00 kswapd0
  113 ?        00:00:00 kseriod
  187 ?        00:00:00 kjournald
 1014 ?        00:00:00 udevd
```

```
1641 ?         00:00:00 kjournald
1642 ?         00:00:00 kjournald
1892 ?         00:00:00 syslogd
1896 ?         00:00:00 klogd
1917 ?         00:00:00 portmap
1937 ?         00:00:00 rpc.statd
1970 ?         00:00:00 rpc.idmapd
2040 ?         00:00:00 nifd
2070 ?         00:00:00 mDNSResponder
2083 ?         00:00:00 smartd
2093 ?         00:00:00 acpid
2105 ?         00:00:00 cupsd
2141 ?         00:00:00 sshd
2152 ?         00:00:00 xinetd
2172 ?         00:00:00 sendmail
2180 ?         00:00:00 sendmail
2191 ?         00:00:00 gpm
2201 ?         00:00:00 crond
2227 ?         00:00:00 xfs
2246 ?         00:00:00 atd
2265 ?         00:00:00 dbus-daemon-1
2278 ?         00:00:00 cups-config-dae
2289 ?         00:00:13 hald
2299 tty1      00:00:00 mingetty
2339 tty2      00:00:00 mingetty
2340 tty3      00:00:00 mingetty
2411 tty4      00:00:00 mingetty
2447 tty5      00:00:00 mingetty
2464 tty6      00:00:00 mingetty
2587 ?         00:00:00 gdm-binary
2763 ?         00:00:00 gdm-binary
2773 ?         00:03:37 X
3000 ?         00:00:00 ssh-agent
3226 ?         00:00:00 gconfd-2
3352 ?         00:00:00 dhclient
3452 ?         00:00:00 artsd
5226 ?         00:00:00 gnome-session
5254 ?         00:00:00 ssh-agent
5281 ?         00:00:00 dbus-daemon-1
5282 ?         00:00:00 dbus-launch
5286 ?         00:00:01 gconfd-2
5289 ?         00:00:00 gnome-keyring-d
5291 ?         00:00:00 bonobo-activati
5293 ?         00:00:03 metacity
5295 ?         00:00:00 gnome-settings-
5301 ?         00:00:03 gam_server
5310 ?         00:00:00 xscreensaver
5316 ?         00:00:00 gnome-volume-ma
5318 ?         00:00:01 gnome-panel
5320 ?         00:00:10 nautilus
5325 ?         00:00:00 eggcups
5331 ?         00:00:00 evolution-alarm
5333 ?         00:00:02 gnome-terminal
5335 ?         00:00:04 gedit
5337 ?         00:00:01 rhythmbox
5342 ?         00:00:00 evolution-data-
```

```
5361 ?          00:00:00 gnome-vfs-daemo
5369 ?          00:00:00 mapping-daemon
5371 ?          00:00:00 nautilus-throbb
5373 ?          00:00:03 wnck-applet
5375 ?          00:00:00 pam-panel-icon
5376 ?          00:00:00 pam_timestamp_c
5389 ?          00:00:00 gnome-pty-helpe
5394 pts/1      00:00:00 bash
5404 pts/2      00:00:00 bash
5409 pts/3      00:00:00 bash
5441 ?          00:00:00 notification-ar
5443 ?          00:00:00 mixer_applet2
5454 ?          00:00:00 clock-applet
5456 ?          00:00:00 gnome-netstatus
5458 ?          00:00:00 gweather-applet
5502 ?          00:00:00 scsi_eh_0
5503 ?          00:00:00 usb-storage
5619 ?          00:00:51 soffice.bin
5689 ?          00:00:00 firefox
5706 ?          00:00:00 run-mozilla.sh
5711 ?          00:00:04 firefox-bin
5857 pts/3      00:00:00 ps
```

How It Works

The `-e` command-line option tells the `ps` command to list every process. Most people use the `-e` option with `-f`, for full output. In this example, however, the goal is to get the command name and skip the rest of the output; therefore, this uses only `-e` and not `-ef` as command-line options to `ps`.

Note that on BSD-derived Unix systems, such as Mac OS X, the ps option will be aux instead of -e.

This example ran on a desktop system. Note that on a server system, you would likely have a lot more processes.

You can place this type of check into a script, of course, leading to the next example.

Try It Out   Verifying Processes Are Running

Enter the following script and name the file `processcheck`:

```
#!/bin/sh

# Checks to see if a given process is running.
# Pass in a command-line argument of the pattern
# to look for. The script will output all the
# occurrences.

pattern=$1

ps -e | grep -v $$ | grep $pattern | awk '{print $4}'
```

When you run this script, you need to pass a pattern for `grep` to use to search for the processes, as shown in this example:

```
$ ./processcheck k
ksoftirqd/0
khelper
kacpid
kblockd/0
khubd
kswapd0
kseriod
kjournald
kjournald
kjournald
klogd
gnome-keyring-d
wnck-applet
clock-applet
awk
```

Alternately, you can try a longer pattern, such as the following:

```
$ ./processcheck gnome
gnome-session
gnome-keyring-d
gnome-settings-
gnome-volume-ma
gnome-panel
gnome-terminal
gnome-vfs-daemo
gnome-pty-helpe
gnome-netstatus
```

How It Works

The processcheck script calls the ps command to list all the processes running on the system. The script directs the output of the ps command to the grep -v command. This command filters out the current process, which should always match the pattern, as the pattern is a command-line argument. (This is called a *false positive match*.)

> *The $$ variable is described in Chapter 9.*

The script next takes the first command-line argument and passes this to the grep command, filtering out all but the process entries that match the pattern. Finally, the awk command strips out the extraneous data, leaving just the process names. The process names are important in case you pass a partial name as the pattern to match. For example, many system kernel-related processes start with the letter *k*. Similarly, many desktop applications that are part of the KDE desktop environment also start with the letter *k*. Without seeing the full process names, you cannot tell what is running.

> *Note that if you use ps with the aux option, you need to change the awk command to print $11 instead of $4.*

Removing Minor Annoyances

Minor annoyances are anything that bugs you (anything small, that is, so Windows security issues don't count). You can use the capabilities of scripts to perform the necessary setup work for commands, so you don't have to.

Whenever possible, let the script do the work, as in the following example.

Try It Out   Running a Command in a Directory

Enter the following script and name the file `jabber`:

```
#!/bin/sh
cd $HOME/java/im/BS211-complete ; sh buddySpace.sh
```

When you run this script, you'll see output like the following:

```
$ ./jabber
loading preferences...
initializing core...
loading GUI...
loading sounds...
initializing plug-ins...
loading conferencing...
loading mapping...
loading html view...
loading browse...
```

This script launches the BuddySpace window, shown in Figure 13-1. This simple script performs one task: This version of BuddySpace won't start unless you launch it from its installation directory. Having to change directories prior to launching a program, and having to do this every day, counts as a minor annoyance.

Figure 13-1

How It Works

BuddySpace provides an instant messaging, or IM, client using the Jabber protocol. Jabber gateways then enable connections to MSN, AOL, Yahoo!, and other IM networks.

See www.jabber.org for more information on the Jabber protocol. See kmi.open.ac.uk/projects/buddy-pace for more information about the BuddySpace client application. BuddySpace is written in Java, so it runs on Mac OS X, Windows, Linux, Solaris, and other versions of Unix. BuddySpace also includes an extensive set of frequently asked questions.

Whenever you face a similar situation, you can write a similar script to remove the annoyance. The next script follows a similar concept.

Try It Out Playing Your Favorite Songs

Enter this script and name the file `favs`:

```
#!/bin/sh
xmms $HOME/multi/mp3/fav_playlist.m3u
```

How It Works

This is another tiny script. It launches the XMMS multimedia player application and passes XMMS the name of a playlist file, telling XMMS which songs to play. Again, the whole point of this script is to save typing.

These examples, while short, should give you some ideas about what you can do with scripts. Once you start scripting the small things, larger things become a lot easier.

Cleaning Up Data

Many programs, systems, and devices log information or can describe themselves, sometimes in excruciating detail. It's the detail that is the problem. You can become overwhelmed by the massive amount of information to slog through just to get to the useful bits. As you'd suspect, scripts can help here as well.

Try It Out Viewing Linux USB Port Details

On a Linux system, you can gather a lot of information on the USB ports by looking at the special file `/proc/bus/usb/devices`:

```
$ cat /proc/bus/usb/devices

T:  Bus=03 Lev=00 Prnt=00 Port=00 Cnt=00 Dev#=  1 Spd=12  MxCh= 3
B:  Alloc=  0/900 us ( 0%), #Int=  0, #Iso=  0
D:  Ver= 1.10 Cls=09(hub ) Sub=00 Prot=00 MxPS= 8 #Cfgs=  1
P:  Vendor=0000 ProdID=0000 Rev= 2.06
S:  Manufacturer=Linux 2.6.9-1.681_FC3 ohci_hcd
S:  Product=OHCI Host Controller
S:  SerialNumber=0000:00:02.1
C:* #Ifs= 1 Cfg#= 1 Atr=e0 MxPwr=  0mA
I:  If#= 0 Alt= 0 #EPs= 1 Cls=09(hub ) Sub=00 Prot=00 Driver=hub
```

```
E:   Ad=81(I) Atr=03(Int.) MxPS=    2 Ivl=255ms


T:   Bus=03 Lev=01 Prnt=01 Port=00 Cnt=01 Dev#=  7 Spd=12   MxCh= 0
D:   Ver= 1.10 Cls=00(>ifc ) Sub=00 Prot=00 MxPS= 8 #Cfgs=  1
P:   Vendor=0781 ProdID=8888 Rev= 1.00
C:*  #Ifs= 1 Cfg#= 1 Atr=80 MxPwr=100mA
I:   If#= 0 Alt= 0 #EPs= 3 Cls=08(stor.) Sub=06 Prot=50 Driver=usb-storage
E:   Ad=81(I) Atr=02(Bulk) MxPS=   64 Ivl=0ms
E:   Ad=02(O) Atr=02(Bulk) MxPS=   64 Ivl=0ms
E:   Ad=83(I) Atr=03(Int.) MxPS=    2 Ivl=1ms


T:   Bus=02 Lev=00 Prnt=00 Port=00 Cnt=00 Dev#=  1 Spd=12   MxCh= 3
B:   Alloc= 14/900 us ( 2%), #Int=  1, #Iso=  0
D:   Ver= 1.10 Cls=09(hub  ) Sub=00 Prot=00 MxPS= 8 #Cfgs=  1
P:   Vendor=0000 ProdID=0000 Rev= 2.06
S:   Manufacturer=Linux 2.6.9-1.681_FC3 ohci_hcd
S:   Product=OHCI Host Controller
S:   SerialNumber=0000:00:02.0
C:*  #Ifs= 1 Cfg#= 1 Atr=e0 MxPwr=  0mA
I:   If#= 0 Alt= 0 #EPs= 1 Cls=09(hub  ) Sub=00 Prot=00 Driver=hub
E:   Ad=81(I) Atr=03(Int.) MxPS=    2 Ivl=255ms


T:   Bus=02 Lev=01 Prnt=01 Port=01 Cnt=01 Dev#=  2 Spd=1.5 MxCh= 0
D:   Ver= 1.10 Cls=00(>ifc ) Sub=00 Prot=00 MxPS= 8 #Cfgs=  1
P:   Vendor=046d ProdID=c00b Rev= 6.10
S:   Manufacturer=Logitech
S:   Product=USB Mouse
C:*  #Ifs= 1 Cfg#= 1 Atr=a0 MxPwr=100mA
I:   If#= 0 Alt= 0 #EPs= 1 Cls=03(HID  ) Sub=01 Prot=02 Driver=usbhid
E:   Ad=81(I) Atr=03(Int.) MxPS=    8 Ivl=10ms


T:   Bus=01 Lev=00 Prnt=00 Port=00 Cnt=00 Dev#=  1 Spd=480 MxCh= 6
B:   Alloc=  0/800 us ( 0%), #Int=  0, #Iso=  0
D:   Ver= 2.00 Cls=09(hub  ) Sub=00 Prot=01 MxPS= 8 #Cfgs=  1
P:   Vendor=0000 ProdID=0000 Rev= 2.06
S:   Manufacturer=Linux 2.6.9-1.681_FC3 ehci_hcd
S:   Product=EHCI Host Controller
S:   SerialNumber=0000:00:02.2
C:*  #Ifs= 1 Cfg#= 1 Atr=e0 MxPwr=  0mA
I:   If#= 0 Alt= 0 #EPs= 1 Cls=09(hub  ) Sub=00 Prot=00 Driver=hub
E:   Ad=81(I) Atr=03(Int.) MxPS=    2 Ivl=256ms


T:   Bus=01 Lev=01 Prnt=01 Port=00 Cnt=01 Dev#=  8 Spd=480 MxCh= 0
D:   Ver= 2.00 Cls=00(>ifc ) Sub=00 Prot=00 MxPS=64 #Cfgs=  1
P:   Vendor=0781 ProdID=7108 Rev=20.00
S:   Manufacturer=SanDisk Corporation
S:   Product=Cruzer Titanium
S:   SerialNumber=00000000000000104629
C:*  #Ifs= 1 Cfg#= 1 Atr=80 MxPwr=100mA
I:   If#= 0 Alt= 0 #EPs= 2 Cls=08(stor.) Sub=06 Prot=50 Driver=usb-storage
E:   Ad=81(I) Atr=02(Bulk) MxPS= 512 Ivl=0ms
E:   Ad=02(O) Atr=02(Bulk) MxPS= 512 Ivl=31875us
```

How It Works

In this example, the Linux box has four USB ports, two on the front and two on the back. Three devices are plugged in: a Logitech USB mouse and two USB flash drives. One of the USB flash drives requires a USB 2.0 port, at least on Linux. Note that although this system has four USB ports, it contains extra entries where devices are plugged in.

Entries with a speed of 480 are USB 2.0 ports. In this data, speed appears as Spd. Entries with a speed of 12 are USB 1.1 ports. USB mice typically reduce the speed. For example, the mouse shown here indicates a speed of 1.5.

USB ports are odd ducks. You can plug in more than one device to each port if the first device has another port or is itself a USB hub with more than one port. Therefore, the system needs to report on any connected devices along with the capabilities of the ports themselves.

Note that reading /proc/bus/usb/devices can take a long time. This is not a real file but part of the pseudo-file system, /proc. You can speed things up with the lsusb command, a Linux-specific command, as shown in the next Try It Out.

Try It Out   **Using the lsusb Command**

The lsusb command provides a quick overview of the USB ports and devices on a system:

```
$ /sbin/lsusb
Bus 003 Device 001: ID 0000:0000
Bus 002 Device 002: ID 046d:c00b Logitech, Inc. MouseMan Wheel
Bus 002 Device 001: ID 0000:0000
Bus 001 Device 003: ID 0781:7108 SanDisk Corp.
Bus 001 Device 001: ID 0000:0000
```

The lsusb command can also output data in tree mode, as shown here:

```
$ /sbin/lsusb -t
Bus#  3
`-Dev#   1 Vendor 0x0000 Product 0x0000
  `-Dev#   2 Vendor 0x0c76 Product 0x0003
Bus#  2
`-Dev#   1 Vendor 0x0000 Product 0x0000
  `-Dev#   2 Vendor 0x046d Product 0xc00b
Bus#  1
`-Dev#   1 Vendor 0x0000 Product 0x0000
  `-Dev#   3 Vendor 0x0781 Product 0x7108
```

The preceding example shows the three USB buses, each with a connected device.

You can ask the lsusb command for more information, but you usually must be logged in as the root user to do so. You will also need a kernel at version 2.3.15 or newer. The -v option, for example, tells the lsusb command to output verbose information, as shown here:

```
# /sbin/lsusb -v -s 003

Bus 001 Device 003: ID 0781:7108 SanDisk Corp.
Device Descriptor:
```

```
    bLength                18
    bDescriptorType         1
    bcdUSB               2.00
    bDeviceClass            0 (Defined at Interface level)
    bDeviceSubClass         0
    bDeviceProtocol         0
    bMaxPacketSize0        64
    idVendor           0x0781 SanDisk Corp.
    idProduct          0x7108
    bcdDevice           20.00
    iManufacturer           1 SanDisk Corporation
    iProduct                2 Cruzer Titanium
    iSerial                 3 00000000000000104629
    bNumConfigurations      1
    Configuration Descriptor:
      bLength               9
      bDescriptorType       2
      wTotalLength         32
      bNumInterfaces        1
      bConfigurationValue   1
      iConfiguration        0
      bmAttributes       0x80
      MaxPower          100mA
      Interface Descriptor:
        bLength             9
        bDescriptorType     4
        bInterfaceNumber    0
        bAlternateSetting   0
        bNumEndpoints       2
        bInterfaceClass     8 Mass Storage
        bInterfaceSubClass  6 SCSI
        bInterfaceProtocol 80 Bulk (Zip)
        iInterface          0
        Endpoint Descriptor:
          bLength           7
          bDescriptorType   5
          bEndpointAddress  0x81 EP 1 IN
          bmAttributes      2
            Transfer Type        Bulk
            Synch Type           none
            Usage Type           Data
          wMaxPacketSize  0x0200 bytes 512 once
          bInterval       255
        Endpoint Descriptor:
          bLength           7
          bDescriptorType   5
          bEndpointAddress  0x02 EP 2 OUT
          bmAttributes      2
            Transfer Type        Bulk
            Synch Type           none
            Usage Type           Data
          wMaxPacketSize  0x0200 bytes 512 once
          bInterval       255
    Language IDs: (length=4)
       0409 English(US)
```

How It Works

This example just prints out verbose information on one device, 003 (Bus 001 Device 003 from the previous example). One line in particular indicates that this system supports at least one USB 2.0 port:

```
bcdUSB                  2.00
```

You can use the grep command to search for this entry on all USB devices:

```
# /sbin/lsusb -v | grep bcdUSB
bcdUSB                  1.10
bcdUSB                  1.10
bcdUSB                  1.10
bcdUSB                  2.00
bcdUSB                  2.00
```

The USB 2.0 ports indicate that a given system can support more sophisticated USB devices. You can look for them with the following script.

Try It Out   Checking for Modern USB Ports

Enter the following script and name the file usbcheck:

```
#!/bin/sh

# Checks for the USB version support, typically 1.1 or
# 2.0, for USB ports on a given Linux system.
#
# NOTE: You must be logged in as root to run this script.

echo "USB support:"
/sbin/lsusb -v | grep bcdUSB | awk '{print $2}'
```

When you run this script, you'll see output like the following:

```
# ./usbcheck
USB support:
1.10
1.10
1.10
2.00
2.00
```

How It Works

Remember that you must be logged in as root to run this script. This script starts with the lsusb command in verbose mode, which outputs far too much information to be useful. The script redirects the output of the lsusb command to the grep command to search for the entries on USB specification support, such as 2.0. The script redirects the output of the grep command to the awk command, to remove the odd bsdUSB text and just show the USB version numbers.

In addition, the script outputs a header line of its own, to help explain the output.

Ironically, this script and the information extracted from /proc/bus/usb/devices helped determine that an older Linux box had two USB 2.0 ports, on the rear of the machine, of course. The front USB ports are all USB 1.1. This is important because certain devices won't work on Linux connected to a 1.1 port. The Sandisk Cruzer Titanium, listed in the previous output, is one such device.

Automating Daily Work

Anything you do day in and day out falls into this category. Use the techniques shown in the previous examples, as well as the previous chapters. Once you have created a script to automate some aspect of your work, you can schedule that script to run at a particular time.

The `cron` scheduler, introduced in Chapter 12, enables you to run commands on a periodic schedule. You can use `cron` by setting up a `crontab` file that specifies when to run the script. Other than the scheduling, however, this type of scripting is the same as any other kind.

Summary

Scripts are an administrator's best friend. They can remember things for you, speed up your work, and sort through yucky output, extracting just the nuggets of useful information necessary to make informed decisions.

This chapter focused on using scripts, and spending very little time writing them, for a big return in time saved for common administrative work. The scripts in this chapter are intended to provoke discussion and further thought about what you can do with scripts.

In the administrative arena, scripts can help you with the following:

- ❏ Remembering complicated commands, command-line options, and command-line arguments for you
- ❏ Troubleshooting, such as checking the amount of available disk space and whether certain types of processes are running
- ❏ Removing minor annoyances
- ❏ Digesting voluminous data and extracting useful information
- ❏ Repetitive tasks you do every day
- ❏ Anything else that bothers you or you think is ripe for scripting

The next chapter switches gears from boring administrative work to fun, graphical, splashy desktop automation. You can use scripts to help with desktop applications as well, especially on that most graphical of systems, Mac OS X.

Exercises

1. Identify some issues at your organization and discuss how you can use scripts to help reduce the problems. (Stick to issues related to your computer systems, rather than annoying colleagues or dim-witted managers.)

2. Look at the online documentation for the ps command. Discuss at least three useful things ps can report.

3. Write a script to determine whether a given file system or mount point is mounted, and output the amount of free space on the file system if it is mounted. If the file system is not mounted, the script should output an error.

Scripting for the Desktop

This chapter introduces scripting for the desktop, or common user applications and the desktop environment. It describes how to script such tasks as playing music, controlling word processors, and the like. Special focus is given to Mac OS X and its unique Apple Open Scripting Architecture, or OSA, that enables the shell environment to interact with applications such as Photoshop or Microsoft Word. While you can do a lot with just the operating system, at some point you're going to want to start gluing various applications together. If you think about it, that's what shell scripting is: gluing applications together. However, it's not limited to things such as sed, awk, and other traditional Unix applications. You can even glue design applications and music applications together with scripting, shell and otherwise.

> While part of this chapter focuses on Mac OS X and linking the shell to AppleScript, the basic concepts apply to any application. For example, OpenOffice contains an extensive scripting implementation that is syntactically very similar to Microsoft's Visual Basic for Applications (VBA). Microsoft Word on the Mac has a full VBA implementation that can be called from AppleScript, which can be called from the shell environment. In other words, regardless of which language an application uses, if it runs on some form of Unix, you can probably get to it from the shell.

This chapter covers scripting for the desktop, including the following:

❑ Scripting office applications, such as the AbiWord word processors and the OpenOffice.org office suite

❑ Scripting Mac OS X applications using AppleScript to drive OSA-enabled applications

❑ Scripting audio players and video players

❑ Tips on scripting other desktop applications

Scripting Office Applications

Office applications provide nice foundations upon which to create scripts. This includes both scripting within an application, such as using Visual Basic for Applications (VBA) inside Microsoft Office, and gluing applications together, such as creating documents for the OpenOffice.org suite.

Scripting the OpenOffice.org Suite

The OpenOffice.org suite includes a word processor, spreadsheet, presentation program, database front end, and a whole lot more. Designed as a drop-in replacement for Microsoft Office, the applications in the OpenOffice.org suite can load and save most Microsoft Office files. In fact, the majority of this book was written using the OpenOffice.org suite.

Note that the name OpenOffice is owned by a company not associated with the free office suite—hence the awkward name OpenOffice.org, often shortened to OOo. You can download the suite from www.openoffice.org. The suite runs on Unix, Linux, Windows, and Mac OS X. For Mac OS X, you can run OpenOffice.org from the X11 environment or download NeoOffice/J from www.neooffice.org for a Macintosh-native version of the OpenOffice.org suite. The suite comes with most Linux distributions.

The suite supports OpenOffice.org Basic, a built-in programming language similar to BASIC or Microsoft's Visual Basic for Applications (VBA). With OpenOffice.org Basic, you can create simple macros or complex programs that run within the OpenOffice.org environment. This is very useful for operations you need to perform repeatedly. OpenOffice.org even includes an integrated development environment (IDE), for creating, testing, and debugging OpenOffice.org Basic add-ons.

OpenOffice.org also supports a programming API, which enables access from Java, C++, Perl, Python, and other programming languages. You can program far more than you'd ever imagine possible using the OpenOffice.org API. Furthermore, all native file formats are textual XML files, which makes it a lot easier to modify these files from your scripts or programs.

Scripting OpenOffice with the Shell

OpenOffice.org can be run from a single command, `ooffice`. By using command-line arguments and options, you can tell the program to print files, run macros, or start in a particular mode. The most useful command-line arguments and options appear in the following table.

Command	Usage
-invisible	Starts in invisible background mode.
-writer	Starts the word processor with an empty document.
-p *filename*	Prints the file *filename*.
macro:///library.module.method	Runs the macro *method* in the given *module* in the given *library*.
'macro:///library.module.method ("Param1","Param2")'	Runs the macro *method* in the given *module* in the given *library*, passing the given parameters (two in this case). You likely need to quote the whole command-line argument.
-calc	Starts the spreadsheet with an empty document.
-draw	Starts the drawing program with an empty document.
-math	Starts the math program with an empty document.
-global	Starts with an empty global document.
-web	Starts with an empty HTML document.
-impress	Starts the presentation program with an empty document.

You can use these command-line arguments in your scripts to launch `ooffice`. For example, the background `-invisible` option is especially useful when `ooffice` is called by a script.

With the macro argument, you can tell `ooffice` to run a given macro, written in OpenOffice.org Basic.

Scripting OpenOffice.org in Basic

BASIC is one of the older programming languages. It was designed long ago for newcomers to programming. Since that time, BASIC has matured into a sophisticated programming environment. Microsoft's Visual Basic for Applications (VBA), provides a way to write BASIC programs that run within the Microsoft Office environment. OpenOffice.org Basic similarly provides a way to write BASIC programs that run within the OpenOffice.org environment. As such, you can write BASIC programs, or program snippets called *macros*, to manipulate documents, update spreadsheets, and so on. Furthermore, you can combine OpenOffice.org Basic with the OpenOffice.org database module to provide a simplified interface for writing programs that access databases.

All of this is rather neat, but best of all is the fact that you can call these OpenOffice.org Basic programs from shell scripts. The scripts can launch the OpenOffice.org suite and run your BASIC programs, all from convenient shell scripts. Note that this exercise isn't trivial. To do this, you need to combine the OpenOffice.org suite, programs written in OpenOffice.org Basic, and shell scripts that run from the shell's command line. This is really an attempt to marry two disparate environments.

OpenOffice.org Basic organizes macros into modules and modules into libraries. Libraries are stored inside objects, such as the OpenOffice.org suite itself, or within a document file.

What's in a Name?

A *module* is a program written in OpenOffice.org Basic. A module contains multiple subroutines and functions.

These subroutines and functions are collectively called *methods*, especially when you invoke a method from shell scripts. The same subroutines and functions are called *macros* as well. You edit macros inside the OpenOffice.org suite.

A *library* is a collection of modules or programs.

All these terms can be quite confusing. The OpenOffice.org documentation doesn't always make it clear what each item represents. This is further complicated by the fact that you can program in Java, which uses the term *methods;* C++, which uses the term *functions;* Perl, which uses the term *subroutines;* Python, which supports *functions* and *methods;* and Basic, which uses *functions* and *subroutines.*

To get started, the first step is to create a library and a module inside that library, as shown in the following Try It Out. Just consider these storage locations for your Basic program code.

Creating an OpenOffice.org Basic Module

Launch an OpenOffice.org application, such as the Writer word processor. Select Tools ⇨ Macros ⇨ Macro, and you'll see the Macro window, much like the window shown in Figure 14-1.

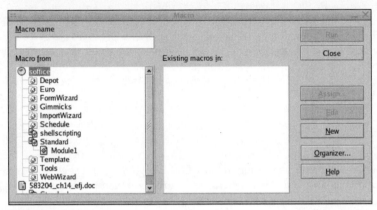

Figure 14-1

Note that the look of each version of the OpenOffice.org suite varies. Therefore, you may see a slightly different window displayed. Luckily, OpenOffice.org comes with a very good set of on-line help.

Click the Organizer button. This displays the Module and Library Organizer window, as shown in Figure 14-2.

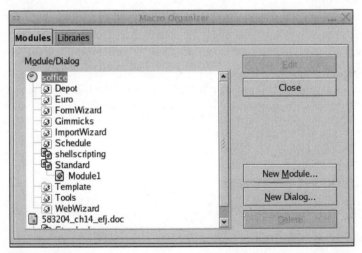

Figure 14-2

Click the Libraries tab, shown in Figure 14-3.

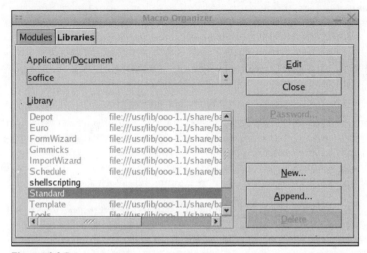

Figure 14-3

You need to start with a library. The Application/Document drop-down list shows *soffice*. This drop-down list may be hard to find because it is small and appears in a way that does not stand out. Leave the setting at *soffice*. Click the New button to create a new library. Name the library shellscripting, as shown in Figure 14-4.

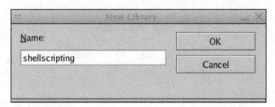

Figure 14-4

Next, you need to create a module within the library. Click the Modules tab in the Macro Organizer window and then click the New Module button. Enter a name of scriptingmodule in the dialog box, as shown in Figure 14-5.

Figure 14-5

You now have a container to hold your new macros.

How It Works

You need to create a library and a module as a place to hang your OpenOffice.org Basic macros. You can use names of your choice. The names shown in this example are used in later examples in this chapter.

Starting with a library, you can place the library inside an application or a document. If you place the library inside the application, you can call on the library from anywhere in the OpenOffice.org suite. If you place the library within only a document, you can only access the macros when editing that document.

Sun Microsystems sells a commercialized version of the OpenOffice.org suite as StarOffice. With StarOffice, the name for the executable program is `soffice`. Thus, you'll sometimes see `ooffice` or `soffice` used interchangeably in the OpenOffice.org on-line help and libraries. For example, to create a library that is accessible anywhere within OpenOffice.org, you create the library with the Application/Document setting as `soffice`, not `ooffice`, even though you are running OpenOffice.org.

Once you have a module set up, you can start to create macros, another word for Basic subroutines and functions, as shown in the next example.

Try It Out   Creating an OpenOffice.org Basic Macro

Select Tools ⇨ Macros ⇨ Macro, and you'll see the Macro window. Click the Organizer button to see the Macro Organizer window. In this window, select the library and then the `scriptingmodule` module you created in the preceding example, as shown in Figure 14-6.

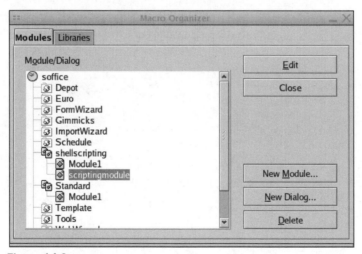

Figure 14-6

Next, click the Edit button. You'll see the OpenOffice.org Basic IDE, as shown in Figure 14-7.

Figure 14-7

Figure 14-7 shows the default empty module just created. The next step is to edit the module. Enter the following code and click the Save icon or menu option:

```
REM  *****  BASIC  *****

Sub Main
    REM Call our macros, for testing.
    call ShowUserName
End Sub


REM Shows a dialog with the user name.
```

```
Sub ShowUserName
    userName = Environ("USER")
    MsgBox "User name is " + userName, 0, "User"
End Sub
```

Figure 14-8 shows the final macro.

Figure 14-8

Click the Run icon, indicated in Figure 14-9, to run the macro.

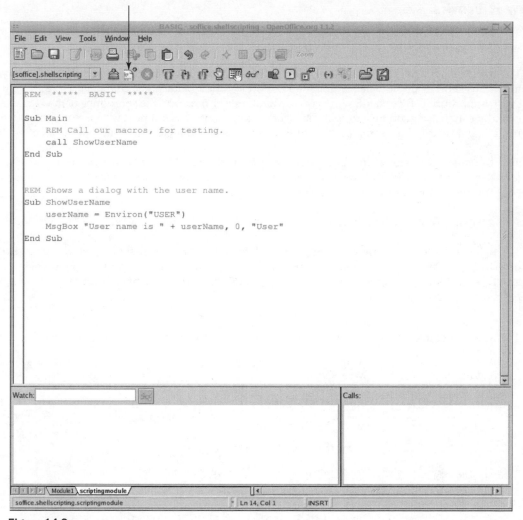

Figure 14-9

When you click the Run button, you will see a window like the one shown in Figure 14-10 (with your username, of course).

Figure 14-10

You have now written and executed a Basic macro in OpenOffice.org.

How It Works

You only need to enter the code marked in bold. OpenOffice.org created the rest for you when you defined a new module.

The BASIC language is not that hard to learn. You can probably grasp enough to get started just by looking at this short example. The REM command, short for *remark*, indicates a comment. The Sub command starts a subroutine. By default, when you run a module or program, the subroutine named Main is what is actually run. It is a good idea to split your work into separate subroutines and not clutter the Main subroutine, but to test, this example shows the call command calling the new subroutine ShowUserName.

The ShowUserName subroutine gets the name of the user from the *USER* environment variable. (Sound familiar?) In OpenOffice.org Basic, call the Environ function to get the value of this environment variable and return that value into the *userName* variable.

A *function* in BASIC is a subroutine that returns a value. By default, subroutines return no value.

The MsgBox command displays a dialog box with the given text. The first parameter, "User name is " + userName, holds the text that should appear within the dialog window. The second parameter, 0, is a special code that indicates what kind of dialog box to create. The third parameter, "User", holds the text for the dialog box's title bar.

The following table lists the numeric codes for the dialog box types supported by the MsgBox command.

Code	Meaning
0	Show the OK button
1	Show the OK and Cancel buttons
2	Show the Cancel and Retry buttons
3	Show the Yes, No, and Cancel buttons
4	Show the Yes and No buttons
5	Show the Retry and Cancel buttons, reversed from above
16	Place the Stop icon in the dialog box
32	Place the Question icon in the dialog box
48	Place the Exclamation icon in the dialog box
64	Place the Information icon in the dialog box
128	Make the first button the default button (if the user presses the Enter key)
256	Make the second button the default button
512	Make the third button the default button

These codes control the buttons and icons shown in the dialog box. You can combine codes to see more than one option. You can find these values, and more, in the on-line help. Look for the document titled *Help About OpenOffice.org Basic.*

Note that the current version of the OpenOffice.org Basic IDE does not support using the Ctrl-S key combination to save your work. This is very, very frustrating. You need to click the Save icon on the toolbar, or select the Save option from the File menu, to save your work. Save often.

Instead of editing in the OpenOffice.org Basic IDE, you can also record your interactions with the OpenOffice.org suite and save the recording as a macro to be called again later.

You can also use the Shell function to run a shell script or program from within the OpenOffice.org environment. With this scenario, you might end up with a shell script calling an OpenOffice.org Basic module, which in turn calls a shell script.

Try It Out   Running an OpenOffice.org Macro from the Command Line

You can run the macro you created in the preceding example from the command line, using a command like the following:

```
$ ooffice -quickstart macro:///shellscripting.scriptingmodule.ShowUserName
```

You should see the same message box dialog window shown previously.

How It Works

This example shows you how to bring the power of OpenOffice.org Basic macros to the shell.

If the OpenOffice.org suite is not running, the ooffice command will start the application and then display the dialog window. If the OpenOffice.org suite is already running, the message box dialog window should appear.

The -quickstart command-line option tells the ooffice command to skip the display of the startup screen.

When you click the OK button, the ooffice command will quit (if OpenOffice.org was not already running when you ran the command).

The macro shown so far requires no parameters. It can get all the data it needs from within the OpenOffice.org environment. Often, however, you'll need to pass a parameter or two to the macro to give the macro the information it needs. The following example shows how to do that.

Try It Out   Passing Parameters from the Command Line to OpenOffice.org

Edit the previous macro definition to appear as follows:

```
REM  *****  BASIC  *****

Sub Main
    REM Call our macros, for testing.
    call ShowUserName
    call ShowMsgBox "Hello from OpenOffice.org", "Hello"
End Sub


REM Shows a dialog with the user name.
```

```
Sub ShowUserName
    userName = Environ("USER")
    MsgBox "User name is " + userName, 0, "User"
End Sub

REM Shows a handy message dialog.
Sub ShowMsgBox(pMessage as String, pTitle as String)
    MsgBox pMessage, 0 + 48 + 128, pTitle
End Sub
```

The new text is indicated in bold. Click the Run icon, and you will see the dialog box shown in Figure 14-11. Note that you will first see the username message dialog. Click the OK button, and you should see the following window.

Figure 14-11

Run the subroutine from the command line. Enter the following command:

```
$ ooffice -quickstart \
'macro:///shellscripting.scriptingmodule.ShowMsgBox("Hi there","Howdy")'
```

You should see the window shown in Figure 14-12. Note the different text.

Figure 14-12

How It Works

The ShowMsgBox subroutine expects two parameters: the text to display and the title for the message window. You can pass these parameters within OpenOffice.org Basic subroutines or, more important, from the command line or a shell script. This example shows how to pass parameters to the OpenOffice.org Basic subroutines from the command line. To do this, you use parentheses around the parameters, using the same *library.module.method* naming scheme used so far from the ooffice command line.

Because the first parameter has a space, you need to quote the Basic parameter value. In addition, to avoid any conflicts with the shell, it is a good idea to surround the entire macro:/// argument in quotes. The two different types of quotes, ' and ", enable you to clearly distinguish these purposes.

The ShowMsgBox subroutine also adds several numeric codes together to get a display that shows the exclamation icon (48), sets the first (and only) button to the default (128), and displays only one button, OK (0).

You can write OpenOffice.org Basic programs to create files, such as word processor documents. The following example shows how to create a TPS report reminder.

Try It Out   **Creating Files from Scripts**

Edit the previous macro definition to appear as follows:

```
REM  *****  BASIC  *****

Sub Main
    REM Call our macros, for testing.
    REM call ShowUserName
    REM call ShowMsgBox "Hello from OpenOffice.org", "Hello"
    call CreateTpsReport("tps1.doc", "This is my TPS Report")
End Sub


REM Shows a dialog with the user name.
Sub ShowUserName
    userName = Environ("USER")
    MsgBox "User name is " + userName, 0, "User"
End Sub

REM Shows a handy message dialog.
Sub ShowMsgBox(pMessage as String, pTitle as String)
    MsgBox pMessage, 0 + 48 + 128, pTitle
End Sub


REM Create a TPS report from text passed in.
Sub CreateTpsReport(fileName, fileText)
    fileNum = Freefile
    Open fileName For Output As #fileNum
    Print #fileNum, fileText
    Close #fileNum

    MsgBox "TPS Report " + fileName + " created.", 64, "Done"
End Sub
```

The new text is indicated in bold.

Next, create the following shell script (remember those?) and name the file `tps_create`:

```
#!/bin/sh

# Launches OpenOffice.org to create a TPS report reminder.
# Pass the name of the report file and the date required
# on the command line, in order. Both arguments
# are optional.
#

dir=`pwd`

if [ $# -lt 1 ]
then
```

```
        filename="$dir/tpsreport.doc"
else
        filename="$dir/$1"
fi

if [ $# -lt 2 ]
then
        date_required=today
else
        date_required=$2
fi

# Build the message as one long line.
msg=$(tr "\n" " " <<EndOfText
"Please complete all TPS reports and have them
on my desk by EOB $date_required."
EndOfText
)



# Send the message
echo "[$msg]"

macro=macro:///shellscripting.scriptingmodule.CreateTpsReport
ooffice -quickstart "${macro}(\"$filename\", $msg)"

echo "Message sent"
```

When you run this script, you should see output like the following:

```
$ ./tps_create
["Please complete all TPS reports and have them on my desk by EOB today." ]
Message sent
```

You should also see a message box like the one shown in Figure 14-13.

Figure 14-13

If no errors appear, you should see the document shown in Figure 14-14 in your current directory.

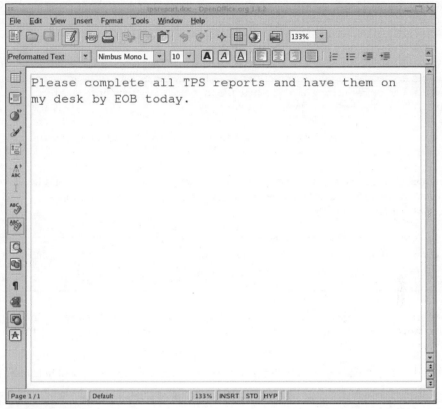

Figure 14-14

How It Works

This is a fairly complicated example because it contains so many parts.

In the OpenOffice.org Basic macro, the CreateTpsReport subroutine opens a file for writing, writes out the passed-in message, and then closes the file. The Freefile function returns a file number, much like the file descriptor introduced in Chapter 5. You need this number because the Open command requires it. (In other words, this is a quirk of OpenOffice.org Basic.)

The Open command opens a file for writing (Output), using the passed-in file name. The Print command prints text to a file number, and the Close command closes a file represented by a file number.

You can test the CreateTpsReport subroutine from within the OpenOffice.org Basic IDE by clicking the Run icon, as shown previously.

Next, the Bourne shell script tps_create invokes the OpenOffice.org Basic macro.

The tps_create script is similar to the tps_report1 and tps_report2 scripts from Chapter 5.

The `tps_create` script gets the current directory from the `pwd` command. This ensures that OpenOffice.org creates files in the current directory. Optionally, you can pass the file name to create (a document file) and the date the TPS reports are required.

The next command in the `tps_create` script creates a message. It is important that this message be only one line due to the way in which the script passes the message as a parameter to the OpenOffice.org Basic macro. The `tr` command acts on a here file to remove any new lines and replace them with spaces. In addition, the text should not contain any commas.

The `tps_create` script uses the `echo` command to output the created message. This helps diagnose problems in the script.

Next, the `tps_create` script calls the `ooffice` command. Because the command line is so long, the script uses a variable for the long name of the OpenOffice.org Basic macro, `shellscripting.scriptingmodule.CreateTpsReport`.

> **The parameters passed to the OpenOffice.org Basic macro must be in quotes. Otherwise, you can crash the OpenOffice suite.**

Together, all of this enables you to script OpenOffice.org applications. See the on-line help on OpenOffice.org Basic as well as the office applications for more information on writing macros.

In addition to OpenOffice.org, you can script other office applications, mentioned here briefly to spur ideas.

Scripting AbiWord

AbiWord provides another word processor. Unlike the OpenOffice.org suite, however, AbiWord is just a word processor, not a full suite. Nonetheless, AbiWord provides an extremely fast and small word processor, especially when compared to Microsoft Word. AbiWord starts faster than Microsoft Word or OpenOffice.org Write, but it does not support the Microsoft file formats or OpenOffice.org.

Find out more about AbiWord at www.abisource.com. AbiWord runs on many platforms, including Unix, Linux, Windows, QNX, and Mac OS X.

AbiWord, like every other major application, supports the capability to plug in add-ons to the application. Two very useful add-ons for scripting are as follows:

❑   The AbiCommand plug-in enables you to run the `abiword` command from shell scripts or the command line.

❑   The ScriptHappy plug-in works inside the AbiWord application. With the ScriptHappy plug-in, you can run a shell script or command from within AbiWord. The word processor will capture the output of the script or command and insert that text into the current document.

To do this, your script *must* be set up as an executable script. It must have execute permissions, as well as the magic first-line comment, such as the following:

```
#!/bin/sh
```

This first-line commend indicates that this script is a Bourne shell script. See Chapter 4 for more information on the magic first-line comment.

Scripting NEdit

The NEdit text editor, which ships with most Linux distributions and can run on most Unix platforms, provides a server mode that you can access from scripts. To use this mode, launch the `nedit` command with the `-server` command-line argument, as shown in the following example:

```
$ nedit -server &
```

Once you do this, the `nedit` command will listen for requests—in most cases, requests to open text files for editing. The `nc` command then sends messages to the `nedit` command. Without any special options, pass the file name to the `nc` command to call up the file in the text editor.

> **Due to an unfortunate coincidence, another command named `nc` may very well be on your system. Short for netcat, or network concatenate, this `nc` command does not work with the `nedit` command. Check which command you have. On Linux systems, for example, `nedit` and its `nc` command should be located in /usr/X11R6/bin/ by default, whereas the netcat `nc` command will be in /usr/bin.**

You can also download the application from www.nedit.org. NEdit requires the X Window System to run.

Another text editor called jEdit also supports a server mode. See Chapter 2 for more information on text editors.

Scripting for the Desktop on Mac OS X

Let's assume that you're one of those hard-working people who needs to be reminded when it's time to go home. (You are a computer geek, right?) You could probably find a dozen tools that will act as an alarm clock for you in Mac OS X, or Linux, or anything else, but where's the fun in that? The following Try It Out combines the shell with AppleScript and iTunes in Mac OS X to accomplish this, because that's what being a geek is all about!

Try It Out   Building Your Own Alarm Clock

In this Try It Out, you begin by setting up an AppleScript to control iTunes. Next, you set up a shell script to be run by `cron` to talk to that AppleScript, and finally, you set up cron to run that shell script.

1. Set up the AppleScript to control iTunes. (You'll learn more about AppleScript shortly; for now, just follow along.) From /Applications/AppleScript/, open Script Editor. You are presented with a blank script window. Type the following code into that window:

```
ignoring application responses
    tell application "iTunes"
        activate
        play
    end tell
end ignoring
```

Click the Compile icon, and the code will be nicely formatted for you. This script is a relatively simple one. The first and last lines are an `ignoring` block. You don't want this script to run until iTunes isn't playing anymore. Instead, you want it to start, start iTunes, send it a command or two, and then get out of the way, and `ignoring applications responses` is how you do that in AppleScript. The second and fifth lines are a `tell` block. With AppleScript, each application has unique terms that apply only to that application. It wouldn't make much sense to tell Word to import CD audio or to tell iTunes to print the fourth paragraph of a document. To avoid that, you use `tell` blocks, which target the lines inside the block at the specific application — namely, iTunes. The third line tells iTunes to start (if it isn't running) and become the frontmost application. (Even if your sound is turned off, you're going to see iTunes coming up). The fourth line tells iTunes to just play anything.

2. You now have a script that will start iTunes and play it, but you still have to link that into `cron`. Due to security and operational issues, you can't directly run an AppleScript from `cron`. You can, however, run a shell script, and shell scripts can talk to AppleScripts in several ways. The simplest way to do this is to save the script as an application in your home directory. You can save it directly or create a folder called cronscripts (or whatever you like), and save the script as an application in there. For the options, make sure the Run Only, Startup Screen, and Stay Open boxes are unchecked. Give it a name like `itunesalarm`, press Save, and that part's done.

    To hook this to `cron`, you need to create a shell script that `cron` can run by taking advantage of a shell command created for NextSTEP (the OS that Apple bought when it bought NeXT, which contributed most of Mac OS X's architecture), the `open` command. This command will enable you to run the AppleScript application you just created as though you were double-clicking on it. (Yes, you could just open iTunes, but it wouldn't play, so that would only be half of it.) This script is really simple, only two lines:

```
#! /bin/sh
open /Users/jwelch/cronscripts/itunesalarm.app
```

Change the path to match that of your script application.

    That's it. Two lines. The first one sets up the shell you're going to use, and the next one opens the script application. Save the script as `itunesalarm.sh` or whatever you like (I suggest saving it in the same folder as the script app), and change the permissions so that it's executable (`chmod 755`).

3. You now have a shell script and an AppleScript application that you need to tie into cron. You don't want to add it to the root `crontab` file in /etc, as it would run as root (bad idea), and it would try to run even if you weren't logged in. Because iTunes won't run outside of a user login, that's a prescription for errors. Instead, take advantage of `cron`'s ability to run user-specific `cron` jobs. (See the `man crontab` page for more details.) First, you need to create your own `crontab` file and name it `mycrontab`. The file itself is short and simple:

As before, substitute your own paths for the ones shown here.

```
# /Users/jwelch/mycrontab
SHELL=/bin/sh
PATH=/etc:/bin:/sbin:/usr/bin:/usr/sbin
HOME=/Users/jwelch/Library/Logs
#
#minute  hour  mday  month  wday  who  command
#
# Run daily/weekly/monthly jobs.
55  16  *  *  *  sh /Users/jwelch/cronscripts/itunesalarm.sh
```

Most of the lines here should be obvious to you. The first line is a comment, so you know where this file is going to live. The next three lines set up the shell, your path, and the path to where you want any logs resulting from this to live. The last line is where all the fun happens. 55 is the minute when the script runs, and 16 is the hour (4 P.M.). Therefore, the script will run every day at 4:55 P.M. (You can get far more specific with cron, but then this would be a cron tutorial). You can't leave the other spaces blank, so use a series of asterisks (*), each preceded by a tab to ensure that cron knows that this doesn't run weekly or monthly and isn't a "standard" job. The last line is the command, telling sh to run the itunesalarm shell script. That's the crontab file for your alarm clock.

4. One step left: telling cron to use the script. To do this, use the crontab command as follows:

```
sudo crontab -u jwelch /Users/jwelch/mycrontab
```

This tells crontab to create a crontab for user jwelch, and use /Users/jwelch/mycrontab as the source. Because you have to run as root, you use the sudo command to run crontab as root. When it's done, if you look inside of /var/cron/tabs/, you see a file named jwelch. If you look at the contents of this file, you see the crontab info you created, along with some things that crontab adds, such as dire warnings not to directly edit this file. That's it. You now have quite the little alarm clock, and you didn't need to be a shell or AppleScript wizard to do it.

How It Works

This alarm clock is pretty simple in function. crontab sets up the crontab file, which is used by cron. (cron searches the /var/cron/tabs/ directory for crontab files named after valid users on that system. It looks there once per minute. When it finds a file, it reads it. If it's time to run any of the jobs, cron runs the jobs specified in the crontab.) In this case, cron runs a shell script that opens an AppleScript that opens iTunes and tells it to start playing. Therefore, with only two applications, one daemon, and one script, you can play music at 4:55 P.M. every day to remind you to go home. Is Unix cool or what?

Obviously, this specific method is only going to work on Mac OS X systems, but the principles will apply to any Unix systems; just change the application you use to make noise at 4:55 P.M. However, Mac OS X is one of the few Unix-based operating systems that enable you to combine a shell script with major commercial apps such as Photoshop, or even Microsoft Word, so from a shell scripting point of view, it's interesting. Mac OS X also has a very well defined scripting architecture, which I touch on in the next section, and that's kind of neat too.

Open Scripting Architecture

When I talk about linking the shell to "native" OS X applications, I'm referring to using the Open Scripting Architecture, or OSA, to connect different environments. OSA has been a part of the Mac OS since the System 7 days and is conceptually just a glue mechanism. It creates a set of interfaces, or APIs, to the Interapplication Communications mechanisms in Mac OS X.

When I talk about "native" Mac OS X applications, it's perhaps easier to define what I'm *not* talking about:

❑   Command-line applications such as shell scripts

❑   Applications that require the X11 environment to function

❑   Older applications that require Mac OS 9 (or earlier) or the Classic Compatibility Environment to run

Everything else is native.

> *Interapplication Communication, or IAC, is simply the way that applications or, more correctly, processes share data. Each OS has several different methods for doing this, from shared memory to copy and paste.*

If developers take advantage of OSA when they write their application, then you, the scripter, can use an OSA language, such as AppleScript, to control that application, which brings us to another major point about OSA.

It is an all-too-common myth that the only way to use OSA and OSA-enabled applications is with AppleScript. This has never been true, and with Mac OS X, it's especially not true. OSA is not a language. It's just a set of APIs that enable you to use an OSA-supported language to get work done. AppleScript is the most traditional language used, and with AppleScript Studio, you can do a lot of really nifty things with it, but it's not the only game in town. Late Night Software has a JavaScript OSA implementation that you can download for free from its web site (www.latenightsw.com), and OSA connectors for Perl, Python, and more are available.

In other words, if you don't want to use AppleScript but want the power that OSA gives you in Mac OS X, relax. You don't need to learn AppleScript if you don't want to (but it's really cool, albeit different from almost every other language).

AppleScript Basics

Even though you can use all kinds of other languages with OSA, the examples in this section use AppleScript, mostly because it has explicit support for interaction with the shell, and Apple has supplied shell applications that enable you to interact with AppleScript.

As I mentioned earlier, AppleScript syntax can be different. One reason for this is to enhance accessibility by people who aren't going to ever be hardcore programmers. The syntax had to be more inviting than traditional programming languages. This is good in that it's somewhat easier to dope out AppleScript syntax when you're first getting into it, but it's bad in that AppleScript's verbosity can result in some very bizarre statements, such as the following:

```
set theiChatStatusMessageText to the contents of text field "iChatStatusMessage" of
window "iChatStatusSet"
```

That's AppleScript referring to something that in dot notation, à la Visual Basic, would look more like this (or something similar):

```
iChatStatusSet.iChatStatusMessage.contents
```

This book is not meant to be a tutorial on AppleScript, but this section does show you some neat tricks you can do with shell and AppleScript and Mac OS X applications, and explain what the script is doing on both sides.

You do need background on one aspect of AppleScript for the examples, and that's *targeting applications*, as this is critical to using AppleScript. Unlike a lot of languages, AppleScript has dynamic syntax that is application specific. In other words, depending on the application you're trying to target, doing the exact same thing can be syntactically different.

For example, suppose you want to create a new signature for an email application and set it to "Custom Sigs ROCK." If you use Microsoft Entourage, you would use this syntax:

```
tell application "Microsoft Entourage"
  make new signature with properties {name:"Shell Scripting Book Sig",
content:"--\rCustom Sigs ROCK", include in random:false}
end tell
```

However, if you're targeting Apple's Mail application, you have to use this:

```
tell application "Mail"
  make new signature with properties {name:" Shell Scripting Book Sig ",
content:"Custom Sigs ROCK"}
end tell
```

While both operations are similar, there's a minor difference or two. For one thing, Entourage has a parameter or property in AppleScript for making this signature appear randomly. Because I didn't want this, I set it to false, as it's a boolean value. Because Mail doesn't support this, I don't use it for Mail. Entourage requires you to add the -Space, which is the standard signature precedent line for email signatures, as a part of the contents, whereas Mail doesn't. Therefore, with Entourage, the sig starts with -- \r, which inserts the <dash><dash><space><return> characters needed for the signature.

The thing to remember is that AppleScript terminology is dynamic and can change depending on what application you're talking to. However, it's not like you have to guess or go searching in obscure locations for documentation that may or may not be current. Every scriptable application carries within itself a guide to how you can script it: the AppleScript Dictionary.

AppleScript Dictionaries

The dictionary is just what it sounds like: a guide to the AppleScript terms and functions that exist for use with that application. Dictionaries can range in size from nonexistent (meaning the application is not scriptable) to hundreds of pages in size (Adobe InDesign, Microsoft Word).

Every scriptable application and OSAX (Open Scripting Architecture extension) has its own dictionary, and they all work the same, with one exception: If you are using an application's dictionary, you have to use a tell block of some kind, whereas with an OSAX you don't need the tell block — you just use the terms.

The following figures show some examples of dictionaries from three applications: Figure 14-15 shows Camino, a Mac OS X–only web browser based on the Mozilla project's Gecko rendering engine. Figure 14-16 shows Firefox, a cross-platform Web browser also based on Gecko, and Figure 14-17 shows Adobe InDesign CS. As you can see, even though Camino and Firefox are based on the same engine, Camino is more scriptable, and InDesign is more scriptable than both of the others combined. InDesign's UI suite (in AppleScript terms, a collection of similar scripting terms within a dictionary) is almost bigger than Camino's and Firefox's combined. You can do *a lot* with AppleScript in InDesign.

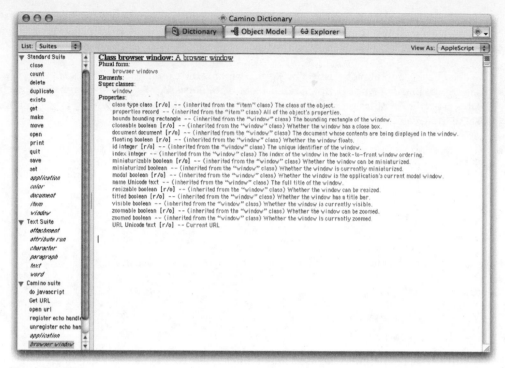

Figure 14-15

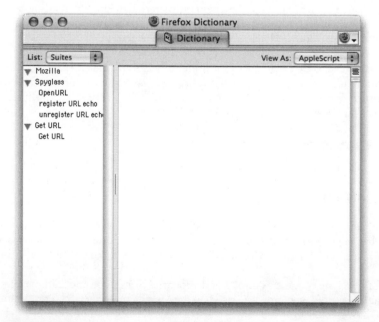

Figure 14-16

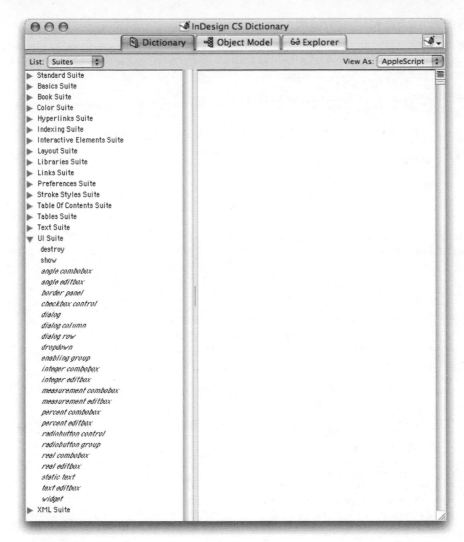

Figure 14-17

Opening a dictionary is simple. Start up Script Editor in /Applications/AppleScript/, and select Open Dictionary in the File menu. Navigate to the application for which you want to open the dictionary, and voila! Dictionary!

Now you can figure out what terms an application directly supports. However, that's not the entire syntax of AppleScript. AppleScript is a programming language with its own syntax, just like C, or Java, or COBOL. Apple has created a language guide for you: *The AppleScript Language Guide,* available as a PDF from Apple at http://developer.apple.com/documentation/AppleScript/Conceptual/AppleScriptLangGuide/AppleScript LanguageGuide.pdf, is the best general guide available, and it's free. If you want to develop a good understanding of the building blocks of AppleScript, it's the best place to start.

AppleScript's Shell Support

How do you actually link AppleScript and shell script together? As you saw in the earlier example, you can use a shell script to start an AppleScript application. What if you can't prebuild the script ahead of time, or you need to talk to the shell environment from AppleScript? Worry not, Apple has taken care of that.

Going from Shell to AppleScript

You can use three shell commands to connect a shell script to AppleScript:

- osalang
- osacompile
- osascript

osalang is the command that enables you to see what OSA languages are installed on a given Mac. If I run osalang with the -L switch on the Mac on which I'm writing this chapter, which gives me all the available languages and their capabilities, I get the following:

```
[Aurora:~] jwelch% osalang -L
Jscr LNS  cgxe-v-h  JavaScript (JavaScript Scripting System)
asDB asDB cgxe-v-h  AppleScript Debugger (Script Debugger's AppleScript debugger)
ascr appl cgxervdh  AppleScript (AppleScript.)
scpt appl cgxervdh  Generic Scripting System (Transparently supports all installed
OSA scripting systems.)
```

The output shows that I have a few different potential languages with different capabilities. The capabilities of the languages translate as follows:

```
c     compiling scripts.
g     getting source data.
x     coercing script values.
e     manipulating the event create and send functions.
r     recording scripts.
v     ``convenience'' APIs to execute scripts in one step.
d     manipulating dialects.
h     using scripts to handle Apple Events.
```

In other words, by using osalang and grep, you can test for a given language or set of capabilities. For example, to look for JavaScript and get its feature set, you use the following:

```
osalang -L|grep "JavaScript"
```

The preceding command would return the following:

```
Jscr LNS  cgxe-v-h  JavaScript (JavaScript Scripting System)
```

Therefore, if you need a specific OSA language, osalang is a handy way to test for that.

osacompile is the second part of the command line AppleScript trio, and a very powerful one. This command enables you to create a compiled script, or script application, from shell input or a text file. You can also specify the OSA language you wish to use; in fact, you can even use different languages depending on the capabilities of the system you're running. For example, you could test for Perl and

JavaScript while using AppleScript as a fallback by taking the output of `osalang` and using that to test for the languages you want. `osacompile` has a nice set of switches that give you a lot of power (see the `man osacompile` page for full details), but the following list shows the major switches:

❑ `-l` enables you to specify the language in which you want the script compiled. For example, if you want the script compiled as JavaScript, use `osacompile -l JavaScript`.

❑ `-e` enables you to enter the script commands as part of the statement. This can be tricky because AppleScript uses a lot of characters that need to be escaped or properly quoted to make it past the shell correctly. You can use multiple lines here by using the forward slash (\) character in the script command. For example, a single line script to display a dialog box would look like `osacompile -e 'display dialog "boo"'`. Note how the full command is enclosed in single quotes and the text part of the command is in double quotes inside the single quotes. A multi-line command would look like `osacompile -e 'display dialog "boo"\< return>display dialog "who"'` and would create a compiled script with two separate commands: `display dialog "boo"` and `display dialog "who"`. Obviously, this is not going to be the way you want to create a large script; the quoting and escaping alone will make you quite insane (not as insane as my former co-worker who composed personal letters in raw PostScript code, but close). To specify an input text file, simply place the path to the file after all the switches in the `osacompile` command, and it will use that as an input file. As long as the input file is valid code for the language you're using, `osacompile` will use it the same way that Script Editor will.

❑ `-o` enables you to specify the name of the script file to be created. If you don't use a name, then the output file is `a.scpt`, and it's placed in whatever directory you happen to be in. If the name of the output file ends in `.app`, then a double-clickable application, or *droplet* (a special AppleScript that runs when files or folders are dropped on it), is created.

You do not make a full GUI application just because you use an .app file. For that, you really need AppleScript Studio, which is a part of Apple's Developer tools, or FaceSpan from DTI. A whole host of tasks is involved in that process, which osacompile isn't doing alone, although it's involved heavily in the process.

❑ `-x` enables you to create a run-only script or application. Normally, scripts and applications include the source code, but if you don't want people doing silly or evil things to your script, you can use the `-x` option to strip the source code out of the compiled script or application. This is also handy for commercial applications for which you don't want people using your source code sans permission.

❑ `-u` enables you to have a startup screen if you're creating an application. This is not a splash screen à la Photoshop, but rather a little screen of text that pops up every time the application runs. They're usually annoying, so most folks don't bother with them.

❑ `-s` creates a stay-open application. Normally, AppleScripts and AppleScript applications run and then stop at the end of the script. Creating a stay-open application enables the script to remain running constantly. AppleScripters use this for several reasons, and as you get more familiar with AppleScript, you'll find reasons to use it too.

If it seems as though I'm avoiding AppleScript Studio, you're right. I am. Not because it's not a great way to create fully featured Mac OS X applications, because it is. Rather, AppleScript Studio is an umbrella name for a huge development environment that can take up entire books, and even a casual discussion of it would take up half of this book and be way off topic. If you're interested in AppleScript Studio, the best place to start is at the AppleScript site's Studio section, at www.apple.com/applescript/ studio.

The final part of the AppleScript shell command triumvirate is `osascript`, which is the complement to `osacompile`. `osascript` executes a given script file or input command but doesn't create a script. It has similar flags to `osacompile`; in fact, the `-l` and `-e` flags are identical. The `-s` flag is for setting options that specify how the script output and errors should be handled. Normally, the output of a script is in human-readable format, so the command `osacompile -e 'set foo to {"listitem1","listitem2"}'` followed by `osascript a.scpt` returns `listitem1, listitem2`. However, if you use the s option for the `-s` flag, `osascript -s s a.scpt`, on the same script, you get the results in the "real" form, which could be compiled into another script: `{"listitem1", "listitem2"}`. Normally, `osascript` passes errors to stderr, not the screen. If you want to see runtime errors (not compile errors; those always go to the screen), use `-s o` with `osascript`.

There are some limitations with `osascript` and `osacompile`. First, you can't play outside your sandbox. If you want to play with things that are above your authentication level, it's not going to work unless you use `sudo` or `su` to run the command. Second, you can't use `osascript` to run scripts that require user interaction. Therefore, while you can use `osacompile` to create scripts that require user interaction, you can't use `osascript` to run them. Considering that user interaction in AppleScripts happens outside of the command-line environment, this makes sense. However, you could use the `open` command, as in the alarm-clock example shown earlier, to run an AppleScript application that requires user interaction. Finally, you can't get too interactive with these commands. The only result you can directly get from an AppleScript is the last one. For anything else, you'll need to have the script write results to a text file.

Going from AppleScript to Shell

While going from shell to AppleScript is really cool, it's only half the story. You can run shell scripts directly from AppleScript via the `do shell script` command. `do shell script` is a fairly self-explanatory command, with a limited set of parameters. From the Standard Additions dictionary:

```
do shell script string  -- the command or shell script to execute.  Examples are
'ls' or '/bin/ps -auxwww'
[as type class] -- the desired type of result; default is Unicode text (UTF-8)
[administrator privileges boolean] -- execute the command as the administrator
[password string] -- use this administrator password to avoid a password dialog
[altering line endings boolean] -- change all line endings to Mac-style and trim a
  trailing one (default true)
[Result: string]  -- the command output
```

There's not a lot to do here, parameterwise. You can specify how you want the result. You can run the shell script as root, but if you do, you have to provide a password. You can enter the password in more than one way: as part of a displayed dialog box (somewhat secure), embedded in the script (not secure at all, not even if it's run-only), or by fetching the password from the user's secure password storage, aka the Keychain or the Keychain Scripting application. (I'll leave the Keychain scripting up to you as an extra-credit trick, but it's really cool, and the only way to get the password is to have an event tap or read it directly from RAM. If someone has cracked your machine to that level, you have greater problems than a shell script.) Altering line endings enables you to have the script output results as a Mac-style string, not a Unix-style string. Change that setting to `false` for Unix line endings.

This feature is a huge hit among the AppleScript community, because it enables them to leverage the strengths of other languages without having to resort to bizarre workarounds. Therefore, if you need high-level text manipulation, instead of trying to do it in AppleScript (a tedious proposition), you can use `do shell script`, and connect to a Perl or shell routine that will manipulate text far faster and more efficiently. It's also handy for doing things when you don't feel like waiting for others. For example, until quite recently, Virex, an antivirus utility for the Mac, couldn't automatically scan items. You had to manually invoke the scan engine in the UI or use the shell command, `vscanx`, manually or via `cron`. Of course, that's not the same as autoscanning a file as soon as it's downloaded. Therefore, I used `do shell script` to create a routine for scanning files with `vscanx`.

First, I set a property that contained the command I needed with all the arguments that I wanted to use:

```
property theScan : "/usr/local/vscanx/vscanx --allole --dam --delete --one-file-
system --recursive --secure --summary "
```

This command scans every kind of file (`--secure`, `--allole`) inside of any folder it's presented with (`--recursive`), cleans all macros from a potentially infected file (`--dam`), deletes any infected file (`--delete`), resides on a single file system (`--one-file-system`), and prints a summary to the screen of what it found (`--summary`). (Note that because Unix can make remote file systems look like a part of the local file system, and because the AFS distributed file system can make entire global networks look like part of the local file system, the `--one-file-system` option is *important*.) This way, I could use `theScan` instead of the full command line and parameters.

Next, I created another property that would use `grep` to scan the results of the viral scan for an infected file result:

```
property theGrep : "|grep \"Possibly Infected\""
```

That was only part of it, however. AppleScript in OS X uses something it calls *folder actions,* commands that run as part of something that happens to a folder, such as adding a file to a folder — that is, downloading a file to the Desktop. Using that and some `do shell script` wizardry, I built an autoscan system for Virex that did not need to interact with OS X at the kernel level (as do most of these systems). It was fast, and I had it working a year before McAfee was able to get a stable version of Virex that had autoscan out the door. The full code, with explanations, follows:

```
property theScan : "/usr/local/vscanx/vscanx --allole --dam --delete --one-file-
system --recursive --secure --summary "
```

The property statement uses a variable for the `scan` command with the full path to `vscanx`; that way, I didn't have to rely on user shell configurations.

```
property theGrep : "|grep \"Possibly Infected\"" --this will check for infected
file result
```

The preceding line checks for the infected file indicated in the summary.

```
property theResult : ""
```

`theResult` is a placeholder text variable.

```
property theMessage : ""
```

`theMessage` is a placeholder text variable.

```
on adding folder items to this_folder after receiving added_items
```

421

This line is part of the folder action handler (AppleScript lingo for *subroutine*) that deals with adding items to a folder. `this_folder` and `added_items` are standard names in this statement, and almost every example of this kind of folder action uses them. I used an example from Apple's AppleScript web site to help me out on this.

```
tell application "Finder"
        set the folder_name to the name of this_folder
end tell
```

Because the Finder is the standard file and folder manipulation application, I use its capabilities to get the name of `this_folder` and put that in `folder_name`.

```
-- find out how many new items have been placed in the folder
set the item_count to the number of items in the added_items
```

The preceding step gets the number of items that have been added to the folder and puts that number in `item_count`.

```
repeat with x in added_items
```

`repeat` loops are AppleScript's version of `for-next` and `while` loops. In this case, I am using the number of items in `added_items` as the control for the loop; and for each iteration, I assign a new item to x.

```
set theFileInfo to info for x --get info for the downloading file(s)
```

`info for` is a record (a list where each item has a label) that is an array of properties for a file, so I put that record into `theFileInfo`.

```
set theBaseSize to size of theFileInfo --get initial size
```

I want to get the current size of the file and use it as a baseline (I'll explain why in a second).

```
delay 3 --wait 3 seconds
set theFileInfo to info for x --get info again
```

This code refreshes the information in `theFileInfo`.

```
set theCompareSize to size of theFileInfo --get a newer size
```

This line gets the most current size of the file.

```
repeat while theCompareSize   theBaseSize --if they don't equal, loop until
they do
```

As of Panther, Mac OS X 10.3, it's hard to tell when a file is still downloading. While the Finder does have a `busy` flag, it's not used if you are transferring files, say, via `ftp`, `sftp`, or some other command-line option. (Well, it may or may not, but as of version 10.3, it's not reliable). Therefore, to work around that, I wrote a loop that compares the starting size with the current size every three seconds. Even on a slow link, the size should change by a byte or two in three seconds. If they aren't equal, `theBaseSize` is set to `theCompareSize`, the system waits three seconds, refreshes `theFileInfo`, gets a new `theCompareSize`, and checks again. Eventually, the two sizes will match, and as far as the script is concerned, the download is done. The next five lines handle this:

```
                set theBaseSize to theCompareSize --new base size
    delay 3 --wait three seconds
    set theFileInfo to info for x --get info
    set theCompareSize to size of theFileInfo --get a newer size
                end repeat --once the sizes match, the download is done

            set thePath to " \"" & (POSIX path of x) & "\"" --this quotes the file
    path so that odd characters are handled correctly
```

In Mac OS X, path delimiters aren't a / (slash) character but a : (colon). The shell environment only uses slashes, so to get around this, use the POSIX path command to get the shell-compatible path of the file from the Mac OS X path. Because it needs to have quotes in it, I insert those by escaping them with the \" character:

```
            set theCommand to theScan & thePath & theGrep as string --build the
    entire command, but only caring if infected files are found
```

Now build the command. Take the theCommand variable, set its contents to the theScan variable concatenated with the thePath variable I just created, and then concatenate *them* with the theGrep variable. And make sure the entire thing is a string, as that's what's needed in the next step:

```
            set theResult to do shell script theCommand --run the command
```

Run vscanx against the current item in added_items, and set that to text:

```
    set theTextResult to theResult as text --text version of the result
```

Even though this is normally a string, I like to be sure, so I use the as text coercion:

```
    set oldDelims to AppleScript's text item delimiters --temp store Applescript
    current delimiters
```

Because the result is going to contain a lot of words and spaces (and I only care about one thing), I'm going to parse it. Normally, Apple uses the null character as a text delimiter. I want to use a space, so I first store the current delimiter in a variable for safekeeping. oldDelims is traditionally used for this.

```
    set AppleScript's text item delimiters to " " --use spaces as the current delimiter
```

The preceding line sets the text item delimiters to a space.

```
    set theNewResult to (every text item of theTextResult) --this turns the text into a
    list, with the number at the end
```

Now turn the result from a single text line to a list of words. When vscanx returns a summary, the number of items found is always the last word/item in the line. Therefore, I turn this into a list, and the last item in the list is going to indicate how many infected items were found and deleted.

```
    set theTest to the last item of theNewResult as number --since the last item is the
    number of possibly infected files, let's treat it as one
```

Remember that in a string, a number character is just that: a character. It's not a number, but we need it to be one, as numerical tests are really easy and reliable compared to text tests. Set theTest to the last item of the newly created list from the summary to force, or *coerce,* that value to be a number.

```
if theTest   0 then --only display a dialog if possible infections are found
```

As long as it's not zero, it's a positive integer. (If it returns a negative, then vscanx is way buggy, and we can't possibly work around that here anyway. In any event, I've never seen that happen or heard of it happening.)

```
set theTest to theTest as text --display dialog only likes text
```

A nonzero return indicates a possible bad virus, and because the file's already been deleted, I should probably tell the user. To do that, I need a display dialog step, and that requires text, so I coerce theTest back to a text variable.

```
display dialog theTest & " possibly infected files were found in
" & thePath & ", and deleted!" --give the user the number of infected files and
location
```

The preceding code tells the user how many infected files were deleted and where they were. I put this in the repeat loop, so if users wanted to kill the scan on the spot, they could by hitting the Cancel button in the dialog box. It creates an error that kills the script. It's a bit abrupt, but it works well here, and it definitely stops the script from running, which is what I want.

```
end if
```

This is the close of the if statement, aka fi in shell. AppleScript closes things with an end *whatever*. More verbose, but in many cases clearer, and much nicer if you're a tad dyslexic.

```
set AppleScript's text item delimiters to oldDelims
```

Because I can't always count on the script's ending cleanly, I restore the delimiters to the state they were in before each iteration. I haven't seen that this creates a noticeable slowdown.

```
--display dialog theResult --add some grep routines to parse for actual infections
```

The preceding line is a reminder of stuff I should do one day.

```
end repeat
```

This line closes the repeat loop.

```
end adding folder items to
```

Finally, the preceding line ends the folder action.

This is a great, albeit not glamorous, use for do shell script, and it shows how it can be a force multiplier for AppleScript. I could use the GUI Virex application here, but if it's not running, the user has to deal with it popping up, eating CPU even in the background, taking up space in the Dock, and so on, even if there's no virus to be found. This way, everything is scanned (regardless of the folder to which you attach this action), and the only time the user is bothered is when a virus is found. Because this happens within three seconds of the file's completing a download, it's unlikely that the user will be able to open the file before the scan happens. True, you have to manually assign this script to every folder on which you want it to run, but it enabled me to enjoy autoscan in a safe, nonkernel patching manner a year before McAfee could offer it. Viruses don't pose the same worry on the Mac as they do on Windows, so this is a more than acceptable level of virus protection for the platform.

Like using osacompile and the others, do shell script has some limitations. First, it's a one-shot deal. You can't use it to create user or even script interactions between shell and AppleScript. The command runs, and you get a return. It's no more interactive than that. You can have the shell script write results to a text file and use AppleScript to read those, but that's it. Second, unless you use an ignoring application responses block, as in the iTunes alarm-clock example, AppleScript will pause script or application execution until the script ends. If you use ignoring application responses with do shell script, you can't get the result of the do shell script step with any reliability. Finally, do shell script uses sh for its environment, and you can't change it unless you include the specific shell in the do shell script statement or in the script you're running. For full details on do shell script, read Apple Technical Note TN 2065, available at http://developer.apple.com/technotes/tn2002/tn2065.html. It is the authoritative answer to almost every do shell script question you'll ever have.

There, in a nutshell, are the basics of AppleScript and shell interaction. You can do a lot more with these two very powerful languages, but I leave that for your own inventive/demented needs.

Mac OS X Terminal Window Settings

Although you can use xterm windows in Mac OS X, most folks use the Terminal application as their shell interface. It's there by default, and you don't have to fire up another windowing environment to get to it. Terminal has the standard features that you find in any terminal window application, plus some pretty spiffy uncommon ones.

Terminal has two areas for settings, Preferences and Window Settings, both accessed from Terminal's application menu, as shown in Figure 14-18.

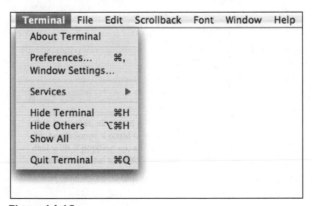

Figure 14-18

The Preferences for Terminal are fairly basic. You can set the initial shell and the initial terminal type, and you can specify a .term file to run when Terminal starts, as shown in Figure 14-19.

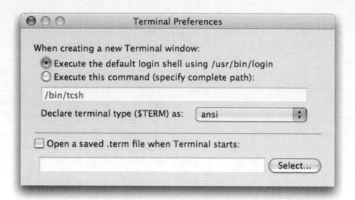

Figure 14-19

However, it's in the Window Settings that you find the juicy Terminal goodness. You'll notice quite a few settings here. One thing to note right away is that by default, these settings only apply to the active Terminal window. If you want them to apply to all future windows, click the Use Settings as Defaults button at the bottom of the window.

The first setting is the Shell setting, shown in Figure 14-20. This is where you set the window behavior when the shell exits. The options are self-explanatory. Just remember that the shell runs inside the window, so it is the window behavior when you quit the shell that you set here.

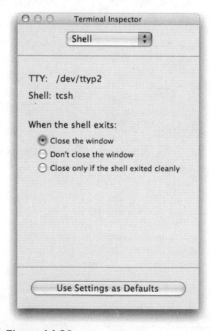

Figure 14-20

Next are the Processes settings. These settings, shown in Figure 14-21, have two major functions: to show you the current process in the frontmost Terminal window and to set the window (not shell or application) closing behavior. The main feature here is that you can insert processes that you should be reminded are running before the window closes, as opposed to always being prompted or never being prompted. This can be handy if you have a script that takes a long time to run and you don't want to accidentally close the window on it while it's running, but you don't want to be *always* prompted.

Figure 14-21

The Emulation settings, shown in Figure 14-22, contain the basic terminal emulation options, including non-ASCII character handling, newline pasting behavior, bell behavior, and cursor positioning.

Scrollback settings specifying the size of the scrollback buffer are handled via the Buffer settings. Also included here are settings for line-wrap behavior and scroll behavior on input, as shown in Figure 14-23.

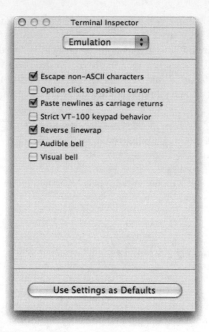

Figure 14-22

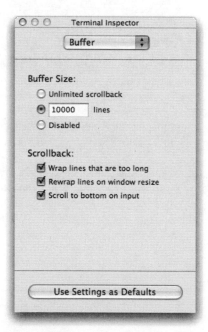

Figure 14-23

Shown in Figure 14-24 are the Display settings. This could just as easily be called Type because this is where you set your type and cursor settings. Because Mac OS X is fully Unicode capable (indeed, all text strings are actually stored as Unicode and translated on the fly to your default encoding), you can specify how to handle Japanese/Chinese and other "larger" character sets. You can also set blinking text options, how dragging text into and around the window is handled, and what font you want to use.

It is worth mentioning here that Terminal in Mac OS X enables you to get the full path to a folder or file by dragging the folder or file into the Terminal window. This can be handy when you are looking inside frameworks, where the path is long and repetitive, or when a lot of special/nonstandard characters are contained in the path name.

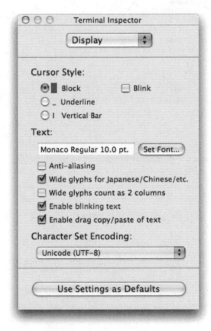

Figure 14-24

Next up are the Color settings, where you can set text colors, background colors, or even a background image in your window. The last setting, Transparency, however, is the coolest thing about Terminal. It enables you to set individual or default transparency for Terminal windows. This is where Mac OS X's imaging model and alpha channels support really shine. It's hard to describe, but Figure 14-25 shows a transparent Terminal window overlaying an opaque Terminal window and a Microsoft Word file, illustrating why this is a definite "ooooooooh" feature.

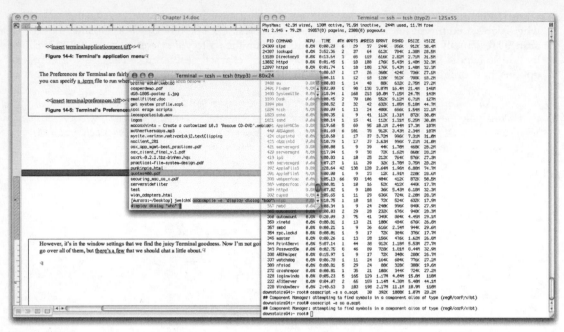

Figure 14-25

The Color settings dialog box is shown in Figure 14-26.

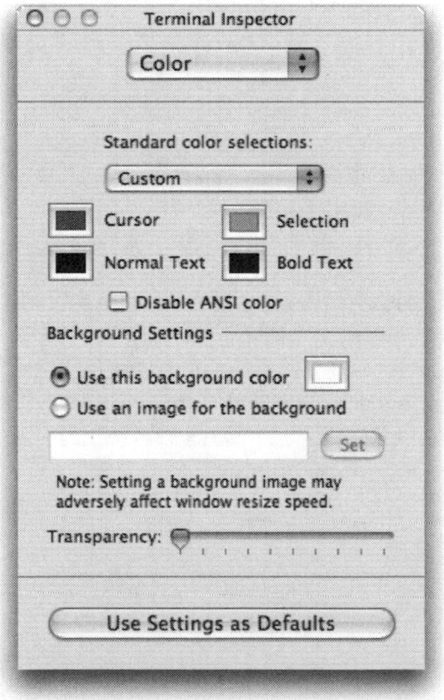

Figure 14-26

The penultimate Terminal dialog box, Window, is shown in Figure 14-27. This is where you set the default width of the window, the primary title for the window that shows in the title bar, and any other bits of information you want in the title bar, such as active process name, shell command name, TTY name, dimensions, .term filename, and the command key combo you need to enter to bring this window to the front.

Figure 14-27

The final Terminal settings dialog box, Keyboard, is shown in Figure 14-28. This can be one of the most critical settings if you are dealing with custom Terminal environments, such as tn3270 or tn5250, where you need to be able to customize the actual codes sent by the forward delete key, the function keys, and so on. You can also set your Mac keyboard's option key to the Terminal meta key (critically important for EMACS users) and just map the forward key to backspace.

That covers all of the UI settings for Terminal. (There is at least one more hidden setting, but you can figure that out on your own for another extra-credit project. It's not that hard; Google should find it quite fast.) Mac OS X gives you a wide range of settings for the Terminal application itself, in addition to the nearly infinite number of ways you can customize your shell environment. Between that and the excellent shell-to-desktop-application connections provided by Apple, you can do a lot with shell at virtually every layer of Mac OS X.

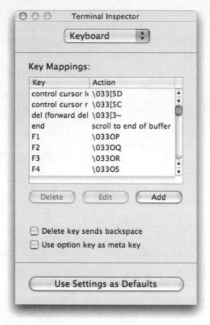

Figure 14-28

Scripting Multimedia

Two of the main Linux and Unix audio players include the X Multi-Media System (XMMS) and Rhythmbox. XMMS looks a lot like the Windows application Winamp. Rhythmbox looks a lot like the Macintosh application iTunes. Both applications can be controlled from the command line, which means, of course, that both applications can be controlled from scripts.

In addition, the Totem movie player can be controlled from the command line.

The following sections provide an overview of the command-line options available to control these applications.

Scripting the XMMS Music Player

The XMMS application, xmms, creates one or more windows to play music, visualize the music, and manage playlists, or lists of songs. Figure 14-29 shows xmms in action.

Once started, you can run the xmms command from the shell or a script to control the already-running xmms by passing command-line options that manipulate the current playlist. For example, to jump ahead to the next song on the playlist, use the following command:

```
$ xmms --fwd
```

Notice the two dashes in front of fwd. When you run this command, xmms jumps to the next song in the playlist.

Figure 14-29

The following table shows the most useful xmms commands for scripting.

Command	Usage
xmms --rew	Jump to the previous song in the playlist
xmms --fwd	Jump to the next song in the playlist
xmms --pause	Pause the music
xmms --play	Play the music, resuming from pause mode

Scripting Rhythmbox

The Rhythmbox player presents a larger user interface by default, as shown in Figure 14-30.

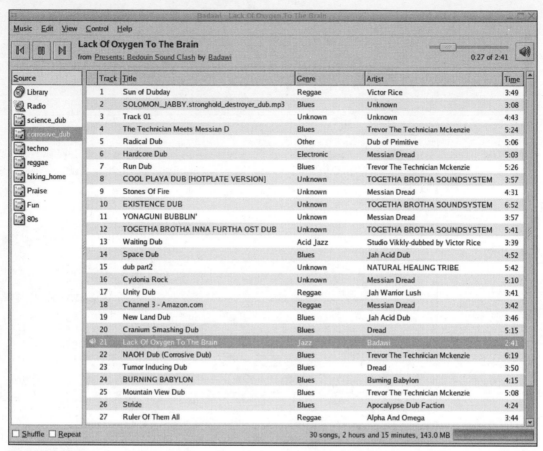

Figure 14-30

You can script the Rhythmbox music player in a similar fashion to XMMS. Launch the `rhythmbox` command normally and then run a second `rhythmbox` command with a special command-line option. For example, to jump to the next song in the playlist, use the following command:

```
$ rhythmbox --next
```

When you run this command, the display should change to show the next song.

The following table shows the most useful `rhythmbox` commands for scripting.

Command	Usage
rhythmbox --previous	Jump to the previous song in the playlist
rhythmbox --next	Jump to the next song in the playlist
rhythmbox --volume-up	Raise the volume
rhythmbox --volume-down	Lower the volume

Command	Usage
rhythmbox --play-pause	Toggle the play or pause mode — if playing music, then pause; otherwise, play music
rhythmbox --toggle-mute	Toggle the mute mode — if muting, then resume normal volume; otherwise, mute

One odd aspect to Rhythmbox is the use of toggles. The --play-pause option switches the state of Rhythmbox, but it is highly dependent on the initial state. The --toggle-mute options works similarly. If you do not know the initial state, then toggling the state will leave the application in an unknown state as well.

Scripting the Totem Movie Player

The totem command-line arguments are very similar to those for the Rhythmbox music player. The main command-line options appear in the following table.

Command	Usage
totem --previous	Jump to the previous movie or chapter
totem --next	Jump to the next movie or chapter
totem --volume-up	Raise the volume
totem --volume-down	Lower the volume
totem --play-pause	Toggle the play or pause mode — if playing, then pause; otherwise, play video
totem --seek-fwd	Tells Totem to seek forward 15 seconds
totem --seek-bwd	Tells Totem to seek backward 15 seconds
totem --quit	Tells Totem to quit

Scripting Other Desktop Applications

In addition to the desktop applications listed here, you can do a lot more with scripts. Any time you type in a complex command, think of scripting the command instead. Furthermore, any application, be it a server program or desktop suite, can be scripted, so long as you can launch the application from a command line. If you can do this, you can launch the application from a shell script.

Some applications, however, work better for scripting than others. For example, the Totem movie player works better with scripts than other movie-playing applications, such as Xine or mplayer. That's simply because the Totem application supports more useful command-line parameters.

Some tips when scripting desktop applications include the following:

❑ Look for applications that support several command-line options and arguments. These applications typically work better for scripting than other applications.

❏ Look for a listing of the command-line options and arguments. On Unix and Linux systems, you can view the on-line manuals with the man command. Some applications, notably the OpenOffice.org suite, seem to go to great lengths *not* to describe the command-line options and arguments.

❏ If a desktop application has a *server* or *background* mode, chances are good that the application was meant to be controlled by other applications. Such applications work well in scripts. The terms *server* and *background* are used in a lot of desktop application documentation.

❏ As always, test the commands you want to script from the command line. Work out all the needed parameters. Then add these commands to your scripts.

Where to Go from Here

By now, you should feel comfortable writing scripts, as well as choosing what will script well and what will be more difficult. Even though this book is titled *Beginning Shell Scripting,* it has covered a lot of tough topics. After getting this far, you should be able to start scripting on your own.

Furthermore, you should be able to perform web searches to find additional information. The Internet is by far the best source for specific information on ever-changing environments and commands. For example, you can find an early paper by Steven Bourne, creator of the Bourne shell, at laku19.adsl.netsonic.fi/ era/unix/shell.html, or the Advanced Bash-Scripting Guide at www.tldp.org/LDP/abs/html/.

Summary

Most users think of scripting and server-related systems as if these two were joined at the hip, but you can also do a lot with desktop applications and shell scripts:

❏ Office applications such as the OpenOffice.org suite and the AbiWord word processor offer several ways to script their applications. The OpenOffice.org suite is especially interesting. You should be able to write scripts that run on multiple platforms that can update documents and fill out forms.

❏ Despite a long history of hostility to the command line, modern Mac OS X systems are surprisingly ready for scripting. You can automate large portions of the desktop with AppleScript as well as traditional shell scripts.

❏ Multimedia applications are also open to scripting, especially the XMMS, Rhythmbox, and Totem media-playing programs.

This chapter should spur a number of ideas as to what you can use scripts for in your environment.

Exercises

1. What is the name of the OpenOffice suite? What is the command that launches the suite?

2. In OpenOffice.org Basic, what are methods, macros, modules, and libraries? What is the difference between subroutines and functions?

3. Can you pass parameters from a shell script to an OpenOffice.org Basic subroutine? If so, how?

4. What is the name of the architecture Apple created to enable scripting of applications in Mac OS X?

5. What is the AppleScript command used to run shell scripts from within an AppleScript?

6. What is the shell command used to compile AppleScript code from the shell environment?

Answers to Exercises

Chapter 2

1. It is good to learn vi and emacs, if only because those editors are available nearly everywhere. Which you choose depends on your preferences. Don't worry if you dislike the choices made by your colleagues. The key is to find an editor that works for you.

   Some criteria that may help choose an editor:

   - ❑ Does it work on the platforms you need to use? For example, at a university, does the editor work in the computer labs as well as on the computers you have available where you live?

   - ❑ Is the performance good enough? Some editors, especially high-end Java Integrated Development Environments, or IDEs, can run painfully slow on systems without at least 1 GB of RAM.

   - ❑ Do you like the "feel" of the editor? This is very subjective but quite important. You may never quite get into the feel of emacs, for example.

2. Vi can be a real pain in the rear end. It can also be very, very productive. Some of the best features of vi include:

   - ❑ Its speed. Vi starts fast and runs fast.

   - ❑ The dot command (.), which repeats the previous operation. This can be very powerful.

   - ❑ The ability to execute a command a number of times, such as 4yy (yank four lines) or 100dd (delete 100 lines).

   - ❑ All the enhancements in vim. Vim really creates a new, and much better, editor.

   Emacs can be a real pain in the rear end. It can also be very, very productive. Some of the best features of emacs include:

   - ❑ The multiple buffers. You can really make use of separate buffers when performing complex edits.

❑   The integrated shell. You can execute shell commands from within the context of the editor.

❑   The directory browser. You can look through directories, selecting files to edit.

❑   The ability to edit the same file in multiple places.

❑   The ability to program the editor. Anything your computer can do can be done within emacs.

3.   This is just one example of the extreme ugliness you can create with shell scripts:

```
# See if you can come up with more statements than this.
# This is ugly. In case we forget, this script outputs:
# A man, a plan, a canal, Panama

a=A
echo -n "$a"
unset a
a=" "
echo -n "$a"
unset a
a="m"
echo -n "$a"
unset a
a="a"
echo -n "$a"
unset a
a="n"
echo -n "$a"
unset a
a=","
echo -n "$a"
unset a
a=" "
echo -n "$a"
unset a
a="a"
echo -n "$a"
unset a
a=" "
echo -n "$a"
unset a
a="p"
echo -n "$a"
unset a
a="l"
echo -n "$a"
unset a
a="a"
echo -n "$a"
unset a
a="n"
echo -n "$a"
unset a
a=","
```

```
echo -n "$a"
unset a
a=" "
echo -n "$a"
unset a
a="a"
echo -n "$a"
unset a
a=" "
echo -n "$a"
unset a
a="c"
echo -n "$a"
unset a
a="a"
echo -n "$a"
unset a
a="n"
echo -n "$a"
unset a
a="a"
echo -n "$a"
unset a
a="l"
echo -n "$a"
unset a
a=","
echo -n "$a"
unset a
a=" "
echo -n "$a"
unset a
a="P"
echo -n "$a"
unset a
a="a"
echo -n "$a"
unset a
a="n"
echo -n "$a"
unset a
a="a"
echo -n "$a"
unset a
a="m"
echo -n "$a"
unset a
a="a"
echo -n "$a"
unset a
a="."
echo -n "$a"
unset a

echo
```

4. The following scripts show how you can create commands, store those commands within a variable, and then access the variable to execute the command:

```
# Starting script.
DIRECTORY=/usr/local
LS=ls
CMD="$LS $DIRECTORY"
$CMD      # Note how the command is executed indirectly.


# Add a -1 (one) command-line option.
DIRECTORY=/usr/local
LS=ls
LS_OPTS="-1"
CMD="$LS $LS_OPTS $DIRECTORY"
$CMD


# Even more indirect script.
DIRECTORY=/usr/local
LS=ls
LS_OPTS="-1"
LS_CMD="$LS $LS_OPTS"
CMD="$LS_CMD $DIRECTORY"
$CMD
```

5. This is about the smallest change to make the script apply to Canadian users:

```
echo -n "Please enter your first name: "
read FIRSTNAME
echo -n "Please enter your last name: "
read LASTNAME
echo -n "Please enter the name of the province where you live: "
read PROVINCE

FULLNAME="$FIRSTNAME $LASTNAME"
MESSAGE="Well, $FULLNAME of $PROVINCE, welcome to our huge"
MESSAGE="$MESSAGE impersonal company."

echo "$MESSAGE"
echo "You will now be known as Worker Unit 10236."
```

6. You don't need to be a guru. You don't have to show off. Just pick an editor that works for you.

7. There is a reason modern keyboards have Page Up, Page Down, Home, End, arrows, and other keys: these keys have proved useful.

Chapter 3

1. Do it. Really. You may want to discuss why many applications allow you to click on long choices like this or provide some other means to quickly make selections. Any script that interacts with the user has a user interface, and it behooves you to make an interface that at least isn't difficult to understand.

2. This example extends the `myls` script. You can use the same technique for the `myls2` script:

```
# This example extends the myls script.

# Change to the directory
# so the file listing is all relative file names.
cd /usr/local

# List the files.
for filename in *
do
     echo $filename
done
```

Note how this script uses the `cd` command to change to the target directory. This means that the `for` loop will list all relative file names, such as bin, and not absolute file names, such as /usr/local/bin.

You can also take an approach such as the following:

```
for filename in /usr/local/*
do
     echo $filename
done
```

This example will output absolute file names, however.

3. These scripts extend the ones from the previous question.

```
# This example extends the myls script.

DIRECTORY=/usr/local

# Change to this directory
# so the file listing is all relative file names.

cd $DIRECTORY

# List the files.
echo "Listing $DIRECTORY"

for filename in *
do
     echo $filename
done
```

The second approach that outputs absolute file names looks like the following:

```
DIRECTORY=/usr/local

for filename in $DIRECTORY/*
do
     echo $filename
done
```

4. This problem is solved by adding a `read` command to read in the directory name, rather than setting the name to a fixed directory:

```
# This example extends the myls script.

echo -n "Please enter the directory to list: "
read DIRECTORY

# Change to this directory
# so the file listing is all relative file names.

cd $DIRECTORY

# List the files.
echo "Listing $DIRECTORY"

for filename in *
do
    echo $filename
done
```

5. Try the `ls -CF1` (C, F, one) command to get an idea how this output should look. To do this, use the file-specific test options of the `test` command:

```
# This example extends the myls script.

echo -n "Please enter the directory to list: "
read DIRECTORY

# Change to this directory
# so the file listing is all relative file names.

cd $DIRECTORY

# List the files.
echo "Listing $DIRECTORY"

for filename in *
do
    if [ -d $filename ]
    then
        echo "$filename/"
    elif [ -x $filename ]
    then
        echo "$filename*"
    else
        echo $filename
    fi
done
```

Chapter 4

1.

```
#unset SHELL

if [ "$SHELL" == "" ]
then
    echo "SHELL not set."
    echo "Bailing out."
    exit -1
fi
```

Uncomment the unset SHELL line to run the script with the *SHELL* environment variable not set, and verify the script works with both cases.

2.

```
for arg in $*
do
    if [ "$arg" != "" ]
    then
        echo "Arg: $arg"
    fi
done

echo "Total args: $#"
```

This exercise combines the for loop and if statement from Chapter 3 with the command-line arguments introduced in this chapter.

3. This may seem like a total cheat:

```
echo "All arguments [$*]"
```

The crucial point here is that while the C shell uses a different variable to hold the number of command-line arguments, the variable $* works in all of the listed shells and, conveniently enough, holds all the command-line arguments.

4. This exercise requires one loop to iterate over the command-line arguments, each of which names a directory, and a second, nested loop to iterate over the files within each directory:

```
# Assumes each command-line argument
# names a directory to list.

for directory in $*
do
    echo "$directory:"
    cd $directory
    for filename in *
    do
        echo $filename
    done
    echo
done
```

Chapter 5

1.

```
# Locks down file permissions.

for filename in *
do

    # Lock down the file permissions.
    chmod g-rwx,o-rwx $filename

done
```

2.   Add the following text to the first line of the script:

```
#! /bin/sh
Then, mark the script with execute permissions.
$ chmod a+x lockdown
The full script then appears as follows:
#!/bin/sh

# Locks down file permissions.

for filename in *
do
    # Initialize all permissions.
    r=""
    w=""
    x=""

    # Check to preserve existing permissions.

    if [ -r $filename ]
    then
        r="r"
    fi

    if [ -w $filename ]
    then
        w="w"
    fi

    if [ -x $filename ]
    then
        x="x"
    fi

    # Lock down the file permissions.
    chmod u+$r$w$x,g-rwx,o-rwx $filename

done
```

3.   There are a number of ways to do this, but one of the simplest is to reverse the tests from less-than comparisons to greater-than or equal checks. For example:

```
# If the user forgets to pass the command-line
# arguments, fill in defaults.

pithy_statement="Action, urgency, excellence"

if [ $# -ge 1 ]
then
    date_required=$1

    if [ $# -ge 2 ]
    then
        pithy_statement=$2
    fi
else
    date_required=today
fi


wall <<EndOfText
Please complete all TPS reports and have them
on my desk by EOB $date_required.

Your cooperation in this matter helps the smooth
flow of our departmental structure.

$pithy_statement!
-Dick
EndOfText

echo "Message sent"
```

4.   Again, there are a number of ways to approach this. Here is the most straightforward:

```
# If the user forgets to pass the command-line
# arguments, fill in defaults.

case $# in
0)
    pithy_statement="Action, urgency, excellence"
    date_required=today
    ;;
1)
    pithy_statement="Action, urgency, excellence"
    date_required=$1
    ;;
*)
    pithy_statement=$2
    date_required=$1
    ;;
esac


wall <<EndOfText
Please complete all TPS reports and have them
on my desk by EOB $date_required.
```

```
Your cooperation in this matter helps the smooth
flow of our departmental structure.

$pithy_statement!
-Dick
EndOfText

echo "Message sent"
```

5. Here is one such script:

```
# First script, outputs a second, that in turn, outputs a third.

cat <<'End1'

    # This is a comment in a script.
    cat <<'End2'
        echo "This is the next output script."
        echo "It doesn't do anything."
End2

End1
```

Note that the end markers must start at the beginning of a line.

When you run this script, it outputs the following:

```
# This is a comment in a script.
    cat <<'End2'
        echo "This is the next output script."
        echo "It doesn't do anything."
End2
```

Save this text to a file, and run this script. When run, it outputs the following:

```
        echo "This is the next output script."
        echo "It doesn't do anything."
```

Save this text to a file, and run this script. When run, it outputs the following:

```
This is the next output script.
It doesn't do anything.
```

Chapter 6

1.

```
cat /etc/passwd | sed '5!d'
```

2.

```
cat /etc/passwd | sed -n '10~5d'
```

3.

```
cat /etc/passwd | sed '10~d' or cat /etc/passwd | sed '10~0d'
```

4.

```
ls -l $HOME | sed 's/micah/hacim/'
```

5.

```
ls -l $HOME | sed '1,10s/micah/hacim'
```

6.

```
#! /bin/sed -f

1 i\
<html>\
<head><title>Converted with sed</title></head>\
<body bgcolor="#ffffff">\
<pre>\

s/&/\&amp;/g
s/</\&lt;/g
s/>/\&gt;/g

$ a\
</pre>\
</body>\
</html>
```

7.

```
#! /bin/sed -f

1 i\
<html>\
<head><title>Converted with sed</title></head>\
<body bgcolor="#ffffff">\
<pre>\

s/&/\&amp;/g
s/</\&lt;/g
s/>/\&gt;/g
s/trout/<b>trout<\/b>/g
s/^$/<p>/g

$ a\
</pre>\
</body>\
</html>
```

8. You can do this in many different ways, but one of the easiest solutions is to put the dash out-side of the backreference:

```
cat nums.txt | sed 's/\(.*\)\)\(.*\)-\(.*$\)/Area code: \1 Second: \2 Third: \3/'
```

9.

```
#!/bin/sed -f

1!G
h
$!d
```

Chapter 7

1.

```
$ cat /etc/passwd | awk -F: '{print $6}'
```

2.

```
awk '{ print "Number of cell phones in use in " $1 ": " $6 }' countries.txt
```

3.   Note that many different answers are possible. Here's one possibility:

```
BEGIN { myformat="%-15s %3s %16s %11s %12s %15s\n"
        printf myformat,
                "Country", "TLD", "Area in sq. km", \
                "Population", "Land lines", "Cell phones"
        printf myformat,
                "-------", "---", "--------------", \
                "----------", "----------", "-----------" }
      { printf myformat, $1, $2, $3, $4, $5, $6 }
```

4.   Note that many different answers are possible. Here's one possibility:

```
{celltotal += $6; landtotal += $5 }
END { print "Cell phones make up " landtotal/celltotal "% of landlines" }
```

5.   There are many different ways to do this. Here's one method:

```
BEGIN { myformat="%-15s %3s %16s %11s %12s %12s\n"
        printf myformat,
                "Country", "TLD", "Area in sq. km", \
                "Population", "Land lines", "Cell phones"
        printf myformat,
                "-------", "---", "--------------", \
                "----------", "----------", "-----------" }
      { printf myformat,
                $1, $2, $3, $4, $5, $6
        areatot += $3
        poptot += $4
        landtot += $5
        celltot += $6 }

END { printf myformat,
                "\nTotals:", NR, areatot, poptot, landtot, celltot "\n"  }
```

Chapter 8

1. The key points come from the focus on shell scripts. These include:

- ❑ Sending data to stdout
- ❑ Sending data to stderr
- ❑ The exit code, or value a command can return (used in `if` statements)

In addition, of course, you can add:

- ❑ Writing to network sockets.
- ❑ Writing UDP datagrams.
- ❑ Creating a device driver to output directly to a device.
- ❑ Outputting graphics. Note that with the X Window System on Unix and Linux, this is a networking operation.
- ❑ Printing.

Going more esoteric, you can add:

- ❑ System V Unix shared memory
- ❑ System V Unix message queues
- ❑ FIFOs and named pipes
- ❑ The Windows Event system

Can you name any more?

2. You can do this simply by using the following command:

```
$ tail -f filename.txt >>  filename.txt
```

Make sure there are a few lines in the file `filename.txt` at the start. Press Ctrl-C to kill the command line.

3.

```
cut -d: -f1,5,6,7 /etc/passwd |
    grep -v sbin |
    grep home   |
    grep sh     |
    sort        |
    cut -d: -f1,2,4 > users.txt


awk -F':' ' { printf( "%-12s %-40s\n", $1, $2 )   } ' users.txt

# Clean up the temporary file.
/bin/rm -rf users.txt
```

In this example, the `grep home` filter passes only those lines that have the text `home`. This is another assumption, that users have home directories in /home or something similar.

Chapter 9

1. Note: This will work on Linux only.

The following script shows the current process ID and then waits for you to press the Enter or Return key:

```
echo "The current process ID is $$."
echo "Press return to continue."
read var
When you run this script, you should see output like the following:
$ sh exercise_09_01
The current process ID is 12048.
Press return to continue.
```

While the script awaits the Enter or Return key, you can switch to another shell window and view /proc/12048 (the number will differ on your system).

2. This script outputs the same data as the `tick_for` example script:

```
echo "Using a wildcard glob in a for loop."
cd /usr/local
for filename in *
do
    echo $filename
done
```

A big difference is that this script changes the directory to the /usr/local directory. The original script did not. You can get around this by saving the current directory and then using the `cd` command to return to that directory.

3. Here is a script that comes out close:

```
# Using expr for math.
# Calculates sales tax.

echo -n "Please enter the amount of purchase: "
read amount
echo

echo -n "Please enter the total sales tax: "
read rate
echo

tax_base=`expr $amount \* $rate`


tax=`expr $tax_base / 100`

total=`expr $amount + $tax`

result=$total

echo "The total with sales tax is: \$ $result."
When you run this script, you'll see:
$ sh exercise_09_03
Please enter the amount of purchase: 107
```

```
Please enter the total sales tax: 7

The total with sales tax is: $ 114.
Compare this with the math2 script:
$ sh math2
Please enter the amount of purchase: 107

Please enter the total sales tax: 7

The total with sales tax is: $ 114.49.
```

Chapter 10

1. The more you experiment, the more familiar you will become with the way functions work.

2. While it is possible to create a function called ls, it isn't recommended, because this is an existing command and you would create an infinite loop when you ran it. The function ls would look something like this:

```
$ ls () {
ls -F --color=auto
}
```

You would call this function by typing ls on the command line. This would then execute the code block that contains ls, the shell would call the ls function, this would execute the code block in the function, and this would be repeated over and over very quickly and could cause your system to no longer respond properly.

3. At first glance, shell functions appear to be very similar to shell aliases. However, on closer inspection you can see many differences. The most basic difference is that aliases are defined using the alias built-in command. Another difference is that you can redefine a command with an alias and you will not have an infinite-loop problem, as you did in Exercise 2. Some other differences are that aliases are simply name substitutions for existing single commands; they also do not contain multiple commands like functions can; and they do not contain logic or positional arguments. This means you cannot manipulate the $@ argument list. In shell scripts, because aliases are very limited, they are not typically used.

Aliases were first introduced in csh and then later adopted by ksh, bash, and zsh. Most implementations of the Bourne shell do not support aliases.

4. Here's one possible answer:

```
#!/bin/sh
#
# This script takes at minimum one argument: the time that the alarm should go off
# using the format hh:mm, it does only rudimentary checks that the format is
# specified is correct. An optional second argument specifies what should be done
# when the alarm goes off. If no second argument is supplied, a simple shell bell
# is used.
#
# Be sure this bell works before you go to sleep!
#
# If the second argument is included and the alarm method is more than one command,
# it will need to be enclosed in quotes.
```

```
# First check that the required minimum arguments have been supplied, and that
# the time is of the format hh:mm. If not exit with the proper usage.

if [ $# -eq 0 ]
then
        echo "Usage: $0 hh:mm [alarm-method]"
        echo "eg. $0 13:30 \"mplayer /media/music/dr_octagon/01.mp3\" "
        exit 1
else
        alarm_time="$1"

        # Check that the format for the alarm time is correct, the first digit
        # should be a number between 0-2, followed by a colon, and ending with a
        # number between zero and 60. NB: This check is not perfect.

        if [ ! `echo "$alarm_time" | sed -n '/[0-2][[:digit:]]:[0-60]/p'` ]
        then
                echo "Incorrect time specified, please use format hh:mm"
                exit 1
        fi

fi

# Set the number of seconds in a minute
seconds=1

# Test to see if a second argument is supplied, if it is not then set the
# bell to a shell bell. The -e argument to echo specifies that echo should
# enable interpretation of the backslash character, and \a is defined in
# the echo(1) man page as a bell.

if [ ! $2 ]
then
        bell="echo -e \a"
else

        bell=$2
fi

# The wait_between_checks function sleeps for the specified number of
# seconds and then calls the check_time function when it is done sleeping.
# This makes the script only check the time once a minute, instead of constantly.

wait_between_checks ()
{
        sleep $seconds
        check_time
}

# The check_time function looks at the current time (in hh:mm format) and
# compares it to the $alarm_time, if they match, then it calls the wakeup function
# otherwise it goes back to sleep by calling the wait_between_checks function
again.
```

```
check_time ()
{
        current_time=`date +%H:%M`

        if [ "$current_time" = "$alarm_time" ]
        then
                wakeup
        else
                wait_between_checks
        fi

}

# The wakeup function simply rings the bell over and over until the script
# is interrupted.

wakeup ()
{
        echo -n "Wake up! Hit control-c to stop the madness"
        $bell
        sleep 1
        wakeup
}

# Finally the main body of the script simply starts things up by calling the
# wait_between_checks function

wait_between_checks
```

5.

```
#!/bin/sh

recurarrg () {
  if [ $# -gt 0 ] ; then
    echo $1
    shift
    recurarrg "$@"
  fi
}

recurarrg one two three four
```

Chapter 11

1.   This script runs, which makes it appear to be correct. It is not. It appears to be a script that acts similarly to the 1s command. It should change to the given directory (passed as the first positional variable on the command line, $1) and then list the files in that directory. If a file is executable, it should append a *. If the file is a directory, it should append a /. This output is similar to the 1s -CF command.

This script, however, has a few things wrong, including the following:

❑ The first `if` statement should be negated with a `!`. That is, if the passed-in directory does not exist, then use /usr/local. The way it reads, if the directory exists, it will execute the `then-fi` block. This script really should output an error message if the directory does not exist, not silently list another directory.

❑ The `then-fi` block sets the variable `directroy`, not `directory`.

❑ The `cd` command changes to the directory held in the variable `directroy`.

❑ The `elif` condition is negated. Remove the exclamation mark.

The following script is an improvement. The error message could be better:

```
# Assumes $1, first command-line argument,
# names directory to list.

directory=$1

if [ ! -e $directory ]
then
    echo "Error: You must pass in the name of a directory."
    exit -1
fi

cd $directory
for filename in *
do
    echo -n $filename

    if [ -d $filename ]
    then
        echo "/"
    elif [ -x $filename ]
    then
        echo "*"
    else
        echo
    fi
done
```

2. This script is a front-end for a very primitive electronic shopping system. It calculates the sales tax and then checks whether the amount is larger than $200. If so, it offers free shipping.

This script is missing two double quotes, starting with the first `echo` statement. The free shipping `echo` statement is also missing a double quote. The missing quotes should flag an error with the (yes or no) text, as this text appears to be calling a subshell.

A corrected script follows:

```
#!/bin/sh

# Using bc for math,
# calculates sales tax.

echo -n "Please enter the amount of purchase: "
read amount
echo
```

```
echo -n "Please enter the total sales tax rate: "
read rate
echo

result=$( echo "
scale=2; tax=$amount*$rate/100.00;total=$amount+tax;print total" | bc )

if [ $( expr "$result > 200" ) ]
then
    echo You could qualify for a special free shipping rate.
    echo -n Do you want to? "(yes or no) "
    read shipping_response
    if [ $shipping_response -eq "yes" ]
    then
        echo "Free shipping selected."
    fi
fi

echo "The total with sales tax = \$ $result."
echo "Thank you for shopping with the Bourne Shell."
```

Chapter 12

1. Anything that you can monitor externally would be monitored the same if called from any system or run on any system. For example, a web server can be monitored externally, with the monitoring scripts answering the question of how long it takes to retrieve a certain web page.

As another example, SNMP MIBs are standardized. (A MIB is similar to an XML schema for SNMP data.) If a Windows system or a Unix system provides data via SNMP, you can monitor both types of systems the same way, by reading SNMP values.

2. The quick answer is to follow the guidelines listed in the chapter:

❑ Try out the commands you think will provide the data points you need.

❑ Write a script to monitor the data points you need.

❑ Test your script.

❑ Configure MRTG to run your script and produce the output you want.

❑ Test MRTG running your script.

You may need to repeat a number of steps as you tweak how your script or MRTG should run.

For a database system such as Oracle or Postgres, you can look into two ways to monitor:

❑ Run a database-specific client program and see if it works or how long it takes to perform some operation.

❑ Try a remote query of a table in the database and see how long this takes. The advantage of this approach is that you don't have to run MRTG on the same system as the database.

3. Your answer will depend on the packages you select. Of all these packages, however, mon is very similar to MRTG in that mon is written in Perl and was designed to be extended by your scripts. These two details are very much like MRTG. MRTG focuses on drawing graphs, whereas mon wants to monitor the health of systems. Mon, for example, can page an administrator when a problem occurs.

HP OpenView is also similar to MRTG, with the focus on using SNMP to gather data and control systems. (OpenView, however, is a whole suite of products.)

The real goal of this exercise, however, is to see some other packages that are available and start to make choices as to which packages can help in your environment.

Chapter 13

1. Of course, it is more fun to talk about those dimwits. The important thing to remember is to stay focused on a few problems that are solvable. Use the techniques shown in this chapter to help guide the discussion.

2. Some things you can use ps to do include the following:

❏ Determine whether a given process is running at all. This comes from an example, so you should have gotten it.

❏ List all processes owned by a given user. Desktop users should have a lot of processes. Users logged in over a network link, using ssh, telnet, and so on, should have far fewer processes running.

❏ In tree mode, the ps command can report on a hierarchy of processes, such as which process begat which.

❏ List the cumulative CPU time used by each process. You can find the most CPU-intensive processes.

❏ List how many copies of a given process are running. Web servers often launch a number of processes.

❏ On Linux, ps can output information about threads (essentially subprocesses). Enterprise applications such as Oracle, WebSphere, WebLogic, and so on, use many threads.

See if you can come up with more.

3. You can approach this in a number of ways. You can simply run the df command with the name of the given file system. Or you can write a script like the following:

```
#!/bin/sh


# Output warnings if a given file system is not mounted.
# Oftentimes, this could be due to a network issue or
# a hard disk failure.

# Pass the name of the file system or the mount point
# as the first command-line argument.
filesystem=$1

df "$filesystem" > /dev/null 2&>1
result=$?

if [ "$result" == 0 ]
then
```

```
    entry=`df -k $filesystem | tail -1`

    # Split out the amount of space free as well as in-use percentage.
    free=`echo $entry | cut -d' ' -f4`
    in_use=`echo $entry | cut -d' ' -f5 | cut -d'%' -f1 `

    echo "Filesystem $filesystem is $in_use% used with $free KB free."
else
    echo "ERROR: Filesystem $filesystem not found."
fi
```

Chapter 14

1. The suite is called OpenOffice.org. The command that launches the suite is `oofice`.

2. A method is a macro, and a subroutine is a function. A module is like a program, and it holds subroutines and functions. A library holds one or more modules.

Subroutines do not return values. Functions return values. This is the main difference.

3. Try the following, using the name of your library, module, and subroutine:

```
$ oofice -quickstart 'macro:///library.module.SubroutineName("param1", "param2")'
```

4. The Open Scripting Architecture

5. `do shell script`

6. `osacompile`

Useful Commands

The commands on your system form the building blocks that you can glue together in your scripts. The following sections cover some of the more useful commands from a scripting point of view, divided into related sections. The listings here appear in a brief format. As always, however, you can find detailed information on these and other commands by perusing the online documentation.

Because of differences between Unix, Mac OS X, Linux, and the Cygwin environment on Windows, the listings here focus on the most common options for these commands. As always, use the ever-handy online manuals to look up the full documentation on each command.

Navigating the System

These commands help you interact with the operating system.

exit

```
exit exit_code
```

Description

Exits the current shell. You can pass an optional exit code, a number. An exit code of 0 (zero) indicates the script executed successfully. A nonzero value indicates an error.

Example

```
$ exit
```

Exits the current shell.

Options

None.

file

```
file options filename
```

Description

Attempts to classify the type of each file passed on the command line. Usually, the `file` command does this by reading the first few bytes of a file and looking for matches in a file of magic values, `/etc/magic`. This isn't really magic but simple comparisons. For example, the `file` command should be able to determine ASCII text files, executable programs, and other types of files.

The file command does not always classify correctly, but it usually does a good job.

Examples

```
$ file `which sh`
/bin/sh: symbolic link to `bash'
```

Prints the type of file of sh. On this system, sh is implemented by bash.

```
$ file vercompare.py
vercompare.py: a /usr/bin/python script text executable
```

Checks the type of a Python script.

Options

Option	Usage
-c	Outputs a checking printout of the magic file
-f *file*	Reads in a given file and then runs the command on each file name in that file, assuming one file name per line
-m *file:file:file*	Uses the named files as the magic files instead of /etc/magic

kill

```
kill options process_IDs
```

Description

Sends a signal to the given process or processes. In most cases, the processes die upon receipt of the signal.

You can send signals only to processes that you own, unless you are logged in as the root user.

Examples

```
$ kill -SIGKILL 4753
```

Sends the kill signal (SIGKILL) to process number 4753.

```
$ kill -9 4754
```

Sends the kill signal (9) to process number 4754.

```
$ kill -l
 1) SIGHUP       2) SIGINT       3) SIGQUIT      4) SIGILL
 5) SIGTRAP      6) SIGABRT      7) SIGBUS       8) SIGFPE
 9) SIGKILL     10) SIGUSR1     11) SIGSEGV     12) SIGUSR2
13) SIGPIPE     14) SIGALRM     15) SIGTERM     17) SIGCHLD
18) SIGCONT     19) SIGSTOP     20) SIGTSTP     21) SIGTTIN
22) SIGTTOU     23) SIGURG      24) SIGXCPU     25) SIGXFSZ
26) SIGVTALRM   27) SIGPROF     28) SIGWINCH    29) SIGIO
30) SIGPWR      31) SIGSYS      34) SIGRTMIN    35) SIGRTMIN+1
36) SIGRTMIN+2  37) SIGRTMIN+3  38) SIGRTMIN+4  39) SIGRTMIN+5
40) SIGRTMIN+6  41) SIGRTMIN+7  42) SIGRTMIN+8  43) SIGRTMIN+9
44) SIGRTMIN+10 45) SIGRTMIN+11 46) SIGRTMIN+12 47) SIGRTMIN+13
48) SIGRTMIN+14 49) SIGRTMIN+15 50) SIGRTMAX-14 51) SIGRTMAX-13
52) SIGRTMAX-12 53) SIGRTMAX-11 54) SIGRTMAX-10 55) SIGRTMAX-9
56) SIGRTMAX-8  57) SIGRTMAX-7  58) SIGRTMAX-6  59) SIGRTMAX-5
60) SIGRTMAX-4  61) SIGRTMAX-3  62) SIGRTMAX-2  63) SIGRTMAX-1
64) SIGRTMAX
```

Lists the signals and their numbers.

Options

Option	Usage
-l	Lists the available signals
-number	Sends the given signal by its number, such as 9 for SIGKILL
-signal	Sends the given named signal, such as SIGHUP

man

```
man options command
```

Description

Displays the online manual entry for the given command.

Example

```
$ man man
man(1)                                                          man(1)

NAME
       man - format and display the on-line manual pages
```

```
SYNOPSIS
       man  [-acdfFhkKtwW]  [--path] [-m system] [-p string] [-C config_file]
       [-M pathlist] [-P pager] [-S section_list] [section] name ...

DESCRIPTION
       man formats and displays the on-line manual  pages.  If  you  specify
       section,  man  only looks in that section of the manual.  name is nor-
       mally the name of the manual page, which is typically the  name  of  a
       command,  function,  or  file.   However, if name contains a slash (/)
       then man interprets it as a file specification, so that you can do man
       ./foo.5 or even man /cd/foo/bar.1.gz.

       See  below  for  a  description of where man looks for the manual page
       files.
...
```

Displays help on the man command.

Options

Options differ by platform. Try the man man command to see the options for your platform.

nohup

```
nohup command options arguments &
```

Description

Short for *no hangup,* the nohup command runs a command and keeps that command running even if you log out. Typically, when you log out, all the commands you launched are terminated if they are still running. The "no hangup" terminology comes from the days when users logged in using a modem over a phone line and would literally hang up the phone when exiting.

Example

```
$ nohup xclock &
[1] 4833
nohup: appending output to `nohup.out'
```

Runs the xclock command in the background, preserving the process even if you log out.

Options

None.

printenv

```
printenv environment_variable
```

Description

Prints out the value of a given environment variable or all environment variables if you pass no arguments to this command.

Example

```
$ printenv USER
ericfj
```

Prints the *USER* environment variable.

Options

None.

ps

```
ps options
```

Description

Prints the status of current processes, depending on the command-line options. With no options, ps lists just the current shell and the ps process. With options, you can list all the processes running on the system.

Note that Berkeley Unix-based systems, including Mac OS X, support a different set of options than System V Unix-based systems. The options to list all processes is aux for Berkeley Unix-based systems and -ef for System V Unix-based systems. Linux systems support both types of options.

Examples

```
$ ps
  PID TTY          TIME CMD
 4267 pts/2    00:00:00 bash
 4885 pts/2    00:00:00 ps
```

Lists the current process (the ps command) and its parent shell.

```
$ ps -ef
UID        PID  PPID  C STIME TTY          TIME CMD
root         1     0  0 09:57 ?        00:00:00 init [5]
root      2046     1  0 08:46 ?        00:00:00 klogd -x
rpc       2067     1  0 08:46 ?        00:00:00 portmap
rpcuser   2087     1  0 08:46 ?        00:00:00 rpc.statd
root      2290     1  0 08:46 ?        00:00:00 /usr/sbin/sshd
root      2340     1  0 08:46 ?        00:00:00 gpm -m /dev/input/mice -t imps2
root      2350     1  0 08:46 ?        00:00:00 crond
xfs       2376     1  0 08:46 ?        00:00:00 xfs -droppriv -daemon
dbus      2414     1  0 08:46 ?        00:00:00 dbus-daemon-1 --system
root      2427     1  0 08:46 ?        00:00:00 cups-config-daemon
...
```

Lists all processes in System V Unix style (-ef).

```
$ ps aux
USER       PID %CPU %MEM    VSZ   RSS TTY      STAT START   TIME COMMAND
root         1  0.0  0.0   3488   560 ?        S    09:57   0:00 init [5]
root         2  0.0  0.0      0     0 ?        SN   09:57   0:00 [ksoftirqd/0]
```

```
root        3  0.0  0.0     0    0 ?      S<    09:57   0:00 [events/0]
root        4  0.0  0.0     0    0 ?      S<    09:57   0:00 [khelper]
root        5  0.0  0.0     0    0 ?      S<    09:57   0:00 [kacpid]
root       27  0.0  0.0     0    0 ?      S<    09:57   0:00 [kblockd/0]
root       28  0.0  0.0     0    0 ?      S     09:57   0:00 [khubd]
root       37  0.0  0.0     0    0 ?      S     09:57   0:00 [pdflush]
root       38  0.0  0.0     0    0 ?      S     09:57   0:00 [pdflush]
root       40  0.0  0.0     0    0 ?      S<    09:57   0:00 [aio/0]
root       39  0.0  0.0     0    0 ?      S     09:57   0:00 [kswapd0]
root      113  0.0  0.0     0    0 ?      S     09:57   0:00 [kseriod]
root      187  0.0  0.0     0    0 ?      S     08:46   0:00 [kjournald]
root     1014  0.0  0.0  1612  448 ?      S<s   08:46   0:00 udevd
...
```

Lists all processes in Berkeley Unix style (aux).

Options

Option	Usage
-a	Lists information on all processes except group leaders and processes not associated with a terminal
-d	Lists information on all processes except group leaders
-e	Lists information on every process
-f	Lists full information on processes
a	List all processes with a terminal
u	Displays data in the user-oriented format
x	Lists processes without a terminal

sleep

```
sleep number_of_seconds
```

Description

Sleeps for a given number of seconds. You can use an m suffix to indicate minutes and an h suffix for hours.

Examples

```
$ sleep 2
```

Sleeps for two seconds.

```
$ sleep 3h
```

Sleeps for three hours.

Options

None.

type

```
type options command_name
```

Description

Determines the type of command, such as a command on disk or a shell built-in command.

Examples

```
$ type sleep
sleep is /bin/sleep
```

Returns the type of the `sleep` command.

```
$ type type
type is a shell builtin
```

Returns the type of the `type` command.

```
$ type -t type
builtin
```

Returns the type name of the `type` command.

```
$ type -p sleep
/bin/sleep
```

Returns the path to the `sleep` command.

```
$ type -t sleep
file
```

Returns the type name of the `sleep` command.

```
$ type -a true
true is a shell builtin
true is /bin/true
```

Returns information on all instances found of the `true` command.

Options

Option	Usage
-a	Searches for all places for a command and lists them all
-f	Don't look for built-in commands
-P	Forces a search over the command path
-p	Returns the name of the file for the command or nothing if the command is built in
-t	Returns a one-word type of the command, either alias, built-in, file, function, or keyword

uname

```
uname option
```

Description

Prints information on the system. Short for *Unix name*.

Examples

```
$ uname -p
powerpc
```

Lists the processor type.

```
$ uname
Darwin
```

Lists the Unix name.

```
$ uname -o
GNU/Linux
```

Lists the OS name.

```
$ uname -s
Linux
```

Lists the kernel name (OS name, really).

```
$ uname --hardware-platform
i386
```

Lists the hardware platform, similar to the processor type.

Options

Option	Usage
-a	Prints all information
-o	Prints the operating system
-p	Lists the processor type
-s	Prints the kernel name

who

```
who options files
```

Description

Shows who is logged on, as well as information about the system.

Examples

```
$ who am i
ericfj   pts/1      Jan 16 15:28 (:0.0)
```

Lists who the user is.

```
$ who -b
          system boot  Jan 16 08:46
```

Lists the last boot time.

```
$ who
ericfj   :0         Jan 16 15:28
ericfj   pts/1      Jan 16 15:28 (:0.0)
ericfj   pts/2      Jan 16 15:28 (:0.0)
ericfj   pts/3      Jan 16 15:28 (:0.0)
```

Lists all logged-in users. Note how it thinks the same user is logged in multiple times. The pts 1, 2, and 3 values come from shell windows.

```
$ who -H
NAME     LINE       TIME         COMMENT
ericfj   :0         Jan 16 15:28
ericfj   pts/1      Jan 16 15:28 (:0.0)
ericfj   pts/2      Jan 16 15:28 (:0.0)
ericfj   pts/3      Jan 16 15:28 (:0.0)
```

Adds a header line to the normal who output.

```
$ who -q
ericfj ericfj ericfj ericfj
# users=4
```

Lists in quick mode.

```
$ who -r
         run-level 5  Jan 16 08:46                       last=S
```

Lists the system run level. On Linux, run level 5 usually means the X Window System has been started for graphics.

Options

Option	Usage
am i	Returns your username
-a	Same as all the other options combined
-b	Prints time of last system boot
-d	Prints dead processes
-H	Inserts a line of column headings
-l	Prints the system login process
-p	Lists processes launched from the init command that are still running
-q	Quick mode, lists user names and a count
-r	Prints the current run level
-s	Short output, default
-t	Prints last system clock change
-T	Adds a +, -, or ? for the status of each user
-u	Prints users logged in

whoami

```
whoami
```

Description

Prints out the username of the current user.

Examples

```
$ whoami
ericfj
```

Lists who the user is.

Options

None.

Working with Files and Directories

Many scripts need to work with files. These commands are among the oldest in Unix history, as files have always been important.

basename

```
basename path suffix
```

Description

Extracts the base file name from a long path. The optional suffix allows you to extract a file-name extension, such as .txt.

Examples

```
$ basename /home/ericfj/rpms/thunderbird-1.0-1.fc3.i386.rpm
thunderbird-1.0-1.fc3.i386.rpm
$ basename /home/ericfj/rpms/thunderbird-1.0-1.fc3.i386.rpm .rpm
thunderbird-1.0-1.fc3.i386
```

Options

None.

cat

```
cat options files
```

Description

Concatenates files to standard output. You can concatenate one or more files. With just one file, cat prints the file to standard output, and you can use this to display the contents of short files. With multiple files, cat prints them all to standard output, allowing you to combine files together. You'll often use output redirection such as > or >> with cat.

Examples

```
$ cat /etc/passwd
root:x:0:0:root:/root:/bin/bash
bin:x:1:1:bin:/bin:/sbin/nologin
daemon:x:2:2:daemon:/sbin:/sbin/nologin
adm:x:3:4:adm:/var/adm:/sbin/nologin
lp:x:4:7:lp:/var/spool/lpd:/sbin/nologin
sync:x:5:0:sync:/sbin:/bin/sync
shutdown:x:6:0:shutdown:/sbin:/sbin/shutdown
halt:x:7:0:halt:/sbin:/sbin/halt
...
```

Shows the contents of the file /etc/password.

```
$ cat /etc/shells
/bin/sh
/bin/bash
/sbin/nologin
/bin/ash
/bin/bsh
/bin/ksh
/usr/bin/ksh
/usr/bin/pdksh
/bin/tcsh
/bin/csh
/bin/zsh
```

Shows the contents of the file /etc/shells.

Options

Options differ by platform. See your online documentation for details on your platform.

chmod

```
chmod option mode filenames
```

Description

Changes the mode, the permissions, on a file.

The following table lists the numeric modes for the chmod command. Note that these modes are all in octal, base 8, numbers.

Value	Meaning
400	Owner has read permission.
200	Owner has write permission.
100	Owner has execute permission.
040	Group has read permission.
020	Group has write permission.
010	Group has execute permission.
004	All other users have read permission.
002	All other users have write permission.
001	All other users have execute permission.

You then need to add these values together, as in the following table.

Value	Meaning
400	Owner has read permission.
200	Owner has write permission.
100	Owner has execute permission.
040	Group has read permission.
020	Group has write permission.
004	All other users have read permission.
764	Total

This example results in a total of 764.

In addition to the numeric modes, you can use the symbolic modes, as shown in the following table.

Value	Meaning
u	The user who is the owner.
g	Group.
o	All other users.
all	Sets permissions for all users. Can also use *a*.
+	Adds the permissions following.
-	Removes (subtracts) the permissions following.
=	Assigns just the permissions following and removes any old permissions on the files.
r	Read permission.
w	Write permission.
x	Execute permission.
l	Locks the files during access.

Examples

```
$ chmod a+x script1
```

Adds execute permissions for all users to script1.

```
$ chmod 764 script1
```

Allows the user to read, write, and execute `script1`, the members of the group to read and write, and everyone else to just read.

Options

Option	Usage
-R	Goes recursively through all subdirectories and files, changing the permissions on all

chown

```
chown option owner files
```

Description

Changes the ownership of files. You must be the owner of the file or files.

Example

```
$ chown ericfj  script1 script2 script3
```

Options

Option	Usage
-R	Goes recursively through all subdirectories and files, changing the ownership on all

cp

```
cp options sourcefiles destination
```

Description

Copies a file or files. If you copy multiple files, then the destination must be a directory. If you just copy one file, then the destination can be a file name or a directory.

Examples

```
$ cp * /usr/local/bin
```

Copies all files in the current directory to /usr/local/bin.

```
$ cp report.txt report.backup
```

Copies a file to a backup file.

Options

Option	Usage
-i	Interactive mode that prompts you before overwriting a file
-f	Forces a copy by removing the target files if needed and trying again
-p	Preserves file permissions on the copy
-r	Same as -R
-R	Goes recursively through all subdirectories and files, copying all

df

```
df options filesystems_or_directories
```

Description

Short for *disk free*, df returns the amount of space used and available on all mounted file systems. With no arguments, df lists information for all mounted file systems. You can pass the name of the file systems, either the file system or the mount point, to list information on just those file systems. You can also provide the name of a directory, and df displays information on the file system that contains that directory. This is very handy so you don't have to remember all the file system names.

For example, an all-too-frequent problem occurs when the /tmp, or temporary, directory fills up. On some systems, /tmp is mounted as its own file system (and disk partition). On other systems, /tmp is part of the root, or /, file system. You can pass /tmp as the name of a file system to the df command. Even if /tmp is not mounted as part of its own file system, the df command will display information on the file system holding /tmp.

Examples

```
$ df
Filesystem           1K-blocks     Used Available Use% Mounted on
/dev/hda2             24193540  3979392  18985176  18% /
/dev/hda1               101086    10933     84934  12% /boot
none                    501696        0    501696   0% /dev/shm
/dev/hda5             48592392 26391104  19732904  58% /home2
```

Lists all mounted file systems.

```
$ df /tmp
Filesystem           1K-blocks     Used Available Use% Mounted on
/dev/hda2             24193540  3979392  18985176  18% /
```

Lists the information for the file system containing /tmp.

Options

Option	Usage
-k	Returns the output in 1K blocks
-l	Displays information on local file systems only.

du

```
du filenames
```

Description

Lists the amount of disk space used for a given set of files or directories. Technically, du estimates the amount of disk usage. You can use du on a file or a directory. The command will traverse all subdirectories and report on the total for each directory it examines. Command-line options can modify this behavior.

Examples

```
$ du
360      ./mrtg/html
632      ./mrtg/working
1100     ./mrtg
328      ./marketing
88       ./web_files
18860    ./figures/tmp/chap14
19460    ./figures/tmp
20       ./figures/.xvpics
136      ./figures/chap1
1416     ./figures/chap2
9872     ./figures/chap14_1
8996     ./figures/chap14_2
53508    ./figures
2228     ./scripts/foo
37284    ./scripts
18688    ./chapter12
5076     ./author_review
122364   .
```

Shows the size of the current directory and all subdirectories.

```
$ du -s
122364   .
```

Runs the same command but in silent mode, showing just a total size.

Options

Option	Usage
-a	Prints a line of output for each file, rather than just one line per directory.
-s	Silent mode. Displays only the total line.

find

```
find start_at conditions actions
```

Description

The `find` command searches the files on disk from a given starting location, `start_at`, looking for files and directories that match the given conditions and then taking the given actions, such as printing out the file names.

This is a very complex command. It is often used to make backups (finding the list of files modified since the last backup), report on large files (finding the list of files larger than a certain size), or in fascist environments, remove all old files (finding all files older than a given date and then removing them).

In some cases, you'll want to combine the output of `find` with other commands. But the number of actions available to the `find` command itself means that you can often just run the command alone.

Older versions of the find command did not print out the names found, in a very stupid default. Most modern versions of find print out the names of the files or directories found. If your system uses the stupid default, add a –print option at the end of the find command to print out the results.

Examples

```
$ find . -ctime -1 -print
./scripts
./scripts/nohup.out
./583204_appb_efj.doc
```

Finds all files in the current directory and below that have been modified in the last day. The `-print` option is not necessary.

```
$ find $HOME -name 'script*'
./scripting_outline.txt
./scripts
./scripts/script1
./scripts/script3
./scripts/script2
./scripts/script_q
./scripts/script1.sh
./scripts/script_y
```

```
./scripts/script5
./scripts/script4
./scripts/script8
./scripts/script6
./scripts/script7
./scripts/script9
./scripts/script10
./scripts/script11
./scripts/script12
./scripts/script13
./scripts/script14
./scripts/script15
./scripts/script16
./scripts/script17
./scripts/script18
```

Finds all files in the user's home directory (and below) with a name that starts with `script`.

Options

See the online manual entry on `find`, as there are a huge number of options that differ by platform.

grep

```
grep options pattern files
```

Description

Searches for text based on a pattern (called a *regular expression*). The lines of text that match the pattern are printed. You need to tell `grep` what to look for and which files to examine.

Other related commands include fgrep and egrep.

Examples

```
$ grep while *
whilepipe:while read filename; do
```

Looks for all files in the current directory for the text *while*. This is found in one file.

```
$ grep -h while *
while read filename; do
```

Performs the same search but does not output the names of the files.

```
$ grep -o while *
whilepipe:while
```

Performs the same search but outputs only the pattern match.

Options

Option	Usage
-h	Does not return the names of the files.
-i	Ignores case when searching.
-l	Just lists the file names, not the matched text.
-q	Quiet mode. Used when you just want to check the program's exit status.
-s	Suppresses error messages.
-v	Looks for lines that do not contain the match.

In addition to these options, you'll find a number of platform-specific options in your online manuals.

head

```
head options files
```

Description

Displays the beginning of a text file. By default, head prints out the first ten lines in the file.

Examples

```
$ head /etc/passwd
root:x:0:0:root:/root:/bin/bash
bin:x:1:1:bin:/bin:/sbin/nologin
daemon:x:2:2:daemon:/sbin:/sbin/nologin
adm:x:3:4:adm:/var/adm:/sbin/nologin
lp:x:4:7:lp:/var/spool/lpd:/sbin/nologin
sync:x:5:0:sync:/sbin:/bin/sync
shutdown:x:6:0:shutdown:/sbin:/sbin/shutdown
halt:x:7:0:halt:/sbin:/sbin/halt
mail:x:8:12:mail:/var/spool/mail:/sbin/nologin
news:x:9:13:news:/etc/news:
```

Lists the first ten lines of /etc/passwd.

```
$ head -2 /etc/passwd
root:x:0:0:root:/root:/bin/bash
bin:x:1:1:bin:/bin:/sbin/nologin
```

Lists the first two lines of /etc/passwd.

Options

Option	Usage
-number	Displays the given number of lines

ls

```
ls options files_or_directories
```

Description

Lists file names. You can display a long listing or a short listing. This is a surprisingly complex command for such a simple purpose.

Examples

```
$ ls /usr/local
bin  etc  games  include  lib  libexec  man  sbin  share  src
```

Lists the files in /usr/local.

```
$ ls -CF /usr/local
bin/  etc/  games/  include/  lib/  libexec/  man/  sbin/  share/  src/
```

Lists the files in /usr/local with a slash after directory names, an @ for links, and a * for executable files.

```
$ ls -l /usr/local
total 80
drwxr-xr-x  2 root root 4096 Dec  9 00:00 bin
drwxr-xr-x  2 root root 4096 Aug 12 12:02 etc
drwxr-xr-x  2 root root 4096 Aug 12 12:02 games
drwxr-xr-x  2 root root 4096 Aug 12 12:02 include
drwxr-xr-x  2 root root 4096 Aug 12 12:02 lib
drwxr-xr-x  2 root root 4096 Aug 12 12:02 libexec
drwxr-xr-x  3 root root 4096 Nov 15 20:35 man
drwxr-xr-x  2 root root 4096 Aug 12 12:02 sbin
drwxr-xr-x  4 root root 4096 Nov 15 17:17 share
drwxr-xr-x  2 root root 4096 Aug 12 12:02 src
```

Presents a long listing of the files in /usr/local.

Options

Option	Usage
-1	Lists one item per line
-a	Lists all files, including hidden (dot) files
-b	Prints octal values of characters you don't see
-c	Lists by last modified time
-C	Lists in columns (the default)
-d	Lists only the name of directories, not the files in them

Option	Usage
-F	Appends an indicator to show directories (/), executable files (*), links (@), and pipes (|)
-g	Lists in long form but without the owner's name
-l	Lists information in long form
-L	Lists the names links are linked to
-m	Lists files across the screen separated by commas
-n	Lists in long form, but with user and group numbers instead of names
-o	Lists in long form but omits the group
-q	Lists nonprintable characters as a question mark, ?
-r	Lists items in reverse order
-R	Recursively goes into all subdirectories
-s	Lists file sizes in blocks, not bytes
-t	Sorts the files by the modification time
-u	Sorts by last access time
-x	Sorts entries by lines instead of by columns

In addition to these options, you'll find a number of platform-specific options in your online manuals.

mkdir

```
mkdir options directory_names
```

Description

Creates one or more directories.

Examples

```
$ mkdir tmp
```

Creates directory tmp.

```
$ mkdir -m 664 tmp
$ ls -dl tmp
drw-rw-r--  2 ericfj ericfj 4096 Jan 16 20:58 tmp
```

Creates directory tmp with the given permissions (verified by the ls command).

481

Options

Option	Usage
-m *mode*	Defines the permissions mode for the new directories

mv

```
mv options source target
```

Description

Moves a file or files. If you move multiple files, the target must be a directory. If you move one file, the target can be a file name or a directory name (naming the directory in which to move the file).

Examples

```
$ mv *.html old_web
```

Moves all HTML files to the directory named old_web.

```
$ mv index.htm index.html
```

Renames the file index.htm to index.html.

Options

Option	Usage
-f	Forces the move, ignoring the -i option
-i	Asks for confirmation if the command would overwrite a file

rm

```
rm options files
```

Description

Removes (deletes) files.

Examples

```
$ rm -rf ./tmp
```

Removes the tmp subdirectory and all files and directories in it.

```
$ rm -i index.html
rm: remove regular file `index.html'? y
```

Removes the file named index.html but requires you to confirm the deletion (a smart option).

Options

Option	Usage
-f	Forces the move, ignoring the -i option
-i	Asks for confirmation if the command would overwrite a file
-r	Recursively removes files and directories

rmdir

```
rmdir options directories
```

Description

Removes (deletes) directories. The directories must be empty to be deleted. Watch out for hidden files (files with names that start with a period), because you won't see these files, but their presence will stop rmdir from deleting a directory.

Examples

```
$ rmdir tmp
```

Removes the subdirectory tmp.

Option

Option	Usage
-p	Removes the directory and any parent directories as long as they are empty

tail

```
tail option files
```

Description

Prints out the last ten lines of a file. You can define the number of lines. The -f option tells the tail command to output forever, checking the file periodically for new lines and then printing those. This is most useful with log files for a service or when building a huge software package.

Examples

```
$ tail /etc/passwd
mailnull:x:47:47::/var/spool/mqueue:/sbin/nologin
smmsp:x:51:51::/var/spool/mqueue:/sbin/nologin
pcap:x:77:77::/var/arpwatch:/sbin/nologin
apache:x:48:48:Apache:/var/www:/sbin/nologin
squid:x:23:23::/var/spool/squid:/sbin/nologin
webalizer:x:67:67:Webalizer:/var/www/usage:/sbin/nologin
```

```
xfs:x:43:43:X Font Server:/etc/X11/fs:/sbin/nologin
ntp:x:38:38::/etc/ntp:/sbin/nologin
gdm:x:42:42::/var/gdm:/sbin/nologin
ericfj:x:500:500:Eric Foster-Johnson:/home2/ericfj:/bin/bash
```

Lists the last ten lines of `/etc/passwd`.

```
$ tail -2 /etc/passwd
gdm:x:42:42::/var/gdm:/sbin/nologin
ericfj:x:500:500:Eric Foster-Johnson:/home2/ericfj:/bin/bash
```

Lists the last two lines of `/etc/passwd`.

```
$ tail -f /var/log/dmesg
EXT3 FS on hda1, internal journal
EXT3-fs: mounted filesystem with ordered data mode.
SELinux: initialized (dev hda1, type ext3), uses xattr
SELinux: initialized (dev tmpfs, type tmpfs), uses transition SIDs
kjournald starting.  Commit interval 5 seconds
EXT3 FS on hda5, internal journal
EXT3-fs: mounted filesystem with ordered data mode.
SELinux: initialized (dev hda5, type ext3), uses xattr
Adding 4096564k swap on /dev/hda3.  Priority:-1 extents:1
SELinux: initialized (dev binfmt_misc, type binfmt_misc), uses genfs_contexts
```

Outputs the contents of the log file `dmesg` forever (until killed).

Options

Option	Usage
-number	Prints the given number of lines.
-f	Forever or follow mode. Prints the end of the file as new lines are added. Usually used with log files.
-s *seconds*	Sleeps for the given number of seconds between checks. Used only with -f.

touch

```
touch options files
```

Description

By touching a file, you modify it. (Think of what happens when children touch something.) At the most basic level, `touch` is used to update the time a file was last modified. You can also set the time to a particular value.

Typically, if a file doesn't exist, `touch` will create it, making it 0 (zero) bytes in size.

To set the time to a particular value, use one of the following formats: CCYYMMddhhmm, YYMMddhhmm, MMddhhmm, or MMddhhmmYY. The following table explains the formats.

Format	Holds
MM	Month, 1–12
dd	Day of month, 1–31
hh	Hour of the day, 00–23
mm	Minute of the hour, 00–59
CC	Century, such as 20
YY	Year in century, such as 06 for 2006

Examples

```
$ touch *.c
```

Updates the modification date for all files ending in .c to the current time.

```
$ touch -t 201012251159 mozilla_coffee_order.html
$ ls -l mozilla_coffee_order.html
-rw-rw-r--  1 ericfj ericfj 7663 Dec 25  2010 mozilla_coffee_order.html
```

Sets the modification time to Christmas in 2010 for the given file and verifies the time with the ls command.

Options

Option	Usage
-a	Changes only the last access time
-c	Does not create a new file if none exists
-m	Changes only the modification time
-t *timestamp*	Sets the time to the given timestamp

Manipulating Text

In addition to working with files and directories, there are quite a few commands that manipulate text. (Some of these distinctions are arbitrary.) These commands are used primarily to output text, while the commands in the following Transforming Data section are used primarily for modifying text.

awk

```
awk '/somedata/ { actions }' filenames
```

Description

The `awk` command runs a program, typically placed between single quotes (as shown here) or in a separate file. The `awk` command searches the files passed to it for the pattern `/somedata/` and then applies the given actions to all lines matching the pattern.

See Chapter 7 for a lot of information on `awk`. This is a very complex command.

Example

```
$ awk -F':' '/eric/ { print $5 }' /etc/passwd
Eric Foster-Johnson
```

Searches for the pattern `eric` in the file `/etc/passwd` and then prints out the fifth field from all matching lines. Sets the field separator to a colon (`:`) instead of the default spaces because of the format of the `/etc/passwd` file.

Options

Option	Usage
-f *program_file*	Loads the awk program from the given file
-F *field_separator*	Changes the default field separator to the given value

echo

```
echo option text
```

Description

Echoes its data to standard output. If you place the data in double quotes, `echo` expands variables inside text strings.

Examples

```
$ echo $HOME
/home2/ericfj
```

Lists the user's home directory.

```
$ echo "User ${USER}'s home directory is ${HOME}."
User ericfj's home directory is /home2/ericfj.
```

Lists the user's username and home directory.

```
$ echo hello    there
hello there
```

Outputs the two arguments, with one space in between.

```
$ echo "hello    there"
hello    there
```

Outputs the same data with the embedded spaces included.

```
$ echo -n "What is your name? "
What is your name?
```

Outputs the question and leaves the cursor after the question mark.

Options

Option	Usage
-n	Doesn't output a new line

Transforming Data

These commands modify data, usually assuming that the data are all text.

cut

```
cut options files
```

Description

Extracts data as columns, based on a field separator, usually a space.

Example

```
$ cut -d':' -f1,5 /etc/passwd
root:root
bin:bin
daemon:daemon
adm:adm
lp:lp
sync:sync
shutdown:shutdown
halt:halt
mail:mail
news:news
uucp:uucp
operator:operator
games:games
gopher:gopher
ftp:FTP User
nobody:Nobody
dbus:System message bus
vcsa:virtual console memory owner
nscd:NSCD Daemon
```

```
rpm:
haldaemon:HAL daemon
netdump:Network Crash Dump user
sshd:Privilege-separated SSH
rpc:Portmapper RPC user
rpcuser:RPC Service User
nfsnobody:Anonymous NFS User
mailnull:
smmsp:
pcap:
apache:Apache
squid:
webalizer:Webalizer
xfs:X Font Server
ntp:
gdm:
ericfj:Eric Foster-Johnson
```

Cuts the first and fifth fields from the /etc/passwd file.

Options

Option	Usage
-d*Delimiter*	Sets the field separator to the given delimiter character. Usually, you need to place this in quotes.
-s	Suppresses the output of lines that don't have a field separator.

sed

```
sed options 'program' files
```

Description

A stream, or noninteractive, text editor. Use sed to modify files in a programmed manner.

See Chapter 6 for a lot of information on sed.

Example

```
$ cat /etc/passwd | sed 'p' | head -10
root:x:0:0:root:/root:/bin/bash
root:x:0:0:root:/root:/bin/bash
daemon:x:1:1:daemon:/usr/sbin:/bin/sh
daemon:x:1:1:daemon:/usr/sbin:/bin/sh
bin:x:2:2:bin:/bin:/bin/sh
bin:x:2:2:bin:/bin:/bin/sh
sys:x:3:3:sys:/dev:/bin/sh
sys:x:3:3:sys:/dev:/bin/sh
sync:x:4:65534:sync:/bin:/bin/sync
sync:x:4:65534:sync:/bin:/bin/sync
```

Sends the contents of the `/etc/passwd` file to the `sed` command. The `'p'` program tells `sed` to print out the lines. This output is redirected to the `head` command, which shows only the first ten lines.

Options

Option	Usage
-e 'script'	Uses the given script as the `sed` program
-f script_file	Loads the script from the given file
-n	Disables the automatic printing

sort

```
sort options files
```

Description

Sorts files line by line.

Examples

```
$ printenv | sort | head -4
COLORTERM=gnome-terminal
DBUS_SESSION_BUS_ADDRESS=unix:abstract=/tmp/dbus-LFVLT6j4Fj
DESKTOP_SESSION=default
DISPLAY=:0.0
```

Sorts the data returned by `printenv`.

```
$ printenv | sort | sort -c
$ printenv |  sort -c
sort: -:2: disorder: HOSTNAME=kirkwall
```

Shows how the `-c` option works. If the data are sorted, `-c` tells the `sort` command to do nothing. Otherwise, it generates an error on the first out-of-order line.

Options

Option	Usage
-b	Ignores leading blank space or tab characters.
-c	Checks if the file is sorted. Does not sort.
-d	Sorts in dictionary order, ignoring punctuation.
-f	Ignores case when sorting.
-i	Ignores nonprinting characters.
-m	Merges already-sorted files. Does not sort.

Table continued on following page

Option	Usage
-M	Assumes the first three letters of each line is a month abbreviation and then sorts by months.
-n	Sorts numerically.
-o *filename*	Sends output to the given file instead of standard output.
-r	Sorts in reverse order.
-u	Throws away duplicate lines.

strings

```
strings options files
```

Description

Searches for printable strings in a file or files and then outputs these strings.

Example

```
$ strings `which awk` | grep opyright
copyright
         -W copyright           --copyright
Copyright (C) 1989, 1991-%d Free Software Foundation.
```

Searches the awk command for the string opyright (short for *copyright*).

Options

Option	Usage
-n *number*	Searches for blocks of printable text with at least the given number of characters. Four is the default.

tr

```
tr options set1 set2
```

Description

Translates or deletes characters.

Example

```
$ cat /etc/passwd | tr ':' ' ' | tail -4
xfs x 43 43 X Font Server /etc/X11/fs /sbin/nologin
ntp x 38 38  /etc/ntp /sbin/nologin
gdm x 42 42  /var/gdm /sbin/nologin
ericfj x 500 500 Eric Foster-Johnson /home2/ericfj /bin/bash
```

Translates the colon in the `/etc/passwd` file to a space, for easier reading. Prints the last four lines.

Options

Option	Usage
-c	Complements. Uses all characters not in set1.
-d	Deletes all characters in set1.
-s	Squeezes the output by eliminating repeats.

Resolving Expressions

Shell scripts don't work that well with mathematical expressions. That's because the shells really treat most values as text strings. If you do need to resolve mathematical expressions, the following commands may help.

bc

```
bc options filenames
```

Description

Provides a programmable calculator. The `bc` command supports its own mini programming language. You can enter commands in the `bc` language at the command line or pipe the text of the commands to `bc`.

In `bc`, the basic data element is a number. You can then use math statements to modify numbers, or you can invoke functions. As a programming language, there are quite a few commands within `bc`.

Example

```
$ bc
bc 1.06
Copyright 1991-1994, 1997, 1998, 2000 Free Software Foundation, Inc.
This is free software with ABSOLUTELY NO WARRANTY.
For details type `warranty'.
scale=2
x=10
x + 10
20
x
10
tax=100*7/100
tax
7.00
x = x + tax
x
17.00
print x
17.00
quit
```

Options

Option	Usage
-l	Loads the math library
-s	Runs bc in POSIX standard mode

expr

```
expr expression
```

Description

Evaluates an expression, usually a numeric expression. Note that expr works only with whole numbers (integers). For floating-point numbers, use bc.

Examples

```
$ expr 40 + 2
42
```

Adds 40 plus 2.

```
$ expr 40 / 10
4
```

Divides 40 by 10.

```
$ expr 42 % 10
2
```

Returns the remainder after dividing 42 by 10.

Options

None.

Index